LIBERALIZATION AND DEVELOPMENT

'A long awaited welcome collection by a leading thinker on development and one of India's foremost economists. An important counterpoint to neoclassical perspectives.'

—Joseph Stiglitz, Professor, Columbia University and
Nobel Laureate in Economics 2001

'This collection constitutes an important contribution to our understanding of the theory and practice of development. The essays are articulate, perceptive and humane, critical of orthodoxy and constructive in opposition. Students and development practitioners should use them as a stimulating and enlightening reality check against commonly accepted theory and policy.'

—Frances Stewart, Professor of Development Economics,
University of Oxford

'Deepak Nayyar is a superb academic, macro and international, economist. He is a distinguished and effective policy practitioner. His essays in these two volumes bridge both worlds. His combination of theory and policy is particularly refreshing because it is founded on a heterodox perspective infinitely more relevant to India and developing countries than the tired slogans and nostrums of orthodox economics. These two volumes cover a wide range of topics: trade, industrialization, globalization and the macroeconomics of development, with concrete policy proposals. They will be essential reading about economics as it should be used to make the real world a better place for a long time to come.'

—Lance Taylor, Professor of Economics, New School for Social Research

'Professor Nayyar deserves the gratitude of the economics profession for the essays presented in these volumes, which combine beautifully theory, history and policy with practical sense. They display deep scholarship with remarkable lucidity of expression, a must reading for students, teachers, and researchers alike.'

—Amit Bhaduri, Emeritus Professor, Jawaharlal Nehru University and
Professor of Economics, University of Pavia

'These two volumes of essays by Deepak Nayyar on trade, globalization and development constitute economic heterodoxy at its best. Whether one agrees with him or not, these masterly essays, written by an economist with a flair for writing, deserve to be read, understood, and mulled over by all.'

—Kaushik Basu, C. Marks Professor and Director, Centre for
Analytic Economics, Cornell University

LIBERALIZATION
AND
DEVELOPMENT

DEEPAK NAYYAR

OXFORD

UNIVERSITY PRESS

YMCA Library Building, Jai Singh Road, New Delhi 110 001

Oxford University Press is a department of the University of Oxford.
It furthers the University's objective of excellence in research, scholarship,
and education by publishing worldwide in

Oxford   New York
Auckland   Cape Town   Dar es Salaam   Hong Kong   Karachi
Kuala Lumpur   Madrid   Melbourne   Mexico City   Nairobi
New Delhi   Shanghai   Taipei   Toronto

With offices in
Argentina   Austria   Brazil   Chile   Czech Republic   France   Greece
Guatemala   Hungary   Italy   Japan   Poland   Portugal   Singapore
South Korea   Switzerland   Thailand   Turkey   Ukraine   Vietnam

Oxford is a registered trade mark of Oxford University Press
in the UK and in certain other countries.

Published in India
by Oxford University Press, New Delhi

ISBN-13: 978-0-19-568676-0
ISBN-10: 0-19-568676-4

Typeset in Agaramond 11/13
by Eleven Arts, Keshav Puram, Delhi 110 035
Printed in India at Roopak Printers, Delhi 110 032
Published by Oxford University Press
YMCA Library Building, Jai Singh Road, New Delhi 110 001

For Rohini

CONTENTS

TABLES AND FIGURES

TABLES

FIGURES

PREFACE

This book and its companion volume, *Trade and Globalization*, bring together thirty of my selected papers published earlier. In a sense, the omnibus collection of essays reflects my intellectual journey over the past three decades. In these travels, the stopovers and the detours have been just as important as the destination. The relevance lies in the process of learning and the evolution of ideas. There are some old questions, persistent problems or hardy perennials, which remain contemporary concerns. There are some new questions which would have been difficult to imagine, let alone anticipate, even twenty years ago. There are some questions which may no longer matter in a changed world but have an analytical or historical relevance. For the author, of course, there is a charm not very different from discovering old photographs in an album. But the utility or the value is for the reader to judge.

In selecting and editing the essays, I have sought to drop those with a focus on the conjuncture and remove portions that are time specific. More important, perhaps, I have attempted to minimize the overlap. Some overlap is inevitable and may even be necessary, to develop nuances and build arguments from similar ideas in different contexts. The essays are not presented in chronological order of publication, for that may not have been conducive to a thematic cohesion. What is more, it would have meant an uneven distribution over time in a collection that is front-loaded. In the two volumes taken together, one-half of the essays have been published after 2000 and more than one-fourth have been published since 2006. Resisting natural temptation, the essays are also not divided into conventional categories, such as theory and policy or the world economy and India. Instead, the essays are grouped in thematic clusters. The introduction in each of the volumes highlights the common themes and the analytical cohesion to explain the unity in the diversity.

The papers in the two volumes have been written and published over a long span of time, during which I have interacted with, and learnt from, teachers, colleagues, students, readers, and listeners. The list could be endless but must be finite. I owe an intellectual debt to my teachers who influenced and shaped my thinking at the outset. As an undergraduate at St Stephen's College, Delhi, it was Pankaj Ganguli who made economics lively and stimulating much beyond the mundane world of textbooks. At the Delhi School of Economics, as an MA student, I fondly remember Amartya Sen, an inspiring teacher with an amazing clarity of thought, and Sukhamoy Chakravarty, with his reticence and depth, both of whom imparted not only elegance but also excitement to the study of economic theory. At Oxford, to start with, as a student of what is now termed the MPhil in Economics, Max Corden guided me with clinical precision on neoclassical trade theory. In doing so, he taught me about the wonderful utility of diagrams in exposition and analysis. Subsequently, at Oxford, I learnt to resist the authority of the printed word, question conventional wisdom, and attempt different answers, from Paul Streeten who was my supervisor as a doctoral student. He also brought home to me the significance of the heterodox and the unorthodox in economics, particularly in thinking about development. Later in life, at the other end of the classroom, I have learnt much from my students, too numerous to name, over the years.

At different stages of my professional life, a wide range and large number of persons have provided me with comments, suggestions, or assistance on early thinking, seminar presentations, and preliminary drafts. I would like to thank, in particular, Yilmaz Akyuz, Rashid Amjad, Alice Amsden, Amiya Bagchi, Paul Bairoch, Jacques Baudot, Sheila Bhalla, Rajeev Bhargava, Manfred Bienefeld, Amitava Bose, Terence Byres, Partha Chatterjee, Andrea Cornia, Arvind Das, Bhagirath Das, Meghnad Desai, Nitin Desai, Jean Drèze, John Eatwell, Richard Falk, André Gunder Frank, Winston Fritsch, Dhruva Ghosh, Ananya Ghosh-Dastidar, Murray Gibbs, Hans van Ginkel, Martin Godfrey, Andrew Graham, Keith Griffin, John Harriss, Barbara Harriss-White, Gerry Helleiner, Rolph van der Hoeven, Angus Hone, Akmal Hussain, Bimal Jalan, Jomo KS, Vijay Joshi, Raphael Kaplinsky, Devesh Kapur, Michael Kaser, Martin Khor, Rajni Kothari, Richard Kozul-Wright, John Langmore, Eddy Lee, Julian Legrand, Patrick Low, Bagich Minhas, Mritiunjoy Mohanty, Mansoob Murshed, Edward Nell, Maria Angela Parra, Prabhat Patnaik, Utsa Patnaik, Anna Piergrossi, C. Rangarajan, S.K. Rao, C.H. Hanumantha Rao, Venugopal Reddy, Gerry Rodgers, Dani Rodrik, Rubens Ricupero, Ignacy Sachs, Gary Sampson, Amal Sanyal, Abhijit Sen, Sunanda Sen, Arjun Sengupta, Anthony Shorrocks, Hans Singer, Ajit Singh, Ram Singh, Juan

Somavia, T.N. Srinivasan, Guy Standing, Ramesh Thakur, Romila Thapar, John Toye, Achin Vanaik, and Adrian Wood.

I would be remiss if I did not mention three professional colleagues and close friends who are no longer alive: Sanjaya Lall at the University of Oxford, Pramit Chaudhuri at the University of Sussex, and Krishna Bharadwaj at Jawaharlal Nehru University who were patient listeners, careful readers, and constructive critics. Discussions with them were always a learning experience.

For engaging discussion, critical comments, and valuable suggestions relating to my research and writing, at different stages, I am deeply indebted to Nirmal Chandra, Ha-Joon Chang, Padmanabha Gopinath, Abid Hussain, Satish Jain, Ashok Mitra, Anjan Mukherji, Jose Antonio Ocampo, Shrirang Shukla, Frances Stewart, Joseph Stiglitz, and Lance Taylor. And I owe a special intellectual debt to Amit Bhaduri, close friend and professional colleague, collaborator and critic, who has been a sounding board for many underdeveloped ideas and a willing reader of several preliminary drafts, over a period of almost twenty-five years.

Nitasha Devasar and Manzar Khan at Oxford University Press persuaded me to put together this collection of essays. I deeply appreciate their patience and understanding through a long period of gestation, as the volumes took much longer than both of them, and even I, had expected. The interregnum of five years as Vice Chancellor at the University of Delhi provides a part, but only a part, of the explanation, because even as I abandoned the classroom I continued to research and write, sometimes almost by stealth as I snatched time whenever possible from weekends, late nights, and long journeys. I can only hope a better collection compensates my publishers for the time lag.

My wife, Rohini, has provided the moral and the intellectual support over a lifetime, beginning even before my first paper was published. She has been a sounding board for ideas. She has been a patient listener. She has been a perceptive reader. She has been sagacious in advice. And she has been a remarkable source of strength in my hours of frustration and moments of despair that are an integral part of the life of anyone who attempts to write. This book is dedicated to her.

New Delhi   Deepak Nayyar
July 2008

ABBREVIATIONS

CSO	Central Statistical Organization
GATT	General Agreement on Tariffs and Trade
GDP	gross domestic product
ILO	International Labour Organization
IMF	International Monetary Fund
LDCs	less developed countries
NDP	net domestic product
NICs	Newly Industrializing Countries
OECD	Organization for Economic Cooperation and Development
PPP	purchasing power parity
R&D	Research and Development
SDRs	Special Drawing Rights
WTO	World Trade Organization

INTRODUCTION

This book brings together selected essays on development and liberalization published earlier. The themes explored in the selection range from macroeconomics through industrialization to development with reference to the changed context shaped by liberalization. Even so, there is an underlying unity in the apparent diversity, for the essays are on the macroeconomics of development: some in macroeconomics, some on development economics, and some at the intersection of the two domains. And my engagement with both domains goes back a long time. There are two other dimensions of coherence that run through the essays which deserve emphasis. In a world where much of development economics in concerned with micro-theoretic analysis, these essays provide a macroeconomic analysis of development. Hence, the focus is on the 'macrocosm' rather than the 'microcosm'. This is in conformity with my instinctive preference for the wider canvas. What is more, the approach is heterodox and unconventional. It questions orthodox economics, not only in its prescriptions but also in its analysis and diagnosis of problems in development. There is an irony that would be easy to miss. At a time when development economics is in fashion in the mainstream of the profession, most of the essays on development in this volume are unfashionable economics.

It is also worth noting an important characteristic of this collection which makes it somewhat different. The essays in the volume cannot be divided into the usual categories of abstract economic theory or systematic empirical analysis but lie somewhere in between. This unusual blend of theory and policy is probably attributable to my professional life in two worlds: the ivory tower of academia and the hurly-burly of public policy. I learnt about macroeconomics, industrialization, and development in the classroom, as a student and a teacher, and through research on these subjects over a lifetime as an academic, much like everybody in the profession. But I also learnt from the experience of redesigning trade policies, rethinking industrial policies, and reformulating macroeconomic policies, some of it in periods of crisis and reform. This experience enriched my understanding. And I hope that it provides a somewhat different perspective on development in the context of liberalization.

The rationale for such a volume is almost obvious. It is not significantly different from that for similar collections or anthologies. Of course, the author cannot claim that the whole is greater than the sum total of the parts. That would violate the laws of arithmetic. It would also transgress the virtue in modesty. But it is plausible to suggest that the whole is different from the parts by themselves. What is more, articles in journals and papers in edited volumes, widely dispersed in space and time, are difficult to find for readers, particularly students. And I hope that this volume of collected essays will make access easier for the reader. I also hope that the book as a whole can reach out to a larger audience than each essay might have done. It would certainly interest those who are not persuaded by orthodoxy in development economics. In a world of specialization, it might also tempt readers who find something interesting, other than what they set out to read, between these covers.

The structure of the book, which provides a framework and a sequence, is simple. The essays are grouped in four thematic clusters: theory, development, industrialization, and liberalization.

THEORY

The first set of essays is on economic theory, contextualized in developing countries. Orthodox theory, which dominates thinking about development, is characterized by two important limitations, which suggest that it may not be appropriate, let alone adequate, for an understanding of reality in developing countries. The obvious limitation is that much of economic theory evolved to analyse problems in industrialized countries. But the nature of relationships and the direction of causation in economics are significantly influenced by the actual setting and the institutional context. What is more, orthodoxy does not quite recognize alternative perspectives or unconventional thinking which may be relevant if we wish to analyse problems in developing countries. The selected essays seek to relate economic theory to the institutional setting and explore heterodox perspectives to further understanding. Consider, for instance, macroeconomics. It was developed in, and for, industrialized countries. This corpus of knowledge, with its competing schools of thought, is sought to be used in developing countries without any significant modification. It is by no means clear that such application is either justified or appropriate. Similarly, the discourse on structural adjustment in developing countries, in response to macroeconomic disequilibria or crisis, is constrained by the almost singular orthodox perspective which excludes pluralism in thinking. It does not recognize that different schools of thought stress different objectives, make different assumptions, and differ in their analysis of how an economy functions or adjusts. The introduction of such different perspectives on the macroeconomics of adjustment shows that there are alternatives, other than orthodox prescriptions, for economies in crisis. Economic theorizing in the contemporary orthodox tradition assumes away the political context almost as a rule. On the rare occasion that it does not, the experience of industrial societies is invoked to suggest that markets and democracy, which ensure efficiency and equity, are both necessary and sufficient for development. The fundamental problem of orthodoxy is that it treats the two spheres of market economy and political democracy as separate from each other. For, in isolation, each provides the freedom to choose. This is a convenient abstraction. But it is not a correct presumption. In reality, it is the interdependence and the interaction that shape outcomes.

Chapter 1 analyses the differences between the economies of industrialized countries and developing countries, which have important implications for macroeconomics in terms of theory and policy. It considers the differences in macroeconomic objectives and examines why the range and reach of macroeconomic policies is different in the two sets of countries. It shows that the relative importance of trade-offs in macroeconomics depends on the context, and analyses why processes of adjustment in developing countries, conditioned by their structural characteristics, might turn out to be very different from those in industrialized countries. It argues that the distinction between short-run macroeconomic models and long-term growth models is not quite appropriate in the context of developing countries, where macroeconomic constraints on growth interact across time horizons and short-term policies have long-term consequences. The essential point that emerges from the essay is that the nature of relationships and the direction of causation in macroeconomics, which shape analysis, diagnosis, and prescription, depend on the institutional setting and not on the analytical structure of models. It also shows that there are systematic differences between industrialized countries and developing countries, just as there are significant differences among developing countries. And even if some laws of economics are universal, the functioning of economies can be markedly different. Therefore, good economic theory and good policy analysis should recognize rather than ignore such myriad differences.

Chapter 2 discusses the process of structural adjustment in developing countries. Its focus is on macroeconomic stabilization in the short-term, but the analysis is situated in a wider context to consider how it relates to the implications of structural reform in the medium term and the prospects for economic growth in the long-term. It begins by setting out the contours of the orthodox, the Keynesian, and the heterodox perspectives on stabilization and adjustment to highlight their differences. It argues that the relationship between stabilization and growth is characterized by interconnections rather than trade-offs and suggests that outcomes depend on modes of adjustment. It also provides a macroeconomic analysis of government deficits and public finances, which are critical in the process of stabilization and adjustment. This highlights the macroeconomic significance of government deficits and points to the fallacies of deficit fetishism based on accounting frameworks. The intersection of economics and politics in the design and implementation of macroeconomic policies is also explored. Going beyond a critique of orthodox stabilization programmes, it shows that there are alternatives in macro-management for economies in crisis, for which it is necessary to shift the focus from the financial to the real economy, from the short-term to the long-term, and from equilibrium to development. Thus, the objective of macroeconomic policies should extend beyond managing inflation and the balance of payments to creating employment and fostering growth. In conclusion, the essay attempts to develop an alternative framework, which straddles time horizons, to understand the restructuring of economies over time.

Chapter 3 has an unusual theme, contrary to the ideology of our times, that markets and democracy may not ensure prosperity for everyone, but may, in fact, exclude a significant proportion of people, particularly the poor, from the process of development. It explains why markets and democracy provide no magic wand. Markets are responsive to the demands of rich people and not to the needs of poor people. Democracies are more responsive to people with a voice than to people at large. There is an interaction between exclusion from markets in the economic sphere and exclusion from democracy in the political sphere. This is because economy and polity are connected and interdependent. Moreover, there is no equality among economic agents or political citizens in terms of their economic or political freedom to choose. There is, in fact, a hierarchy of freedoms, with more for some and less for others, where there is a significant overlap between the economic and political spheres. Indeed, the liberal paradox runs much deeper. Markets exclude people without entitlements, assets or capabilities. It is in the logic of markets. Yet, markets would like to include as many people as possible, to enlarge the size of the market. In contrast, democracy includes people by a constitutional right to vote. It is the foundation of democracy. Yet, political processes seek to exclude or marginalize those without a voice, for that is what the exercise of political power is about. The irony of this paradoxical situation is striking.

DEVELOPMENT

The second set of essays is on development, in a world that has witnessed enormous change. The retreat of the State and the advance of the market have changed the national context while the gathering momentum of globalization has changed the international context. Both have significant implications for development. The selected essays explore some of these implications, in part on a wide canvas and in part with smaller pictures. In times to come, markets and globalization may not turn out to be the fast lane to development, as orthodoxy believes, for their spread has also reduced the space for, and autonomy to formulate policies in the pursuit of national development objectives. Even so, in this constrained world, redesigning development strategies can create choices and possibilities for latecomers. The necessity of questioning conventional wisdom at this juncture is borne out by the story of development during the second half of the twentieth century. There is a mismatch between ideology and experience. Outcomes in development did not quite conform to belief systems about development. The doctrinal swing in thinking, which borders on a shift in paradigm, has been associated with a profound change in the concern of public policies for development. The object of stability in the short-term and the quest for efficiency in the medium-term has led to a neglect of development objectives in a longer-term perspective. In this process, in the orthodox literature, employment is almost a residual outcome rather than a primary objective of development. But it must be recognized that work and livelihoods are most important determinants of the well-being of people.

Chapter 4 seeks to reflect on development in prospect, not retrospect, in the wider international context of globalization. It sets the stage by outlining conflicting perceptions about globalization as a *mantra* for development. It argues that globalization has diminished the policy space so essential for countries that are latecomers to development. It suggests that there is a need to reflect on the meaning of, and rethink the focus on development, which has narrowed with the passage of time. The basic theme is that, to use the available policy space for development, it is necessary to redesign strategies by introducing correctives and to rethink development by introducing different perspectives, if development is to bring about an improvement in the well-being of people. In redesigning strategies, some obvious correctives emerge from an understanding of theory that recognizes the limitations of orthodoxy and a study of experience embedded in both successes and failures that recognizes not only the diversity but also the complexity of development. In rethinking development, it is imperative to recognize the importance of initial conditions, the significance of institutions, the relevance of politics in economics, and the critical role of good governance. Redesigning strategies and rethinking development in the national context is essential. But the international context also needs some change so that it is more conducive to development. Even if it is difficult, there is a clear need to create more policy space for national development, by reshaping the rules of the game in the world economy and contemplating some governance of globalization.

Chapter 5 sketches a picture, with broad strokes on a wide canvas, of thinking about, and outcomes in, development during the second half of the twentieth century, to stress the importance of learning and unlearning from experience. In doing so, it considers the pattern of growth in the world economy from 1951 to 2000, characterized by uneven development over time and across space. It also questions the caricature distinctions between success and failure at development, in a world where outcomes were mixed. This is vividly illustrated by a tale of two countries: China and India. In this span of time, thinking about development witnessed a complete swing of the pendulum, from the Development Consensus to the Washington Consensus. These shifts in paradigm, which reshaped strategies of development, were strongly influenced by history and conjuncture, reinforced by the dominant political ideology of the times. However, changes in development strategies did not lead to the expected outcomes. In fact, there was a discernible mismatch between turning points in thinking and performance. The dramatic changes in perceptions about China and India, from role models in the early 1950s to disaster stories in the mid-1970s and star performers in the early 2000s, almost coincided in time with the swings in doctrines about development. But it would be a mistake to attribute cause-and-effect simply to the temporal sequence. For development strategies in China and India did not conform to caricature versions associated with doctrinal swings in thinking. In fact, both countries used unorthodox or heterodox policies for orthodox objectives. Of course, the experience of the past 50 years did lead to some rethinking about development. This learning from experience, however, was selective. And it differed across schools of thought. For it was shaped only in part by outcomes. It was also significantly influenced by priors in thinking and ideology in perspectives. Thus, attempts to unlearn from development, which questioned beliefs or changed priors embedded in ideologies, were few and far between.

Chapter 6 examines the consequences of short-termism in public policies for economic development. In doing so, it analyses some long-term implications of short-termism. It uses the examples of trade liberalization and financial liberalization to show that *hysteresis*—the effects of short-term policies that persist over time to influence outcomes in the long-term—may have an adverse effect on the performance of an economy. It argues that such changes in policy regimes may stifle the capabilities of domestic firms through *hysteresis* effects and may adversely affect the investment behaviour of firms through an increase in uncertainty or risk. But that is not all. This may further dampen investment at a macro level through an interaction of the multiplier mechanism and the acceleration principle. The preoccupation with the short-term, this paper suggests, also leads to a systematic neglect of long-term objectives such as the development of human resources and the acquisition of technological capabilities. Yet, there is no country that has succeeded at industrialization without attaining these objectives. Insofar as economic policies are, at present, characterized by such short-termism, this phenomenon assumes special significance in the contemporary debate on development.

Chapter 7 attempts to analyse the implications of the changed national context, characterized by a growing enthusiasm for liberalization, and the changed international context, shaped by the gathering momentum of globalization, for work, livelihoods, and rights, from a development perspective. It would seem that markets and globalization have transformed the world of work, which has consequently become more complex and diverse. There is an explicit shift in the focus from labour to work. And there is an implicit shift in emphasis from workers as a class to workers as individuals. The changes in the nature of work also mean that livelihoods no longer depend on employment alone, and thus are at risk in a world where income opportunities for most people are provided by insecure or casual employment. At the same time, the narrow legal perspective of rights at work is being replaced by a concern about rights of people in the wider context of development situated in the much broader arena of social ethics. This mismatch between emerging reality and emerging thinking is striking. It is possible to bridge the gap only through correctives and interventions in national development strategies. The realization of rights as a part of the development agenda would also reshape the world of work and of livelihoods.

INDUSTRIALIZATION

The third set of essays is on industrialization. Of the four essays, two focus on the international context, while two focus on India. This selection highlights both change and continuity in the debate on industrialization. The international relocation of manufacturing production, in part by transnational corporations, contributed to a rapid growth in manufactured exports, hence industrialization, in a few small East Asian countries. However, their characterization as success stories that approximated to free trade and *laissez-faire* was caricature history, for their export orientation was not the equivalent of free trade, just as the visible hand of the State was much more in evidence than the invisible hand of the market. In retrospect, it is clear that there is more to trade policies than the choice between import substitution and export promotion, or outward and inward orientation, just as there is more to industrialization than trade policies. The debate on industrialization in India, which is relevant for other late industrializers, provides an interesting complement to the literature on the subject. For one, it highlights the significance of the macroeconomic determinants of, and constraints on, industrial growth. For another, in considering the relationship between foreign trade and the industrialization process, it suggests that the causation runs in both directions and that the macroeconomics of the external sector is critical for an understanding.

Chapter 8 studies the international relocation of manufacturing production as a process, to analyse its implications for industrialization in developing countries. Its focus is on the period 1960–80, when it became fashionable to cite Hong Kong, Singapore, South Korea, and Taiwan as role models in development. It begins with a broad quantitative assessment of the participation by developing countries in world industrialization and trade, which highlights the striking asymmetries in the distribution of industrial output and manufactured exports between countries at that time. In 1975, for instance, the East Asian-4 accounted for just about 2 per cent of the population of the developing world and less than 10 per cent of its manufacturing value-added but as much as 50 per cent of its manufactured exports. It then narrows the focus to examine the relocation of manufacturing production in developing countries by transnational corporations to analyse the underlying factors. The question posed is whether this experience of export-led industrialization could be replicated elsewhere. The essay argues that it would not be possible to generalize this East Asian experience simply because such a prescription suffered from the fallacy of aggregation, for the consequent expansion in manufactured exports could never be absorbed by the world economy. What is more, the East Asian economies were characterized by specificities in time and space which could not be ignored. Indeed, the essay further suggests that economic policies in these countries were not in conformity with their caricature model of markets and openness. Some time later, this proposition came to be widely accepted.

Chapter 9 explores selected themes in trade and industrialization situated in the wider context of development. The stage is set by explaining the rationale of departures from free trade in economic theory. The essay then sets out the orthodox critique of the experience with industrialization in developing countries, which highlights the sins of import substitution and State intervention to stress the virtues of openness and markets. The neoclassical critique and the neo-liberal prescription, it argues, are characterized by theoretical and analytical limitations. Indeed, it would seem that the mainstream literature on trade and industrialization is narrow in its focus just as it is selective in its use of theory and experience. Significant themes are neglected. Hence, the paper situates trade in a macroeconomic perspective, highlights the importance of the demand side, outlines the implications of demand–supply linkages, and stresses the problems associated with missing out on the technology factor. It recognizes that in the changed international context, attributable to globalization, an increase in the degree of openness of economies is inevitable while the degrees of freedom for nation states are bound to be fewer. But it would be a mistake to consider necessity as a virtue. The degree of openness and the nature of intervention are strategic choices in the process of industrialization, which cannot be defined, and should not be prescribed, once-and-for-all for they depend on the stage of development and must change over time. The role of the State in the process of industrialization remains critical. But it cannot be more of the same. It needs to be redefined.

Chapter 10 explores the problems of industrialization in India from a macroeconomic perspective. In retrospect, it is possible to discern four phases of industrialization in India: the phase of rapid industrial growth from the early 1950s to the mid-1960s, the phase of stagnation from the mid-1960s to the late 1970s; the phase of revival and growth in the 1980s; and the phase of rapid growth that began in the late 1990s. This essay analyses the factors underlying the deceleration in industrial growth and the persistent quasi-stagnation in the second phase, with some discussion on the necessary or sufficient conditions for a return to the path of sustained growth. It made an important contribution to the lively debate on the subject at the time. It starts with an examination of trends in industrial production and establishes the fact of deceleration in growth. It then provides a critical review of the alternative explanations for stagnation in the industrial sector ranging from supply constraints and the policy regime to performance of the agricultural sector, the level of investment particularly public investment in the economy, and the nature of the demand constraint implicit in income distribution. This leads to the development of a unified hypothesis that explains the rapid industrial growth during 1950–65 and the near stagnation during 1965–80, with a focus on the demand factor and the critical importance of the domestic market for sustained industrialization in India. The issues analysed remain central to any discussion about the macroeconomic determinants of, and constraints on, industrial growth in India.

Chapter 11 is somewhat different from the extensive literature on the subject which analyses export performance or evaluates import substitution in independent India. It seeks to situate the foreign trade sector in the wider context of planning for industrialization, to develop a macroeconomic overview, and to analyse the interaction between foreign trade and the national economy since 1950 until 1990. At the outset, it outlines the changes in perceptions about foreign trade in the planning process, over four decades in retrospect, and considers the underlying factors. Thereafter, it develops a simple analytical framework on the macroeconomics of the external sector, in which cumulative causation could lead to both virtuous circles and vicious circles. In this framework, the essay then examines the possible impact of the foreign trade sector on the economy as a whole to suggest that it had a qualitative significance rather than a quantitative importance. The nexus between investment and exports that could have created a virtuous circle of cumulative causation did not materialize. In contrast, developments in the national economy, beginning in the late 1970s, had implications for the external sector. The regime of industrial and trade policies had a direct impact on foreign trade while the regime of fiscal policies had an indirect impact on the external sector, to drive a vicious circle of cumulative causation that led to the external debt crisis in the early 1990s. The essential message of the essay is that macroeconomic causation is crucial for an understanding of connects between the external sector and the industrialization process.

LIBERALIZATION

The fourth set of essays is on liberalization. Its focus is on India. There are four selected essays. Of these, the first two essays analyse the Indian experience with adjustment and reform that began in the early 1990s, for the period since then is long enough to attempt an assessment. The other two essays situate economic liberalization in India in its wider political and historical context. In response to the macroeconomic crisis of 1991, the government set in motion a process of stabilization along with fiscal adjustment and structural reform. The short-term compulsions were to manage the balance of payments situation and restrain inflation, but more needed to be done in terms of resolving the fiscal crisis and restoring economic growth. This needs evaluation. It is just as important to evaluate the medium-term experience with economic reforms, because the debate tends to focus on what is said or done but does not consider what is not said or not done. Some important dimensions are missed. What is more, outcomes are shaped by transition paths over time and there are long-term implications which must be recognized. Economic liberalization, which was crisis-driven rather than strategy-based, was superimposed on a process of economic development in a framework of political democracy that had evolved in India over a period spanning four decades. It is essential to explore this interaction of economics and politics. Similarly, as assessment of economic performance since the onset of liberalization cannot be done in isolation, but must be situated in longer-term historical perspective in comparison with the period since independence and the earlier colonial era. This intersection of economics and history also needs to be explored.

Chapter 12 attempts to analyse the short-term effects, the medium-term consequences, and the long-term implications of stabilization and adjustment in India in response to the macroeconomic crisis in India. The short-term effects of stabilization present a mixed picture. There was a build-up of foreign exchange reserves but it was based on an accumulation of external debt and a reliance on capital inflows that were short-term or could be withdrawn on demand. Double-digit inflation persisted for some time. And the inflation would have been higher were it not for a succession of good monsoons. The medium-term consequences were also a cause for concern. The quality of fiscal adjustment was poor. It did not provide a sustainable solution to the fiscal crisis. What is more, the burden of adjustment was distributed in an unequal manner, as it squeezed resources available for social sectors and the poor. Of course, India fared much better than most countries in Latin America and sub-Saharan Africa insofar as the slowdown was short-lived and the economy returned to earlier rates of growth than might have been expected. Yet, the longer-term implications of stabilization need to be recognized, because the process of macroeconomic adjustment was based on an investment squeeze, although higher levels of investment, particularly public investment, would have been more conducive to growth. Just as important, perhaps, the process of economic growth, when restored, did not create adequate employment opportunities.

Chapter 13, with a focus on structural economic reforms in India, seeks to develop an understanding of the factors that made reforms possible and to analyse the lessons that emerge from the experience. It does not attempt to provide an assessment or evaluation of economic reforms. Instead, it endeavours to explore the context, economic and political, in which reforms began life. The conjuncture was an important underlying factor. The external debt crisis, juxtaposed with the uncertain political situation, allowed the reforms to be introduced, while the changed international context following the collapse of communism indirectly supported this process. Some lessons are clearly discernible from the experience of more than a decade. The lessons learnt from the experience are that: competition in the market is desirable; marketization, in itself, is not always desirable; and the speed and sequence of change matter. The lessons not yet learnt from the experience are that: a prudent macro-management of the economy is essential; infrastructure is of critical importance; and the role of the State in a market economy must be redefined. It is clear that the debate on economic reforms does not pay sufficient attention to transition paths over time and to interactions across time horizons. What is more, some essentials, such as employment creation, distributional outcomes, and good governance, are forgotten. This needs correctives. It must also be recognized that economic reforms in India turned out to be a success, in significant part, because of the essential foundations laid, and the initial conditions created, in the preceding forty years.

Chapter 14 reflects on the theme of democracy and development. It situates the process of economic development in the wider context of political democracy to explore the interaction between economics and politics in independent India. At the beginning, it sets out an analytical framework which explains why markets and democracy provide no magic wand. It suggests that the real issue is the tension between the economics of markets, which excludes poor people, and the politics of democracy, which includes the same poor people. For the purpose of analysis, the essay divides the long period of 50 years into three phases. In the first phase, 1947–66, the strategy of development was shaped by a political consensus and a long-term perspective, with a conscious effort to accommodate the poor even if it was long on words and short on substance. In the second phase, from 1967 to 1990, there was an erosion of the political consensus and the capacity of the State to mediate between conflicting interests. Those with a political voice made economic claims on the government. The response of the State was a mix of mediation, co-option, patronage, and populism. The third phase, from 1991 onwards, was characterized by an absence of consensus and a presence of short-termism, in which the economics of liberalization and the politics of empowerment moved the economy and the polity in opposite directions. The need for conflict resolution was greater than ever before. But the task became more difficult. And, strangely enough, the effort was much less.

Chapter 15 situates the economic performance of independent India in a historical perspective to evaluate the past and to reflect on the future. It shows that the turning point in economic growth was *circa* 1951 in the long twentieth century and *circa* 1980 in the period since independence. And it is clear that the turning point in the early 1950s was much more significant than the structural break in the early 1980s. In any case, 1991 was not a watershed. Thus, it is not possible to attribute the turnaround in India's economic performance to economic liberalization. During the period 1950–80, economic growth in India was respectable, for it was a radical departure from the colonial past and no worse than the performance of most countries. During the period 1980–2005, economic growth in India was impressive, indeed much better than that in most countries. The real failure in both these periods was India's inability to transform this growth into development, which would have brought about an improvement in the living conditions of its people. And India's unfinished journey in development cannot be complete as long as poverty, deprivation, and exclusion persist. Even so, with correctives, the essay argues, it should be possible to reach the destination. The conclusion is clear. It is only an India which provides capabilities, opportunities, and rights to people, ordinary people, which can also deliver prosperity and power for the nation, so cherished by some.

PART 1
THEORY

Chapter 1

MACROECONOMICS IN DEVELOPING COUNTRIES*

M‍acroeconomics was developed in, and for, the industrialized countries. Theory and policy were both concerned with how monetary and fiscal policies should be used in those economies and what might be expected of such policies in terms of attaining full employment, controlling inflation, or stabilizing economic activity. This corpus of knowledge, with its competing schools of thought, is sought to be used in developing countries and without any significant modification. It is by no means clear that such application is either justified or appropriate.

The object of this essay is to analyse the differences between the economies of industrialized countries and developing countries, which have important implications for macroeconomics in terms of theory and policy. Such differences shape not only the descriptive but also the analytical and the prescriptive dimensions of macroeconomics in developing countries. And, even if the foundations of macroeconomics are the same, a recognition of these differences is essential for an understanding of reality in the context of developing countries.

The structure of the essay is as follows. The first section suggests that it is the institutional setting, rather than the analytical structure of models, which explains the determinants of causation in macroeconomics. The second section explores the differences in the structural characteristics of developing economies as compared with industrialized economies. The third section considers the differences in macroeconomic objectives and examines why the range and reach of macroeconomic policies is different in the two sets of countries. The fourth section shows that the relative importance of trade-offs in macroeconomics depends on the institutional context, and analyses

*I would like to thank Amit Bhaduri, Anjan Mukherji, Jose Antonio Ocampo, Joseph Stiglitz, and Lance Taylor for helpful comments and valuable suggestions.

why the process of macroeconomic adjustment in developing countries, conditioned by their structural characteristics, might turn out to be very different from that in industrialized countries. The fifth section argues that the distinction between short-run macroeconomic models and long-term growth models is not quite appropriate in the context of developing countries where macroeconomic constraints on growth straddle time horizons. The sixth section sets out some contextual policy debates to illustrate how issues and arguments are shaped by specificities in developing economies. The seventh section concludes.

INSTITUTIONAL SETTING

It is widely recognized that developing economies are significantly different from industrialized economies. Yet, the macroeconomic models used, in terms of analytical constructs, typically follow a similar classification: classical, Keynesian, and monetarist. The consensus among economists, much like fashion, has changed over time. The Keynesian consensus vanished, largely because the focus shifted from unemployment to inflation,[1] but the shift was attributable, in small part, to the difficulties in reconciling the Keynesian world view with behavioural hypotheses about households and firms in standard microeconomic analysis. The increasing focus on inflation and growth also shifted focus from aggregate demand to aggregate supply. This led to the emergence of supply-side economics, which argued for reducing public investment in the hope of stimulating private investment through incentives such as tax-cuts. Thereafter, for some time, the monetarist tradition became the ruling orthodoxy in macroeconomics. It stressed the importance of monetary aggregates and justified a natural rate of unemployment. But in most quarters, there is now a consensus that monetarism too failed.

Both neoclassical and neo-Keynesian models had their day in the sun. The former constructed macroeconomic theories based on standard neoclassical assumptions of methodological individualism. Hence, neoclassical analysis emphasized the role of rational expectations, using representative agent models. As a result, it ignored the fundamental Keynesian distinction between households as savers and firms as investors. Neoclassical theorizing was premised on the idea that markets always cleared. Thereby it assumed away the problem of unemployment. What is more, it ignored the theory and evidence on market imperfections, asymmetric information, and economic irrationalities. Neo-

---

[1]It is plausible to argue but difficult to establish that this shift in focus from unemployment to inflation mirrored a change in the balance between contesting political ideologies.

Keynesian analysis attempted to redefine microeconomics so as to make it consistent with macroeconomic observations. These models sought to focus on wage-price rigidities, but such theoretical explanations for rigidities were little better than the ad hoc models that they were intended to replace.

The implicit theorizing in all of these models has obvious shortcomings in explaining fluctuations in the level of economic activity in industrialized countries. But these are even less satisfactory as macroeconomics in the context of developing countries, where agriculture creates a dualism, where the financial sector is underdeveloped, where the informal sector is large, where markets are not perfect, where prices are often flexible, and where unemployment, often disguised as underemployment, is widespread.[2]

The macroeconomic aggregates are, of course, the same. So are the macroeconomic identities. For an understanding of macroeconomic systems, however, the accounting relations of aggregates need to be combined with an economic analysis of causal determinants, to describe the behaviour of households, firms, and governments. It is here that differences arise. The nature of relationships (between variables) and the direction of causation (what determines what) are both functions of the setting or the context.

The starting point for any macroeconomic analysis is the distinction between exogenous and endogenous variables or that between autonomous and induced changes. Such a distinction is essential in macroeconomic theorizing which seeks to analyse policy implications. It is important to recognize that this distinction is derived not from the analytical structure but from the institutional setting of models.

The most important example, perhaps, is the Keynesian idea that investment is an independent (exogenous) variable to which saving adjusts as a dependent (endogenous) variable. Investment is autonomous, determined by profit expectations of firms, while saving is induced, determined by income of households. The distinction rests on the institutional assumption that firms have access to credit from commercial banks and financial institutions depending on their credit worthiness and the expected profitability of their projects, irrespective of the level of savings by households in the economy. Thus, it is the institutional setting of what Hicks characterized as an 'overdraft economy' which allows investment to be financed in advance of, and independent of, the level of saving in the economy.[3]

[2]In fact, such widespread underemployment, or even open unemployment, in developing countries is often sustained only by the social structure of the family.
[3]See Hicks (1937).

A short digression is worthwhile. If credit is endogenously determined by demand, then the Keynesian perspective emerges in its sharpest focus. The independence of the investment function of firms determines effective demand (hence output), while the financial system merely plays an accommodating role without influencing the level of demand (hence output). On the other hand, if credit is assumed to be exogenously determined by the financial system, the monetarist perspective, or at least a perspective that seeks to focus more on finance, emerges as critical, insofar as banks have a role in influencing the investment decisions of firms by relaxing or tightening credit facilities extended to firms.[4] Or, if firms have to rely mostly on their own capital to finance investment in a financial market without depth, then corporate profits, or savings, largely determine investment.[5] In either case, investment can no longer be treated as exogenous.

The moral of the story is clear. The distinction between exogenous and endogenous variables, or that between the autonomous and induced changes, is essential in macroeconomic models which seek to analyse events or prescribe policies. But this distinction does not derive from the analytical structure of a model; it derives from the underlying institutional setting of the model. Much can change, especially in terms of policy prescriptions, when institutional settings, hence determinants of causation, change. And without some notion of causation, or the sequence of events in time, no policy prescription is possible. Therefore, even equilibrium relations require some causal interpretation, at least for policy analysis.

It follows that macroeconomics developed in the context of industrialized countries cannot simply be transplanted in developed countries. Starting from accounting identities, models can be built based on economic reasoning, but such models must respect institutional facts and recognize different contexts.

---

[4]Monetary authorities can influence the willingness and ability of banks to provide credit. If there is credit rationing, it is not just interest rates but also the availability of credit that determine investment. And even if investment is determined by the interest rate, the latter is effectively determined by the monetary authorities either directly or indirectly through money supply. For a discussion, see Greenwald and Stiglitz (2003).

[5]The monetarist perspective is an attempt to incorporate finance, since it is credit that drives economic activity more than money. But money and credit are highly correlated. The control of central banks over money supply can be thought of as a surrogate for their control over credit supply. Monetarism failed in part because, at critical times, money supply and credit supply do not move in tandem.

STRUCTURAL DIFFERENCES

There are important differences in the structural characteristics of developing economies as compared with industrialized economies. In the world of macroeconomics, there are at least six that deserve to be highlighted. It is, of course, essential to remember that there are important differences among developing countries not only across regions but also within regions.

First, from a Keynesian perspective, in advanced capitalist economies, the main problem is the adequacy of effective demand. Such an economy possesses a productive capacity which matches the existing labour force but capital equipment remains underutilized for lack of demand. It is not as if there are no supply constraints. There are. And recent advances in macroeconomics have emphasized how shocks to the economy can lead to shifts in the aggregate supply curve as well as the aggregate demand curve.[6] But the expansion of output is primarily demand-constrained. The crucial problem in a developing county is different. Even if its productive capacity or capital equipment is fully utilized, it cannot absorb the existing labour force in gainful employment. The problem then is the deficiency of productive capacity and not the anomaly of its underutilization.[7] It is not as if there are no demand constraints. There are. In some sectors of an economy, output may be demand-constrained for some time.[8] In some economies, output may be demand-constrained for some time. And recent stabilization experiences suggest that a contraction in demand can, and does, induce a contraction in output. But the expansion of output is primarily supply-constrained. This structural difference is embedded in differences in stylized facts about the two sets of economies: limited labour and unlimited capital in industrialized countries, as compared with limited capital and unlimited labour in developing countries. This reality has, to some extent, changed over time. And the increasing openness of economies is also influencing this reality.

Second, there may be differences in the degree of price flexibility. In both industrialized economies and developing countries, these may vary across sectors and may change over time. In the institutional context of industrialized countries, macroeconomics sought to focus on the implications of wage-rigidities. But, in developing countries, where formal sector employment is a small proportion of employment in the economy as a whole, the rigidity of money wages, or real

---

[6]See, for example, Greenwald and Stiglitz (2003).
[7]See Kalecki (1976a). See also, Kalecki (1971).
[8]Nayyar (1994). See also, Bhaduri (1986).

wages, is a less critical policy problem.[9] In fact, price formation is dichotomized by the dualistic structure of these economies. In the agricultural sector, prices are determined largely by demand and supply through market-clearing. Indeed, government support prices for agriculture in many developing countries are attributable to this reality. In the non-agricultural sector, particularly manufacturing, prices are determined through mark-ups on a cost-plus basis.[10] Moreover, in some developing countries, wages in the organized sector are characterized by an indexation which imparts rigidity to real wages. In such price–wage interaction, the role of trade unions is often significant but not quite recognized. Obviously, generalizations are difficult. Yet, it can be said that agricultural prices are more flexible than industrial prices, and agriculture is typically more important in developing countries. Historically, oligopolies, with their associated price-rigidities, were more important in industrialized countries than they are now, but such oligopolies remain important in the manufacturing sector in many developing countries. On balance, it is plausible to argue that wages and prices are more flexible in developing countries than in industrialized economies.[11] It is also reasonable to suggest that insofar as there are wage-rigidities in both sets of countries the underlying factors are different.[12]

Third, in the medium-term, the sources of output growth are different. In industrialized economies, output growth is driven by productivity increase

[9]It needs to be said that this generalization is not quite borne out by the Latin American experience, where the widespread adoption of contract indexation created strong real wage rigidities.

[10]This characterization of price formation in developing countries was the essential assumption in Kalecki's writings on macroeconomics with reference to underdeveloped countries. See Kalecki (1976b). This assumption played a strategic role in the literature on structuralist economics that emerged in the 1970s and 1980s, mostly in the Latin American context but also in the Indian context. See, for example, Taylor (1983) and Rakshit (1989).

[11]Some studies suggest that there is more volatility in wages in developing countries, perhaps because trade unions and employment protection are relatively weak. This suggests that there may be more flexibility of wages, but it could also partly be because developing countries are more vulnerable to shocks. See Easterly et al. (2001).

[12]The explanations for wage rigidities may also differ. In very poor countries, the subsistence wage may constitute a floor. Alternatively, the nutritional efficiency wage may be part of the explanation: employers do not want to pay a lower wage, because at a lower wage productivity is significantly lower because nutrition is insufficient. The relationship between productivity and wages is the subject of a vast literature. See, for example, Stiglitz (1976). In other countries, minimum wages may play an important role. In yet other countries, efficiency wage theories based on selection, incentive, or morale effects may provide a more important part of the explanation for real wage rigidity. In this context, it is worth noting that the stylized facts from Latin America conform more closely to industrialized economies than to developing countries.

which, in turn, is a function of the level of investment and the pace of technical progress. In developing economies, output growth is, or at least should be, driven by labour absorption through employment creation in the non-agricultural sector and, in some part, through a shifting of labour from low productivity employment to higher productivity employment in the manufacturing sector or the services sector. In this process, investment plays a critical role. Of course, in most successful developing countries, which eliminate disguised unemployment in the agricultural sector, approximate to full employment in the industrial sector, or close the technological gap between themselves and industrialized countries, productivity increase becomes the primary source of output growth. And, in the long run, growth in output per capita requires productivity gains regardless of labour market conditions. This is borne out by the experience of massive productivity growth in Japan, Korea and, now, China.

Fourth, there are pronounced differences in financial markets. In industrialized countries, financial markets, institutions, and instruments are far more developed than those in developing countries. And there are significant differences in the degree of monetization. Consequently, in developing countries, firms rely more on self-financing than their counterparts in industrialized economies, in part because equity markets are underdeveloped as a source of finance for new investments.[13] Borrowing from informal money markets is common. And debt–equity ratios are, as a rule, higher. In industrialized countries, increasingly, there has been a move away from bank lending towards securitization. These differences are, in important part, attributable to the absence or presence of institutions, as also to the depth of financial markets.[14] However, even the form and availability of financial instruments can make a difference.[15] An important function of financial markets is to transfer and absorb risk. Underdeveloped financial markets in

[13]India is, perhaps, an exception to this rule, insofar as equity markets are a significant, and increasingly important, source of finance for firms. For a discussion on stock markets as a source of corporate financing in developing countries, see Singh (1997).

[14]Rural credit markets provide a striking example of such specificities in developing countries. Moneylenders in the agricultural sector, who have access to the market for credit, transfer the risk entirely to the poor borrower through an undervaluation of collateral assets. See Bhaduri (1977).

[15]In the United States, where most mortgages are fixed rate and do not have significant prepayment penalties, the lowering of interest rates leads to refinancing. In the United Kingdom, however, a more common form of mortgage is the variable rate mortgage with fixed payments, so that lowering interest rates would presumably have a much weaker effect.

developing countries mean that they are less able to absorb shocks than industrialized economies.[16]

Fifth, governments in industrialized countries have little trouble in financing their deficits, whereas governments in developing countries typically face greater financial constraints. In fact, experience suggests that few developing countries can sustain a government deficit that is 5 per cent of gross domestic product (GDP), or more, for long. Of course, borrowing from the central bank is an option. But it cannot be stretched beyond limits for that could be dangerous. Indeed, such excessive deficit financing was an important source of hyperinflation in several Latin American economies. Consequently, most governments in developing countries run pro-cyclical fiscal policies.[17] The financial constraints facing governments exacerbate problems that arise in the private sector. In such a context, underdeveloped financial markets, or inadequately developed financial sectors, impede the ability of developing countries to absorb shocks.

Sixth, in comparison with industrialized countries developing countries are much smaller but more open economies. Of course, in this dimension, generalizations are difficult because there are marked differences between countries in the developing world as also between countries in the industrialized world. Yet, it is plausible to suggest that most developing countries are more open, insofar as exports constitute a larger proportion of GDP and foreign capital inflows finance a larger proportion of domestic investment. The combination of greater openness and smaller size means that economies of developing countries are not only more prone but are also more vulnerable to external shocks. The analysis of macroeconomic fluctuations in the case of a small open economy illustrates many of the deficiencies of orthodox economics. If the standard assumptions were true, an adjustment of the exchange rate would result in an infinite demand for a country's exports. In such a world, any problem of insufficiency of aggregate demand would be easy to solve, so that it would be logical to focus on aggregate supply. But it is simply not appropriate to borrow the small country assumption from orthodox trade theory for macroeconomic analysis in the context of developing countries. These countries have always been vulnerable to terms of trade changes associated with openness in trade. The openness to capital flows has accentuated this vulnerability. And, in a world

---

[16]Of course, even sophisticated capital markets are capable of generating huge messes, such an Enron and LTCM in the United States, or bad debt in Japan, but the much greater depth of financial markets makes it possible to contain such crises.

[17]For a discussion, see Ocampo (2003).

of capital market liberalization, developing countries are far more exposed to, but much less able to cope with, exogenous shocks and financial crises.

OBJECTIVES AND POLICIES

The differences are not only structural. Macroeconomic objectives in developing countries are, or should be, different from those in industrialized countries. In the industrialized economies, the traditional policy objectives were internal balance and external balance.[18] Internal balance was defined as full employment combined with price stability. External balance was defined as equilibrium in the balance of payments, primarily with reference to the current account and, more precisely, in terms of the distinction between autonomous and accommodating transactions.[19] The conception of internal balance, now, is confined to price stability. And full employment is no longer an integral part of the objective. Presumably, this is partly attributable to the belief that if the government achieves price stability, then the market will automatically achieve the objective of full employment. But there is little reason to believe that this is in fact the case, in either industrialized or developing countries. In a world of capital account liberalization, the meaning of external balance is less than clear. It extends much beyond the current account as most capital account transactions are autonomous rather than accommodating.[20]

In developing economies, the traditional concern was economic growth in the long-term. The emphasis was on savings and investment. The focus shifted to macro-management in the short-term, after many developing

[18]The distinction between internal balance and external balance was first made by Meade (1951). These were the policy objectives of the model. There were two sets of policy instruments: income adjustments (though fiscal and monetary policies) and price adjustments (through exchange rate variations or wage flexibility).

[19]The distinction between autonomous and accommodating transactions in the balance of payments was also first made by Meade (1951). Autonomous transactions are undertaken for their own sake, for the profit or the satisfaction they yield. They do not depend on other transactions. Accommodating transactions, by contrast, are not undertaken for their own sake. They depend on other (autonomous) transactions. Hence, they are a residual that accommodates gaps. External balance is, then, defined as a situation where receipts and payments on account of autonomous transactions are equal so that accommodating transactions are zero.

[20]At the time that Meade made the distinction, as also for a long period thereafter, the current account, in which all transactions were autonomous, was the major component of the balance of payments. Thus, autonomous transactions in the capital account were modest, while accommodating transactions were shaped mostly by the current account balance. The significance of the capital account in the balance of payments has increased enormously with capital mobility. So has the importance of autonomous transactions in the capital account.

countries, particularly the so-called emerging economies in Latin America, as also the transition economies in Eastern Europe, ran into debt crises or other forms of macroeconomic disequilibrium if not turbulence. Again, the reason often put forward was that, if the government succeeded in achieving price stability in the short-run, all else, including growth would follow. Even so, the essential objective in developing countries is to step up the rate of growth as much as possible. Faster growth will lead to higher incomes and more employment. Clearly, the growth has to be sustainable. There is a presumption that it will not be sustainable if inflation soars or if the balance of payments gets too far out of line. Thus, it is sometimes postulated that the objective of macroeconomic policy should be to maximize growth subject to two constraints: that inflation remains within limits of tolerance and that the current account deficit in the balance of payment remains within manageable proportions. And, often, it is very difficult to anticipate which of these problems will arise or which of the constraints will become binding. Maximizing growth typically means maximizing current output and employment, if labour productivity growth is constant or exogenous.

Macroeconomic policies are the same. The traditional policy instruments, in both industrialized economies and developing economies, are fiscal policy and monetary policy. But the range and the reach of these policies differ in the two sets of countries.

Any consideration of fiscal policy should make a distinction between revenue and expenditure of the government. In developing countries, tax revenues are based less on direct taxes and more on indirect taxes as compared with industrialized economies. Moreover, in developing countries, almost without exception, the base for taxation is significantly narrower while tax compliance is significantly lower (which is attributable to tax avoidance and tax evasion). Thus, governments find it very difficult to increase their income through tax revenues.[21] This is a problem because, as a rule, tax–GDP ratios in developing countries are much lower. In industrialized economies, where tax–GDP ratios are much higher, the debate is about tax-cuts. In the sphere of expenditure, developing countries are characterized by proportionately larger government sectors where degrees of freedom are circumscribed by political compulsions, possibly more than in industrialized economies. What is more, in developing countries, the proportion of investment expenditure in total public expenditure is higher than in industrialized economies because

---

[21]Indeed, governments find it exceedingly difficult to tax certain sectors, groups, or classes. For this reason, the tax–GDP ratio in countries such as India and Mexico is much too low, even when compared with some developing countries.

private investment in infrastructure is not always forthcoming. Yet, in difficult times, it is such investment expenditure that is axed because governments find it very difficult to cut consumption expenditure. This means that excessive fiscal stringency imposes a high cost in terms of lost growth. In industrialized economies, the proportion of public expenditure on social security and social sectors is significantly higher than that in developing countries, even if the need for such expenditure is as strong in the latter. Because so many more individuals are near subsistence, even small cuts in these social expenditures can have large consequences. In industrialized countries, a cut in educational expenditures will lead to slightly larger class sizes and, arguably, a reduction in the quality of education. In developing countries, a cut in educational expenditures will mean that more children will not go to school. On the whole, it is clear that governments in industrialized economies have much more fiscal flexibility than their counterparts in developing countries.

Monetary policy clearly highlights the differences, which are much more pronounced, particularly in terms of reach, because money markets are often segmented, if not underdeveloped, in developing countries. Insofar as the effects of monetary policy are more narrowly directed, the economic costs of reliance on monetary policy may be greater and its effectiveness lower. Open market operations are obviously a limited option in thin markets. In the past, many developing countries sought to use interest rates as a strategic instrument for guiding the allocation of scarce investible resources in a market economy.[22] In such a context, it is not surprising that, in developing countries, the volume of credit was always perceived as more effective than the price of credit as an instrument of monetary policy. The practice has changed in the recent past since the deregulation of domestic financial sectors has led to the emergence of markets for financial assets. This should have made interest rates a more potent instrument. Ironically enough, it has not, because capital account convertibility has curbed flexibility in the use of interest rates. Industrialized economies are not immune from the fetters of international financial markets, but the reach of monetary policy is significantly greater than in developing countries.

It is also important to recognize the somewhat different macroeconomic implications of the interaction between fiscal and monetary policy in developing countries. For example, the monetary impact of fiscal policy is perhaps greater

[22]The striking examples of such a strategic use of interest rates are the East Asian countries, particularly Japan and Korea. See Wade (1990) and Chang (1994). In this context, it is worth noting that the deregulation of domestic financial markets in developing countries is bound to limit the use of the structure of interest rates, say a differentiation between short-term rates and long-term rates, as a means of influencing the allocation of scarce resources.

in developing countries because a much larger proportion of the fiscal deficit is financed by borrowing from the central bank. In a shallow capital market, the alternatives are few and far between. And, in developing countries, borrowing from the central bank is the principal source of reserve money which makes it the most important determinant of monetary expansion. This is no longer the case in most Latin American economies, but remains the reality in most other developing countries. Similarly, the fiscal impact of monetary policy is perhaps greater in developing countries, because, in situations where public debt is large as a proportion of GDP and interest payments on such debt are large as a proportion of government expenditure, even modest changes in interest rates exercise a strong influence on fiscal flexibility.

The orthodox belief system that higher interest rates would help reduce macroeconomic imbalances is not always borne out by the reality of experience with the use of monetary policy in developing countries.[23] Higher interest rates do not necessarily reduce government borrowing in situations where it is difficult to increase income or reduce expenditure of the government. But higher interest rates almost certainly make public debt less manageable.[24] Conceivably, higher interest rates also feed into inflation through cost-push mechanisms.

In a changed international context, it is also important to recognize that countries which are integrated into the world financial system are constrained in using an autonomous management of demand to maintain levels of output and employment. Expansionary fiscal and monetary policies—large government deficits to stimulate aggregate demand or low interest rates to encourage domestic investment—can no longer be used, as easily as in the past, because of an overwhelming fear that such measures could lead to speculative capital flight and a run on the national currency.[25] The problem exists everywhere. But it is far more acute in developing countries.

Standard macroeconomics seeks to focus on fiscal policy and monetary policy. But there is an increasing recognition of the importance of other policy instruments, while increasing attention is devoted to the microeconomic aspects of conventional policy instruments. Traditional Keynesian economics, of course, had a very simple model of firms and households. Firms paid attention only to interest rates, whereas households paid attention only to income. Thus, the only aspect of tax policy that mattered was disposable household income, and the only aspect of monetary policy that mattered was interest

---

[23]See Nayyar (2001).
[24]The most obvious examples of this syndrome are Argentina, Brazil, and Turkey.
[25]For a more detailed discussion on this issue, see Nayyar (2003).

rates. Similarly, neoclassical models, as also real business cycle models, had very simple models of firms and households, in which inter-temporal substitution effects played a more important role while current income played a less important role. Hence, temporary income taxes had a negligible effect. But temporary consumption taxes had a significant effect. Recent developments in macroeconomics have attempted to build models with more realistic descriptions of both household and firm behaviour. Households do not fully pierce the corporate veil. Both households and firms may be credit constrained. Bank regulators can influence the availability as well as the price of credit.

TRADE-OFFS AND ADJUSTMENT

There are important trade-offs in macroeconomics, particularly in the sphere of macroeconomic policies, which must be recognized. However, the significance of such trade-offs depends on the context. The trade-off between inflation and unemployment is much more important in industrialized economies than it is in developing countries. The trade-off between short-term macro-management and long-term objectives is much more important in developing countries than it is in industrialized countries.

The conventional trade-off between inflation and unemployment is epitomized in the Phillips Curve. But this construct is much too limited.[26] In the near-obsessive concern of governments with the control of inflation, driven more and more by international financial markets, it is often forgotten that the management of inflation is not an end in itself. And, beyond a point, reducing inflation is at the cost of not only employment but also growth. Of course, even in industrialized economies, the focus now is on deflation now that the macroeconomic context has changed. In fact, debt-deflation has been a major issue in economies where asset price bubbles have burst or crashed. In developing countries, there is no well defined Phillips curve. Indeed, it is difficult to conceptualize a negative relationship between the rate of inflation and the rate of unemployment in economies where non-participation in the labour force, disguised unemployment in the subsistence agricultural sector, underemployment in the urban informal sector, and wage employment in the formal (manufacturing and services) sector coexist in a spectrum without any clear lines of demarcation.

In developing countries, as also in transition economies, in recent years, public policies have come to be preoccupied with macro-management in the short-term and re-structuring of economies in the medium-term. The former

[26]For a discussion, see Jung (1985). See also, Bagchi (1994).

is driven by the quest for stabilization. The latter is prompted by the quest for efficiency. This is in conformity with the orthodoxy embodied in the Washington Consensus. There is, however, an important trade-off between short-term concerns and long-term objectives. For one, there are some long-term consequences of short-termism. Macroeconomic policies implemented with a short-term objective may have adverse consequences for the performance of the economy in the long-term, through *hysteresis*, if the effects of short-term policies persist over time to influence outcomes in the long-term.[27]

It is possible to cite several examples which show that the preoccupation with short-term management and medium-term restructuring may have damaging consequences in the long-term.[28] Trade liberalization, which leads to the exit of domestic firms on a significant scale, ultimately affects the capacity of an economy to respond to changes in relative prices. The reason is simple. Exit is easy but re-entry is difficult. Similarly, financial liberalization, which leads to a persistent, if not mounting, overvaluation of the exchange rate, may force domestic firms to close down.[29] By the time the overvaluation is undone, *hysteresis* effects could be strong. This means that re-entry becomes difficult, for domestic firms must create new capacities to capture the opportunities created by the changed set of relative prices. But that is not all. The workers who are unemployed as a consequence of closures may lose their skills with the passage of time and become less productive when employment opportunities appear after a lag. It is also possible that their old skills, even if retained, are less relevant after a time.

Furthermore, a preoccupation with the short-term often leads to a systematic neglect of long-term development objectives. There are two reasons for this. First, in the sphere of economics, such objectives cannot be defined in terms

[27]It might seem that the concept of trade-off, which refers to choices at a point in time, is diluted by the notion of hysteresis, which refers to effects that persist even long after the cause is removed. But it is not, because the trade-off between short-term concerns and long-term objectives is discernible only across time horizons.

[28]For an analysis of this issue, see Nayyar (1998).

[29]Such an overvaluation, with similar consequences, may be attributable to monetary contraction or fiscal expansion, for example, in the United States during the first half of the 1980s. There is literature that examined the hysteresis effects of the persistent overvaluation of the US dollar. The upshot of this literature was that overvaluation leads to an accumulation of adverse trade effects which ultimately need to be remedied through an overdepreciation. The reason is that, in the presence of hysteresis, a period of sustained undervaluation is needed to bring forth the required investment. For a discussion, see Dornbusch (1987). This parable conveys an important lesson about the significance of the long-term real exchange rate.

of oversimplified performance criteria set forth by the Bretton Woods institutions. Second, in the realm of politics, such objectives do not bring tangible gains which can be exploited by governments or administrations within their term of office. In a longer time horizon, the development of human resources and the acquisition of technological capabilities are examples of such objectives, the neglect of which could turn out to be most problematic.[30] Conventional macroeconomics simply does not recognize this trade-off. Orthodoxy believes that an adjustment of the mix of instruments, say, tighter fiscal policy coordinated with looser monetary policy, can be used to achieve whatever growth objective the government wants at the same time that the desired employment objective is achieved.

The process of adjustment in economies at a macro level differs not only over time but also across space. Single models cannot suffice. And generalizations are perilous. All the same, it should come as no surprise that, as in most of economic theory, a mechanism of adjustment or a process of change must work either through prices or through quantities or through some combination of both. Yet, the mode and speed of adjustment at a macro level are different in developing countries from those in industrialized economies.

Considerable evidence suggests that there is much greater economic volatility in developing countries than in industrialized countries. This is partly because the economies are smaller, less diversified, and exposed to greater shocks, which they are less equipped to absorb. Their adjustment processes work less well and more slowly. Markets that function well have the capacity to absorb shocks and dissipate them through the economy. In developing countries, as a rule, markets work less well. Hence, it should come as no surprise that such economies respond less well to shocks. The exact nature of the failure, however, is subject to some contention and way well differ across countries. In some cases, there may be greater price rigidities. In such situations, economies adjust at a macro level through changes in output rather than changes in prices. Moreover, the greater the rigidity in prices, the greater the burden that is placed on quantity (income or output) adjustments.[31]

On the other hand, there is also some evidence that prices and wages are more volatile in developing countries, consistent with the hypothesis that they are more, not less, flexible. It is the imperfections of capital markets which shape differences in how shocks are absorbed, or amplified, in the economy.

[30]See Nayyar (1998).
[31]See Stiglitz (1999).

Equity markets are better at risk-sharing than debt markets, and developing countries rely more heavily on debt.[32] Countries with very high debt–equity ratios (as was the case for many East Asian countries before the 1997 financial crises) become highly vulnerable to certain kinds of shocks, and the process of adjustment, which entails recapitalizing financial institutions, is much more complicated.[33]

There is another significant difference between industrialized economies and developing economies which lies in the speed of adjustment. In general, the speed of adjustment in developing countries, particularly on the supply side, is slower than it is in industrialized countries. The reason is simple. Resources are not perfectly mobile across sectors or substitutable in uses; and prices, particularly of factors, are not completely flexible. These problems are accentuated in developing economies which are characterized by structural rigidities. The dynamics of demand are fast in expansion and in contraction. In contrast, the dynamics of supply are slow in expansion (which is partly attributable to the limitations in financial markets) even if somewhat faster in contraction.

CONSTRAINTS ON GROWTH

In the context of industrialized countries, there is a distinction between macroeconomic models, where the focus is on the short-run, and growth models, where the time horizon is the long-term. The interconnections are important. But these are not explored enough in such analysis. The dichotomy extends to theorizing about developing countries. This is obviously not appropriate, particularly because structural constraints characteristic of these economies have several different dimensions. Some of the dimensions of these constraints can be depicted in short-run macroeconomic models. Others must be built into long-term growth models. But there are some that can only be analysed through models that link short-run macroeconomic adjustments with long-term patterns of growth. Such models are few.

In the context of developing countries, there is a literature around the theme of macroeconomic constraints on growth.[34] But this literature remains

[32]Theories based on the economics of information (asymmetries in information) explain not only the limitations of equity markets but also why they play a much smaller role in developing countries as compared with industrialized economies.

[33]Of course, the social arrangements for saving, not to mention financial churning, also matter and differ across countries. In China and Russia, for example, where private saving is high, capital flight is a possible outcome. The high private saving in Japan, in contrast, leads to more direct foreign investment.

[34]There is an extensive literature on two-gap models. The earliest contributions were McKinnon (1964) and Chenery and Strout (1966).

in the domain of development economics. It is not an integral part of macroeconomics for development. Yet, arguably, it should be. This literature suggests that, at a macro level, economic growth in developing countries may be limited by a savings constraint, a foreign exchange constraint, a wage goods constraint, or a fiscal constraint. Such models start from the premise that, given a capital–output ratio, the rate of investment determines the rate of growth in an economy. The focus, then, is on what constitutes, at the margin, the effective constraint on increasing investment. A saving constraint represents a situation where investment cannot be raised because consumption is at a minimum acceptable level. A foreign exchange constraint represents a situation where available savings cannot be transformed into investment because the requisite investment goods cannot be imported. A wage goods constraint represents a situation where the rate of growth of supply of necessities does not allow the level of investment to be raised any further.[35] A fiscal constraint represents a situation where limits on public investment mean that total investment cannot be increased beyond a level because there is a complementarity between public investment and private investment. Of course, these models are simple analytical abstractions. The essential message is that the cost of alleviating the binding macroeconomic constraint on growth, at the margin, is high in developing countries.

There is a literature on 'gap models' that debates which of these constraints might be dominant and explores the macroeconomic implications or consequences of the interaction between these constraints.[36] Of course, in equilibrium, these constraints are always satisfied. Indeed, the constraints only exist *ex ante*, but cannot be there *ex post* because there can be no gaps in accounting identities. Embedded in the discussion of 'gap models' are certain assumptions about which variables are exogenous and which are endogenous, or which elements of economic behaviour can be altered by economic policy and which cannot. Such analytical constructs may not be important in themselves. But the moral of the story is important. They draw our attention to the variety of ways by which policy can affect macroeconomic equilibrium and the variety of interactions that need to be taken into account. Most important, perhaps, these models focus on the possible trade-offs that have to be faced in formulating macroeconomic policies.

Given such macroeconomic constraints, irrespective of which particular constraint is dominant, any attempt to step up the rate of growth in an economy spills over into an acceleration in the rate of inflation or a difficult balance of

---

[35]In analysing macroeconomic constraints on growth in underdeveloped countries, Kalecki sought to focus on the wage goods constraint. See Kalecki (1970).

[36]See Bacha (1990) and Taylor (1994).

payments situation. The threshold of tolerance for inflation, determined by polity and society, may vary from as little as 5 per cent per annum to as much as 100 per cent per annum. The manageability of a difficult balance of payments situation depends on the willingness and ability of creditors in the outside world to lend, or to finance current account deficits; this willingness and ability varies significantly from country to country and that depends on the historical context. But that is not all. The essential point is that an understanding of macroeconomic constraints on growth, in the context of developing countries, is important because it highlights macroeconomic interactions between the short-run and the long-term.

CONTEXTUAL POLICY DEBATES

There are salient issues that are a subject of debate in the context of macroeconomics for developing countries. These debates focus on the nature of relationships and the direction of causation between macroeconomic variables. The points of contention are frequently about whether or not there are specificities in developing economies. It may be worth citing two illustrative examples of the positions staked out in these debates. The first concerns the determinants of price behaviour and the second considers the relation between public and private investment.

The most important illustration, perhaps, is provided by the debate on the determinants of price behaviour. At one level, it is concerned with what causes inflation. At another level, it is concerned with what should be done about inflation. It would be no exaggeration to state that it provides a touchstone to distinguish orthodox (or monetarist) thinking from heterodox (or structuralist) thinking. The competing schools of thought, in terms of both perception and prescription, are the monetarists and the structuralists.[37] The monetarist theory about inflation is a demand and supply fable which emphasizes the role of money supply. It ultimately reduces to a simple proposition that monetary expansion drives inflation. The structuralist theory of inflation is, on the one hand, about relative price shifts which are a part of the distributional conflict. On the other hand, it is about a set of rules of price formation which provide an institutional mechanism through which inflation escalates. Structuralist theorizing about inflation is ultimately a story about imbalances in markets for goods and for factors. In this discourse, the Keynesian view about aggregate supply–demand imbalances, or the Kalecki view about real

---

[37]For a discussion on competing hypotheses about inflation, see Taylor (1991).

disproportionalities and distributional conflict, is no longer centre stage. Of course, these may be important determinants of price behaviour in developing countries.

Obviously, both the contending views about inflation are relevant. In the context of markets where firms set prices (most industrialized economies), it is the perceptions of firms about the demand (curves) and cost (curves) they face that determine their price decisions. In the context of competitive markets, it is gaps between demand and supply at existing prices that determine price adjustments. But aggregate demand (and possibly aggregate supply), and thus the demand (and supply) for particular goods, is affected by monetary policy. Monetarism stresses monetary policy as the source of inflation. Structuralist hypotheses emphasize other sources, which depend upon the context. Of course, it must be recognized that even if structural changes initiate a bout of inflation, monetary expansion can accentuate inflation. But the reverse is also true. And it is seldom recognized.

In reality, inflation processes are pretty *sui generis*, each one combining its own brew of structuralist and monetarist factors. The responses of governments to inflationary situations can range from an indifference to, or an obsession with, inflation. Much depends on the context and the experience of the decision-makers.[38] However, there are very few anti-inflation policies. The few available choices are austerity, pegging some key nominal prices such as wage rates or the exchange rate, or attracting capital inflows. Monetary policy can also be used to bring inflation under control, though often at a high price in terms of output foregone.

It is clear that no single explanation can suffice across countries or over time. The analysis and the prescription in developing countries must depend on the circumstances in particular and the institutional setting in general.

Another interesting example of contending views is provided by the debate on the relationship between public investment and private investment. Orthodoxy, contextualized in the industrialized economies, believes that public investment crowds-out private investment. The argument is simple. Government borrowing to finance public investment raises interest rates, which depresses private investment. The unorthodox view, contextualized in developing

[38]There is a marked difference in attitudes towards, and concerns about inflation, between Latin America and Asia. This is not limited to policymakers. It extends to economists as well. This difference is attributable to experiences embedded in history. Thus, the focus of macroeconomic policy in Latin America is on the management of inflation. In contrast, macroeconomic policy in Asia tends to focus much more on growth. The past experience of high inflation in Latin America and low inflation in Asia probably explains this difference.

countries, argues that public investment crowds-in private investment.[39] The experience of developing countries, in general, suggests that public investment and private investment are complements rather than substitutes. This may be so for several reasons. For one, public investment, particularly in infrastructure, may reduce the cost of inputs used by the private sector or increase the demand for goods produced by the private sector. For another, public investment may stimulate private investment insofar as it increases the degree of capacity utilization in the economy. But this relationship may change with levels of income and stages of development.

CONCLUSION

The essential point that emerges from this essay is that the nature of relationships and the direction of causation in macroeconomics, which shape analysis, diagnosis, and prescription, depend upon the institutional setting. This essay also demonstrates that there are systematic differences between industrialized economies and developing countries, just as there are significant differences among developing countries. And even if some laws of economics are universal, the functioning of economies can be markedly different. Therefore, good economic theory and good policy analysis should recognize, rather than ignore, such myriad differences.

REFERENCES

Bacha, E.L. (1990), 'A Three-gap Model of Foreign Transfers and GDP Growth Rates in Developing Countries', *Journal of Development Economics*, Vol. 32, No. 2, pp. 279–96.

Bagchi, A.K. (1994), 'Macroeconomics', *Journal of Development Planning*, No. 24, pp. 19–88.

Bhaduri, Amit (1977), 'On the Formation of Usurius Interest Rates in Agriculture', *Cambridge Journal of Economics*, Vol. 1, No. 4, pp. 341–52.

_____ (1986), *Macroeconomics: The Dynamics of Commodity Production*, Macmillan, London.

Chang, H.-J. (1994), *The Political Economy of Industrial Policy*, Macmillan, London.

Chenery, H.B. and A. Strout (1966), 'Foreign Assistance and Economic Development', *American Economic Review*, Vol. 56, No. 4, pp. 679–733.

Dornbusch, R. (1987), 'Exchange Rate Economics', *Economic Journal*, Vol. 97, No. 1, pp. 1–18.

Easterly, W., R. Islam, and J.E. Stiglitz (2001), 'Shaken and Stirred: Explaining Growth Volatility', *Annual Bank Conference on Development Economics*, World Bank, Washington, pp. 191–211.

[39]See Nayyar (1994).

Greenwald, Bruce and J.E. Stiglitz (2003), *Towards a New Paradigm in Monetary Economics*, Cambridge University Press, Cambridge.

Hicks, J.R. (1937), 'Mr Keynes and the Classics: A Suggested Interpretation', *Econometrica*, Vol. 5, No. 2, pp. 147–59.

Jung, W.S. (1985), 'Output-inflation Trade-offs in Industrial and Developing Countries', *Journal of Macroeconomics*, Vol. 7, No. 1, pp. 101–13.

Kalecki, M. (1970), 'Problems of Financing Economic Development in a Mixed Economy', in W. Eltis, M. Scott, and J. Wolfe (eds), *Induction, Growth and Trade: Essays in Honour of Sir Roy Harrod*, Oxford University Press, Oxford, pp. 91–104.

—— (1971), *Selected Essays on the Dynamics of Capitalist Economies*, Cambridge University Press, Cambridge.

—— (1976a), 'The Difference between Crucial Economic Problems of Developed and Underdeveloped Non-socialist Economies', in *Essays on Developing Economies*, Harvester Press, Hassocks, pp. 20–27.

—— (1976b), 'The Problem of Financing Economic Development', in *Essays on Developing Economies*, Harvester Press, Hassocks, pp. 41–63.

McKinnon, R. (1964), 'Foreign Exchange Constraints and Economic Development', *Economic Journal*, Vol. 74, No. 294, pp. 338–409.

Meade, J. (1951), *Theory of International Economic Policy: The Balance of Payments*, Oxford University Press, Oxford.

Nayyar, D. (ed.) (1994), *Industrial Growth and Stagnation: The Debate in India*, Oxford University Press, New Delhi.

—— (1998), 'Short-termism, Public Policies and Economic Development', *Economies et Societies*, Vol. 32, No. 1, pp. 107–18.

—— (2001), 'Macroeconomic Reforms in India: Short-term Effects and Long-term Implications', in W. Mahmud (ed.), *Adjustment and Beyond: The Reform Experience in South Asia*, Palgrave, London, pp. 20–46.

—— (2003), 'Globalization and Development Strategies', in J. Toye (ed.), *Trade and Development: New Directions for the Twenty-first Century*, Edward Elgar, Cheltenham, pp. 35–61.

Ocampo, J.A. (2003), 'Developing Countries' Anti-cyclical Policies in a Globalized World', in A.K. Dutt and J. Ros (eds), *Development Economics and Structuralist Macroeconomics: Essays in Honour of Lance Taylor*, Edward Elgar, Cheltenham, pp. 374–405.

Rakshit, M. (ed.) (1989), *Studies in Macroeconomics of Developing Countries,* Oxford University Press, New Delhi.

Singh, A. (1997), 'Financial Liberalization, Stock Markets, and Developing Countries', *Economic Journal*, Vol. 107, No. 442, pp. 771–82.

Stiglitz, J.E. (1976), 'The Efficiency Wage Hypothesis, Surplus Labour, and the Distribution of Income in LDCs', *Oxford Economic Papers*, Vol. 28, No. 2, pp. 185–207.

—— (1999), 'Towards a General Theory of Wage and Price Rigidities and Economic Fluctuations', *American Economic Review*, Vol. 89, No. 2, pp. 75–80.

Taylor, L. (1983), *Structuralist Macroeconomics*, Basic Books, New York.
_____ (1991), *Income Distribution, Inflation, and Growth*, The MIT Press, Cambridge.
_____ (1994), 'Gap Models', *Journal of Development Economics*, Vol. 45, No. 1, pp. 17–34.
Wade, R. (1990), *Governing the Market: Economic Theory and the Role of Government in East Asian Industrialization*, Princeton University Press, Princeton.

Chapter 2

MACROECONOMICS OF STRUCTURAL ADJUSTMENT AND PUBLIC FINANCES IN DEVELOPING COUNTRIES*

The last quarter of the twentieth century witnessed a striking change in the concerns of macroeconomics. In industrialized countries, the conventional concern of macroeconomics was maintaining short-term equilibrium. The objectives of full employment and price stability were sought to be achieved through fiscal and monetary policy instruments. The slowdown in growth shifted the focus to productivity increase and economic growth in the long-term. In developing countries, the traditional concern of macroeconomics was economic growth in the long-term, with an emphasis on savings and investment. The focus shifted to macro-management in the short-term after many developing countries, as also transition economies, ran into debt crises or other forms of macroeconomic disequilibrium, if not turbulence.

The objective of this essay is to analyse the process of structural adjustment in developing countries that experienced such crises. In doing so, it seeks to focus on macroeconomic stabilization in the short-term, but this discussion is situated in a wider context to consider how it relates to the implications of structural reform in the medium-term and the prospects for economic growth in the long-term. It also endeavours to provide a macroeconomic analysis of government deficits and public finances, which are critical in the process of stabilization and adjustment. Going beyond a critique of orthodox stabilization programmes, it shows that there are alternatives in macro-management for economies in crisis, which would be conducive to development.

The structure of the essay is as follows. The first section outlines the contours of the orthodox, Keynesian, and heterodox perspectives on stabilization and adjustment to highlight their differences. The second section discusses problems of transition from crisis to stabilization and from stabilization

*I would like to thank Jose Antonio Ocampo and Joseph Stiglitz for useful comments and valuable suggestions. I am also grateful to Amit Bhaduri and Lance Taylor for helpful discussion on the subject over the years.

to growth, mostly in terms of theory, but with some reference to experience. The third section considers the relationship between stabilization and growth, which is characterized by interconnections rather than trade-offs, to suggest that much depends on the modes of adjustment. The fourth section examines the concept of twin-deficits, which is at the core of the orthodox belief about adjustment, to trace the underlying economic causation that shapes outcomes. The fifth section analyses government deficits to show that it is necessary to focus on their macroeconomic significance rather than on accounting frameworks, and points to the fallacies of deficit fetishism. The sixth section explores the intersection of economics and politics in the design and implementation of macroeconomic policies. The seventh section develops an alternative framework, which straddles time horizons, to understand the restructuring of economies over time. The eighth section concludes.

MACROECONOMIC ADJUSTMENT: DIFFERENT PERSPECTIVES

In a situation of deep macroeconomic disequilibrium, whether it is a balance of payments crisis or a sharp acceleration of the rate of inflation, stabilization is an imperative. This is widely accepted. Yet, economists cannot agree on how this is to be done. The extensive literature on the subject, which draws on both theory and experience, is characterized by widely divergent perspectives on macroeconomic adjustment. Obviously, the most important differences lie in the prescriptions. But there are significant differences even in analysis and diagnosis. It is possible to make a distinction between three such perspectives: the orthodox perspective, the Keynesian perspective, and the heterodox perspective. There is, of course, some differentiation, just as there are fine nuances, within each of these perspectives. Nevertheless, the differences between the three schools of thought, in theory and policy, are clear enough. It is interesting that these differences are much more visible in the academic debate than in the real world. For in practice, stabilization policies have been essentially similar across a wide range of developing countries and transition economies, primarily because most economies in crisis have been guided by the International Monetary Fund (IMF) and the World Bank in their stabilization and adjustment programmes.

In these programmes of macroeconomic stabilization, there are two fundamental objectives. The first objective is to pre-empt a collapse of the balance of payments situation in the short-term and to reduce the current account deficit in the medium-term. The second objective is to curb inflationary pressures and expectations in the short-term and to reduce the rate of inflation as soon as possible thereafter. The principal instruments of stabilization are fiscal policy and monetary policy, which seek to reduce the level of aggregate demand in the economy, and are often used in conjunction with a devaluation, which seeks to stem destabilizing expectations. This perspective is, of course, based on the presumption that the problems are attributable to rising fiscal deficits, the associated monetary expansion, and an unsustainable exchange rate.

In response to a macroeconomic crisis, stabilization is often combined with adjustment and reform. Such programmes of structural adjustment, based on policy reform advocated by the international financial institutions, are concerned with the supply side in an endeavour to raise the rate of growth of output. Structural reform seeks to shift resources: (a) from the non-traded goods sector to the traded goods sector and within the latter from import competing activities to export activities; and (b) from the government sector to the private sector. Apart from resource allocation, structural reform seeks to improve resource utilization by: (a) increasing the degree of openness of the economy and (b) changing the structure of incentives and institutions, which would reduce the role of State intervention to rely more on the market place, dismantle controls to rely more on prices, and wind down the public sector to rely more on the private sector.

It should be obvious that these are the essential components of orthodox stabilization programmes drawn up as part of an arrangement with the IMF and structural adjustment programmes drawn up as part of an arrangement with the World Bank. Such programmes were adopted by most countries in Latin America, sub-Saharan Africa, South Asia, and Eastern Europe in response to macroeconomic crises. It is worth noting that it was not possible for a country to enter into a stabilization programme with the IMF unless it entered into a structural adjustment programme with the World Bank. In spite of this cross-conditionality, which meant that one was not possible without the other, the relationship between macroeconomic stability and structural reforms has been largely ignored in the conventional literature on the subject.

The prescriptions of the IMF and the World Bank are derived from orthodox economics. The orthodox perspective, in turn, is based on neoclassical economics which assumes competitive markets, profit-maximizing firms, and rational consumers. In this world of abstractions, economies function smoothly in an efficient manner. The episodes of unemployment are only temporary, as there are strong restorative forces. Given the belief that economies, almost always, are at full employment, orthodoxy worries about inflation rather than unemployment. And inflation is seen as policy-induced. It could be the outcome of an expansionary fiscal policy or monetary policy. There is a presumption that government expenditure, whether on consumption or on investment, is unproductive. What is more, fiscal deficits are counterproductive because they erode investor confidence and lead to lower investment. An expansionary monetary policy, it is believed, results in higher prices, not more output, because money affects only price levels and has no impact on output levels. The focus, then, is on inflation and deficits, which are sought to be addressed through a restrictive fiscal policy and a tight monetary policy. In conformity with the monetarist view, the emphasis is on the quantity of money, which translates into domestic credit control in IMF financial programming. Of course, in this belief system, governments are a part of the problem rather than a part of the solution. Even so, it is recognized that if there is a macroeconomic crisis, stabilization policies are essential.

The Keynesian perspective provides a sharp contrast because it is concerned with unemployment and stagnation, which are sought to be addressed through expansionary fiscal and monetary policies. The focus, then, is on levels of employment and output. Thus, in an economic downturn, the prescription is to increase government expenditure, reduce taxes and lower interest rates to stimulate the economy.[1] In developing countries, Keynesians have some preference for monetary policy because lower interest rates and easier credit access would stimulate investment and foster growth. The emphasis is on the interest rate rather than on money supply. However, it is recognized that when an economy is in a severe downturn, or when there is large excess capacity, or when there are supply constraints, an expansionary monetary policy may fail to induce investment. In such circumstances, the Keynesian view advocates the use of fiscal policy. Stepping up government investment is seen as the best method, for it would bring tangible results and yield social benefits. It would also foster growth. However, in the short-term, even unproductive investment or consumption expenditure by the government would lead to an expansion of output through the multiplier effect. Obviously, for a developing country in an economic downturn, short-term macro-management would be conducive to growth in the medium-term if it encourages investment. It may be possible to stimulate private investment through lower interest rates or easier credit access. But this process can be supported by increases in public investment. Indeed, in developing countries, public investment, particularly in infrastructure, crowds-in private investment. The merits of such a counter-cyclical approach are obvious. Of course, there are two implications of expansionary macroeconomic policies that must be recognized. For one, excessive stimulation may lead to

[1] See Keynes (1936).

inflation but this is acceptable within limits if it leads to higher levels of output and employment. For another, expansionary policies could enlarge the current account deficit in the balance of payments and it may be difficult to find the requisite external finance following a debt crisis.

The heterodox perspective differs not only from the orthodox view but also from the Keynesian view. It explores alternative approaches and unconventional methods to stabilize the economy, combat inflation, increase employment, and stimulate growth.[2] In this process, the role of the government is seen as very important. The heterodox view argues for a wider range of instruments and a larger range of mechanisms through which economic policies can help achieve macroeconomic objectives. Hence, much more emphasis is placed on supply side effects, implications for income distribution, the role of expectations, and a broad range of balance-sheet effects at the micro level. The heterodox view is critical of the orthodox view for using models of firm and household behaviour which abstract so much from reality. It starts from the premise that markets are not competitive, households are often not rational, and neither have perfect information. Thus, asymmetries in information, juxtaposed with risk, shape their behaviour. More realistic assumptions in models, based on observed behaviour of firms and households, provide a strong rationale for government intervention in the economy and more instruments to stabilize the economy. In contrast with the Keynesian view which emphasizes aggregate demand, the heterodox view also recognizes the importance of aggregate supply. If there are wage–price rigidities, a leftward shift in either the aggregate demand curve or the aggregate supply curve would lead to a reduction in the levels of output and employment. But that is not all. Shocks to the economy which reduce aggregate demand also simultaneously reduce aggregate supply.

Conversely, an increase in aggregate demand can also have positive effects on the supply side. This deserves explanation. An increase in market size facilitates the realization of scale economies, thus bringing about a cost reduction, just as a reduction in costs, and hence prices, induces a demand expansion. Over time, the underlying factors are dynamic scale economies and increases in labour

---

[2]The heterodox approach, itself, is diverse. It is, therefore, worth citing some references. The tradition goes back to the work of Kalecki. See, in particular, Kalecki (1971 and 1976). Some of the more important contributions of this tradition, combined with contributions from other schools of thought, have been developed by Lance Taylor. See, in particular, Taylor (1991 and 2004). The heterodox approach, in the Kalecki tradition, is also developed in Bhaduri (1986). The Latin American structuralist tradition, too, played an important role. See, for example, Furtado (1971) and Ffrench-Davis (2000).

productivity. This cumulative causation which is complex but virtuous is often termed the 'Kaldor–Verdoorn Law'.[3] Such cumulative causation can also be the opposite of virtuous.[4] In this world, demand and supply are intertwined, which must be recognized rather than ignored in the formulation of stabilization policies. For one, it exercises an important influence on the effectiveness of monetary and fiscal policies in different situations. For another, it highlights the importance of distributional conflicts underlying inflationary processes.

Such different perspectives on the macroeconomics of adjustment are attributable to the following reasons. First, different schools of thought stress different objectives. For some, price stability is an end in itself. For others, the essential objective is to increase growth and reduce poverty. For most, however, controlling inflation is a means whereas more rapid, stable, and equitable growth is the end. Second, different schools of thought differ in their understanding of, or belief about, how an economy functions or adjusts. This leads to genuine differences in thinking about outcomes. Third, different schools of thought make different assumptions. Sometimes these differences in assumptions remain unstated because they are implicit rather than explicit. Inevitably, this accentuates their differences.

PROBLEMS OF TRANSITION

In any process of stabilization, adjustment, and reform, economies experience problems of transition so that their return to a path of sustained growth, combined with stability in the price level and the balance of payments situation, is not assured. It is possible to consider such problems of transition at two levels.[5] First, in terms of analysis, we can consider such problems that arise from the interaction between the demand side and the supply side, problems that arise largely on the demand side or problems that arise mostly on the supply side. Second, in terms of actual experience, there are problems which have emerged from IMF programmes of stabilization and World Bank programmes of structural adjustment in Latin America, sub-Saharan Africa, East Europe, and South Asia. The distribution of the burden of adjustment, in the process of transition, is a problem that surfaces at both levels.

The fundamental problem of transition arises from the fact that the speeds of adjustment on the demand and supply sides are considerably different. Fiscal adjustment and monetary discipline can be used to squeeze aggregate

---

[3]See Kaldor (1978).

[4]For an interesting analysis of cumulative causation with negative consequences in this link between growth and productivity, see Ocampo and Taylor (1998).

[5]For a detailed discussion, see Nayyar (1995). See also Bhaduri (1992).

demand so that, in response to inflation, the speed of adjustment on the demand side is fast. The response of demand to expansionary fiscal and monetary policies is just as rapid. On the other hand, the speed of adjustment on the supply side is inevitably slow, because resources are not perfectly mobile across sectors or substitutable in uses; moreover, prices, particularly of factors of production, are not completely flexible. This is so even if all the price incentives of a market economy can be brought to perfect function. The problems are accentuated in economies characterized by structural rigidities which obviously constrain the response to structural reforms. Supply adjustment based on an expansion of output requires structural changes through creation of capacity, alleviation of infrastructural bottlenecks, streamlining of input supplies, reorientation of public utilities and so on, all of which take time. In contrast, supply adjustment based on a contraction of output is, in some instances, as rapid as demand adjustment. Therefore, the dynamics of demand are fast in both expansion and contraction, whereas the dynamics of supply are slow in expansion but faster in contraction. These asymmetries have four macroeconomic implications which are crucial in the process of stabilization and adjustment.

First, stabilization policies which are meant to reduce demand may, at the same time, reduce supply even more, for the simple reason that a substantial fiscal adjustment and a tight monetary policy squeeze both investable resources and working capital. As an economy contracts from both sides, the current account deficit may possibly be reduced but inflation would not be restrained. Second, insofar as aggregate demand remains greater than aggregate supply, or the sectoral composition of demand does not match the sectoral composition of supply, and balance of payments constraints prevent excess demand from being met through imports, inflation persists. Third, the initial effects of structural reform, particularly in situations where the balance of payments constraint is binding, may lead to a contraction of output in some sectors before an expansion of output in other sectors. This tends to increase excess demand in the system and exacerbates the problem of inflation. Fourth, fiscal contraction and monetary discipline which squeeze aggregate demand in the short-term may constrain supply responses in the medium-term. Yet, without a foundation of macroeconomic stabilization in the short-term, policy reform simply cannot produce the desired results in the medium-term. This is the crux of the problem when economies begin adjustment processes in a situation of deep macroeconomic disequilibrium.

On the demand side, the optimistic scenario implicit in IMF stabilization programmes is that inflation would come down and the current account deficit would be reduced, while the economy would adjust at a macro-level through a fall in prices and a rise in output. This outcome, however, is by no means certain. Nor is the transition from crisis to stabilization. In fact, it is perfectly possible that fiscal austerity and monetary discipline may not reduce the current account deficit and the rate of inflation. Reduced fiscal deficits do not always translate into reduced current account deficits if the impact of the consequent deflation is largely on non-traded goods, so that reduced domestic absorption may not stimulate exports and dampen imports. Restrictive monetary policies, which combine a credit squeeze with high interest rates, do not always curb inflation if inflationary pressures and expectations are influenced not only by excess liquidity but also by real disproportionalities or structural rigidities, and if price formation is based on mark-ups, administered-pricing, and cost-indexation rather than market-clearing.[6] The impact of macroeconomic adjustment on output, from the demand side, is also crucial. In principle, adjustment is possible either through an increase in output or through a decrease in expenditure. In practice, however, economies in crisis would not readily forego output and borrow to meet expenditure. Economic retrenchment, in which countries are forced to cut expenditures, is thus the more probable outcome.[7] This tends to impact output through aggregate demand and, if there are wage–price rigidities, the mode of macroeconomic adjustment may then be a reduction in output rather than in prices. At the same time, a significant devaluation, which is often an integral part of stabilization programmes,[8] may exacerbate the rise in prices and reinforce the contraction in output at least in the short-run.[9] Devaluations escalate inflation directly through cost-push and indirectly through mark-ups. The consequent cut in real wages, and the possible deterioration in the terms of trade following a devaluation, may reduce real income in the economy, leading to a contractionary effect on output.[10] It would appear that the transition path to stabilization is like walking a tight rope. If inflation does not slow down or the balance of payments does not stabilize, the intended virtuous circle is easily transformed into an unintended

[6]For a discussion of alternative hypotheses on inflation, see Taylor (1988).

[7]See Cooper (1992).

[8]It is worth noting that orthodox policy prescriptions on the exchange rate are different in different contexts. In the African context, for example, devaluation is considered desirable since it is supposed to improve the trade balance. In the Latin American context, however, a strong exchange rate is considered desirable for price stability and for portfolio investment.

[9]There is also a temporal dimension, which cannot be ignored and should be recognized. In the medium-term, a devaluation could be an important policy instrument for development.

[10]For an analysis of the possible contractionary effects of a devaluation, see Krugman and Taylor (1978).

vicious circle, as the exchange rate and the price level chase each other. In these situations, particularly where the mode of macroeconomic adjustment is contraction of output, stagflation is a probable scenario.[11]

On the supply side, the optimistic scenario implicit in liberalization programmes guided by the Bretton Woods institutions is that structural reform would impart both efficiency and dynamism to the growth process in the medium-term. The transition from stabilization to growth, however, is by no means assured. The sequence and the pace of restructuring must be such that it can be absorbed by the economy. If this is not the case, things can go wrong. Trade policy reform may stimulate output by creating economic efficiency gains, but it can also move an economy from a situation of too much protection to a situation of too little protection and if the manufacturing sector is unable to cope with such a rapid transition the outcome may be forced de-industrialization. Industrial deregulation, which removes barriers to entry and limits on growth, may increase competition among firms and improve resource utilization. However, it often leads to retrenchment or closures and cannot wish away barriers to exit, particularly in economies where income levels are low, unemployment levels are high, and social safety nets are absent. Deregulation in the financial sector, unless it is paced with care, can be perilous not just in terms of bubbles that burst or scandals that surface, but also if it diverts scarce resources from productive uses into speculative activities. Public sector reform, which is based on the sale of government assets and rudimentary forms of privatization, may not resolve the real problems of efficiency or productivity, but it can end up socializing the costs and privatizing the benefits. Capital market liberalization imposes constraints on macroeconomic policies. Lower interest rates can no longer be used to encourage domestic investment, just as higher government deficits can no longer be used to expand aggregate demand, for fear that this might provoke massive capital outflows. And such integration into international financial markets, which is often premature, makes the economy far more vulnerable.[12] Therefore, the content, sequence, and speed of policy reform must be planned and calibrated in a careful manner, such that it recognizes structural rigidities where they exist instead of assuming structural flexibilities where they do not exist. In sum, supply response may be induced but cannot be assured by policy regimes alone, for resources are neither as substitutable in use nor as flexible in price as neoclassical economics suggests.

[11]This did happen in Latin America where the 1980s are, in retrospect, described as the lost decade. Many countries in Eastern Europe, in their process of transition from planned systems to market economies, experienced similar difficulties.

[12]For a more detailed discussion of this issue, see Nayyar (2003a).

The actual experience of stabilization, adjustment, and reform programmes in Latin America and sub-Saharan Africa, guided by the IMF and the World Bank in a medium-term perspective, also reflects problems of transition. The critical evaluation of these programmes in the literature on the subject points to significant dangers.[13] First, almost without exception, there is an adverse impact on poverty insofar as the burden of adjustment is borne largely by the poor. Second, these programmes tend to stifle long-term growth prospects so that a return to the path of sustained growth is often a hope rather than a reality. Third, such programmes tend to overestimate export prospects and the availability of external finance and, when this does not materialize, economies are forced into a deflation that imposes social costs and squeezes supply responses. Fourth, there is a steady externalization of policy formulation. For one, responsiveness to changing and evolving situations is significantly reduced as policy prescriptions are characterized by an analytical absolutism: if you have a balance of payments problem the answer lies in liberalizing trade and if you have a fiscal crisis the answer lies in reducing tax rates. For another, sensitivity to social and political realities is sharply eroded as national policies are shaped without reference to the context.[14]

The experience of stabilization and adjustment in the transition economies of Eastern Europe, during the early 1990s, was similar. And the outcomes were almost the same.[15] It would seem that the IMF and the World Bank did not learn from their experience in Latin America and sub-Saharan Africa during the 1980s. In fact, not much changed in Latin America during the 1990s.[16] Indeed, the same mistakes were repeated following the financial crises in East Asia during the late 1990s. More recently, the story was no different in Argentina. In response to the crises, the IMF stabilization programmes in Korea, Indonesia, Thailand, and Argentina adopted contractionary fiscal and monetary policies despite clear signs of a severe economic downturn in these

[13]There is an extensive literature on this subject. See, for example, Williamson (1983 and 1990); Killick (1984), and Taylor (1993).

[14]In the policy lending programmes of international financial institutions, conditionalities begin with the classical areas of economic policy, but then extend to social institutions such as civil service systems or legal frameworks and political areas such as governance, human rights, and democracy. Soon, these policy engineers find themselves doing nothing short of what political leaders are supposed to do. This is a serious mistake, for it imposes outside intervention in what must be national policies. And, for all the rhetoric about ownership, there has been no significant change in this reality.

[15]See, for example, Amsden et al. (1994).

[16]For a careful analysis of the Latin American experience with macroeconomic stabilization and structural reforms, see Ocampo (2004).

countries. The prescriptions continued to be based on the approach that one-size-fits-all. It was simply not recognized that the East Asian crises, unlike the Latin American crises in previous decades, were not caused by large government deficits or loose monetary policies. And it is hardly surprising that contractionary macroeconomic policies made the downturns worse. The high interest rates imposed high social costs, in terms of output and employment foregone, because firms in these economies were highly leveraged.[17] Malaysia did not follow orthodox prescriptions. Instead, it introduced capital controls.[18] Consequently, perhaps, Malaysia's downturn was shorter and shallower. Even the IMF now accepts that it made a mistake in East Asia.[19] A study by the IMF Independent Evaluation Office also shows that the IMF consistently overestimated investment and growth prospects, particularly in economies in crisis.[20]

In evaluating experiences across countries, it is difficult to define and then identify 'success' or 'failure' because actual outcomes span a wide spectrum from moderate successes at one end to real disasters at the other. But the diverse experiences do establish that the transitions from crisis to stabilization and from stabilization to growth are characterized by a discernible set of problems.

Macroeconomic adjustment and structural reform are not simply a matter of academic discourse. During the transition period, these processes impose a real burden of adjustment that is distributed in an asymmetric manner. Without correctives, the burden of adjustment is inevitably borne by the poor. For all the rhetoric about social safety nets, economies in crisis simply do not have the resources for this purpose. It cannot suffice to assert, as governments often do, that the burden of such adjustment would have to be borne by the affluent simply because it is the rich who have the incomes to immunize themselves from the burdens of structural change. It is obvious that there can be no adjustment without pain, but pain for whom? This is why correctives are necessary. Inflation tends to make the rich better-off as it redistributes incomes from wages to profits and the poor worse-off as it erodes their incomes which are not index-linked. The soft options in fiscal adjustment tend to squeeze public expenditure in social sectors where there are no vocal political constituencies, as the sources allocated for poverty alleviation, health care, education, and

[17]The use of high interest rates advocated by the IMF provides an ironical twist. The monetarist perspective always stressed the quantity of money, while the Keynesian perspective always emphasized the interest rate. This aspect of Keynesianism was revived in a perverse sense because of international capital flows.

[18]For a discussion on the East Asian crises and their aftermath, see Furman and Stiglitz (1998). See also, Jomo (2001).

[19]Lane et al. (1999).

[20]See Independent Evaluation Office (2003).

welfare programmes decline in real terms. Restructuring on the supply side, which follows structural reform, inevitably imposes a burden on wage labour. Such outcomes, borne out by available evidence, can only hurt the poor.[21] Adjustment with a human face is then an illusion.

STABILIZATION AND GROWTH

The meaning of stabilization in economics is much the same as in medicine: just as medical treatment seeks to stabilize the health of a patient in critical condition, economic management attempts to stabilize an economy in deep crisis. The focus of the literature on macroeconomic stabilization is, however, narrow. Much of the discussion is on stabilization of prices. Some of the discussion is on stabilization of balance of payments situations. There is almost no reference to stabilization of output levels or income levels. What is more, the time horizon for such discussion is the short-run. However, what concerns people is the stability of their incomes in the short-run and the growth of their incomes over time. Growth matters because it is cumulative. If the growth in GDP, in real terms, is 2.5 per cent per annum, income doubles in 28 years. But if this growth rate is 5 per cent per annum, income doubles in 14 years. And if this growth rate is 7.5 per cent per annum, income doubles in 9 years.

It is essential to recognize that stabilization cannot, and should not, be separated from growth. There are important reasons. First, short-run stabilization policies have long-term consequences. Second, the relationship between stabilization and growth is characterized by interconnections rather than trade-offs. Third, the objective must be stabilization with growth which cannot be reduced to an either–or choice.

In this context, it is important to recognize two limitations of the orthodox belief system. First, for economies in crisis, orthodox economists advise that governments should not attempt to attain full employment. Instead, governments are urged to accept the pain of adjustment, in the form of lower output today, for a higher output tomorrow. This recommendation conforms to the strong spring analogy: the harder you push the spring down, the greater the force with which it bounces back. But critics believe that a weak spring is a more appropriate analogy for the economy, for when it is pushed too hard, it may simply remain there if its restorative forces are destroyed. This is mere analogy but statistical analysis provides some support for the critics.[22] Second,

---

[21]For evidence on the impact of structural adjustment on the social sectors, nutrition, health, and living standards in developing countries, see Cornia et al. (1987). See also, Mehrotra and Jolly (1997).

[22]See Ben-David and Papell (1998) and Lutz (1999).

orthodox economists place an excessive emphasis on price stability, which is simply not appropriate. Such thinking may have been shaped by the experience of hyperinflation in Latin America during the 1980s and in Eastern Europe during the early 1990s. And hyperinflation did indeed mean huge costs and devastating consequences for those economies. But this hyperinflation was tamed. And countries in Asia, as also Africa, have rarely, if ever, experienced hyperinflation. Indeed, rates of inflation in Asia and Africa have been moderate. Available evidence suggests that moderate rates of inflation have been associated with rapid economic growth in many countries across the developing world.[23] Indeed, Kalecki's macroeconomic analysis of underdeveloped countries suggested that moderate rates of inflation might enable an economy to attain a higher rate of growth than would otherwise be possible.[24] Since the early 1990s, most developing countries and transitional economies have experienced moderate or low inflation. In countries where inflation is already moderate or low, concerted policy efforts to reduce it further, at the margin, may yield only small benefits but impose large costs, for this can only squeeze employment in the short-term and dampen growth in the medium-term.

The implications and consequences of stabilization policies in the short-run for economic growth in the medium-term depend, in part, on the mode of adjustment in the economy at a macro level.

Economies can adjust at a macro level either through changes in prices or through changes in incomes. In a world of wage–price flexibility, which conforms to the orthodox view, the outcome would be price adjustment and the path from stabilization to growth would be smooth. In a world of wage–price rigidities, which conforms to the Keynesian view and the heterodox view, the outcome would be income adjustment. Such beggar-thyself policies are bound to have a negative impact on growth.

Economies in crisis can adjust either through an increase in output or through a decrease in expenditure. Adjustment through output expansion would obviously have a positive impact on growth. This would be easier in situations where there are underutilized capacities. Adjustment through expenditure reduction would obviously have a negative impact on growth. Insofar as economies in crisis are likely to be output-concerned, economic retrenchment, in which countries are forced to cut expenditure, is the more probable outcome. Such macroeconomic adjustment can only place the economy on a slower growth path with effects that would persist in the medium-term.

[23]For a discussion, as also evidence, see Stiglitz et al. (2006).
[24]See Kalecki (1970).

Economic growth can come from an increase in the productivity of investment, but only in part. Ultimately, sustained economic growth also requires an increase in the investment–GDP ratio. In an open economy, at a macro level, the excess of investment over savings corresponds to the excess of imports over exports. The strategy conducive to growth, then, would be to raise the investment–GDP ratio. For economies that are prone to debt crises, or do not have adequate access to external financing, this higher investment rate should be sustained by raising the export–GDP ratio and the domestic savings–GDP ratio, rather than by allowing a compensatory increase in the import–GDP ratio supported by foreign capital inflows. This underlines the significance of increasing exports and raising domestic savings. The former is recognized. The latter is forgotten. Following a debt crisis, or faced with limits on external financing, an economy could also adjust by lowering its investment–GDP ratio, so as to manage with a lower import–GDP ratio that can be supported by available external finance, given the export–GDP ratio and the domestic savings–GDP ratio. This mode of adjustment would obviously not be conducive to growth.

In developing countries, it is more than likely that the mode of adjustment may not be growth-friendly. The reason is that, under normal circumstances, there is a pro-cyclical pattern to macroeconomic policies. This is particularly true of fiscal policy.[25] During downswings of the business cycle, as the economy slows down, tax revenues fall or do not rise as much as expected. The ability of the government to service public debt diminishes. The interest rate on government borrowing rises. And governments find it not only more expensive but also more difficult to borrow in order to finance expenditure. During upswings of the business cycle, the opposite happens. Government revenues recover. So does government expenditure. And governments have more access to cheaper credit.

The social costs of pro-cyclical fiscal policies are high. In downturns, cuts in public expenditure squeeze investment in infrastructure and reduce allocations for social sectors, which can only dampen growth in the long-term. In upturns, readily available finances may be used for investments that yield low returns or even for unproductive consumption expenditure. In general, stop–go cycles are bound to reduce the efficiency of government spending. Yet, there are strong, embedded incentives or disincentives for governments to adopt pro-cyclical fiscal policies. In a downturn, therefore, such pro-cyclical policies can only accentuate difficulties in the short-run and dampen growth in the medium-term.

[25]For a detailed discussion, see Ocampo (2003).

The probability of such outcomes increases with orthodox stabilization programmes, which advocate pro-cyclical macroeconomic policies: a restrictive fiscal policy and a tight monetary policy. This is just the opposite of anti-cyclical macroeconomic policies adopted as a rule by governments in industrialized countries. It is also counter-intuitive insofar as it is the opposite of what students of macroeconomics learn across the world. As a result, growth is dampened, if not stifled.[26]

Clearly, then, it is both necessary and desirable to explore alternative methods of stabilization, which would minimize the negative impact on growth and, if possible, foster growth. In this endeavour, it is important to learn from mistakes in orthodox policies and from experience with unorthodox policies.

A contractionary fiscal policy is often associated with cuts in public investment which constrain growth in the medium-term, in part, because such cuts squeeze investment in infrastructure and, in part, because such cuts dampen private investment. Similarly, a tight monetary policy used to stabilize prices can constrain growth by making funds for investment more expensive and less available. In developing countries, higher interest rates dampen private investment. But that is not all. High interest rates can also lead to more failures in firms and banks. All this inhibits future growth.

Obviously, it would be preferable to consider alternative methods of stabilization. Fiscal adjustment should not rely excessively on expenditure reduction but should also attempt to increase the income of the government. At the same time, it is essential to raise the level and rate of investment in the economy. For this, an increase in public investment, particularly in infrastructure, is perhaps the most effective method, because it could stimulate private investment and ease supply constraints. Similarly, stepping up public expenditure in social sectors would not only protect the poor or the vulnerable but would also help maintain aggregate demand wherever necessary. Easier access to credit, even if selective, or the use of controls on capital inflows, instead of relying on higher interest rates alone, would also reduce the adverse effects of stabilization on growth. What is more, the anti-cyclical stance of such methods, taken together, would be supportive of growth in the medium-term.

Economic policies do matter. And, for an economy in crisis, whether the government raises or lowers expenditure, or raises or lowers interest rates, makes an enormous difference. The mix of policies is obviously important but the trade-off between stabilization and growth is much less than what orthodoxy suggests.

[26]See Easterly et al. (2001).

DEFICITS AND ADJUSTMENT: IDENTITIES AND CAUSATION

The economic philosophy of orthodox stabilization programmes rests on the belief that the internal imbalance in the fiscal situation and the external imbalance in the payment situation are closely related. The macroeconomics of this relationship can be reduced to a simple proposition based on the national income accounting identity: *ex post*, the current account deficit in an economy is the sum of (i) the difference between investment and saving in the private sector and (ii) the difference between expenditure and income in the government sector.[27] Thus, an external (current account) deficit in an open economy requires that either the private sector invests more than it saves or that the government sector spends more than it earns, or some combination of both. And, in an open economy, for any given saving–investment gap in the private sector, there would be a one-to-one correspondence between changes in the current account deficit (surplus) and the government deficit (surplus).

This proposition, derived from the national income accounting identity, forms the analytical basis of the concept of twin-deficits in orthodox macroeconomics, conceptualized and popularized by the IMF. The conclusion drawn is that any reduction in the current account deficit in the balance of payments of an economy requires a reduction in the fiscal deficit of the government. It is possible to reduce this proposition to an even simpler formulation. If the private sector is assumed to make both ends meet, so that income equals expenditure and, given consumption, saving equals investment, the deficit in public finance would be exactly equal to the deficit in the current account in the balance of payments. The excess of expenditure over income in the government sector, then, is matched exactly by an excess of expenditure over income for the economy as a whole which is met by borrowing from abroad. But, as we have seen, even if saving and investment in the private sector are not equal, there is a correspondence between the current account deficit of an economy and the fiscal deficit of its government.

---

[27]The simple national income accounting identity $Y = C + I + X - M$ can be rewritten as $I - S = M - X$, given that $Y - C = S$. Let Ip and Sp denote investment and saving in the private sector. Let Ig, Sg, Cg, Eg, and Yg denote investment, saving, consumption, expenditure, and income, respectively, in the government sector.

$$
\begin{aligned}
\text{Then, } I - S \quad &= \quad (Ip + Ig) - (Sp + Sg) \\
&= \quad (Ip - Sp) + (Ig - Sg) \\
\text{In turn, } (Ig - Sg) \quad &= \quad [Ig - (Yg - Cg)] \\
&= \quad [(Ig + Cg) - Yg] \\
&= \quad (Eg - Yg) \\
\text{Therefore, } (M - X) \quad &= \quad (Ip - Sp) + (Eg - Yg)
\end{aligned}
$$

It must be stressed that an accounting identity does not, and cannot, establish economic causation. For a definitional equality is a mere truism. It is not an explanation. Consider, for example, the statement: 'It rains on a rainy day.' This is a truism. It does not explain why it rains or when rain can be expected. Similarly, the twin-deficit definition does not identify any mechanism by which a reduction in the fiscal deficit will lead to a reduction in the current account deficit. For an understanding of macroeconomic systems, the accounting relations of macroeconomic aggregates need to be combined with an economic analysis of causal determinants. The nature of relationships between variables (what is autonomous and what is induced) and the direction of causation (what determines what) are both functions of the institutional setting. In principle, the mechanism, if it exists, must work either through prices or through quantities or through some combination of both. In practice, the nature of causation would be determined by the institutional context in the economy.

The price adjustment story runs as follows. Given revenues, an increase in government expenditure will mean a higher government deficit, causing inflation, hence raising prices of goods produced at home. As a result, at a given exchange rate, people will buy cheaper foreign goods rather than domestic goods which will widen the trade (current account) deficit, until the government deficit and the external deficit match one another or correspond to restore the definitional identity. A similar mechanism would also work in the opposite direction. A reduction in the government deficit would then correspondingly reduce the trade (current account) deficit by improving the price competitiveness of domestic goods in the world market. This simple theoretical construct can be embellished in many ways with models or statistics. But the basic story line remains. And this is the story line that the IMF advocates.

But there is an alternative story based on quantities, or outputs and incomes, rather than prices. The income adjustment story runs as follows. As the government reduces its expenditure, hence deficit, the purchasing power in the economy falls, directly in the government sector, and then, indirectly, in the private sector for producers and workers who supply to meet the demand from government. The result, through the multiplier, is a magnified fall in purchasing power, much larger than the original reduction in the government deficit. This contraction in purchasing power means a shrinking market at home for domestic producers, leading to a spreading loss of income and employment all around. It is this falling income which reduces imports until the trade (current account) deficit is reduced again to match, or to correspond with, the government deficit. A similar mechanism would work in the opposite direction. And this is the story line that orthodoxy ignores.

There is much that we can learn about this process of adjustment from the experience of orthodox stabilization programmes. A large number of countries in Latin America, Africa, Asia, and Eastern Europe have undergone stabilization, as part of an arrangement with the IMF, over the past 25 years. Available evidence suggests that a substantial reduction in the government deficit reduces the trade deficit very significantly through a reduction in the level of economic activity, employment and output, rather than by simply reducing the rate of inflation in the country attempting stabilization. Thus, reduced government deficits may end up reducing trade deficits, only at considerable social cost, through a reduction in output and employment which is accentuated by multiplier effects. It would seem that the income adjustment story is more probable, and no less plausible, than the price adjustment story.[28]

The orthodoxy about twin-deficits simply assumes that macroeconomic systems are characterized by price adjustment and not income adjustment. This, in turn, rests on the convenient assumption that stabilization through deflation, which reduces government deficits, will not affect output, and even if it does, the impact would be little. The quantity theory of money provides the analytical foundation for this belief on the premise that any fall in the quantity of real output is exogenous, and full employment is always maintained. This thinking is reinforced by the belief that reduced government deficits reduce monetary expansion which lowers prices. But we know that reduced government deficits can also reduce output through the multiplier effect. This is validated by experience in country after country. Therefore, it is not plausible to expect smooth price adjustment and to assume away harsh income adjustment.

It is clear that the concept of twin-deficits is misleading as an analytical construct because an accounting identity does not establish economic causation. But that is not all. It may not even provide an accurate description of real world situations. Starting from the same identity, it can be said that, for any given expenditure–income gap in the government sector, there would be a one-to-one correspondence between changes in the current account deficit (surplus) and the saving–investment gap in the private sector. Insofar as the three gaps must sum to zero, much depends on which one is relatively stable. And if the government deficit (surplus) is relatively stable, the twin-deficits story could be missing out on the reality that the current account deficit (surplus) is shaped by the private sector. It is plausible to suggest that this may be so in much of Asia.

[28]For a discussion, as also evidence on this issue, see Bhaduri and Nayyar (1996). See also, Taylor (1988) and Cooper (1992).

MACROECONOMICS OF PUBLIC FINANCES

In analysing the macroeconomics of structural adjustment, the discussion so far has simply referred to the fiscal deficit of the government. This generic term conceals more than it reveals. There are different measures of deficits in government finances, which are often used in an inter-changeable manner. This can be misleading. Even at the risk of stressing the obvious, therefore, it is worth making an analytical distinction between the gross fiscal deficit, the monetized deficit, the revenue deficit, and the primary deficit.[29]

The gross fiscal deficit measures the difference between revenue receipts plus grants and total expenditure plus net domestic lending, where the latter exceeds the former. In simpler words, it is the difference between the total income and the total expenditure of the government which is financed by borrowing. Therefore, it also provides a measure of the increase in public debt during the year. It is the most complete measure of the deficit in government finances.

The monetized deficit is that part of the gross fiscal deficit which is financed by government borrowing from the central bank. In most developing countries, borrowing from the central bank is the primary source of reserve money. Thus, for any given money multiplier, the monetized deficit is the main determinant of the increase in money supply in the economy.

The revenue deficit or the revenue surplus measures the difference between the revenue receipts of the government (made up of tax revenues plus non-tax revenues) and the non-investment (consumption) expenditure of the government. It seeks to focus on the revenue account in the gross fiscal deficit by excluding the capital account. The distinction between the capital account and the revenue account is most simply stated as follows: transactions which affect the net wealth or debt position of the government enter into the capital account while transactions which affect the income or expenditure of the government enter into the revenue account. Therefore, the revenue deficit provides a measure of government borrowing that is used to support consumption. In this sense, it is an important index of whether a fiscal regime is sustainable.

The primary deficit is the gross fiscal deficit minus interest payments. This is important for two reasons. For one, interest rates can be volatile and are sometimes beyond the control of governments in developing countries. For another, in countries where government debt is large as a proportion of GDP, interest payments constitute a large, pre-emptive component of government

---

[29]See Nayyar (1995).

expenditure.[30] What is more, public debt that has accumulated over a long period of time means that a large gross fiscal deficit will persist for quite some time even after correctives have been introduced. The primary deficit shows more clearly whether the observed change makes the situation better or worse. Governments also need to focus on what they can control at a point in time.

Macroeconomic policy is guided by a focus on intermediate variables such as deficits in government finances. But this can be misleading if accounting frameworks are inappropriate. Even appropriate accounting frameworks are not enough. The reason is simple. Such measures are like a thermometer. If it shows that the body temperature is above normal, it signals that something is wrong. But a thermometer does not provide a diagnosis for a patient. Similarly, an accounting framework can never provide a complete diagnosis, let alone a prescription, for an economy.

The accounting frameworks in use for deficits in government finances are an almost perfect illustration of this problem. And the problem is compounded because different measures are used for different purposes in a manner that is far from consistent. For a meaningful analysis of policy, therefore, it is essential that the use of accounting frameworks is determined by their macroeconomic significance. If the objective is to measure the total borrowing needs of the government, the gross fiscal deficit is the most appropriate. If the objective is to consider the implications of a deficit in government finances for monetary expansion, as an index of inflationary pressures, the monetized deficit is the most appropriate. If the objective is to assess whether a fiscal regime is sustainable over time, the revenue deficit is the most appropriate. If the objective is to examine what governments can do, or have done, to improve the fiscal situation, the primary deficit is the most appropriate.

This conceptual clarity is necessary. But it cannot eliminate ambiguities or anomalies altogether. It is worth citing some examples. First, the distinction between deficit financing of public consumption *versus* public investment is not always clear cut. The reason is simple. The conventional accounting notion of public consumption includes expenditures on health and education which, if well executed, have a large investment component. Second, in developing countries, the IMF has sought to focus on the overall public sector deficit, which includes not only all tiers of government but also government-owned firms. Such a consolidated budget for the public sector in an economy means that an increase in borrowing by public sector firms leads to an increase in

---

[30]Some inflation correction for interest payments would also be appropriate but such an adjustment is difficult to incorporate in accounting frameworks.

the overall public sector deficit. In Europe, however, the IMF does not include borrowing by public sector firms in the government sector. This asymmetrical treatment embedded in accounting frameworks creates anomalies. Third, accounting frameworks in use by the IMF encourage governments to privatize public sector firms, insofar as capital receipts from such asset sales are absorbed in the budget to reduce the gross fiscal deficit of the government, even when such privatization is otherwise not necessary or desirable. From the perspective of the public sector, it would be preferable to use the proceeds from the sale of government equity, at least in part, to restructure public enterprises. In terms of macroeconomic management, it would obviously be desirable to use receipts from such asset sales to reduce (repay) public debt. But conventional accounting frameworks do not provide any credit for such sensible macroeconomics.

Such accounting frameworks also provide the basis for performance criteria that are used by the IMF in monitoring its stabilization programmes. The consequence is a concern about deficits in government finances that borders on fetishism. It is essential to recognize the fallacies of such deficit fetishism.[31]

Orthodoxy believes that reducing gross fiscal deficits is both necessary and sufficient for the macroeconomic adjustment. This is a myth. The size of the fiscal deficit, or the amount of government borrowing, is the symptom and not the disease. And there is nothing in macroeconomics which stipulates an optimum level to which the fiscal deficit must be reduced as a proportion of GDP. Indeed, it is possible that a fiscal deficit at 6 per cent of GDP is sustainable in one situation while a fiscal deficit at 4 per cent of GDP is not sustainable in another situation. The real issue is the allocation and end-use of government expenditure in relation to the cost of borrowing by the government. Thus, government borrowing is always sustainable if it is used to finance investment and if the rate of such investment is greater than the interest rate payable.

In an ideal world, there should be a revenue surplus large enough to finance capital expenditure on the social sectors, as also on defence, where there are no immediate or tangible returns. This would ensure that borrowing is used only to finance investment expenditure which yields a future income flow to the exchequer. So long as that income flow is greater than the burden of servicing the accumulated debt, government borrowing remains sustainable. In the real world, however, government borrowing is sometimes used, at least in part, to support consumption expenditure. In these circumstances, the rate of return on investment, financed by the remainder of the borrowing cannot be high

---

[31]For a discussion, see Nayyar (1996).

enough to meet the burden of servicing the entire debt. This problem is often compounded by IMF conditions in stabilization programmes which raise the cost of government borrowing. For one, governments are forced to cut back sharply on borrowing at low interest rates from the central bank so as to reduce monetary expansion. For another, financial deregulation means that governments have to borrow at a significantly higher cost, from the commercial bank system and the domestic capital market, as interest rates on government securities are raised to market levels.[32]

There is a similar fetishism about monetized deficits. It serves little purpose to eliminate the monetized deficits for fear of inflation if the government continues to borrow as much from elsewhere, instead of the central bank, but at a much higher cost. There are other important macroeconomic consequences of such monetarism. For one, it makes public debt much less manageable and reduces fiscal flexibility for governments as interest payments pre-empt a much larger proportion of government expenditure. For another, high interest rates, which may not dampen government borrowing in the short-run if not in the medium-term, crowd-out private investment, as rates of return on borrowed capital used to finance investment need to be much higher.

POLITICAL ECONOMY OF POLICY DESIGN

Macroeconomic policies are neither formulated nor implemented in a vacuum. It is, therefore, important to recognize the significance of the political context. In any programme of stabilization and adjustment, there are winners and losers. And even if the benefits, which accrue to some, are greater than the costs, which are imposed on others, there are political consequences. For the compensation principle exists only in text books on welfare economics. In reality, the gainers do not compensate the losers. The political process sets out incentives and disincentives for governments. Citizens assess the economic performance of governments. In democracies, voters exercise their choice at the time of elections, which is shaped, at least in part, by the performance of the economy. Even in undemocratic or authoritarian regimes, governments are ultimately accountable to the people. Therefore, what governments can or cannot do in the sphere of macroeconomic policies is also shaped in the realm of politics.

The design and implementation of fiscal policy is often shaped by the constraints embedded in political economy. More often than not, adjustment

---

[32]This is borne out by experience in a wide range of developing countries. For an analysis of the Indian experience, see Nayyar (2001).

through fiscal policies takes the form of reducing the expenditure rather than increasing the income of the government. Governments in developing countries find it very difficult to increase their income through tax revenues, because important political constituencies with a voice have the capacity not only to evade or avoid taxes but also to resist taxes. Orthodoxy does not help matters. For, typically, tax rates are lowered without any systematic effort to improve compliance or broaden the base for taxation. The Laffer Curve belief system is not the only culprit. Tax revenues, as a proportion of GDP, also stagnate, if not decline, since import tariffs are systematically reduced in the process of import liberalization, which is an integral part of stabilization programmes. In contrast, governments in developing countries find it somewhat less difficult to decrease their expenditure, although there are asymmetries. It is easier to cut investment expenditure than to cut consumption expenditure, just as it is easier to reduce public expenditure on social sectors where the economic constituencies are not as organized as elsewhere and the consequences are discernible only after a time-lag.

There is a similar intersection of economics and politics in the sphere of monetary policy. The orthodox view does recognize this but the recognition is limited to the macroeconomic significance of monetized deficits and the independence of central banks.[33] This is no doubt important, but there is more to the political economy of monetary policy. Interest rates are particularly important, for they can be used not only to stimulate investment or aggregate demand but also as a strategic instrument to guide the allocation of scarce investible resources in a market economy. But constraints embedded in political economy reduce the degrees of freedom in the use of interest rates. Property-owning democracies with extensive rentier interests, in developing countries, almost as much as in industrial societies, prefer higher interest rates not only because of higher income from financial assets but also because a wider middle class fears that inflation might erode the real value of their accumulated savings.[34] In developing countries that have carried out capital account liberalization, sources of foreign capital inflows also prefer higher interest rates and lower inflation rates. It is not surprising, then, that any lowering of interest rates is resisted by an emerging rentier class in domestic financial markets which has a political voice, just as any lowering of interest rates is constrained by an integration into international financial markets which also become significant political constituencies for finance ministers. Differential interest rates, which

[33]See, for example, Alesina and Summers (1993).
[34]Bhaduri (2002).

were used effectively in East Asia, are no longer an option after the deregulation of domestic financial sectors. Yet, in segmented and imperfect capital markets, access to credit may turn out to be unequal between sectors or groups depending upon political voice or influence.

There is an interesting twist in the tale, for those excluded by the economics of markets are included by the politics of democracy.[35] Poor people, particularly in poor countries, fear inflation because, in the absence of indexation, an increase in the prices of food or necessities erodes their real incomes and diminishes their well-being. Thus, citizens in a democracy, with a right to vote, often assess the economic performance of a government by the yardstick of inflation. But that is not all. The employment implications and distributional consequences of economic policies are perhaps equally important underlying factors that influence or shape electoral outcomes. In the ultimate analysis, people judge economic performance of governments in terms of employment possibilities, educational opportunities, or health care facilities for themselves and their families. The size of the budget deficit, the internal debt of the government, the external debt of the nation, the balance of payments situation, or the expansion of money supply, are economic abstractions that are somewhat distant from the daily lives of ordinary people.[36]

Stabilization and adjustment, inevitably, have an impact on income distribution at a macro level. But this issue is almost entirely ignored in the orthodox literature on the subject. There is an implicit underlying view that economics should be concerned with efficiency. Hence, if there are any adverse consequences of macroeconomic policies in terms of distribution or welfare, it is theorized that these can be corrected by efficient lump-sum transfers. But orthodoxy believes that this decision must be made in the realm of politics and not in the sphere of economics. In reality, however, issues of distribution cannot be separated from issues of efficiency. And it cannot suffice to say that the outcomes of economic policies should be moderated by social policies. A dichotomy between economic and social policies is inappropriate. In fact, no such distinction is made in industrial societies where there is an integration, rather than separation of economic and social policies.

In sharp contrast, the impact of economic policies on income distribution is centre stage in the heterodox schools of thought. In this world, the effects of macroeconomic policies are significantly influenced by who gains how much

[35]For an analysis of this proposition, see Nayyar (2003b).

[36]This hypothesis about how people assess the economic performance of governments, particularly in democracies, is developed at some length in Bhaduri and Nayyar (1996).

from expansionary policies and who loses how much from contractionary policies. Their respective propensities to consume or to save are also important determinants of outcomes. These consequences are not confined to the short-run, for the consumption decisions of the households and investment decisions of firms, which are influenced by macroeconomic policies, also shape the prospects of growth in the medium-term.

The distributional implications and the social consequences of macroeconomic policies are often neglected. This needs to be corrected. In the short-term, it might be about the distribution of the burden of adjustment. In the medium-term, it might be about cuts in subsidies which squeeze the private consumption of the poor or cuts in public expenditure for social sectors which curb the social consumption of the poor. In the long-term, it might be about the distribution of benefits from economic growth where employment expansion and employment creation are particularly important.

RESTRUCTURING OF ECONOMIES OVER TIME

The restructuring of an economy over time has three dimensions: the management of demand, the management of incentives, and the development of capabilities and institutions. The objective of managing demand is to influence the level and composition of demand, hence output and employment, in the economy, mostly in the short-term. The objective of designing incentives is to induce supply responses and coax productivity increases, mostly in the medium-term. The objective of building capabilities at a micro-level and institutions at a meso-level is to create a milieu that imparts efficiency and dynamism to the growth process, mostly in the long-term.[37]

Each of these dimensions of restructuring has a close correspondence with the respective time horizon. But it is not possible to separate demand, supply, and capabilities or institutions in this manner because there is an interdependence and an interaction which leads to spillovers. It would take too long to set up a complete matrix. Some examples would suffice. For instance, aggregate demand management in the short-term, which is part of a stabilization programme, may squeeze supply responses in the medium-term. Similarly, incentive management, say in the form of import liberalization, may impact the level of demand in the short-term at a macro-level if it switches expenditure away from home-produced goods and may affect capabilities in the long-term if it enforces closures rather than efficiency at a micro-level. And, State intervention

---

[37]The discussion that follows draws upon, and builds on, some earlier work of the author. See Nayyar (1996 and 2004).

meant to support the development of capabilities and institutions in the long-term, say strategic industrial policy, may affect incentive structures in the medium-term and aggregate demand in the short-term.

In this wider context, economic liberalization shaped by orthodoxy, through the influence of the IMF and the World Bank, has three limitations. First, it is overwhelmingly concerned with the management of incentives and the supply side in a medium-term perspective. Some attention is paid to the management of demand in the short-term, but this is limited to the quest for stabilization in a narrow sense insofar as the aim is to stabilize price levels rather than output levels. There is almost no recognition that the development of capabilities and institutions has a long-term significance. Second, it does not recognize the interdependence and interaction between these three dimensions of restructuring that straddle time horizons. In fact, it is necessary to recognize possible contradictions so as to avoid them and potential complementarities so as to exploit them. Third, it makes a commonplace, yet serious, theoretical error in the design of policies, for it confuses *comparison* of equilibrium positions with *change* from one equilibrium position to another. It simply does not consider problems that arise in transition from the starting point to the ultimate destination.

The management of demand, mostly internal but also external, is based on fiscal policy and monetary policy combined with exchange rate policy. It is concerned with stabilization. But the mix of stabilization policies is often inappropriate. Aggregate demand management through fiscal adjustment and monetary policy should squeeze imports and consumption of the non-poor, instead of investment and consumption of the poor. In a situation where incomes are low, consumption levels of the poor need to be protected by restraining inflation and maintaining public expenditure destined for the poor. The mode of adjustment on the demand side is crucial, for it can either stimulate or stifle growth. Therefore, fiscal adjustment should not rely excessively on expenditure reduction but should also attempt to increase the income of the government. At the same time, it is essential to raise the level and rate of investment in the economy. For this, it is necessary to increase public investment, particularly in infrastructure where private investment (whether domestic or foreign) is not readily forthcoming. As far as possible, such public investment should be financed out of higher tax and non-tax revenues. To some extent, borrowing can also be used for this purpose, provided that investments financed by borrowed resources yield adequate returns. The size of the fiscal deficit is less important than the use or the cost of borrowing. It is the revenue deficit, which requires borrowing to finance government consumption expenditures, that must be progressively reduced and rapidly eliminated. The fetishism about reducing the fiscal deficit despite a burgeoning revenue deficit, or eliminating the monetized deficit despite the much higher cost of borrowing, is entirely misplaced. Similarly, the reliance on unsustainable and unstable capital inflows, through capital market liberalization, to finance current account deficits is a mistake. Direct foreign investment which provides non-debt-creating and investment-financing capital inflows is preferable as a source of external finance. But it has implications for domestic capabilities in the long-term that must be recognized.

The management of incentives, motivated by the objective of minimizing costs and maximizing efficiency at a micro-level, is based on a set of policies intended to increase competition between firms in the market place. Domestic competition is sought to be provided through deregulation in investment decisions, in the financial sector, and in labour markets. Foreign competition is sought to be provided through openness in trade, investment, capital, and technology flows. There are the obvious correctives. For one, the speed of change must be calibrated so that it can be absorbed by the economy. For another, the sequence of change must be planned with reference to an order of priorities. In both, whether speed or sequence, deregulation and openness must be consistent with the other dimensions of restructuring in the short-term and in the long-term. There are, however, problems beyond simple correctives that must be addressed and resolved. First, it is essential to establish rules that govern markets, for the market is a good servant but a bad master, whether in the sphere of industrial deregulation, trade liberalization or financial sector reform. Second, a focus on sectoral components of reform may lead to a situation where the structure of incentives as a whole is inappropriate. For instance, the mix of tax reform and financial liberalization rewards finance capital more than industrial capital. But industrial capitalism is made on shop floors and not in stock markets. It is important to avoid the dangers of what Keynes described as 'casino capitalism'. Third, it must be recognized that incentives may be necessary but are not sufficient and that there is nothing automatic about competition. In other words, policy regimes can only create an enabling framework but cannot deliver outcomes. The creation of competitive markets that enforce efficiency may, in fact, require strategic intervention through industrial policy, trade policy, or financial policy.[38]

[38]See Amsden (1989), Singh (1994), and Chang (1996).

The development of capabilities and institutions is an essential foundation for international competitiveness. This is clearly established by the experience of the successful latecomers to industrialization, particularly in Asia but also elsewhere.[39] It would seem that the third dimension of restructuring is often neglected altogether, even by those who wish to capture the benefits from integration with the world economy or dream of becoming global players. This must be corrected so that the long-term objectives of development receive the much-deserved attention. In this context, there are three points that deserve emphasis. First, the importance of education in particular and human resource development in general cannot be stressed enough. It is vital. Second, the acquisition of technological and managerial capabilities is absolutely essential. It must be ensured that the structure of incentives helps in building, and does not end up stifling these capabilities. Third, the creation of institutions that would regulate, streamline, and facilitate the functioning of markets is clearly necessary. This requires planning and takes time. In each of these pursuits, strategic forms of State intervention are of the essence. Therefore, the government simply cannot afford to abdicate its role in the belief that markets know best. It is only a creative interaction between the State and the market, which evolves in a dialectical manner with the passage of time, that can foster the development of capabilities and institutions in the process of industrialization.[40]

CONCLUSION

It would seem that the concerns of orthodox macroeconomics are much too narrow. What is more, orthodoxy does not recognize the specificities in time and in space that characterize developing countries and transition economies. It is, therefore, necessary to explore alternatives in the management of economies in crisis, from a different perspective. This should shift the focus from the financial to the real economy, from the short-term to the long-term, and from equilibrium to development. It is imperative that the objective of macro-management should extend beyond managing inflation to restoring full employment. In developing countries, which have not yet reached a stage of full employment, macroeconomic policies should be conducive to employment expansion and employment creation. Similarly, it is essential to recognize that

[39]See, in particular, Lall (1990). See also Dahlman et al. (1987), and Bell and Pavitt (1992).

[40]For a detailed discussion on the role of the State vis-à-vis the market in the process of industrialization, see Nayyar (1997). There is, of course, an extensive literature on the subject. See, for example, Stiglitz (1989), Wade (1991), Shapiro and Taylor (1990), Bhaduri and Nayyar (1996), and Lall (1997).

open economy macroeconomics is not simply about exchange rates or capital flows. Indeed, thinking must extend beyond the external sector of economies. The reason is that developments in the external sector spill over into the national economy with significant implications and consequences. It is, of course, important to think about the macroeconomic objectives of internal balance and external balance in the short-term. But it is just as important to think beyond the short-term, about macroeconomic policies that are conducive to economic growth, increased productivity, and employment creation in the long-term. In doing so, it is important to remember the distinction between means and ends. Stabilization is a means. So is macroeconomic management. For that matter, so is economic growth. It is development, for the well-being of people, which is an end.

REFERENCES

Alesina, A. and L. Summers (1993), 'Central Bank Independence and Macroeconomic Performance: Some Comparative Evidence', *Journal of Money, Credit and Banking*, Vol. 25, No. 22, pp. 151–62.

Amsden, Alice (1989), *Asia's Next Giant: South Korea and Late Industrialization*, Oxford University Press, New York.

Amsden, Alice, Jacek Kochanowicz, and Lance Taylor (1994), *The Market Meets its Match*, Harvard University Press, Cambridge.

Bell, M. and K. Pavitt (1992), 'Accumulating Technological Capability in Developing Countries', *Annual Bank Conference on Development Economics*, 1992, Proceedings, pp. 257–81.

Ben-David, Dan and David Papell (1998), 'Slow-downs and Meltdowns: Post-war Growth Evidence from 74 Countries', *Review of Economics and Statistics*, Vol. 80, November, pp. 561–71.

Bhaduri, Amit (1986), *Macroeconomics: The Dynamics of Commodity Production*, Macmillan, London.

—— (1992), 'Stabilization and the East European Transition', in S. Richter (ed.), *The Transition from Command to Market Economies in Eastern Europe*, Westview Press, San Francisco.

—— (2002), 'Nationalism and Economic Policy in an Era of Globalization', in D. Nayyar (ed.), *Governing Globalization: Issues and Institutions*, Oxford University Press, Oxford.

Bhaduri, Amit and Deepak Nayyar (1996), *The Intelligent Person's Guide to Liberalization*, Penguin Books, New Delhi.

Chang, Ha-Joon (1996), *The Political Economy of Industrial Policy*, Macmillan, London.

Cooper, Richard (1992), *Economic Stabilization and Debt in Developing Countries*, The MIT Press, Cambridge.

Cornia, Andrea, Richard Jolly, and Frances Stewart (1987), *Adjustment with a Human Face*, Clarendon Press, Oxford.

Dahlman, C.J., B. Ross-Larson, and L. Westphal (1987), 'Managing Technological Development: Lessons from Newly Industrializing Countries', *World Development*, Vol. 15, No. 6, pp. 759–75.

Easterly, William, R. Islam, and Joseph Stiglitz (2001), 'Shaken and Stirred: Explaining Growth Volatility', *Annual Bank Conference on Development Economics*, World Bank, Washington, DC, pp. 191–212.

Ffrench-Davis, Ricardo (2000), *Reforming the Reforms in Latin America: Macroeconomics, Trade and Finance*, St. Martin's Press, New York.

Furtado, Celso (1971), *Development and Underdevelopment*, University of California Press, Berkeley.

Furman, Jason and Joseph Stiglitz (1998), 'Economic Crises: Evidence and Insights from East Asia', *Brookings Papers on Economic Activity*, No. 2, pp. 1–135.

Independent Evaluation Office (2003), 'Fiscal Adjustment in IMF-Supported Programs', IMF, Washington, DC, September.

Jomo, KS (ed.) (2001), *Malaysian Eclipse: Economic Crisis and Recovery*, Zed Books, London.

Kaldor, Nicholas (1978), *Further Essays in Economic Theory*, Duckworth, London.

Kalecki, Michal (1970), 'Problems of Financing Development in a Mixed Economy', in W. Eltis, M. Scott, and J. Wolfe (eds), *Induction, Growth and Trade: Essays in Honour of Sir Roy Harrod*, Oxford University Press, Oxford.

_____ (1971), *Selected Essays on the Dynamics of the Capitalist Economy*, Cambridge University Press, Cambridge.

_____ (1976), *Essays on Developing Economies*, The Harvester Press, Hassocks.

Keynes, J.M. (1936), *The General Theory of Employment, Interest and Money*, Macmillan, London.

Killick, T. (1984), *The Quest for Economic Stabilization: The IMF and the Third World*, Overseas Development Institute, London.

Krugman, Paul and Lance Taylor (1978), 'Contractionary Effect of Devaluation', *Journal of International Economics*, Vol. 8, No. 2, pp. 445–56.

Lall, Sanjaya (1990), *Building Industrial Competitiveness in Developing Countries*, OECD, Paris.

_____ (1997), 'Imperfect Markets and Fallible Governments: The Role of the State in Industrial Development', in D. Nayyar (ed.), *Trade and Industrialization*, Oxford University Press, New Delhi.

Lane, Timothy et al. (1999), 'IMF-Supported Programs in Indonesia, Korea and Thailand: A Preliminary Assessment', IMF, Washington, DC.

Lutz, G. Matthias (1999), 'Unit Roots versus Segmented Trends in Developing Countries Output Series', *Applied Economic Letters*, No. 6, pp. 181–4.

Mehrotra, Santosh and Richard Jolly (eds) (1997), *Development with a Human Face*, Clarendon Press, Oxford.

Nayyar, Deepak (1995), 'Macroeconomics of Stabilization and Adjustment', *Economic Appliquee*, Vol. 48, No. 3, pp. 5–37.

_____ (1996), *Economic Liberalization in India: Analytics, Experience and Lessons*, Orient Longman, Calcutta.

_____ (1997), 'Themes in Trade and Industrialization', in D. Nayyar (ed.), *Trade and Industrialization*, Oxford University Press, New Delhi.

_____ (2001), 'Macroeconomic Reforms in India: Short-term Effects and Long-run Implications', in W. Mahmud (ed.), *Adjustment and Beyond: The Reform Experience in South Asia*, Palgrave, London.

_____ (2003a), 'Globalization and Development Strategies', in John Toye (ed.), *Trade and Development: New Directions for the Twenty-first Century*, Edward Elgar, Cheltenham.

_____ (2003b), 'The Political Economy of Exclusion and Inclusion: Democracy, Markets and People', in A.K. Dutt and J. Ros (eds), *Development Economics and Structuralist Macroeconomics: Essays in Honour of Lance Taylor*, Edward Elgar, Cheltenham.

_____ (2004), 'Economic Reforms in India: Understanding the Process and Learning from Experience', *International Journal of Development Issues*, Vol. 3, No. 2, pp. 31–55.

Ocampo, Jose Antonio (2003), 'Developing Countries Anti-Cyclical Policies in a Globalized World', in A.K. Dutt and J. Ros (eds), *Development Economics and Structuralist Macreconomics: Essays in Honour of Lance Taylor*, Edward Elgar, Cheltenham.

_____ (2004), 'Latin America's Growth and Equity Frustrations During Structural Reforms', *Journal of Economic Perspectives*, Vol. 18, No. 2, pp. 67–88.

Ocampo, Jose Antonio and Lance Taylor (1998), 'Trade Liberalization in Developing Economies: Modest Benefit but Problems with Productivity Growth, Macro Prices and Income Distribution', *Economic Journal*, Vol. 108, No. 450, September, pp. 1523–46.

Shapiro, Helen and Lance Taylor (1990), 'The State and Industrial Strategy', *World Development*, Vol. 18, No. 6, pp. 861–78.

Singh, Ajit (1994), 'Openness and the Market-Friendly Approach to Development: Learning the Right Lessons from Development Experience', *World Development*, Vol. 22, No. 12, pp. 1811–24.

Stiglitz, Joseph (1989), 'Economic Role of the State: Efficiency and Effectiveness', in A. Heertje (ed.), *The Economic Role of the State*, Basil Blackwell, Oxford.

Stiglitz, Joseph, Jose Antonio Ocampo, Shari Spiegel, R. Ffrench-Davis, and Deepak Nayyar (2006), *Stability with Growth: Macroeconomics, Liberalization and Development*, Oxford University Press, Oxford.

Taylor, Lance (1988), *Varieties of Stabilization Experience*, Clarendon Press, Oxford.

_____ (1991), *Income Distribution, Inflation and Growth*, The MIT Press, Cambridge.

_____ (ed.) (1993), *The Rocky Road to Reform: Adjustment, Income Distribution and Growth in the Developing World*, The MIT Press, Cambridge.

_____ (2004), *Reconstructing Macroeconomics*, Harvard Univesity Press, Cambridge.

Wade, Robert (1991), *Governing the Market*, Princeton University Press, Princeton.

Williamson, John (ed.) (1983), *IMF Conditionality*, Institute for International Economics (IIE), Washington, DC.

—— (1990), *Latin American Adjustment: How Much Has Happened?*, IIE, Washington, DC.

Chapter 3

ON EXCLUSION AND INCLUSION
Democracy, Markets, and People*

INTRODUCTION

In the early twenty-first century, *market economy* and *political democracy* are buzzwords: not only in turbulent Eastern Europe attempting a transition to capitalism, but also across a wide spectrum of countries in the developing world from Latin America through Africa to Asia. This is partly a consequence of the collapse of planned economies and excessive or inappropriate State intervention in market economies. And it is partly attributable to a concern about authoritarian regimes, particularly in countries where there has been no improvement in living conditions of the common people, but even in countries where economic development has been impressive despite which there is no movement towards a democratic polity. Consequently, the mood of the moment is such that markets and democracy are perceived as both virtue and necessity. In this process, some countries are in search of new models of development, while others are attempting to adapt their erstwhile models of development.

The theme of this essay is that, contrary to the ideology of our times, markets and democracy may not ensure prosperity for everyone but may, in fact, exclude a significant proportion of people, particularly the poor, from the process of development. The first section explains why markets and democracy provide no magic wand. It stresses that market economy and political democracy are not separate worlds but are closely interconnected. The second section analyses how markets exclude people. It shows that exclusion and inclusion are in the logic of markets. The third section explores the interaction of economics and politics to question orthodoxy. It argues that there is no equality among economic agents or political citizens in terms of their economic or political freedom to choose.

*I would like to thank Amit Bhaduri and Satish Jain for helpful discussion which clarified my ideas on the subject. I would also like to thank Jean Dreze for useful suggestions.

DEMOCRACY AND MARKETS

The virtues of a market economy, articulated more than two centuries ago by Adam Smith, are spelt out at length in orthodox economic theory.[1] It is efficient as it optimizes production (in terms of resource allocation) and consumption (in terms of utility maximization). It is democratic insofar as it offers an equal opportunity to all. It is libertarian insofar as it gives every person the right of self-determination. For the contemporary enthusiasts, as much as Adam Smith, private initiative is the means and economic prosperity is the end. Similarly, the virtues of a political democracy can be traced to Anglo-Saxon and European thinking about liberalism. Its basic tenets are freedom for individuals, pluralism of values, importance of rights, and equality among people. In such political thought, these tenets are sacrosanct and the limits, if any, are enshrined in a *social contract* where individuals can be coerced by collective decisions only if they have consented to being subjected to the system.[2]

These virtues of market economy and political democracy, stressed by orthodoxy, have come to occupy centre stage in the context of reforms in the contemporary world, particularly in the erstwhile socialist countries but also elsewhere. It is striking that democracy and markets are often considered together as if they are indivisible and are of equal importance. There are two limitations of this world view.

First, there is an underlying presumption that democracy and markets are inseparable and almost ensure each other. This is wrong. The existence of a political democracy is neither a necessary nor a sufficient condition for the functioning of a market economy. The East Asian examples, of market economy without political democracy, provide ample support for this proposition. In terms of logic, it implies that the existence of a market economy is neither a necessary nor a sufficient condition for sustaining a political democracy.

Second, the pairing suggests that democracy and markets are at par. This is questionable. The introduction of democracy in a polity is a fundamental issue, whereas the use of markets in an economy is an institutional matter. For its intrinsic value, democracy is an end in itself. Markets, on the other hand, are means, the use (non-use) of which has to be justified by consequences. For some, economic freedom is an end in itself, so that markets can also have some intrinsic virtues, embedded in free or greater choice. In any event, both cannot be posited as fundamental requirements, for if there

---

[1]This literature began life in the era of classical political economy. The most important contributions were those of Smith (1776) and Mill (1848). See also Hayek (1960).

[2]The classic statements of liberalism are to be found in the writings of Adam Smith, Jean Jacques Rousseau and, in particular, John Stuart Mill. More recent contributions, representing different views, are Berlin (1969), Sen (1970), Rawls (1971), and Sugden (1981).

is a democracy it is up to the people to decide whether or not, or how much, to use markets.[3]

It is, therefore, reasonable to suggest that democracy and markets are distinct from each other. It is also plausible to argue that, even if both are institutions evolved by humankind, democracy and markets are simply not at the same level. Yet, orthodoxy believes that, insofar as democracy is about political freedom for individuals and markets are about economic freedom for individuals, the two together must serve the interests of the people. However, there is little basis for this inference either in theory or in practice.

For one, democracies function on the principle of majority rule or some variant thereof. This is clearly preferable to monarchies or oligarchies associated with the rule of an individual or of a few. But democracy can lead to the *tyranny of majorities*.[4] What is more, in countries characterized by social and economic inequalities that run deep, it is not clear how universal adult franchise alone can create political equality. We must not also forget that universal suffrage is a twentieth century phenomenon even in Europe. Indeed, we would do well to remember that it was property rights, rather than equality, which were at the foundation of liberalism. And, for a long time, it was property that endowed people with a right to vote so that access to political democracy was the privilege of a few and not the right of everyone.

For another, the proposition that markets create equal opportunities for all depends on the critical assumption that the initial distribution of property rights is equal. Thus, any defence of the market on the premise that it is good in terms of actual outcomes must rest on a defence of the initial distribution of property rights. The argument that markets protect the interests of individuals or groups (ethnic, religious, or political),[5] which even democracies cannot, is

---

[3]For a discussion on the importance of democracy, in the context of market economies, see Sen (2000). Democracy, Sen argues, has three distinct virtues: (a) its intrinsic importance; (b) its instrumental contributions; and (c) its constructive role, in the creation of values and norms. Sen recognizes that markets have obvious instrumental virtues. But he also goes on to argue that, if an extension of the choice set is good, a market economy may have intrinsic virtues.

[4]The principle that the will of the majority should always prevail in a democracy has been a matter of debate for a long time. John Stuart Mill, for example, argued that 'the government of the whole by a mere majority of the people', the principle of majority rule, is undemocratic. This was, then, developed into an argument for proportional representation (Mill 1859 and 1861).

[5]The argument is that even when a minority group is treated with hostility by the majority (say, a group of people with extremist political views who wish to produce a newspaper), the market system offers the minority significant protection (say, buying newsprint and employing journalists), see Sugden (1981). Similarly, Friedman (1962) points out that Jewish people were able to survive the hostile environment in medieval Europe largely because they were engaged in commerce and trade. And the economic (self) interest of the population prevailed over religious

limited, for such individuals or groups are not guaranteed access to the market as buyers if they have no incomes or sellers if they have nothing to sell. It is important to recognize that while democracy may be about the *tyranny of majorities,* markets may be about the *tyranny of minorities.*

In practice, we know that the combination of democracy and markets is neither necessary nor sufficient to bring about an improvement in the living conditions of the majority of the people in a society. Consider egalitarian development, which brings about material well-being of people together with some equality of economic opportunities. We have seen such egalitarian development in planned economies without political democracy, as in the erstwhile socialist countries of Eastern Europe, and in market economies without political democracy, as in some East Asian and South East Asian countries. In sharp contrast, markets and democracy together, where these institutions are not sufficiently developed and have not evolved over a long period of time, as in countries of Eastern Europe, have only produced chaos.[6] The outcome is prosperity for a few and misery for the many. Clearly, there are no magic wands. Democracy and markets are both institutions. The outcome depends on how they are used.

The orthodox belief system about market economy and political democracy is obviously open to question. It is clear enough that democracy and markets, together, do not necessarily serve the interests of people. The fundamental problem with orthodoxy is that it treats the two spheres of market economy and political democracy as separate from each other. For, in isolation, each provides freedom to choose. This is a convenient abstraction. But it is not a correct presumption. The reality is very different as the two are simply not separable. In fact, the two are closely interconnected. It is the interaction between market economy and political democracy that shapes outcomes for people. This interaction of economics and politics, which is critical, is explored later in the essay.

EXCLUSION AND INCLUSION

Joan Robinson once said, 'There is only one thing that is worse than being exploited by capitalists. And that is not being exploited by capitalists.' The same goes for participation in markets. For there is an exclusion in the process.[7]

---

discrimination. Becker (1971) argues that markets protect minorities through the force of competition. Firms which discriminate against certain minority groups will be driven out of business by those which do not. This argument is much more limited. It may also be wrong because, under certain circumstances, discrimination can maximize profits.

[6]Amsden et al. (1994). See also, Taylor (1993).

[7]Much the same, I have argued elsewhere, is true of globalization. For a detailed discussion, see Nayyar (2003).

The term *exclusion* has become a part of the lexicon of economists recently, although it has been in the jargon of sociology and the vocabulary of politics in Europe for somewhat longer. The phrase *social exclusion* is used to describe a situation, as also to focus on a process, which excludes individuals or groups from livelihoods and rights, thus depriving them of sources of well-being that have been assumed, if not taken for granted, in industrial countries.[8] The essential point is that economic stratification is inevitable in market economies and societies, which systematically integrate some and marginalize others to distribute the benefits of economic growth in ways which include some and exclude others.

The literature on developing countries has, in contrast, sought to study marginalization or deprivation of majorities through a focus on poverty and inequality. The concept of exclusion may be useful in the context of developing countries if it helps us understand how the spread of markets affects the common people. Exclusion is inherent in the logic of markets. Markets may exclude people as consumers or producers or both.

Markets exclude people as consumers or buyers if they do not have any incomes, or sufficient incomes, which can be translated into purchasing power. In Amartya Sen's terminology, this exclusion is attributable to a lack of *entitlements*.[9] Such people are obviously excluded from the consumption of goods and services which are sold in the market. But they may also be excluded from non-market allocations such as the public provision of goods and services if they live in clusters such as urban slums, or rural settlements, where drinking water, sanitation facilities, roads, electricity, or even street lights are not provided. It is, then, the location of the poor (and not their income) which deprives them of access to public services which may be (almost) free elsewhere.

Markets exclude people as producers or sellers if they have neither *assets* nor *capabilities*. People experience such exclusion if they do not have assets, physical or financial, which can be used (or sold) to yield an income in the form of rent, interest, or profits.[10] Even those without assets could enter the market as producers or sellers, using their labour, if they have some capabilities.[11] Such

[8]See Commission of the European Communities (1993). For an extensive discussion on social exclusion, ranging from conceptual issues through country studies to policy issues, see Rodgers et al. (1995).

[9]This term was first used by Sen (1981) in his work on poverty and famines.

[10]The rural poor in the developing world, who are landless, experience such exclusion. The landless are deprived not only of a source of livelihood but also of a status in society. Exclusion, then, is both economic and social.

[11]In this paper, I use the word *capabilities* to characterize the mix of natural talents, skills acquired through training, learning from experience, and abilities or expertise based on

capabilities, which are acquired through education, training, or experience are different from abilities which are endowed. But the distribution of capabilities may be just as unequal if not more so. It is these capabilities which can, in turn, yield an income in the form of wages. Hence, people without capabilities, the poor who cannot find employment, are excluded. In fact, even people with capabilities may be excluded from employment if there is no demand for their capabilities in the (labour) market.[12] And, in the ultimate analysis, such capabilities must find acceptance, or use, in the market. That is the problem.

In addition, markets exclude people both as consumers and producers or as buyers and sellers if they do not accept, or conform to, the *values* of a market system. The most obvious example of such exclusion is tribal populations or forest communities in market economies. The same can be said, perhaps, for pockets of pre-capitalist formations in what are essentially capitalist systems. Such exclusion may also take other forms. There may be people who are unable or unwilling to sell their assets: for instance, a person may be unable or unwilling to sell an ancestral house in the market. Or, there may be people who are unable or unwilling to sell their capabilities: for instance, a person may be unable or unwilling to charge fees as an astrologer or a musician because of a belief system that such talents cannot and should not be sold. In other words, people who are excluded because of their set of norms can find some kind of inclusion in the market once they accept a different set of norms. In general, the terms of such inclusion are such that it intensifies insecurity and exploitation at least for some time.

---

education, embodied in a person, that enable him or her to use these (capabilities as a producer or a worker) for which there is not only a price but also a demand in the market. It follows that even persons with capabilities may be excluded from employment if there is no demand for their capabilities in the (labour) market. It is essential to note that the same word, *capabilities*, has been used in a very different sense by Amartya Sen, who argues that the well-being of a person depends on what the person succeeds in *doing* with the commodities (and their characteristics) at his command. For example: food can provide nutrition to a healthy person but not to a person with a parasitic disease; or, a bicycle can provide transportation to an able-bodied person but not to a disabled person. Thus, for Sen (1985), *capabilities* characterize the combination of functionings a person can achieve, given his personal features (conversion of characteristics into functionings) and his command over commodities (entitlements).

[12]Open unemployment simply means exclusion from the labour market. But there is also exclusion within the labour market experienced by those who are underemployed in the agricultural sector and by those who are self-employed or in casual employment in the urban informal sector. The segmented labour market means that access to good jobs which are secure and well-paid is exceedingly difficult whereas access to bad jobs which are insecure and poorly paid is easier.

As a concept, exclusion may describe a situation or characterize a process.[13] In describing a situation, whether it refers to a point in time or to a permanent state, the concept of exclusion is much the same as the concept of poverty. The object is to identify the excluded and the poor, respectively. In characterizing a process, the concept of exclusion goes further to focus on how the operation of economic and social forces recreates or accentuates exclusion over time. This may be attributable to the logic of markets, which give to those who have and take away from those who have not, as the process of cumulative causation leads to market-driven virtuous circles and vicious circles.[14] This may be the outcome of patterns of development where economic growth is uneven between regions and the distribution of its benefits is unequal between people, so that there is growing affluence for some combined with persistent poverty for many. This may be the consequence of strategies of development, as a similar economic performance in the aggregate could lead to egalitarian development in one situation, and growth which bypasses the majority of the people in another situation. It is clear that institutional arrangements which mediate between economic development on the one hand and social development on the other are critical. For these institutional mechanisms may accentuate exclusion or foster inclusion, just as they may limit the gains to an affluent minority or spread the gains to the poor majority. The initial distribution of assets and the subsequent distribution of incomes are important determinants of whether the vulnerable sections of the population are marginalized and excluded or are uplifted and included.

It must be recognized that the impact of exclusion from markets is at different levels: individuals, social groups, regional, and national.[15] Individuals are excluded from access to markets if they do not have the requisite entitlements, assets, capabilities, or values. Groups in society such as the landless, the illiterate, the handicapped, the lower castes (as in India), women (in some occupations), migrant workers, or ethnic groups are sometimes excluded from participation in the economy.[16] This could mean that identifiable social groups are at a disadvantage in their access to markets and may even be subjected to systematic

---

[13]Rodgers et al. (1995).

[14]For an analysis of cumulative causation in the process of development, in particular, spread effects and backwash effects, see Myrdal (1968).

[15]For a detailed discussion, see Rodgers et al. (1995), pp. 269–75.

[16]Some, like Becker (1971), argue that women and minorities would be helped by markets which reduce discrimination. But this is not possible if such groups do not have the requisite entitlements, assets, or capabilities. What is more, discrimination persists for social and political reasons.

exclusion from livelihood. Regions within countries, particularly those without natural resources, those with a difficult terrain, those at a distance, or those without skilled labour, may be excluded from development. This may take the form of exclusion from infrastructure, from public goods and services, or from economic and social opportunities. Some of these exclusions from the market also exist at the national level. There are many examples of this in poor countries, such as exclusions from land, from employment, from social protection, from health care, from education, and even from basic human needs such as food, clothing, and shelter.

The analysis so far may suggest that exclusion is bad and inclusion is good. But it is not meant to. It must be said that the nature of inclusion or exclusion matters. Inclusion is not always good. Coercive inclusion by markets, whether child labour, tribal populations or immigrant workers can be exploitative. The employment of women as wage labour on terms inferior to those of men, or the employment of migrants from rural areas in the unorganized urban sector at wages lower than those of workers in the organized sector, provide other examples. The basic point is that inclusion which is coercive or on inferior terms is not desirable. And the terms of inclusion matter. For similar reasons, exclusion is not always bad. To those who do not accept the values of the market system, any voluntary exclusion from markets, on the part of individuals or groups, should be perfectly acceptable.

ECONOMICS AND POLITICS

It has been suggested earlier that market economy and political democracy cannot and should not be separated from each other as if they constitute two different worlds. The reason is simple enough. In every society, economy and polity are closely intertwined. It is, therefore, essential to explore the interaction of economics and politics in this context, which shapes outcomes for people.

The essence of the tension between the economics of markets and the politics of democracy must be recognized. In a market economy, people vote with their money in the market place. But a political democracy works on the basis of one-person-one-vote. The distribution of votes, unlike the distribution of incomes or assets, is equal. One adult has one vote in politics, even though a rich man has more votes than a poor man, in terms of purchasing power, in the market. This tension may be compounded by a related asymmetry between economy and polity. The people who are excluded by the economics of markets are included by the politics of democracy. Hence, exclusion and inclusion are asymmetrical in economics and politics. The distribution of capabilities is also uneven in the economic and political spheres. The rich dominate a market economy in terms of purchasing power. But the poor have a strong voice in a political democracy in terms of votes. And there is a mismatch. It is clear that, in reconciling market economy and political democracy, a sensible compromise must be reached between the economic directions which the market sets on the basis of purchasing power and the priorities which a political system sets on the basis of one-person-one-vote.[17] In this context, it is not surprising that successive generations of economic thinkers and social philosophers have stressed the role of the State in this process of mediation. The reason is important even if it is not obvious. Governments are accountable to their people, whereas markets are not. In a democracy, of course, the government is elected by the people. But even where it is not, the State needs legitimation from the people, most of whom are not rich or are poor. The task of reconciliation and mediation is obviously difficult but clearly necessary.

Markets are responsive to the demands of rich people but not to the needs of the poor people. This is inherent in the logic of markets where decisions about what is produced are based on demand and not on need. Thus, markets produce goods for which there is enough purchasing power. The output-mix depends upon the composition of expenditure and the size of the market. Since the rich have more purchasing power, markets, left to themselves, are likely to produce more cellular phones and not improved ploughs or more soft drinks and not safer drinking water.[18] In this manner, markets include people with entitlements but exclude people without entitlements. In theory, every economic agent has the freedom to choose. In practice, there is a choice for some but not for others. And there is more choice for some than for others.

Democracies are more responsive to people with a voice than to people at large. People without a political voice are often simply neglected. There are, of course, problems associated with majority rule which might lead some democracies to exclude minorities. Even if we abstract from such problems, however, the principle of one-person-one-vote does not make every citizen equal in a political democracy. For, in the real world, social and economic

---

[17]For a discussion of this problem in the Indian context, see Bhaduri and Nayyar (1996).

[18]Similarly, research and deveopment (R&D) which is market-driven is more likely to focus on tomatoes with longer shelf-lives or maize used as poultry-feed and not on drought-resistant crops for dry lands. It is not surprising, then, that only 0.2 per cent of world-wide R&D on health care is devoted to tuberculosis, gastric diseases and pneumonia, even though these account for almost 20 per cent of the disease burden in the world. Vaccines are the most cost-effective technologies known in health care, for they prevent illness with one dose. But the proportion of private R&D expenditure in the pharmaceutical sector on vaccines is negligible because they cannot produce profits year after year.

inequalities are inevitably reflected in the political process. In theory, democracy provides every citizen political freedom in the form of civil rights and political liberties. In practice, there is freedom for some but not for others. And there is more freedom for some than for others.

The orthodox dichotomy between economy and polity simply does not conform to any reality. It is only to be expected that there is an interaction between exclusion from the market in the economic sphere and exclusion from democracy in the political sphere. An economic exclusion from livelihood often creates or accentuates a political exclusion from rights. Thus, for the poor in a democracy, the right to vote may exist in principle, but in practice it may be taken away by coercion or coaxed away by material incentives at the time of elections. Similarly, the very poor are vulnerable to exploitation or oppression because their civil rights or equality before the law exist in principle but are difficult to protect or preserve in practice. The reason is simple. They do not have the resources to claim or the power to assert their rights.

Exclusion extends beyond the economic and the political to the social and cultural spheres. The social manifestations of exclusion can be powerful. This is best illustrated with an example from India where the underprivileged in society, such as the lower castes, are poor because they have the little in the form of entitlements, assets, or capabilities, but even where they are better endowed in terms of these attributes, their exclusion from markets, particularly from the market for land and labour in rural India, persists for social rather than economic reasons. At the same time, economic exclusion accentuates social exclusion, while social exclusion accentuates political exclusion. Similarly, cultural exclusion such as that of immigrant groups, minority communities, or ethnic groups interacts with economic exclusion from the market and political exclusion from democracy.

Clearly, there is an overlap between those excluded by market economy and those excluded by political democracy, just as there is an overlap between those included by market economy and those included by political democracy. The poor who are marginalized in the economy also do not have a voice in the polity, just as the rich who are dominant in the economy also have a strong political voice. Economic deprivation and political marginalization go hand-in-hand in much the same way as economic strength and political power go hand-in-hand. Thus, the real world around us does not conform to the characterization in the orthodox belief system. There are two divergences which yield two propositions. For one, the economy and the polity are connected and interdependent. For another, there is no equality among economic agents or political citizens in terms of their economic or political freedom to choose.

There is, in fact, a hierarchy of freedoms, with more for some and less for others, where there is a significant overlap in the economic and political spheres. These two propositions, which emerge from the analysis in this essay, add to our understanding of markets and democracy.

In conclusion, it needs to be said that the liberal paradox is much deeper. On the one hand, markets exclude people without entitlements, assets, or capabilities. It is in the logic of markets. Yet, markets would like to include as many people as possible. For, in the words of Adam Smith, 'the division of labour is limited by the size of the market'. On the other hand, democracy includes people by a constitutional right to vote. It is the foundation of democracy. Yet, political processes seek to exclude or to marginalize those without a voice. That is what the pursuit and exercise of political power is about. The irony of this paradoxical situation is striking.

REFERENCES

Amsden, A., J. Kochanowicz, and L. Taylor (1994), *The Market Meets its Match*, Harvard University Press, Cambridge.

Becker, G.S. (1971), *The Economics of Discrimination*, University of Chicago Press, Chicago.

Berlin, I. (1969), *Four Essays on Liberty*, Clarendon Press, Oxford.

Bhaduri, A. and D. Nayyar (1996), *The Intelligent Person's Guide to Liberalization*, Penguin Books, New Delhi.

Commission of the European Communities (1993), *Towards a Europe of Solidarity: Intensifying the Fight against Social Exclusion and Fostering Integration*, EC, Brussels.

Friedman, M. (1962), *Capitalism and Freedom*, Chicago University Press, Chicago.

Hayek, F.A. (1960), *Constitution of Liberty*, Routledge and Kegan Paul, London.

Mill, J.S. (1848), *Principles of Political Economy*, with an introduction by W.J. Ashley, Longmans, London.

———— (1946), *On Liberty* (1859) and *Considerations on Representative Government* (1861), with an introduction by W.J. Ashley, Longmans, London.

Myrdal, G. (1968), *Asian Drama: An Inquiry into the Poverty of Nations*, Allen Lane, London.

Nayyar, D. (2003), 'Globalization and Development Strategies', in J. Toye (ed.), *Trade and Development: Directions for the Twenty-first Century*, Edward Elgar, Cheltenham.

Rawls, J. (1971), *A Theory of Justice*, Clarendon Press, Oxford.

Rodgers, G., C. Gore, and J.B. Figueiredo (eds) (1995), *Social Exclusion: Rhetoric, Reality, Responses*, International Labour Organization, Geneva.

Sen, A.K. (1970), *Collective Choice and Social Welfare*, North-Holland, Amsterdam.

———— (1981), *Poverty and Famines: An Essay on Entitlement and Deprivation*, Clarendon Press, Oxford.

———— (1985), *Commodities and Capabilities*, North-Holland, Amsterdam.

_____ (2000), *Development as Freedom*, Oxford University Press, New Delhi.

Smith, A. (1776), *The Wealth of Nations*, with an introduction by Andrew Skinner (1970), Pelican Books, Harmondsworth.

Sugden, R. (1981), *The Political Economy of Public Choice: An Introduction to Welfare Economics*, Martin Robertson, Oxford.

Taylor, L. (1993), *The Rocky Road to Reform: Adjustment, Income Distribution and Growth in the Developing World*, The MIT Press, Cambridge.

PART 2
DEVELOPMENT

Chapter 4

DEVELOPMENT THROUGH GLOBALIZATION?*

Globalization, which gathered momentum during the last quarter of the twentieth century, has created unparalleled opportunities and posed unprecedented challenges for development. Yet, the virtual ideology of our times has transformed globalization from a descriptive word into a prescriptive word. But the reality that has unfolded so far belies the expectations of the ideologues. The exclusion of countries and of people from globalization, which is partly attributable to the logic of markets, is a fact of life. Even so, there is a strong belief and an influential view that globalization is the road to development during the first quarter of the twenty-first century.[1] In a volume that seeks to think ahead about the future of development economics, development through globalization is an appropriate theme. It is even more appropriate, perhaps, with a question marked at the end.

The object of this essay is to reflect on development in prospect, not retrospect, situated in the wider international context of globalization. In doing so, it shall, of course, address the question posed in the title. The main object, however, is to focus on the correctives that would have to be introduced and the rethinking that would have to be done, given the reality of globalization, if development is to bring about an improvement in the living conditions of people, ordinary people.

The structure of the chapter is as follows. The first section outlines the rationale of globalization as a *mantra* for development, to juxtapose it with conflicting perceptions and complex realities. The second section examines the constraints on, and the choices for, latecomers to development at the present

*I am grateful to Amit Bhaduri, Ha-Joon Chang, and Lance Taylor for helpful discussion. I would also like to thank Andrea Cornia, Gustav Ranis, and Frances Stewart for valuable comments.

[1]See, for example, Sachs and Warner (1995), who were among the first exponents of this view. This prescriptive view of globalization is also set out, at some length, by Bhagwati (2004) and Wolf (2004).

juncture, given the asymmetrical consequences of globalization so far. The third section explains the essential meaning and sets out the objectives of development to suggest that we need to rethink the focus. The fourth section considers some important correctives, learning not only from the past but also from the present, for strategies of development. The fifth section argues that some rethinking is essential, from different perspectives, to understand and to foster the process of development, particularly because thinking about development, in terms of both theory and policy, has become narrower with the passage of time. The sixth section explores how the rules of the game for the world economy need to be reshaped to create more space for the pursuit of national development objectives. The last section concludes.

GLOBALIZATION AS A *MANTRA* FOR DEVELOPMENT

Recent years have witnessed the formulation of an intellectual rationale for globalization that is almost prescriptive. It is perceived as a means of ensuring not only efficiency and equity but also growth and development in the world economy. The analytical foundations of this world view are provided by the neo-liberal model. Orthodox neoclassical economics suggests that intervention in markets is inefficient. Neo-liberal political economy argues that governments are incapable of intervening efficiently. The essence of the neo-liberal model, then, can be stated as follows. First, the government should be rolled back wherever possible so that it approximates to the ideal of a minimalist State. Second, the market is not only a substitute for the State but also the preferred alternative because it performs better. Third, resource allocation and resource utilization must be based on market prices which should conform as closely as possible to international prices. Fourth, national political objectives, domestic economic concerns, or even national boundaries should not act as constraints. In this world, domestic economic concerns mesh with, or are subsumed in, the maximization of international economic welfare, and national political objectives melt away in the bargain.

The ideologues believe that globalization led to rapid industrialization and economic convergence in the world economy during the late nineteenth century. In their view, the promise of the emerging global capitalist system was wasted for more than half a century, to begin with by three decades of conflict and autarchy that followed the First World War and subsequently, for another three decades, by the socialist path and a statist world view. The conclusion drawn is that globalization, now as much as then, promises economic prosperity for countries that join the system and economic deprivation for countries that do not.[2] It needs to be stressed that this prescriptive view of globalization is contested and controversial.[3] Yet, for those who have this strong belief, globalization is the road to development in the first quarter of the twenty-first century.[4]

Interestingly enough, the development experience of the world economy in the last quarter of the twentieth century is invoked as supporting evidence, not only by the advocates but also by the critics of this prescription. In caricature form, these conflicting perceptions are almost polar opposites of each other. The pro-globalization advocates argue that it led to faster growth, that it reduced poverty, and that it brought about a decrease in inequality. The anti-globalization critics argue that it led to slower but more volatile growth, that it increased poverty in most parts of the world, and that there was an increase in inequality. Of course, such a broad-brush picture of conflicting perceptions abstracts from the nuances and the qualifications. But it highlights the impasse in a debate that borders on a dialogue of the deaf.

Yet, there is a little dispute about some important dimensions of reality. In conventional terms, the world has made enormous economic progress during the second half of the twentieth century. During this period, world GDP multiplied almost twelve-fold while per capita income more than trebled. The growth has been impressive even in the developing world, particularly when compared with underdevelopment and stagnation in the colonial era during the first half of the twentieth century. But such aggregates conceal more than they reveal. In fact, development has been uneven within and between countries. The pattern of development has been such that it has led to an increase in the economic distance between the industrialized world and much of the developing world. It has also led to an increase in the economic distance between the newly industrializing countries (NICs) at one end and the least developed countries at the other. At the same time, economic disparities between regions and between people within countries have registered a significant increase.

Uneven development is not without consequences for people. Poverty, inequality, and deprivation persist. And there is poverty everywhere. One-

---

[2]See, in particular, Sachs and Warner (1995). For a very different, contrasting, historical perspective on globalization and development, see Nayyar (2006).

[3]In an interesting critique, Samuelson (2004) questions the analytical basis and the theoretical foundations of this prescriptive view. For a critical perspective on the implications of globalization for development, see Stiglitz (2002), Nayyar (2003a), and Kaplinsky (2005). See also, Soros (1998) and Baker, Epstein, and Pollin (1998).

[4]Sachs and Warner (1995), Bhagwati (2004), and Wolf (2004).

eighth of the people in industrial societies are affected by, or live in, poverty. Almost one-third of the people in the developing world live in poverty and experience absolute deprivation insofar as they cannot meet their basic human needs. As many as 830 million people suffer from malnutrition while 1.2 billion people do not have access to clean water, and 2.7 billion people do not have adequate sanitation facilities. More than 250 million children who should be in school are not. Nearly 300 million women are not expected to survive to the age of 40. And 850 million adults remain illiterate. Most of them are in developing countries. But, in a functional sense, the number of illiterate people in industrial societies at 100 million is also large.[5]

In other words, many parts of the world and a significant proportion of its people are largely excluded from development. This may be attributable to the logic of markets which give to those who have and take away from those who have not, as the process of cumulative causation leads to market-driven virtuous circles or vicious circles. This may be the outcome of patterns of development where economic growth is uneven between regions and the distribution of its benefits is unequal between people, so that the outcome is growing affluence for some combined with persistent poverty for many. This may be the consequence of strategies of development as a similar economic performance in the aggregate could lead to egalitarian development in one situation and growth which bypasses the majority of the people in another situation.

CONSEQUENCES, CONSTRAINTS, AND CHOICES

In retrospect, it is apparent that globalization has been associated with simultaneous, yet asymmetrical, consequences for countries and for people. There is an inclusion for some and an exclusion, or marginalization, for many. There is affluence for some and poverty for many. There are some winners and many losers. Joan Robinson once said, 'There is only one thing that is worse than being exploited by capitalists. And that is not being exploited by capitalists.' Much the same can be said about markets and globalization which may not ensure prosperity for everyone but may, in fact, exclude a significant proportion of people.

It would seem that globalization has created two worlds that co-exist in space even if they are far apart in well-being. For some, in a world more interconnected than ever before, globalization has opened the door to many benefits. Open economies and open societies are conducive to innovation,

---

[5]The evidence cited in this paragraph is obtained from UNDP, *Human Development Report*, various issues, and World Commission on the Social Dimension of Globalization (2004).

entrepreneurship, and wealth creation. Better communications, it is said, have enhanced awareness of rights and identities, just as they have enabled social movements to mobilize opinion. For many, the fundamental problems of poverty, unemployment, and inequality persist. Of course, these problems existed even earlier. But globalization may have accentuated exclusion and deprivation, for it has dislocated traditional livelihoods and local communities. It also threatens environmental sustainability and cultural diversity. Better communications, it is said, have enhanced awareness of widening disparities. Everybody sees the world through the optic of their lives. Therefore, perceptions about globalization depend on who you are, what you do, and where you live. Some focus on the benefits and the opportunities. Others focus on the costs and the dangers. Both are right in terms of what they see. But both are wrong in terms of what they do not see.

On balance, it is clear that there is exclusion of countries and of people.[6] Too many people in poor countries, particularly in rural areas or in the informal sector, are marginalized if not excluded. Too few share in the benefits. Too many have no voice in its design or influence on its course. There is a growing polarization between the winners and the losers. The gap between rich and poor countries, between rich and poor in the world's population, and between rich and poor people within countries, has widened. These mounting imbalances in the world are ethically unacceptable and politically unsustainable.[7]

But that is not all. Globalization has diminished the policy space so essential for countries that are latecomers to development. Indeed, the space for, and autonomy to formulate policies in the pursuit of national development objectives is significantly reduced. This is so for two reasons: unfair rules of the game in the world economy and consequences of integration into international financial markets.

In a world of unequal partners, it is not surprising that the rules of the game are asymmetrical in terms of construct and inequitable in terms of outcome. The strong have the power to make the rules and the authority to implement the rules. In contrast, the weak can neither set nor invoke the rules. The problem, however, takes different forms.[8]

First, there are different rules in different spheres. The rules of the game for the international trading system, being progressively set in the World Trade

---

[6]For a detailed discussion, as also evidence, see Nayyar (2003a and 2006).

[7]This proposition is set out, as also explained, in the Report of the World Commission on the Social Dimension of Globalization (2004).

[8]For a more complete discussion on rules of the game, see Nayyar (2002a and 2003a).

Organization (WTO), provide the most obvious example. There are striking asymmetries. National boundaries should not matter for trade flows and capital flows but should be clearly demarcated for technology flows and labour flows. It follows that developing countries would provide access to their markets without a corresponding access to technology and would accept capital mobility without a corresponding provision for labour mobility. This implies more openness in some spheres but less openness in other spheres. The contrast between the free movement of capital and the unfree movement of labour across national boundaries lies at the heart of the inequality in the rules of the game.

Second, there are rules for some but not for others. In the WTO, for instance, major trading countries resort to a unilateral exercise of power, ignoring the rules, because small countries do not have the economic strength even if they have the legal right to retaliate. The conditions imposed by the IMF and the World Bank, however, provide the more familiar example. There are no rules for surplus countries, or even deficit countries, in the industrialized world, which do not borrow from the multilateral financial institutions. But the IMF and the World Bank set rules for borrowers in the developing world and in the transition economies. The conditionality is meant in principle to ensure repayment, but in practice it imposes conditions to serve the interests of international banks which lend to the same countries. The Bretton Woods institutions, then, act as watchdogs for moneylenders in international capital markets. This has been so for some time. But there is more to it now. The IMF programmes of stabilization and World Bank programmes of structural adjustment seek to harmonize policies and institutions across countries, which is in consonance with the needs of globalization.

Third, the agenda for new rules is partisan, but the unsaid is just as important as the said. The attempt to create a multilateral agreement on investment in the WTO, which seeks free access and national treatment for foreign investors, with provisions to enforce commitments and obligations to foreign investors, provides the most obvious example. Surely, these rights of foreign investors must be matched by some obligations. Thus, a discipline on restrictive business practices of transnational corporations, the importance of conformity with anti-trust laws in home countries, or a level playing field for domestic firms in host countries, should also be in the picture.

The process of globalization is already reducing the autonomy of developing countries in the formulation of economic policies in their pursuit of development. These unfair rules also encroach on the policy space so essential for national development. The existing (and prospective) rules of the WTO regime allow few exceptions and provide little flexibility to countries that are latecomers to industrialization. In comparison, there was more room for manoeuvre in the erstwhile General Agreement on Tariffs and Trade (GATT), *inter alia*, because of special and differential treatment for developing countries. The new regime is much stricter in terms of the law and the implementation. The rules on trade in the new regime make the selective protection or strategic promotion of domestic firms *vis-à-vis* foreign competition much more difficult. The tight system for the protection of intellectual property rights could pre-empt or stifle the development of domestic technological capabilities. The possible multilateral agreement on investment, should it materialize, would almost certainly reduce the possibilities of strategic bargaining with transnational firms. Similarly, commitments on structural reform, an integral part of stabilization and adjustment programmes with the IMF and the World Bank, inevitably prescribe industrial deregulation, privatization, trade liberalization and financial deregulation. In sum, the new regime appears rule-based but the rules are not uniform. And it is not clear how or why this is better than discretion. For, taken together, such rules and conditions are bound to curb the use of industrial policy, technology policy, trade policy, and financial policy as strategic forms of intervention to foster industrialization.[9]

At the same time, the consequences of integration into international capital markets also reduce degrees of freedom. Exchange rates can no longer be used as a strategic device to provide an entry into world markets for manufactured goods, just as interest rates can no longer be used as a strategic instrument for guiding the allocation of scarce investible resources in a market economy. What is more, countries that are integrated into the international financial system are constrained in using an autonomous management of demand to maintain levels of output and employment. Expansionary fiscal and monetary policies—large government deficits to stimulate aggregate demand or low interest rates to encourage domestic investment—can no longer be used because of an overwhelming fear that such measures could lead to speculative capital flight and a run on the national currency.[10]

In sum, the existing global rules encroach upon essential policy space. And the problem is compounded by the rapid, and sometimes premature, integration into international financial markets. Therefore, latecomers to

[9]It must be recognized that such State intervention was crucial for development in the success stories among late industrializers during the second half of the twentieth century. For a convincing exposition of this view, see Amsden (1989), Wade (1990), and Chang (1996).

[10]For an analysis of this issue, see Nayyar (2002b).

industrialization would find it difficult to emulate the East Asian success stories. Indeed, the industrialized countries had much more freedom and space in policy formulation at comparable stages of their industrialization.[11]

There is an obvious question that arises. What are the options or choices in this situation for countries that are latecomers to development? First, it is essential to use the available policy space for national development, given the international context. Second, it is important to create more policy space by reshaping the rules of the game in the world economy.

In the national context, therefore, it is necessary to redesign strategies by introducing correctives, and to rethink development by incorporating different perspectives, that would make for egalitarian economic development and a more broad-based social development. In the international context, even if difficult, it is necessary to reshape the rules of the game and contemplate some governance of globalization.

CONCEPTION OF DEVELOPMENT

Before considering these possibilities, it is both necessary and desirable to reflect on the essential meaning of development. For this purpose, a short digression is worthwhile. The reason is that the agenda on development in terms of both theory and policy has, unfortunately, narrowed with the passage of time. So has its meaning and the object of its focus. Hence, there is a need to reflect on the meaning and rethink on the focus.

There is a vast literature on economic development which is rich in terms of range and depth. Yet, there is not enough clarity about the meaning of development. There are many different views. And perspectives have changed over time.

In the early 1950s, conventional thinking identified development with growth in GDP or GDP per capita. The earlier literature emphasized economic growth and capital accumulation at a macro level. The contemporary literature emphasizes economic efficiency and productivity increases at a macro level. Industrialization has always been seen as an essential attribute of development. The emphasis has simply shifted from the pace of industrialization to the efficiency of industrialization. The underlying presumption is that economic growth and economic efficiency are not only necessary but also sufficient for bringing about an improvement in the living conditions of people. From time to time, dissenting voices questioned the conventional wisdom to suggest other indicators of development but these were largely ignored by mainstream

[11]See Bairoch (1993) and Chang (2002a). See also Maddison (1995).

economics. And, even 50 years later, economic growth or increases in per capita remain the most important measure of development.

The early 1970s witnessed the emergence of a literature that suggested other indicators of development such as a reduction in poverty, inequality, and unemployment which would capture changes in the quality of life.[12] This thinking moved further. Development, it was argued, must bring about an improvement in the living conditions of people. It should, therefore, ensure the provision of basic human needs for all: not just food and clothing but also shelter, health care and education.[13] It was stressed that this simple but powerful proposition is often forgotten in the conventional concerns of economics. Such thinking culminated in writings on, and an index of, human development.[14]

In the late 1990s, Amartya Sen provided the broadest possible conception of development as freedom: a process of expanding real freedoms that people enjoy for their economic well-being, social opportunities, and political rights.[15] Such freedoms are not just constitutive as the primary ends of development. Such freedoms are also instrumental as the principal means of attaining development. What is more, there are strong interconnections that link different freedoms with one another. Political freedoms help promote economic security. Social opportunities facilitate economic participation. Economic well-being supports social facilities and reinforces political rights. In this manner, freedoms of different kinds strengthen one another.

The purpose of development, after all, is to create a milieu that enables people, ordinary people, to lead a good life. Development must, therefore, provide all men and women the rights, the opportunities, and the capabilities they need to exercise their own choices for a decent life.

The significance of this abstraction about, or conceptualization of, development is not lost on everyone. But it is the tangible or the measurable that remains dominant in terms of wide use and popular understanding. Per capita income is only an arithmetic mean. Social indicators are also statistical averages. And neither captures the well-being of the poor. Even the human development index is not quite an exception. The quantifiable is obviously important. But it should not shape our thinking about development. In fact, it does. Consequently, the focus is misplaced. It needs to be corrected. And the

---

[12]See, for example, Baster (1972), Seers (1972), and Morris (1979).

[13]See Streeten (1981) and Stewart (1985).

[14]There is an extensive literature on the subject. For a discussion on the conceptual foundations, see Sen (1989) and Haq (1995). For an analysis of issues related to methodology and measurement, see Anand and Sen (1994).

[15]See Sen (1999).

correction has several dimensions. It is essential to make a distinction between means and ends. Economic growth and economic efficiency, or for that matter industrialization, are means. It is development which is an end. Much of the focus in the literature on development is on economies. But aggregates often conceal more than they reveal. Thus, it is important to shift the focus from countries to people. However, people are not just beneficiaries. It is only if people are centre stage in the process of development, as the main actors, that development can empower them to participate in the decisions that shape their lives. The significance of this proposition is highlighted by the medieval distinction between agents and patients, which is invoked by Amartya Sen. He argues that the freedom-centred understanding of economics and of the process of development is very much an agent-oriented view. This is because individuals with adequate social opportunities can effectively shape their own destiny and help each other. They must not be seen primarily as patients, or passive recipients, of the benefits of cunning development programmes.[16]

REDESIGNING STRATEGIES: INTRODUCING CORRECTIVES

The introduction of correctives in the design of strategies for development is easier said than done. Even so, some essential correctives emerge from an understanding of theory and a study of experience that recognizes not only the diversity but also the complexity of development. In this reflection, it is necessary to recognize the limitations of orthodox economic theory and policy prescriptions even if these represent influential thinking about development at the present juncture. It is just as necessary to learn lessons from the history of development experience embedded in both successes and failures without neglecting specificities in time and space.

The first limitation of orthodoxy is its unquestioned faith in the market mechanism. It fails to recognize that there is no magic in the market. Indeed, market failures are not quite an exception but are closer to being the rule. The strong belief in the market mechanism is based on the proposition that market forces, or the invisible hand, achieve a competitive equilibrium. The fundamental theorems of welfare economics establish that this is an efficient state and a desirable state.[17] In spite of the analytical elegance of these theorems, such faith is not quite warranted. The skepticism extends much beyond the critics. Consider, for example, the following quotations from three distinguished economic theorists: Frank Hahn, Amartya Sen, and Joseph Stiglitz.

[16]For a lucid analysis, see Sen (1999).

[17]For a detailed examination of the fundamental theorems of welfare economics, see Arrow (1950).

It showed that it is logically possible to describe a world where greedy and rational people responding only to price signals take actions which are mutually compatible. The theory does not describe the invisible hand in motion but displays it with its task accomplished ... The importance of this intellectual achievement is that it provides a benchmark ... Now one of the mysteries which future historians of thought will surely wish to unravel is how it came about that the Arrow–Debreu model came to be taken descriptively; that is as sufficient in itself for the study and control of actual economies. (Hahn 1984, p. 308)

The intellectual climate has changed quite dramatically over the last few decades, and the tables are now turned. The virtues of the market mechanism are now standardly assumed to be so pervasive that qualifications seem unimportant .... The need for critical scrutiny of standard preconceptions and politico-economic attitudes has never been stronger. Today's prejudices (in favour of the pure market mechanism) need to be investigated and, I would argue, partly rejected. (Sen 1999, pp. 111–2.)

The invisible hand of the market is invisible because it is not there. (Stiglitz 2002.)[18]

There are, in fact, many reasons why these results, which highlight the virtues of the market, may not hold.[19] First, there may be externalities in production or consumption which would lead to market failure. The original solution to this problem was appropriate taxes and subsidies to be introduced by the government. But this went out of fashion with the Coase Theorem, which returned the market to its pedestal.[20] Second, in such a world, markets may not deliver efficient and desirable outcomes if transaction costs are too high or if there is no government that can assign and protect property rights. Third, markets may not function, as textbooks would have us believe, in situations where an enforcement of contracts is difficult or not possible. And this is a common occurrence in developing countries which are significantly different from industrial societies in this sphere. Fourth, markets may cease to function as expected if there is an uncertainty about quality. In other words, doing business in markets is difficult where goods or services are of poor quality and where quality cannot be discerned by consumers before purchase.[21] Fifth, it would seem that the market mechanism needs support to function as it is meant to. The need for such support spans a wide range from taxes-cum-subsidies

[18]Joseph Stiglitz during an interview on WBAI Radio, 15 August 2002, New York.

[19]For a succinct discussion on why these results may not hold, see Mukherji (2005).

[20]See Coase (1960). It is worth noting that Richard Coase was awarded the Nobel Prize in Economics, for this contribution, in 1991.

[21]This proposition was developed by Akerlof (1970) in a seminal contribution.

in the presence of externalities, and laws to enforce contracts or property rights, to certification and regulation in a world of asymmetric information. Even with such support, markets are prone to corrupt practices whenever agents engaged by institutions to enforce regulations or laws are more interested in their own welfare rather than in achieving the goals set for them by institutions established to regulate markets.[22]

The second limitation of orthodoxy is the belief that getting-prices-right is enough. Such thinking makes an elementary, but commonplace, error in the design of policies. It confuses *comparison* (of equilibrium positions) with *change* (from one equilibrium position to another). In the real world, economic policy must be concerned not merely with comparison but with how to direct the process of change. Thus, for example, even if a reduction in protection can, in principle, lead to a more cost-efficient economy the transition path is by no means clear. And the process of change should not be confused with the ultimate destination of the economy that is competitive in the world market.[23]

The third limitation of orthodoxy is the presumption that policy regimes which are necessary are also sufficient.[24] The management of incentives motivated by the object of minimizing costs and maximizing efficiency at a micro level is based on a set of policies that is intended to increase competition between firms in the market place. Domestic competition is sought to be provided through deregulation in investment decisions, in the financial sector, and in labour markets. Foreign competition is sought to be provided through openness in trade, investment, and technology flows. It must, however, be recognized that there is nothing automatic about competition. Policy regimes can allow things to happen but cannot cause things to happen. The creation of competitive markets that enforce efficiency may, in fact, require strategic intervention through industrial policy, trade policy, and financial policy, just as it may require the creation of institutions.

The fourth limitation of orthodoxy is its stress on government failures and its neglect of market failures. However, both market failure and government failure are facts of life. For neither markets nor governments are, or can ever be, perfect. Indeed, markets are invariably imperfect and governments are without exception fallible. The juxtaposition of government failure and market failure in an either–or mode, as if there was a choice to be made, is misleading. It is important to introduce correctives against both market failure and government failure. In such a perspective, the State and the market are complements rather

---

[22]See, for instance, Banerjee (1997).
[23]Bhaduri and Nayyar (1996) and Nayyar (1997).
[24]See Nayyar (1997) and Stiglitz (1998).

than substitutes. What is more, the relationship between the State and the market cannot be defined once-and-for-all in any dogmatic manner but must change over time in an adaptive manner as circumstances change.[25] In this context, it is important to remember that markets are good servants but bad masters. What is more, efficient markets need effective states.

The development experience during the second half of the twentieth century also suggests important correctives for redesigning strategies. There are some important lessons that can be learnt from mistakes and failures of the past.[26] The first lesson to emerge from experience is that competition in the market is desirable. Such competition is essential between domestic firms, between domestic firms and foreign firms, as also between the public sector and the private sector. Industrial deregulation that removes barriers to entry for new firms and limits on the growth in existing firms leads to competition between domestic firms. Trade liberalization which reduces restrictions or tariffs on imports leads to competition between domestic and foreign firms. The dismantling of public sector monopolies leads to competition between the public sector and the private sector. It is such competition between firms, in price and in quality, that creates efficiency among producers and provides a choice for consumers.

The second lesson to emerge from experience is that prudent macro-management of the economy is both necessary and desirable. Soft options, such as borrowing by the government only postpone the day of reckoning. Borrowing to support consumption almost always leads to a fiscal crisis. The problem may be compounded by a reliance on external resources to finance development. And if such borrowing is used to support consumption, a debt crisis is almost inevitable. Even so, it is necessary to recognize the fallacies of deficit fetishism. It must be stressed that the size of the fiscal deficit or the amount of borrowings are symptoms and not the disease. The real issue is the use to which the government borrowing is put in relation to the cost of borrowing by the government. Thus, government borrowing is always sustainable if it is used to finance investment and if the rate of return on such investment is greater than the interest rate payable.

The third lesson to emerge from experience is that excessive and inappropriate State intervention is counterproductive. It is, of course, important to learn from mistakes but it is just as important to avoid over-correction in learning from mistakes, because there are dangers implicit in over-reaction.

[25]For an analysis of the relationship between the State and the market, from this perspective, see Bhaduri and Nayyar (1996).

[26]The discussion on lessons in the following paragraphs draws upon Nayyar (2004).

Clearly, there are things that markets can and should do. However, there are some things that only governments can do. If governments do these badly, it is not possible to dispense with governments or replace them with markets. Governments must be made to perform better. It is, therefore, necessary to reformulate the questions about the economic role of the State.[27] The real question is no longer about the size of the State (how big?) or the degree of State intervention (how much?). The question is now about the nature of State intervention (what sort?) and the quality of the performance of the State (how good?).

The fourth lesson to emerge from experience, in the more recent past, is that the speed and the sequence of change matter. For one, the speed of change must be calibrated so that it can be absorbed by the economy. For another, the sequence of change must be planned with reference to an order of priorities. The significance of speed and sequence emerges clearly in the sphere of trade policy reform and even more clearly from the experience with capital account liberalization. In both, whether speed or sequence, deregulation and openness must be compatible with initial conditions and must be consistent with each other.

Clearly, it is important to learn from failures. Recognition of where things went wrong translates easily into correctives. But it is just as important to learn from successes. And there are two important lessons that emerge from the development experience in countries that are success stories. First, there are specificities in time and space which must be recognized and cannot be ignored. Obviously, one size does not fit all. Second, latecomers to industrialization during the twentieth century—to begin with, in Europe and subsequently in Asia—that succeeded adopted strategies of development which not only varied across countries over time but also differed significantly from the orthodox policy prescriptions now in fashion.[28] Last but not least, there are some forgotten essentials that should form an integral part of any attempt at redesigning strategies of development.

First, it is not quite recognized that economic growth is necessary but not sufficient to bring about a reduction in poverty. It cannot suffice to say that the outcomes of economic policies should be moderated by social policies. The dichotomy between economic and social policies is inadequate just as the dichotomy between economic and social development is inappropriate. In fact, no such distinction is made in industrialized countries. And the

---

[27]For a discussion on the economic role of the State, see Stiglitz (1989) and Killick (1990). See also Lall (1990) and Shapiro and Taylor (1990).

[28]See Amsden (1989), Lall (1990), Wade (1990), and Chang (2002a).

experience of the industrialized world suggests that there is a clear need for an integration, rather than separation, of economic and social policies. Thus, it is important to create institutional mechanisms that mediate between economic growth and social development.

Second, it is often forgotten that the well-being of humankind is the essence of development. Thus, distributional outcomes are important. So are employment and livelihoods. Structural reforms associated with economic liberalization have important implications for employment creation and income opportunities. For one, insofar as such reforms increase the average productivity of labour, through the use of capital-intensive or labour-saving technologies, or through a restructuring of firms, which increases efficiency, it reduces the contribution of any given rate of economic growth to employment growth. For another, insofar as trade liberalization enforces closures rather than efficiency at a micro-level, or switches demand away from home-produced goods to foreign goods at a macro-level, it has an adverse effect on output, hence employment, which is magnified through the multiplier effect. This has important consequences in the medium term. There is a contraction of employment in some sectors without a compensatory expansion of employment in other sectors. And, as employment elasticities of output decline, employment creation slows down. It need hardly be stressed that employment creation is the only sustainable means of reducing poverty. Moreover, employment is also essential for the well-being and dignity of people.

RETHINKING DEVELOPMENT: DIFFERENT PERSPECTIVES

The discourse on theory and policy in development has become narrower with the passage of time. Some rethinking on development is essential. It must incorporate different perspectives. A systematic, let alone complete, analysis of such alternatives would mean too much of a digression. Even so, it is necessary to stress the following as an integral part of any rethinking on development: the importance of initial conditions, the significance of institutions, the relevance of politics in economics, and the critical role of good governance.

It is obvious that initial conditions are important determinants of development. It should also be recognized that initial conditions can and should be changed to foster development. This is an unambiguous lesson that emerges from economic history.[29] In countries that are latecomers to industrialization, State intervention creates conditions for the development of industrial capitalism through the spread of education in society, the creation of a physical infrastructure,

---

[29]For a fascinating historical analysis of the development experience of latecomers to industrialization, see Amsden (2001) and Chang (2002a).

and the introduction of institutional change. This role has always been recognized. The building of managerial capabilities in individuals and technological capabilities in firms is also an important, even if less recognized, dimension of initial conditions, for such capabilities determine technical efficiency in the short-run and competitiveness in the long-run. This has been recognized for some time. The present juncture, however, is characterized by a widespread disillusionment with the economic role of the State and a strong belief in the magic of the market. Hence, orthodoxy neglects the importance of initial conditions. There is an irony in this situation. In the context of globalization, such a role for the State is more necessary than ever before. Indeed, creating the initial conditions is essential for maximizing the benefits and minimizing the costs of integration with the world economy.

The debate on development is, in large part, about policies. The time has come to move beyond policies to institutions. The recent recognition of the importance of institutions, even if late, is welcome.[30] Yet, the understanding of institutions in the profession of economics is, to say the least, limited. Economists have treated institutions as a black box in much the same way as they treated technology for some time. What is more, orthodox economics has sought to harmonize the role as also the form of institutions across the world, irrespective of space and time. This is a serious mistake, since one-size-does-not-fit all. There are specificities in space. Institutions are local and cannot be transplanted out of context. There are specificities in time. Institutions need time to evolve and cannot be created by a magic wand. The blueprints for economic liberalization over the past 25 years have simply not recognized this reality.

The meaning of institutions is not always clear. At one level, institutions refer to the rules of the game. These rules can be formal, as in constitutions, laws, or statutes. These rules can also be informal, as in norms, conventions, or practices. At another level, institutions refer to organizations or entities that are not players. The role of the State is crucial in almost every dimension of institutions. In an economy, the State seeks to govern the market through rules or laws. It does so by setting rules of the game for players in the market. In particular, it creates frameworks for regulating markets. But it also creates institutions, whether organizations or entities, to monitor the functioning of markets. The development of such institutions, which cannot always develop on their own, may need some proactive role for the State, where it needs to

---

[30]See for example, North (1990) and Chang (2002b).

be a catalyst if not leader. Of course, there are institutions that may develop through markets, as in standards or for safety, but these depend on social norms.

In a market economy, social norms are perhaps as important as laws or organizations in the world of institutions.[31] Clearly, there is a world beyond 'methodological individualism' which reduces all social and economic interaction simply to the self-interest of the individual. This proposition is nicely illustrated by Adam Smith's intellectual journey from the *Theory of Moral Sentiments* to the *Wealth of Nations*. The notion of society came to be embedded in a wider range of human moral sentiments. This was Smith's composite notion of 'sympathy'. Such sympathy was not just altruism. It was a complex range of co-existing, often conflicting, human motives that culminated in social norms such as trust in exchange, respect for contracts, or reciprocity in behaviour. Some of these may also have been the outcome of longer-term enlightened self-interest. In this world, exchange and production in markets is sustained by underlying, unwritten, social norms. Indeed, without such social norms, no market economy can function. Unfortunately, social norms, so essential for institutions, are no longer part of the conventional academic discourse, which exaggerates the efficiency of an abstract market mechanism based on an invented auctioneer and neglects the role of the State in preserving or reinforcing these norms.

The literature does not make any clear distinction between forms and functions of institutions. There is, also, little understanding of processes of change in existing institutions or in evolution of new institutions. Much remains to be done so as to improve understanding of institutions and of institutional change in the process of development, which could be the difference between success and failure at development. Such understanding needs not only theory but also history. However, the theory must be non-ideological just as the history must be non-selective.

In every society, economy and polity are closely intertwined. It is the interaction of economics and politics which shapes outcomes for people. Therefore, it is essential to explore the interplay between economics and politics in the process of development.[32] There is, then, a need for a political economy that extends beyond econometric analysis at a micro level, even if it is the fashion of our times. This is easier said than done. But a beginning could be

---

[31]For a lucid discussion on the importance of social norms in market economies, with particular reference to Adam Smith, see Bhaduri (2002).

[32]This is stressed by North (2001) in a short essay on understanding development.

made by exploring the relationship between markets and democracy, democracy and development, and development and empowerment.

The essence of the tension between the economics of markets and politics of democracy must be recognized. In a market economy, people vote with their money in the market place. But a political democracy works on the basis of one-person-one-vote. The distribution of votes, unlike the distribution of incomes or assets, is equal. One adult has one vote in politics even though a rich man has more votes than a poor man, in terms of purchasing power, in the market. This tension may be compounded by a related asymmetry between economy and polity. The people who are excluded by the economics of markets are included by the politics of democracy. The rich dominate a market economy in terms of purchasing power. But the poor have a strong voice in a political democracy in terms of votes. Hence, exclusion and inclusion are asymmetrical in economics and politics. In reconciling market economy and political democracy, successive generations of economic thinkers and political philosophers have stressed the role of the State in this process of mediation. The reason is important even if it is not obvious. Governments are accountable to their people whereas markets are not. In a democracy, however, governments are elected by the people. But even where they are not, the State needs legitimation from the people most of whom are not rich or are poor.[33]

The relationship between democracy and development is also complex. But it is important to reject the view that latecomers to development cannot afford the luxury of democracy. Indeed, thinking ahead, it is clear that democracy is going to be conducive to the process of development. The reason is straightforward. The essential attributes of democracy, transparency and accountability, provide the means for combining sensible economics with feasible politics.[34] The economic priorities of the people will be reflected more and more in the political agenda of parties if there is a transparency in the system. The agenda of political parties will be reflected more and more in the reality of economic development if there is accountability in the system. Once this two-way process gathers momentum, transparency and accountability will create a commitment to the long-term objectives of development in the context of a political democracy where governments are bound to change through elections over time.

The problem is that democracy, while conducive and necessary, is not sufficient to actually produce development. We know that from experience.

[33]The discussion in this paragraph draws upon Nayyar (2003b).
[34]For a more detailed discussion, see Bhaduri and Nayyar (1996).

Development may or may not be provided from above by benevolent governments. It must be claimed from below by people as citizens from governments that are accountable. The empowerment of people, then, is an integral part of any process of change that leads to development. A political democracy, even if it is slow, provides a sure path for two reasons. It increases political consciousness among voters to judge political parties for their performance. At the same time, it increases participation in the political process when it leads to mobilization on some issues. This highlights the significance of Amartya Sen's conception of development as freedom. Expanding freedoms for people at large constitute development. But the same expanding freedoms, which empower people, are instruments that drive the process of change in development.

Governance is critical in the process of development. The real issue is not about more or less government. It is about the quality of government performance. This has two dimensions. The first dimension is more obvious. It is about redefining the economic role of the State in a changed national and international context. In the earlier stages of development, the primary role is to create initial conditions. In the later stages of development, the role is neither that of a promoter nor that of a catalyst. It is somewhat different and spans a range: functional intervention to correct for market failure, institutional intervention to govern the market, or strategic intervention to guide the market.[35] In this era of markets and globalization, surprisingly enough, the role of the State is more critical than ever before and extends beyond correcting for market failures or regulating domestic markets. It is about: (a) creating the initial conditions to capture the benefits from globalization; (b) managing the process of integration into the world economy in terms of pace and sequence; (c) providing social protection and safeguarding the vulnerable in the process of change; and (d) ensuring that economic growth creates employment and livelihoods for people.[36] In sum, governments need to regulate and complement markets so as to make them people-friendly. Thus, the role of the State in the process of development will continue to be important for some time to come, even as the scope of the market increases through liberalization in the wider context of globalization.

The second dimension, good governance, is less obvious. It is, however, more concrete and less abstract. Governance is largely about rules and institutions that regulate the public realm in civil society. A democratic system seeks to provide for equal participation of the rich and the poor, or the strong

[35]Nayyar (1997). See also Bhaduri and Nayyar (1996).
[36]See World Commission on the Social Dimension of Globalization (2004).

and the weak, individuals as citizens in political processes. And good governance is a process characterized by communication and consultation, through which disputes are resolved, consensus is built, and performance is reviewed on a continuous basis. The basis for good governance is a democratic political system that ensures representative and honest governments, responsive to the needs of people. This involves more than simply free and fair elections. It implies a respect for the economic, social, and political rights of citizens. The rule of law is a foundation. An equitable legal framework, applied consistently to everyone, defends people from the abuse of power by State and non-State actors. It empowers people to assert their rights. The need for good governance extends to economic, social, and political institutions required for the functioning of market economy and political democracy. A vibrant civil society, empowered by freedom of association and expression which can voice diversity in views, is just as important for good governance insofar as it provides checks and balances when governments do not act as they should. In sum, good governance, where governments are accountable to citizens and people are centre stage in the process of development, is essential for creating capabilities, providing opportunities, and ensuring rights for ordinary people. Governance capabilities matter. Indeed, the quality of governance is an important determinant of success or failure at development.[37] The moral of the story is not less government but good governance.

INTERNATIONAL CONTEXT: GOVERNING GLOBALIZATION

It is clear that, during the first quarter of the twenty-first century, development outcomes would be shaped, at least in part, by the international context. It is also clear that unfair rules of the game in the contemporary world economy would encroach on policy space so essential for development. This situation needs to be corrected. The correctives should endeavour to make existing rules less unfair, introduce new rules where necessary, and recognize that even fair rules may not suffice. But this endeavour cannot succeed without more democratic structures of governance in the world economy. In this process, interestingly enough, the role of nation states would be critical.

In reshaping unfair rules, it need hardly be said that the nature of the solution depends upon the nature of the problem. Where there are different rules in different spheres, it is necessary to make the rules symmetrical across

---

[37]A striking illustration of this proposition is provided by the wide diversity in economic performance across states in India, despite common policies, similar institutions, and the economic union. There are even more striking examples that emerge from a comparison of economic performance across countries in the developing world.

spheres. Where there are rules for some but not for others, it is necessary to ensure that the rules are uniformly applicable to all. Where the agenda for new rules is partisan, it is imperative to redress the balance in the agenda.[38]

There is a clear need for greater symmetry in the rules of the multilateral trading system embodied in the WTO. If developing countries provide access to their markets, it should be matched with some corresponding access to technology. If there is almost complete freedom for capital mobility, the draconian restrictions on labour mobility should at least be reduced. The enforcement of rules is also asymmetrical. In the Bretton Woods institutions, enforcement is possible through conditionality. Such conditionality, however, is applicable only to developing countries or transition economies that borrow from the IMF or the World Bank. In the WTO, enforcement is possible through retaliation. But most developing countries do not have the economic strength, even if they have the legal right, to retaliate. The reality, then, is that the countries that are poor or weak conform to the rules, whereas countries that are rich or strong can flout the rules. And the hegemonic powers, often, simply ignore the rules. The enforcement of rules for the rich and the powerful is, therefore, essential. In addition, the agenda for the new rules needs careful scrutiny for it is shaped by the interests of industrialized countries while the needs of development are largely neglected. For instance, if the proposed multilateral agreement on investment is so concerned about the rights of transnational corporations, some attention should also be paid to their possible obligations. In any case, such an agreement should not be lodged in the WTO. The issue of labour standards, of course, is simply not in the domain of the WTO.

But that is not all. There are some spheres where there are no rules, such as international financial markets or cross-border movements of people, which are not even on the agenda. The time has come to introduce some rules that govern speculative financial flows constituted mostly by short-term capital movements in search of capital gains, sensitive to exchange rates and interest rates. It is also perhaps necessary to think about a new international financial architecture in which a World Financial Authority would manage systemic risk associated with international financial liberalization, coordinate national action against market-failure or abuse, and act as a regulator in international financial markets.[39] Similarly, it is worth contemplating a multilateral framework for consular practices and immigration laws that would govern cross-border

---

[38]The following discussion on the rules of the game in the world economy draws upon earlier works of the author (Nayyar 2002a and 2003a).

[39]For a discussion on the rationale for, and contours of, such a World Financial Authority, see Eatwell and Taylor (2000).

movements of people, akin to multilateral frameworks that exist, or are sought to be created, for the governance of national laws, or rules, about the movement of goods, services, technology, investment, and information across national boundaries.[40] The essential object should be to create a transparent and non-discriminatory system, based on rules rather than discretion, for people who wish to move, temporarily or permanently, across borders.

Rules that are fair are necessary but not sufficient. For a game is not simply about rules. It is also about players. And if one of the teams or one of the players does not have adequate training or preparation, it will simply be crushed by the other. In other words, the rules must be such that newcomers or latecomers to the game, for example developing countries, are provided with the time and the space to learn so that they can become competitive players rather than push-over opponents. In this context, it is important to stress that, for countries at vastly different levels of development, there should be some flexibility, instead of complete rigidity, in the application of uniform rules. Indeed, uniform rules for unequal partners can only produce unequal outcomes. Thus, we should be concerned with the desirability of the outcomes and not with the procedural uniformity of rules. It is, in principle, possible to formulate general rules where application is a function of country-specific or time-specific circumstances, without resorting to exceptions. It implies a set of multilateral rules in which every country has the same rights but the obligations are a function of its level or stage of development. In other words, rights and obligations should not be strictly symmetrical across countries. And there is a clear need for positive discrimination or affirmative action in favour of countries that are latecomers to development.

The reshaping of rules is easier said than done. Much would depend upon structures of governance. The existing arrangements for global governance are characterized by a large democratic deficit.[41] In terms of representation, the existing system is less than democratic. For one thing, representation is unequal, in part because of unequal weights in representation in institutions such as the IMF and the World Bank, and in part because of exclusion from representation in arrangements such as the P-5 or the G-8 or even the Organization for Economic Cooperation and Development (OECD). For another, representation is incomplete insofar as it is confined mostly to governments, with little that could be described as participation by civil society

---

[40]For a discussion on the rationale for such a multilateral framework to govern cross-border movements of people, see Nayyar (2002c). The World Commission on the Social Dimension of Globalization (2004) makes a similar proposal.

[41]The democratic deficit is analysed, at some length, in Nayyar (2002a).

or corporate entities, let alone people or citizens. In terms of decision-making, the existing system is even less democratic. Where some countries have more votes than others and yet other countries have no votes, the system is obviously undemocratic. Even the principle of one-country-one-vote, however, does not ensure a democratic mode. Much also depends on how decisions are made. The right of veto in the Security Council of the UN is explicitly undemocratic. But decision-making by consensus, as in the WTO, can also be undemocratic if there is bilateral arm-twisting or a consensus is hammered out among a small subset of powerful players, while most countries are silent spectators that are in the end a part of the apparent consensus.

It is difficult to imagine more democratic structures of governance in a world of such disparities, economic and political, between countries. But democracy is not simply about majority rule. It is as much about the protection of rights of minorities. The essential corrective, then, is to create institutional mechanisms that give poor countries and poor people a voice in the process of global governance. Even if they cannot shape decisions, they have a right to be heard. In addition, wherever existing rules constrain autonomy or choices in the pursuit of development, there is a need for the equivalent of an escape clause. Such a provision to opt out of obligations embedded in international rules, without having to forsake rights, could provide countries that are latecomers to development with the requisite degrees of freedom in their national pursuit of development objectives. It is important to recognize that, in democratic situations, *exit* has as much significance as *voice*.

In the international context, where the distribution of economic and political power is so unequal, the nation state is, perhaps, the only institutional medium through which poor countries or poor people can attempt to influence or shape rules and institutions in a world of unequal partners. This is because only nation states have the authority to set international rules. Groups of countries with mutual interests are more likely to be heard than single countries by themselves. There will always be some conflict of interest but there will always be areas where it is possible to find common cause and accept trade-offs. In principle, it is possible to contemplate cooperation among nation states to create rules and norms for the market that transcend national boundaries, just as the nation state created rules and norms for the market within national boundaries. In practice, however, a recognition of the benefits of such cooperation might not be motivation enough. Cooperation among nation states is far more likely to materialize, much like stable coalitions, if and when the costs of non-cooperation cross the threshold of tolerance. In either case, the nation state is the most important player in the game. Therefore, it is not possible to imagine good governance in the world without nation states, just as it is not possible to have good governance in countries without governments.

CONCLUSION

In considering the prospects for development during the first quarter of the twenty-first century, it is time to reflect on a new agenda for development. In this reflection, the concern for efficiency must be balanced with a concern for equity, just as the concern for economic growth must be balanced with a concern for social progress. It is also time to evolve a new consensus on development, in which the focus is on people rather than on economies. Such a consensus must be built on a sense of proportion which does not reopen old ideological battles in terms of either–or choices, and on a depth of understanding which recognizes the complexity and the diversity of development. This thinking should not be limited to the sphere of economics. It must extend to the realm of politics. For substantive democracy, which creates a political accountability of governments to the people, must be an integral part of the new agenda for, and the new consensus on, development. In such a world, ensuring decent living conditions for people, ordinary people, would naturally emerge as a fundamental objective. Development must, therefore, provide all men and women the rights, the opportunities and the capabilities to expand their freedoms and exercise their own choices for their well-being. In this process, people would be participants rather than beneficiaries. The distinction between ends and means would remain critical. And, in the pursuit of development, the importance of public action cannot be stressed enough. It must be an integral part of development strategies, which should not be forgotten in the enthusiasm for markets and globalization.

REFERENCES

Akerlof, G.A. (1970), 'The Market for Lemons: Quality Uncertainty and the Market Mechanism', *Quarterly Journal of Economics*, Vol. 84, No. 3, pp. 488–500.

Amsden, Alice H. (1989), *Asia's Next Giant: South Korea and Late Industrialization*, Oxford University Press, New York.

_____ (2001), *The Rise of the Rest: Challenges to the West from Late Industrializing Economies*, Oxford University Press, New York.

Anand, Sudhir and Amartya Sen (1994), 'Human Development Index: Methodology and Measurement', HDRO Occasional Paper 12, UNDP, New York.

Arrow, Kenneth J. (1950), 'An Extension of the Basic Theorems of Classical Welfare Economics', in J. Neyman (ed.), *Proceedings of the Second Berkeley Symposium in Mathematical Statistics and Probability*, University of California Press, Berkeley.

Bairoch, Paul (1993), *Economics and World History: Myths and Paradoxes*, University of Chicago Press, Chicago.

Baker, Dean, Gerald Epstein, and Robert Pollin (eds) (1998), *Globalization and Progressive Economic Policy*, Cambridge University Press, Cambridge.

Banerjee, Abhijit V. (1997), 'A Theory of Misgovernance', *Quarterly Journal of Economics*, Vol. 112, No. 4, pp. 1289–332.

Baster, Nancy (1972), 'Development Indicators', *Journal of Development Studies*, Vol. 8, No. 3, pp. 1–20.

Bhaduri, Amit (2002), 'Nationalism and Economic Policy in an Era of Globalization', in Deepak Nayyar (ed.), *Governing Globalization: Issues and Institutions*, Oxford University Press, Oxford.

Bhaduri, Amit and Deepak Nayyar (1996), *The Intelligent Person's Guide to Liberalization*, Penguin Books, New Delhi.

Bhagwati, Jagdish (2004), *In Defence of Globalization*, Oxford University Press, Oxford.

Chang, Ha-Joon (1996), *The Political Economy of Industrial Policy*, Macmillan, London.

_____ (2002a), *Kicking Away the Ladder: Development Strategy in Historical Perspective*, Anthem Press, London.

_____ (2002b), 'Breaking the Mould: An Institutionalist Political Economy Alternative to the Neo-liberal Theory of the Market and the State', *Cambridge Journal of Economics*, Vol. 26, No. 5, pp. 539–59.

Coase, Richard (1960), 'The Problem of Social Cost', *Journal of Law and Economics*, Vol. 3, pp. 1–44.

Eatwell, John and Lance Taylor (2000), *Global Finance at Risk: The Case of International Regulation*, The New Press, New York.

Hahn, Frank (1984), *Equilibrium and Macroeconomics*, Basil Blackwell, Oxford.

Haq, Mahbub ul (1995), *Reflections on Human Development*, Oxford University Press, New York.

Kaplinsky, Raphael (2005), *Globalization, Poverty and Inequality*, Polity Press, Cambridge.

Killick, Tony (1990), *A Reaction Too Far: Economic Theory and the Role of the State in Developing Countries*, Overseas Development Institute, London.

Lall, Sanjaya (1990), *Building Industrial Competitiveness in Developing Countries*, OECD Development Centre, Paris.

Maddison, Angus (1995), *Monitoring the World Economy: 1820–1992*, OECD Development Centre, Paris.

Morris, M.D. (1979), *Measuring the Conditions of the World's Poor*, Pergamon Press, Oxford.

Mukherji, Anjan (2005), 'Development Economics and Governance: A Theoretical Perspective', *mimeo*, Centre for Economic Studies and Planning, Jawaharlal Nehru University, New Delhi.

Nayyar, Deepak (1997), 'Themes in Trade and Industrialization', in Deepak Nayyar (ed.), *Trade and Industrialization*, Oxford University Press, New Delhi.

_____ (2002a), 'The Existing System and the Missing Institutions', in Deepak Nayyar (ed.), *Governing Globalization: Issues and Institutions*, Oxford University Press, Oxford.

_____ (2002b), 'Capital Controls and the World Financial Authority: What Can We Learn from the Indian Experience', in John Eatwell and Lance Taylor (eds), *International Capital Markets: Systems in Transition*, Oxford University Press, New York.

_____ (2002c), 'Cross-Border Movements of People', in Deepak Nayyar (ed.), *Governing Globalization: Issues and Institutions*, Oxford University Press, Oxford.

_____ (2003a), 'Globalization and Development Strategies', in John Toye (ed.), *Trade and Development*, Edward Elgar, Cheltenham.

_____ (2003b), 'The Political Economy of Exclusion and Inclusion: Democracy, Markets and People', in Amitava Krishna Dutt and Jaime Ros (eds), *Development Economics and Structuralist Macroeconomics: Essays in Honour of Lance Taylor*, Edward Elgar, Cheltenham.

_____ (2004), 'Economic Reforms in India: Understanding the Process and Learning from Experience', *International Journal of Development Issues*, Vol. 3, No. 2, pp. 31–55.

_____ (2006), 'Globalization, History and Development: A Tale of Two Centuries', *Cambridge Journal of Economics*, Vol. 30, No. 1, pp. 137–59.

North, Douglass C. (1990), *Institutions, Institutional Change and Economic Performance*, Cambridge University Press, Cambridge.

_____ (2001), 'Needed: A Theory of Change', in Gerald M. Meier and Joseph E. Stiglitz (eds), *Frontiers of Development Economics*, The World Bank, Washington, DC.

Sachs, Jeffrey and Andrew Warner (1995), 'Economic Reforms and the Process of Global Integration', *Brookings Papers on Economic Activity*, No. 1, pp.1–118.

Samuelson, Paul A. (2004), 'Where Ricardo and Mill Rebut and Confirm Arguments of Mainstream Economists Supporting Globalization', *Journal of Economic Perspectives*, Vol. 18, No. 3, pp. 135–46.

Seers, Dudley (1972), 'What are We Trying to Measure?', *Journal of Development Studies*, Vol. 8, No. 3, pp. 21–36.

Sen, Amartya (1989), 'Development as Capability Expansion', *Journal of Development Planning*, No. 19, pp. 41–58.

_____ (1999), *Development as Freedom*, Alfred E. Knopf, New York.

Shapiro, Helen and Lance Taylor (1990), 'The State and Industrial Strategy', *World Development*, Vol. 18, No. 6, pp. 861–78.

Soros, George (1998), *The Crisis of Global Capitalism*, Little Brown, New York.

Stewart, Frances (1985), *Planning to Meet Basic Needs*, Macmillan, London.

Stiglitz, Joseph E. (1989), 'Economic Role of the State: Efficiency and Effectiveness', in A. Heertje (ed.), *The Economic Role of the State*, Basil Blackwell, Oxford.

_____ (1998), 'More Instruments and Broader Goals: Moving Toward the Post-Washington Consensus', WIDER Annual Lecture 2, UNU-WIDER, Helsinki.

_____ (2002), *Globalization and its Discontents*, Allen Lane, London.

Streeten, Paul (1981), *First Things First: Meeting Basic Human Needs in Developing Countries*, Oxford University Press, Oxford.

Wade, Robert (1990), *Governing the Market: Economic Theory and the Role of Government in East Asian Industrialization*, Princeton University Press, New Jersey.

Wolf, Martin (2004), *Why Globalization Works*, Yale University Press, New Haven and London.

World Commission on the Social Dimension of Globalization (2004), *A Fair Globalization: Creating Opportunities for All*, ILO, Geneva.

Chapter 5

LEARNING TO UNLEARN FROM DEVELOPMENT*

The study of development in economics, as also in the other social sciences, began life in the early 1950s. It is clear that, throughout the period since then, thinking about development has always been embedded in strong belief systems. Sharp differences, even polar opposite views, are common. These cannot be disguised as differences between schools of thought attributable to abstractions such as intellectual tradition. The real differences lie in implicit or explicit political ideologies. Yet, interestingly enough, there is a mismatch between ideology and experience, for outcomes in development do not quite conform to *a priori* thinking about development.

The object of this essay is to reflect on development in retrospect, during the second half of the twentieth century, to analyse the experience, and draw some lessons. In doing so, it poses, and endeavours to answer, two questions. What can we learn from the development experience to introduce correctives for the future? What must we learn from the experience of development to induce rethinking for the future? Learning from experience is of critical importance. It is about correcting for mistakes. Everybody would agree. But it is just as important to unlearn from experience. It is about questioning long-held beliefs and thinking anew. Most have not thought about it. This provides the rationale for the somewhat unusual title of this essay.

The structure of the essay is as follows. The first section outlines the broad contours of the fundamental changes in thinking about strategies of development during the second half of the twentieth century. The second section highlights how these changes have influenced alternatives in development and shaped perceptions of reality, with a tale of two countries. The third section considers the pattern of growth in the world economy from 1951 to 2000, which has

*This paper is based on my plenary lecture at the 50th Anniversary Conference of Queen Elizabeth House, Oxford, in July 2005. I am indebted to Amit Bhaduri for helpful discussion and Maria Angela Parra for valuable assistance. I would also like to thank Meghnad Desai, Barbara Harriss-White, and John Toye for constructive comments on an earlier draft.

been associated with uneven development over time and across space. The fourth section attempts to assess economic performance across countries, making a distinction between success and failure, to suggest that reality as it has unfolded does not conform to beliefs or expectations in thinking about development. The fifth section explores the anatomy of the new success stories in development, China and India, to analyse the lessons from and implications of the development experience of these two Asian giants. The sixth section concludes.

THINKING ABOUT DEVELOPMENT

It is clear that the development experience of the world economy since 1950 has been uneven and mixed. The attempts to analyse what turned out right and what went wrong have led to both diagnosis and prescription. These have, in turn, meant fundamental changes in thinking about development strategies.

In the post-colonial era, which began soon after the end of the Second World War, most underdeveloped countries adopted strategies of development that provided a sharp contrast with their past during the first half of the twentieth century.[1] First, there was a conscious attempt to limit the degree of openness and of integration with the world economy, in pursuit of a more autonomous development. Second, the State was assigned a strategic role in development because the market, by itself, was not seen as sufficient to meet the aspirations of those who were latecomers to development. Third, industrialization was seen as an imperative in the catch-up process, which had to start from import substitution in the manufacturing sector. These three essentials represented points of departure from the colonial era characterized by open economies and unregulated markets that had been associated with the de-industrialization during the nineteenth century in much of the underdeveloped world. The conjuncture was almost as important as the history, for it shaped aspirations of newly independent countries about economic development in the context of national sovereignty. This approach also represented a consensus in thinking about the most appropriate strategy of development. There were a few voices of dissent. But it was, in effect, the Development Consensus at the time. And this consensus was dominant from the late 1940s to the early 1970s.

The actual industrialization experience during this period led to questions and an emerging critique. The post-mortem of failures led to a diagnosis while the analysis of successes led to strong prescriptions. It was argued that industrialization policies which protected domestic industries from foreign

[1]For a more detailed discussion on strategies of industrialization and development, see Nayyar (1997).

competition and led to excessive or inappropriate State intervention were responsible for the high costs and the low growth in several economies.[2] The prescription followed from the critique to suggest that more openness and less intervention would impart both efficiency and dynamism to the growth process.

Slowly, but surely, thinking about development witnessed a big swing of the pendulum. This swing began in the late 1970s, as the Development Consensus was increasingly subjected to question. Most countries in the developing world, to be followed by transition economies a decade later, began to reshape their domestic economic policies so as to integrate much more with the world economy and to enlarge the role of the market *vis-à-vis* the State. The essentials of this approach, as also the underlying rationale, were shaped, once again, by the history and the conjuncture. It was, in part, a consequence of development experience in the preceding 25 years, often associated with inappropriate or excessive State intervention, which did not lead to the expected outcomes in development and culminated in internal crisis situations in the economy or polity in some countries. This was juxtaposed with the impressive economic performance of a few countries in East Asia which was attributed to markets and openness. And these success stories were portrayed as role models in development.

There were voices of dissent. The critics argued that it was not appropriate to draw lessons from the experience of a few countries which could be generalized and transplanted elsewhere. Even more important, perhaps, it was stressed that this approach was selective in its use of theory and history. For one, there was a striking asymmetry between the unqualified enthusiasm of policy prescriptions advocating free(r) trade, unmindful of the distinction between statics and dynamics or irrespective of time and place, and the formal exposition of the free trade argument in economic theory with its careful assumptions, proofs, and exceptions.[3] For another, the characterization of the success stories as economies which approximated to free trade and *laissez-faire* was partial if

[2]See Little et al. (1970), which attempted a systematic evaluation of the industrialization experience in selected developing countries to question the Development Consensus. See also Krueger (1978).

[3]In an essay on the debate about trade and industrialization, this proposition was set out most succinctly by Diaz-Alejandro (1975, p. 96): 'In the trade and development literature, there has existed for a long time, going back at least to John Stuart Mill, a striking difference between the rigour of formal proofs on the static advantages of free trade, typically involving careful assumptions and caveats, and the impetuous enthusiasm with which most of the professional mainstream advocates free or freer trade policies, on both static and dynamic grounds, for all times and places.'

not caricature history for their export orientation was not the equivalent of free trade just as the visible hand of the State was more in evidence than the invisible hand of the market.[4]

In spite of these limitations, however, the neoclassical critique continued to gather momentum through the 1980s. The policy prescriptions derived from it became increasingly influential as these were adopted by the World Bank, to begin with in its research agenda and subsequently in its policy menu. The process was reinforced by the reality that unfolded. The earlier success stories—Korea, Hong Kong, Taiwan, and Singapore—turned into the East Asian miracle which spread to Malaysia, Thailand and, in the perception of some, even Indonesia. The impressive economic performance of China during the 1980s was also attributed to economic reform that recognized the virtue in markets and openness. The debt-crisis, which surfaced in Latin America, moved to sub-Saharan Africa and ultimately caught up with South Asia. The swing of the pendulum was almost complete. The new orthodoxy was readily accepted by economies in crisis where the IMF and the World Bank exercised enormous influence through their stabilization and adjustment programmes. And it was not long before this approach was described as a new consensus in thinking about development. It came to be known as the Washington Consensus.[5]

The history of outcomes in development, even if selective and partial, was reinforced by the conjuncture in the late 1980s. The political collapse of communism was seen as the economic triumph of capitalism. The advocates of this world view argued that the erstwhile centrally planned economies of East Europe, in particular the former Soviet Union, represented failure, while the open market economies of East Asia epitomized success. In retrospect, there can be no doubt that this caricature juxtaposition of the failure of the State with the success of the market exercised an important influence on thinking about development. The disillusionment with the Development Consensus was complete. And, by the early 1990s, the Washington Consensus acquired a near-hegemonic status in thinking about development.

This hegemony did not last long. The belief system was somewhat shaken by the financial crises in Asia as also elsewhere. What is more, the development experience during the 1990s belied expectations. The orthodox prescriptions

---

[4]In the literature on the development experience of the East Asian success stories—Hong Kong, Singapore, South Korea, and Taiwan—Lee (1981) was among the first to emphasize this limitation. It has come to be recognized far more widely with the subsequent works of Amsden (1989), Wade (1990), and Chang (1996). See also, Singh (1994) and Lall (1997).

[5]This term was, perhaps, coined by Williamson (1994).

were subjected to increasing question. And the questions did not come from the critics alone.[6] Consequently, the dominance of the Washington Consensus began to wane. But it has not been replaced by a new consensus. In fact, in the early 2000s, the situation is somewhat diffused. There are discernible strands in thinking about development. The orthodoxy embedded in the Washington Consensus remains the most influential. But it is modified as a Washington Consensus *plus* with some more dos, or as a Washington Consensus *minus* with some qualified don'ts. Even so, it only validates the proverb that the more things change, more they remain the same. Dani Rodrik (2005, p.12) puts it succinctly: 'The current approach can be summarized with little exaggeration as one of: *do whatever you can, as much as you can, as quickly as you can.*'

It is hardly surprising that the voices of dissent, which question orthodoxy in terms of the underlying theory and the emerging reality, are many more. There is also a revisionism that is discernible in dissenting voices. It accepts that more of the same is not appropriate for strategies of development. It argues that middle-paths may be more appropriate than end-point solutions. It stresses the need to recognize the importance of specificities in time and space. Yet, there is a clear difference between the orthodox belief-system on the one hand and the heterodox, or the unorthodox, perspective on the other. These are competing strands in thinking about development. But, at this juncture, there is no clear consensus as in the past. The history of the experience with the Washington Consensus is perhaps not long enough. And we have obviously not reached a conjuncture that could polarize thinking once again.

In retrospect, it is clear that turning points in thinking about development, which reshaped strategies, were strongly influenced by history (the past), and conjuncture (the present), reinforced by the dominant political ideology of the times. The Development Consensus, in the early 1950s, was shaped by the experience of de-industrialization and underdevelopment in the colonial era and the nationalist aspirations of the newly independent countries with the beginnings of de-colonization. The Washington Consensus, which evolved through the 1980s, was shaped, in part, by the history of outcomes in development over the preceding three decades. The success of a few East Asian countries and failure elsewhere in the developing world were highlighted, even if the history was selective and partial. This was reinforced by the conjuncture in the late 1980s that witnessed the political collapse of communism. The East Asian miracle initiated rethinking about development

[6]See, for example, Stiglitz (1998, 2002) and Easterly (2001). See also Amsden et al. (1994) and Chang (2002).

while the collapse of the centrally planned economies in Europe completed the swing of the pendulum. It was not influenced by events such as stagflation in the industrialized countries, the crisis in the international monetary system, or the strain on the multilateral trading system, which coincided in time. The erosion of the Keynesian consensus and the rise of monetarism, which reshaped thinking in macroeconomic theory and policy around that time, probably exercised a significant influence, insofar as they mirrored a change in the dominant political ideology. It would be reasonable to infer that the swings in thinking about development were driven by a mix of ideology and experience.

ALTERNATIVES IN DEVELOPMENT

Once upon a time, in the early 1950s, there were alternatives in development for countries that were latecomers. There was the capitalist path of market economies with some supportive role from the State. There was the socialist path of the centrally planned economies. There was the middle path of mixed economies—some called them non-capitalist and some called them non-socialist—but it sought to combine the market with a proactive State. Just four decades later, in the early 1990s, the choices vanished and it would seem that, in terms of alternatives, there were none! Indeed, during the 1990s, economic liberalization became a *mantra* for development everywhere in the world so that markets and openness came to be seen as both necessity and virtue. At this juncture, not much more than a decade later, the confidence and the certainty associated with the ideology that was dominant not so long ago have diminished. But no alternatives have emerged, at least so far, possibly because there is no consensus, or not enough clarity, about the most appropriate policies or strategies. Thinking ahead, however, there is a need to evolve alternatives in development.

In retrospect, the story about alternatives in development, in terms of choices and perspectives, is illustrated vividly by a tale of two countries: China and India. In the early 1950s, both were path-setters, if not role models. China adopted the socialist path. But it was different from the Soviet Union. It was a predominantly agrarian economy that had not yet industrialized. What is more, its political revolution was brought about by the peasantry rather than the industrial working class. It was, therefore, a possible model for underdeveloped countries. India adopted the middle path of a mixed economy. This was not altogether new and resembled State capitalism elsewhere. But the conception and the birth of political democracy in independent India was unique (Nayyar 1998). Its economy, which combined roles for the market and the State, and its polity which introduced democracy, were both seen as possible models for underdeveloped countries. There was, then, considerable optimism about both China and India.

Just 25 years later, in the mid-1970s, perceptions were almost the polar opposite. Both China and India became exemplars of almost everything gone wrong. The story about China, in caricature form, ran as follows. The man-made famines were a failure that turned into tragedy. The Cultural Revolution was a disaster. And the totalitarian State was unacceptable. The story about India, in caricature form, ran as follows. The slow growth and the persistent poverty in the economy represented failure.[7] The inefficient industrialization was a disaster. And the political democracy was unaffordable, if not unviable. The critics were partly right in what they saw. But the critics were quite wrong in what they did not see. In both countries, post-revolution China and post-independence India, there were significant achievements that were simply set aside. In sum, the shortcomings were highlighted while the achievements were neglected.

Another 25 years later, in the early 2000s, there was a dramatic change in perceptions once again. The same China and India came to be seen as star performers, if not role models, which did almost everything right.[8] For some, the rapid economic growth in both countries is the focus. For others, the economies of the two Asian giants demonstrate the virtues of markets and openness. Once again, it needs to be said that the observers are right in what they see but are wrong in what they do not see. The economic performance of China and India at a macro-level is indeed impressive compared with most countries of the world. But there are limitations in this performance that cannot be ignored. The rapid economic growth has not been associated with acceptable, let alone desirable, distributional outcomes. In China, there is a sharp increase in economic inequalities. In India, poverty persists and social indicators of development are a cause for concern. In both countries, employment creation has slowed down. In sum, the achievements are highlighted while the shortcomings are forgotten.

It would be reasonable to ask: what has changed? In part, of course, it is the reality of development that has changed in both countries. But, in the world outside, perceptions about their development have changed much more rapidly than the realities. Even more important, perhaps, thinking about

[7]The strongly critical view of the development path in India is articulated by Lal (1998). The critique of the industrialization experience in India was first set out by Bhagwati and Desai (1970).

[8]Such optimism about China and India captured attention following the study on BRICS by Goldman Sachs (Wilson and Purushothaman 2003).

development has changed, so that the optic through which the people view China and India has changed. Indeed, the dramatic changes in perceptions about China and India, from role models in the early 1950s to disaster stories in the mid 1970s, almost coincided in time with the swings in doctrines about development. The perceptions of development outcomes in China and India possibly reinforced changes in thinking about development. The changed thinking, in turn, possibly exercised some influence on the reshaping of development strategies in China and India. However, it is just as important to recognize that, over time, both China and India have learnt from their experience of development. This is reflected in their attempts, sometimes belated, sometimes incomplete, and sometimes inappropriate, to introduce correctives with the object of consolidating strengths and eliminating weaknesses that have surfaced in the process of development. And, when outcomes have not turned out to be what was expected, particularly if the mismatch between the expectations about and the realities of development has persisted over time, there has been some attempt, even if lagged and limited, to unlearn from experience.[9] This has led to the setting aside of some shibboleths, just as it has led to debates that question established belief-systems. On balance, it is plausible to argue, even if impossible to prove, that changes in strategies in China and India were driven more by learning and unlearning from their own development experience than by swings in development doctrines. There is an obvious question that arises. Did changes in development strategies shape the observed development outcomes in China and India? This question is addressed later in the essay.

UNEQUAL GROWTH AND UNEVEN DEVELOPMENT

During the second half of the twentieth century, economic growth in the world economy was rapid, particularly when compared with the preceding 50 years, but this growth was unevenly distributed over time and across space. Table 5.1 presents evidence on rates of growth in GDP and GDP per capita, for each decade in the period 1951–2000, in industrialized countries, developing countries, and regions within the developing world. These figures are computed from Maddison (2003), which provides a complete time series for GDP and GDP per capita in 1990 international Geary-Khamis dollars, which are purchasing power parities (PPP) used to evaluate output and are calculated using a specific method devised to define international prices. This measure facilitates inter-country comparisons over time. In any case, United

[9]For an analysis of changes in thinking about development in China and India, particularly with reference to economic policies, see Nolan (2004) and Nayyar (2004).

Table 5.1: Economic Growth in the World Economy, 1951–2000

(per cent per annum)

GDP

	Maddison Data					United Nations Data		
	1951–60	1961–70	1971–80	1981–90	1991–2000	1971–80	1981–90	1991–2000
World	4.71	5.41	4.24	2.25	3.05	4.65	2.40	3.06
Industrialized Countries	4.52	5.29	3.41	2.53	2.59	3.32	2.54	2.65
Developing Countries	4.75	5.44	4.40	2.20	3.14	4.91	2.38	3.14
Latin America	4.67	4.86	4.58	1.09	2.96	4.76	1.19	3.03
Africa	4.14	4.93	3.34	2.31	2.56	3.82	2.47	2.76
Asia	5.70	6.90	6.30	3.28	4.85	6.66	3.40	4.43
China	6.46	3.63	5.03	7.26	7.46	5.30	9.17	10.42
India	3.94	3.69	3.10	5.59	5.77	2.98	5.84	5.25

GDP per capita

	Maddison Data					United Nations Data		
	1951–60	1961–70	1971–80	1981–90	1991–2000	1971–80	1981–90	1991–2000
World	2.47	2.95	1.82	0.10	1.26	2.22	0.20	1.21
Industrialized Countries	3.48	4.32	2.70	2.05	2.02	2.60	2.04	2.07
Developing Countries	2.28	2.68	1.65	-0.28	1.11	2.14	-0.17	1.04
Latin America	1.92	2.17	2.28	-0.89	1.22	2.40	-0.83	1.26
Africa	2.02	2.41	0.61	-0.47	0.16	1.04	-0.39	0.30
Asia	2.59	3.35	2.80	0.51	2.78	3.10	0.57	2.19
China	4.37	1.53	3.14	5.71	6.31	3.38	7.60	9.34
India	1.98	1.43	0.78	3.38	3.85	0.78	3.68	3.33

Notes: (a) The growth rates for each period are computed as geometric means of the annual growth rates in that period.

(b) The Maddison data and the United Nations data on GDP and GDP per capita are not strictly comparable.

(c) The Maddison data on GDP and GDP per capita, which are in 1990 international Geary-Khamis dollars, are PPP used to evaluate output which are calculated based on a specific method devised to define international prices. This measure facilitates inter-country comparisons.

(d) The United Nations data on GDP and GDP per capita are in constant 1990 US dollars.

(e) The figures in Table 5.1 for the world economy cover 128 countries, of which 21 are industrialized countries and 107 are developing countries.

(f) Latin America includes the Caribbean.

Sources: Maddison (2003), United Nations (2006 b and c).

Nations data on national income accounts at constant prices are available for the period since 1971 but not earlier. The Maddison data and the United Nations data are not strictly comparable. Even so, Table 5.1 also sets out growth rates in GDP and GDP per capita computed from United Nations data, in constant 1990 dollars, for each decade in the period 1971–2000. A comparison of the two sets of growth rates, in each of the three decades for which both sources are available, shows that the numbers correspond closely and significant differences are exceptions.

The evidence in Table 5.1 reveals that economic growth was uneven over time. There was a rapid growth in GDP, in the range of 5 per cent per annum, both in the industrialized countries and the developing world, during the 1950s, 1960s, and 1970s. Growth in GDP per capita in developing countries was distinctly lower than growth in GDP given the high rates of population growth, as death rates declined sharply while birth rates did not. Yet, on an average, growth in per capita income in most developing countries, at more than 2 per cent per annum, was a radical departure from the stagnation or decline in the colonial era. There was a discernible slowdown, indeed downturn, *circa* 1980. During the 1980s, GDP growth rates everywhere, at a little more than 2 per cent per annum, were about half their level in the preceding three decades. In the industrialized countries, with stable populations, growth in GDP per capita was about the same. In the developing world, however, where population growth remained at high levels, growth in GDP per capita was negative. The 1990s witnessed a mild recovery in GDP growth in the developing world, at 3 per cent per annum, while there was no change in the industrialized countries, but growth in GDP per capita remained in the range of 1 per cent per annum in the world economy and in the developing countries.

The evidence in Table 5.1 also shows that economic growth was uneven across space. During the 1950s, 1960s, and 1970s, growth in GDP per capita in the industrialized countries was much higher than that in the developing world, even though growth in GDP was roughly the same. More differences surfaced in the subsequent decades. In the 1980s, the slow-down in GDP growth was much more pronounced in Latin America and Africa, so that GDP per capita declined at a significant rate in both these regions of the developing world. And, in the 1990s, the recovery in GDP growth was slower in Latin America and Africa, so that growth in GDP per capita was negligible in Africa and a little more than 1 per cent per annum in Latin America. By contrast, in Asia, driven in part by the rapid growth in China and India, the downturn was not as sharp in the 1980s while the recovery was more substantial in the 1990s. During the 1980s and 1990s, in the industrialized countries, growth in GDP, even if slower, was steady, while growth in GDP per capita was sustained at 2 per cent per annum.

In this context, it is important to note that the faster growth in the 1950s, 1960s, and 1970s was associated with stability whereas the slower growth in the 1980s and 1990s was associated with volatility. A recent study by the United Nations (2006a) shows that, during the 1960s and 1970s, nearly 50 out of a sample of 106 developing countries experienced one or more prolonged episodes of high and sustained per capita income growth at more than 2 per cent per annum. During the 1980s and 1990s, however, there were only 20 developing countries that experienced such periods of sustained growth, while 40 developing countries suffered growth collapses in which there was no growth, or there was a decline, in per capita incomes for periods of five years or longer. Such collapses in growth were most common among the least developed countries and in sub-Saharan Africa. In the 1960s and 1970s, such growth collapses, which affected less than 10 developing countries, were a rare occurrence.[10]

It is not surprising that this uneven distribution of growth over time and across space was associated with a divergence in levels of income and development between countries. Evidence available provides confirmation. It is worth citing some statistics. The ratio of GDP per capita in the 20 richest countries to GDP per capita in the 20 poorest countries of the world rose from 54:1 during 1960–2 to 121:1 during 2000–2.[11] The ratio of GDP per capita in the richest country to GDP per capita in the poorest country of the world rose from 268:1 in 1960 to 615:1 in 2000.[12] This comparison is based on data in constant prices but at nominal exchange rates. In terms of PPP, the difference is not as high but the widening of the gap over time is more pronounced. The Maddison (2003) data, in 1990 international Geary-Khamis dollars, show that the ratio of GDP per capita in the richest country to GDP

[10]United Nations (2006a, pp. vi–vii and pp. 7–13). The analysis reported here is largely based on the evidence presented in Ocampo and Parra (2005). Hausmann et al. (2004) consider the period 1950–98 and come to similar conclusions about sustained periods of rapid acceleration in economic growth.

[11]Between 1960–2 and 2000–2, in constant 1995 dollars, GDP per capita in the 20 richest countries rose from 11417 to 32339, while GDP per capita in the 20 poorest countries barely increased from 212 to 267 (*World Development Indicators 2003*, World Bank).

[12]In 1960, among 100 countries for which data are available, in constant 1995 dollars, Switzerland had the highest GDP per capita at 26,245 while Malawi had the lowest GDP per capita at 98. In 2000, among 181 countries for which data are available, in constant 1995 dollars, Luxembourg had the highest GDP per capita at 58,464 while Congo had the lowest GDP per capita at 95 (*World Development Indicators 2004*, World Bank).

per capita in the poorest country of the world rose from 32:1 in 1960 to 129:1 in 2000.[13] Clearly, the income gap between rich and poor countries widened during the second half of the twentieth century. It is worth noting that this gap widened more rapidly in the period 1981–2000, when compared with the period 1951–80, because of the increased divergence in growth of per capita incomes.[14] Such inter-country income inequalities are a reason for concern, because studies of income inequality among all the people in the world show that as much as 70 per cent is explained by inequality between countries while just 30 per cent is explained by inequality within countries.[15]

The story is similar for intra-country income inequalities. Income distribution within countries also worsened. This is borne out by a study on trends in the distribution of income, during the period from the 1960s to the 1990s, for 73 countries comprising developed, developing, and transitional economies. It shows that income inequality increased in 48 countries, which account for 59 per cent of the population and 78 per cent of the PPP-GDP in the sample of 73 countries. Income inequality remained the same in 16 countries which account for 36 per cent of the population and 13 per cent of the PPP-GDP in the sample of 73 countries. Income inequality decreased only in nine countries which account for 5 per cent of the population and 9 per cent of the PPP-GDP in the sample of 73 countries (Cornia and Kiiski 2001). The increase in income inequality was striking in some industrialized countries. Between 1975 and 2000, the share of the richest 1 per cent in gross income rose from 8 per cent to 17 per cent in the United States, from 8.8 per cent to 13.3 per cent in Canada, and from 6.1 per cent to 13 per cent in the United Kingdom (Atkinson 2003).

At the end of the twentieth century, the divide between rich and poor countries was clearly reflected in their unequal participation in the world economy. Consider some evidence, for 2000, on international trade, international investment, and international finance (Nayyar 2006a). Industrialized countries accounted for 64 per cent of world exports, while developing countries accounted for 32 per cent and transitional economies for the remaining 4 per cent. Industrialized countries accounted for 82 per

[13]The Maddison (2003) data, in 1990 international Geary-Khamis dollars, show that, in 1960, Switzerland had the highest GDP per capita at 12,457 while Guinea had the lowest GDP per capita at 392, whereas, in 2000, US had the highest GDP per capita at 17,224 while Zaire had the lowest GDP per capita at 218.

[14]For a discussion of, and evidence on, this divergence, see United Nations (2006a).

[15]See Bourguignon and Morrison (2002), Milanovic (2005), and United Nations (2006a).

cent of direct foreign investment inflows in the world economy, whereas developing countries accounted for 16 per cent and transitional economies for the remaining 2 per cent. Industrialized countries accounted for 95 per cent of cross-border mergers and acquisitions in terms of purchases whereas developing countries accounted for just 4 per cent and transitional economies accounted for a mere 1 per cent.

This sharp divide between rich and poor countries is no surprise but there is also a clear divide within the developing world. Just twelve economies— Argentina, Brazil, and Mexico in Latin America; and China, Hong Kong, India, Indonesia, Korea, Malaysia, Singapore, Taiwan, and Thailand in Asia—account for much of the engagement of developing countries with the world economy. During the 1990s, these countries accounted for 70 per cent of total exports from the developing world and 75 per cent of manufactured exports from the developing world, absorbed almost 72 per cent of foreign investment flows to the developing world, and received about 90 per cent of portfolio investment flows to the developing world (Nayyar 2006a). At the other end of the spectrum, the least developed countries, as also countries in sub-Saharan Africa, are peripheral to the process.

ASSESSING ECONOMIC PERFORMANCE

It is necessary but not sufficient to outline the broad contours of the development experience during the second half of the twentieth century. The next step is to assess the economic performance of developing countries. For this purpose, it may be necessary and appropriate to divide this long period of time into two periods. The preceding discussion provides a pointer. There was a significant transformation in thinking about development *circa* 1980. It is clear that growth rates also witnessed a discernible change *circa* 1980. It would seem that turning points in thinking and performance coincided closely in time. Therefore, it would be appropriate to compare the period from 1951 to 1980 with the period from 1981 to 2005. Any such periodization is obviously arbitrary but it serves an analytical purpose.

Table 5.2 provides a comparison of rates of growth in GDP and GDP per capita, during the periods 1951–80 and 1981–2005, for the world economy, for industrialized countries, for developing countries, and for regions within the developing world. It also provides such a comparison of growth rates for China and India. The figures for the period 1951–80 are based on Maddison data because United Nations data are not available before 1971. The figures for the period 1981–2005 are based on United Nations data because Maddison

Table 5.2: Comparison of Growth Performance, 1951–80 and 1981–2005
(Selected Country-groups, Regions, and Countries)

(per cent per annum)

	Maddison Data		United Nations Data		Maddison Data		United Nations Data	
	1951–80	1981–2000	1981–2000	1981–2005	1951–80	1981–2000	1981–2000	1981–2005
	GDP				GDP per capita			
World	4.77	2.64	2.72	2.95	2.40	0.66	0.69	0.99
Industrialized Countries	4.40	2.56	2.59	2.50	3.50	2.04	2.06	1.96
Developing Countries	4.84	2.65	2.74	3.04	2.19	0.39	0.42	0.80
Latin America	4.69	2.01	2.09	2.26	2.11	0.15	0.20	0.44
Africa	4.12	2.42	2.60	2.97	1.66	-0.17	-0.06	0.39
Asia	6.28	4.04	3.90	4.06	2.90	1.61	1.36	1.63
China	5.03	7.36	9.80	9.73	3.01	6.01	8.46	8.51
India	3.57	5.68	5.54	5.79	1.40	3.62	3.50	3.83

Notes: (a) The growth rates for each period are computed as geometric means of the annual growth rates in that period.
(b) The Maddison data and the United Nations data on GDP and GDP per capita are not strictly comparable.
(c) The Maddison data on GDP and GDP per capita, which are in 1990 international Geary-Khamis dollars, are PPP used to evaluate output which are calculated based on a specific method devised to define international prices. This measure facilitates inter-country comparisons.
(d) The United Nations data on GDP and GDP per capita are in constant 1990 US dollars.
(e) The figures in Table 5.2 for the world economy cover 128 countries, of which 21 are industrialized countries and 107 are developing countries.
(f) Latin America includes the Caribbean.
Sources: Maddison (2003), United Nations (2006 b and c).

data are not available after 2001. These two sources are not strictly comparable. For the period 1981–2000, however, data are available from both sources. To facilitate a comparison, Table 5.2 also presents figures on growth rates, during 1981–2000, computed separately from Maddison data and United Nations data. A comparison of the two sets of growth rates, during the period 1981–2000 for which both sources are available, shows that the numbers correspond closely and the only significant differences are in the figures for China. Therefore, it is reasonable to infer that the growth rates for the periods 1951–80 and 1981–2005, even if computed from different sources, are comparable.

A study of Table 5.2 clearly shows that growth in GDP and GDP per capita during 1981–2005 was much slower than it was during 1951–80. This was so for the world economy, for industrialized countries, and for developing countries. Growth in GDP was in the range 4–5 per cent per annum during 1951–80 and in the range of 2–3 per cent per annum during 1981–2005 almost everywhere, except Asia where it was 6 per cent and 4 per cent per annum, respectively. Growth in GDP per capita slowed down considerably even in the industrialized countries, from 3.5 per cent per annum to 2 per cent per annum but the slowdown was more pronounced for developing countries, from 2.2 per cent per annum to 0.8 per cent per annum. In Latin America and Africa, during 1981–2005, growth in GDP per capita was less than 0.5 per cent per annum, while Asia fared better at more than 1.5 per cent per annum. It is worth noting that China and India were the exceptions. In both countries, growth rates in the second period were much higher than the perfectly respectable growth rates in the first period. So much so that, between 1951–80 and 1981–2005, average annual growth in GDP per capita almost trebled in both China and India. This was attributable in part to higher GDP growth rates and in part to lower population growth rates.

Such an overview of growth performance is necessary. But it cannot be sufficient because aggregates sometimes conceal as much as they reveal. An assessment of economic performance, which must be based on outcomes in development, is a far more complex exercise. It must be carried out at a more disaggregated level. However, that is beyond the scope of this essay. Even so, it is possible to draw some meaningful conclusions from an analysis which provides an overview of secular changes in doctrines and outcomes. In retrospect, it is clear that, in both periods, reality as it unfolded did not conform to expectations implicit in the belief systems of the times about development. In fact, as it turned out, changes in development strategies did not lead to the expected changes in development outcomes.

The experience during the period 1951–80 led to some rethinking about development. This learning from experience, however, was selective. And it was not the same everywhere. For it was shaped only in part by outcomes. It was also significantly influenced by priors in thinking and ideology in perspectives. This often led to generalized prescriptions which did not quite recognize that development was characterized by specificites in time and space.

The proponents of the Development Consensus realized that it was not sufficient to focus on the pace of industrialization and the rate of economic growth. And it came to be recognized that the levels of, or trends in, per capita income were not quite appropriate as indicators of development. After all, per capita income is only an arithmetic mean. Social indicators are also statistical averages. And neither captures the well-being of the poor. In fact, distributional outcomes left much to be desired. In most developing countries, economic growth, which was impressive by historical standards, did not lead to a significant reduction in absolute poverty and did not bring about an improvement in the living conditions of ordinary people. This was both recognized and emphasized by scholars who noted that, during this period, growth was not transformed into development. Thus, the early 1970s witnessed the emergence of a literature that suggested other indicators of development, such as a reduction in poverty, inequality, and unemployment which would capture changes in the quality of life.[16] This thinking moved further. Development, it was argued, must bring about an improvement in the living conditions of people. It should, therefore, ensure the provision of basic human needs for all: not just food and clothing but also shelter, health care, and education.[17] It was stressed that this simple but powerful proposition is often forgotten in the conventional concerns of economics. Such thinking culminated in writings on, and an index of, human development.[18] In this literature, the ends were much more clearly specified than the means. Correctives were, of course, suggested, to ameliorate absolute poverty and foster human development. However, the underlying fundamental questions were not addressed. For instance, why did economic growth not lead to employment creation and poverty eradication? Or, was it necessary to redefine the respective roles of the State and the market? Hence there was little in terms of rethinking strategies of

---

[16]See, for example, Baster (1972), Seers (1972), and Morris (1979).

[17]See Streeten (1981) and Stewart (1985).

[18]There is an extensive literature on the subject. For a discussion on the conceptual foundations, see Sen (1989) and Haq (1995).

development. In other words, there was some learning from what went wrong but not enough unlearning from why it went wrong.

The concerns of mainstream economics were elsewhere. It largely ignored this focus on people. And it continued to emphasize economic growth, but sought to stress economic efficiency as the primary criterion to assess the economic performance of countries. The orthodox critique of the industrialization experience in developing countries, which also surfaced in the early 1970s, argued that the policy framework in most developing countries, which was based on the Development Consensus of the early 1950s, led to economic inefficiency and resource misallocation while the cumulative effect of these policies became an obstacle to growth.[19] The essential message was that outcomes could have been much better in terms of efficiency and growth and not that outcomes should have been better in terms of the well-being of people. Clearly, little attention was paid to an important dimension of failure in the strategy it sought to criticize. There was an implicit assumption that economic growth was both necessary and sufficient to bring about development.

This focus on the performance of countries sought to contrast failures with successes. The success stories that came to be portrayed as role models were Hong Kong, Singapore, South Korea, and Taiwan. The lessons drawn from the experience of these few countries were sought to be generalized and transplanted elsewhere.[20] The new orthodoxy did not recognize, or chose to ignore, the fact that economic policies and development practices in these countries were not in conformity with their caricature model of markets and openness.[21] What is more, it did not recognize that the distinction between success and failure, while important, is not exhaustive. In fact, actual outcomes in development were a complex mix, which could not be characterized simply in an either–or mode. Industrialization in developing countries was characterized by success stories in a few, muddling-through in some, and near-failure in others. And it is not as if all countries could be unambiguously classified into one of these categories. The development experience within countries was also an uneven mix of success and failure. Thus, generalizations in diagnosis and prescription, which ignored the specificities of economies in time and space, were often not appropriate.

[19]Little et al. (1970) and Krueger (1978).

[20]In this context, the research publications and the policy advice of the World Bank exercised significant influence. See, for example, *World Development Report 1987* and World Bank (1993).

[21]Amsden (1989), Wade (1990), and Chang (1996).

The second period from 1981 to 2005, the era of markets and globalization, witnessed economic liberalization and economic reform across-the-board in developing countries and transition economies. More openness and less intervention was the bottom-line. There was a rapid increase in the degree of openness of economies. There was also a profound change in the structure of incentives and institutions which reduced the role of the State to rely more on the market. This happened almost everywhere. And the experience with such reforms is now long enough to assess performance in terms of development outcomes. It is plausible to argue, though impossible to prove, that the reality as it has unfolded does not conform to beliefs, or expectations, in orthodox thinking about development. There is now a growing recognition that the response to these reforms has been less than spectacular.[22] What is more, it would seem that there is a mismatch between regime change and economic performance. Yet, this experience during the period 1981–2005 has not persuaded orthodoxy to learn from outcomes in development even in terms of contemplating correctives. The belief system remains firmly embedded, so that there is no attempt to unlearn from development. There are, of course, concerns voiced by critics. And there is some rethinking about development from a heterodox perspective which draws upon experience.

Consider first, the countries that were conformists, which adopted the reform agenda of the Washington Consensus almost in its entirety. Most countries in Latin America, sub-Saharan Africa, and Eastern Europe belong to this group. It is clear that these liberalizers have under-performed or not performed. Some can even be described as dismal failures. In fact, during this period, the performance of Latin America, sub-Saharan Africa, and Eastern Europe, in terms of economic growth and distributional outcomes, was not only much worse than other parts of the world, particularly Asia in the same period, but was also distinctly worse than their own performance in the preceding period 1951–80.

Consider next, the countries that were non-conformists, which did not quite adopt the reform agenda of the Washington Consensus. There are only a few countries that belong to this group. The most important examples are China and India since the late 1970s, followed by Vietnam since the late 1980s. These countries are now recognized as star performers in terms of economic growth if not distributional outcomes. But these performers are not the

---

[22]For a discussion of, and evidence on, this proposition, see Rodrik (2005). See also, Taylor (2007).

liberalizers, at least not in the conventional sense when compared with the conformists in Latin America or sub-Saharan Africa. Generalizations are difficult. Even so, it is plausible to suggest that these countries used unorthodox or heterodox policies for orthodox objectives in much the same way as the East Asian tigers did during the preceding period.

What are the lessons that emerge from the development experience during the second period 1981–2005? And what conclusions can we draw from the contrast in economic performance between the conformists and the non-conformists? It must be said that the answers are strongly influenced by ideological perspectives on development. Orthodox economists draw a simple conclusion. In countries where performance has belied expectations, economic reforms have been either too slow or not enough. The solution, in their view, is an enlarged policy agenda, with a second, third, or even fourth generation of reforms. This adds up to an augmented Washington Consensus. It suggests that there are many more things which remain to be done. It also suggests some modifications and qualifications in the original menu. The heterodox view argues that this is a false alternative.[23] The reason invoked is simple. In situations where the first-best cannot be attained because all the necessary conditions cannot be satisfied, more reform, faster reform, or deeper reform cannot be a solution, because the second-best outcome may require the satisfaction of a completely different set of conditions. Instead, it suggests a diagnostic approach that moves away from blanket prescriptions towards a more nuanced strategy which recognizes that constraints and possibilities are country-specific so that the design of policies and institutions depends upon the context.[24] Unorthodox economists draw a stronger conclusion from the contrasting experience of the conformists and the non-conformists, to suggest that the solution advocated by the Washington Consensus could turn out to be worse than the problem. It is stressed that unfettered markets and unconstrained openness are neither necessary nor desirable. Indeed, it is argued that the nature of State intervention and the degree of openness are strategic choices, which cannot be defined once-and-for-all as they depend on the stage of development and must change over time. Thus, it is essential to redefine the role of the State *vis-à-vis* the market and manage integration with the world economy in a strategic manner. The unorthodox perspective would recommend such a non-conformist path.

[23]For an analysis and evaluation of the augmented Washington Consensus, see Rodrik (2005).

[24]This argument is developed, at some length, by Rodrik (2005). See also, Rodrik (2003).

A comparison of the two periods reveals some striking asymmetries. In the first period, 1951 to 1980, economic growth across the developing world was sustained at a respectable pace, which was a radical departure from the stagnation in the colonial era. But this growth did not translate into well-being for ordinary people. The advocates of the Development Consensus sought to introduce correctives without rethinking strategies, while orthodoxy sought fundamental changes in economic policies for faster growth and greater efficiency. The swing of the pendulum in thinking about development was almost complete by 1980. And it was not long before the Washington Consensus reshaped policies and strategies across the developing world. But outcomes in development belied expectations and promises. In fact, during the second period, 1981 to 2005, economic growth across the developing world, except for China and India, was much slower and more volatile than in the preceding three decades. What is more, there was a discernible increase in economic inequalities between countries and between people, while poverty persisted in large parts of the developing world. It would seem that the doctrinal swing which changed strategies did not transform outcomes in development. Yet, there is little to suggest that orthodoxy has learned, let alone unlearned, from the development experience during this second period.

It is also possible to discern asymmetries in thinking. The experience during 1951–80 prompted more rethinking on development in the orthodox perspective than in the unorthodox perspective. The experience during 1981–2005 prompted more rethinking on development in the unorthodox perspective than in the orthodox perspective. In both periods, there was some rethinking on development in the heterodox perspective.[25] There was learning from development, even if limited or selective, everywhere, although its extent varied over time and across space. It is plausible to argue though impossible to prove the following hypothesis. Dominant ideologies were always reluctant to question their belief systems. It meant ceding intellectual or political space. Hence, the attempts to unlearn from development, which changed priors or thinking, were few and far between. And it should come as no surprise that non-dominant doctrines were more willing to learn from the development experience. It meant capturing intellectual or political space. Yet, once the tables were turned, such that non-dominant doctrines became dominant

[25]For an analysis of changing perspectives in development economics, during the period 1950–2000, see Toye (2003). For some discussion on the orthodox, heterodox, and unorthodox perspectives on development, in the context of the debate on liberalization, see Bhaduri and Nayyar (1996). And, for a further analysis of the debate about development in the wider context of globalization, see Nayyar (2007).

ideologies, they also became reluctant to learn, and unwilling to unlearn, from experience. It would seem that the willingness to learn and the capacity to unlearn changed with the times. Beyond this conflict between doctrinal world views, there are two other conclusions that can be drawn. But these call for some departures from priors that are shaped by ideological perspectives.

For one, the problem is neither about means nor ends, in themselves. The real issue is the path from means to ends. And there is a commonplace error in the design of policies. It confuses *comparison* (of equilibrium positions) with *change* (from one equilibrium position to another). In the real world, economic policy must be concerned not merely with comparison but with how to direct the process of change. Similarly, it cannot suffice to enunciate general principles, such as managing integration with the world economy, maintaining macroeconomic stability through prudent public finances, or putting in place institutions. The real issue is the transition path from the use of policy instruments to the realization of policy objectives.

For another, it is essential to recognize the specificities of economies in time and space. It is just as important to recognize the complexities of the growth process. Such recognition is critical because constraints on growth can be very different in different situations and at different times. Therefore, even if the ends are common, the means, whether policies or institutions, may have to be different across countries at a point in time. Indeed, even in the same country, policies and institutions may have to be adapted as circumstances change over time. Obviously, simple generalizations are perilous, because one size does not fit all. But this does not mean that we cannot learn from experience. Nor should it suggest that analysis, diagnosis, and prescriptions are *passé*. It is just that there can be no unique solutions even for similar, yet differentiated, situations, let alone for a multiplicity of different situations.

ANATOMY OF SUCCESS STORIES

Much has been said and much has been written on the East Asian miracle, the metaphor used to describe the success stories in development during the period from 1960 to 1980. Indeed, there is an extensive literature on the subject. And it would mean too much of a digression to enter into a discussion here. Suffice it to say that, except for Hong Kong, the East Asian economies simply did not conform to their caricature characterization in the policy

---

[26]See, for example, Akyuz (1999) and Rodrik (2005).
[27]Amsden (1989), Wade (1990), and Lall (1990).

prescriptions. There is now an extensive literature on the subject which shows that the East Asian tigers used strategic forms of intervention and unorthodox economic policies to attain conventional objectives.[26] Strategic intervention by the State, particularly in the realm of industrial policy and technology policy but also in the sphere of trade policy, rather than a reliance on market forces alone, was used to promote competition, calibrate openness, and foster capabilities.[27] Similarly, unorthodox means were used to preserve macroeconomic stability, stimulate private investment, and encourage technological development.[28] This is now fairly widely accepted. Hence, repetition of the argument and the evidence would serve little purpose. But there are other important dimensions that are largely ignored: history, politics, and conjuncture. It was history that shaped land reforms, particularly in Taiwan, with important distributive consequences. It was politics in the Cold War era that provided economic and political support for the small East Asian countries. It was the conjuncture in the world economy that created expanding marketing opportunities for the East Asian tigers without the constraints and the reciprocity now implicit in the multilateral trading system.

Much less has been said and much less has been written about the more recent success stories in Asia, particularly China and India. Even if we do not subscribe to the arithmetic of compound rates set out in the Goldman Sachs study, on the BRICs in 2050, China and India are seen as star performers by those who advocate markets and openness as the road to development. Interestingly enough, there is a strong and influential belief that these two Asian giants, in slumber until then, awoke to a new dawn with economic liberalization: China after 1978 and India after 1991. Such oversimplified conclusions are unwarranted, in part because they do not situate the economic development of China and India in historical perspective. It must be stressed that, if we consider the twentieth century, both China and India experienced their first turning point in economic growth during the early 1950s. This marked a complete break from, and a sharp contrast with, the near-stagnation during the period 1900–50. It is worth noting that in this period of the colonial era, China and India were among the most open and the least regulated economies in the world. Yet, the outcome was the de-industrialization and underdevelopment. In fact, during the first half of the twentieth century, in real terms, growth in national income was 0.3 per cent per annum in China and 0.8 per cent per annum in India, whereas growth

[28]Chang (2003) and Rodrik (2005).

in per capita income was negative at –0.3 per cent per annum in China and –0.1 per cent per annum in India.[29] In sharp contrast, during the period from 1951 to 1980, at constant prices, growth in GDP was 5 per cent per annum in China and 3.6 per cent per annum in India, whereas growth in GDP per capita was 3 per cent per annum in China and 1.4 per cent per annum in India (Table 5.2).

During the second half of the twentieth century, for China after the revolution and for India since independence, the turning point in economic growth was *circa* 1980. In the period from 1981 to 2005, at constant prices, growth in GDP has been 9.7 per cent per annum in China and 5.8 per cent per annum in India, while growth in GDP per capita has been 8.5 per cent per annum in China and 3.8 per cent per annum in India (Table 5.2). It is worth noting that the acceleration in the rate of growth in India, which constituted a departure from the proverbial Hindu rate of growth, began around 1980, more than a decade before economic liberalization.[30] Therefore, in drawing inferences about cause-and-effect for India, it is not possible to reason even on a *post hoc ergo propter hoc* basis. For China, it is possible, although it is not logical, to reason on a *post hoc ergo propter hoc* basis. Much more important, perhaps, such watersheds or thresholds in time are altogether ahistorical in their understanding of the process of economic growth. Both China and India are, in fact, stories of changes with continuity, where the past has not only shaped the present but would also influence the future. It is plausible to suggest that the stories of economic development in China after the revolution, and in India since independence, are more about introducing correctives and implementing changes that sought to eliminate weaknesses and build on strengths, in discrete steps over time than about big bang changes that sought to erase the past.

It is, of course, possible to engage in debates about the timing of the changes, or the periods of transition, in both countries. But that is another matter. The critical point is that the three decades in China after the revolution (1949–78) and the four decades plus in India since independence (1947–91), created the initial conditions and laid the essential foundations without which economic reforms could not have produced, or led to, the observed

---

[29]These compound growth rates have been computed from data on GDP and GDP per capita, in international dollars at 1980 prices, for China and India in 1900 and 1950 (Maddison 1989).

[30]For a detailed discussion on turning points in economic growth in independent India, see Nayyar (2006b). See also, Rodrik and Subramanian (2004).

outcomes that are now depicted as success stories. In China, it was the spread of education in society, the building of a physical infrastructure, the establishment of a capital goods sector, the creation of capabilities among people, a prudent macro-management of the economy, and effective implementation of public action. In India, a system of higher education was developed, a physical infrastructure was built, a capital goods sector was established, entrepreneurial abilities were nurtured in individuals, managerial capabilities were fostered in firms, while social institutions and the legal framework necessary for a market economy were put in place. The transition economies in Eastern Europe and Central Asia did not have these essential foundations so that big bang economic reforms led to disastrous outcomes in the short-run.[31] Similarly, in developing countries that had not created the requisite initial conditions and institutional capacities, economic reforms did not produce a take-off in growth. It is hardly surprising, then, that the spate of economic reforms did not lead to the expected outcomes, predicted by orthodoxy, in sub-Saharan Africa or Eastern Europe.

There are both similarities and differences between China and India. Thus, it is important to ask what is common and what is not? The similarities are mostly in the economy. Both created the initial conditions. Both opted for gradualism in change rather than big bangs. Both attempted an adaptation and a contextualization of changes that were introduced. The differences are mostly in the polity. India is a vibrant political democracy. Its strength lies in the institutional checks and balances, as also in the capacity to manage conflict that democracy provides. Its weakness lies in the capacity to implement public action which is constrained by competing claims of a democratic system. China, which is a one-party State, does not have a political democracy. Its strength lies in its strong capacity to implement public action. Its weakness lies in the reality that there are not enough institutional checks and balances, and there is little capacity to manage conflict, because it does not have a democratic political system.

There is something else that China and India have in common for the period 1981–2005. In terms of economic growth, they have performed much better than the industrialized countries which experienced a slow-down in growth, the transition economies which did badly, and much of the developing world apart from a few countries in Asia. Obviously, economic

---

[31]There is an extensive literature on this subject. See, for example, Amsden et al. (1994) and Cornia and Popov (2001).

growth is absolutely essential. China and India are doing well in that domain. But economic growth is not sufficient. And distributional outcomes are of critical importance. So are employment and livelihoods. It is neither feasible nor desirable to separate economic growth from distributional outcomes because they are inextricably linked with each other. This link is provided by employment creation and employment opportunities. Neither is doing well in these domains. In China, distributional outcomes are significantly worse. In India, poverty reduction has slowed down while employment elasticities of output have declined to levels much lower than ever before.

In spite of the shortcomings, the mega economies of Asia, China and India, are widely cited as the success stories in development, with the prospect of even more promise during the first quarter of the twenty-first century. The rise of these economies has often been attributed to their integration with the world economy through markets and openness. This is as much of a caricature characterization as that of the East Asian tigers a quarter of a century earlier. The success of China and India, such as it is, is attributable much more to national development strategies. What, then, are the lessons from, and the implications of, the development experience of the new tiger and the older dragon?

The lessons are clear enough: (a) create initial conditions in terms of education, infrastructure, capabilities, and institutions; (b) manage strategic integration, rather than passive insertion, into the world economy; (c) opt for gradualism in change and hasten slowly with liberalization, keeping in view the pace and the sequence; and (d) recognize specificities of, and differences between, economies despite apparent similarities.

It is clear that the development experience of China and India during the second half of the twentieth century is much too complex for simplified conclusions or broad generalizations. It may be tempting to reason on a *post hoc ergo propter hoc* basis, as some do: that the 'bad' economic performance of China and India during the period 1951–80 was attributable to 'flawed' strategies of development, or that the 'good' economic performance of China and India during the period 1981–2005 is attributable to 'wise' strategies of development. But, as shown above, it would be a serious mistake to attribute cause-and-effect, simply in terms of temporal sequence, to changes in development strategies and changes in development outcomes. The reasons deserve emphasis. First, development strategies in China and India do not conform to caricature versions associated with doctrinal swings in thinking about development. In fact, both countries were significantly different from most developing countries—almost unique in the period 1951–80 and clearly non-conformist in the period 1981–2005. Second, in both countries, economic performance during the period 1951–80 was perfectly respectable in terms of economic growth and impressive compared with the preceding 50 years, so much so that in a longer-term perspective, 1950 was a turning point in economic growth, although there were shortcomings and failures in other aspects. Third, in both countries, economic performance during the period 1981–2005 was even better in terms of economic growth, but this growth was not inclusive, as poverty persisted in India and inequalities rose in China. Fourth, in both countries, the impressive economic performance during the period 1981–2005 was, in significant part, attributable to the initial conditions that were created and the essential foundations that were laid, during the period 1951–80.

There is a related question that arises. Is it possible to replicate the development experience of China and India elsewhere? The fallacy-of-composition argument is less powerful for China and India, as compared with the original East Asian tigers, simply because the mega economies are so large. Therefore, it should be possible for a few, indeed many more, countries to follow in their footsteps without straining the absorptive capacity of the world economy. But China and India are more difficult to replicate in as much as size and space are connected, so that smaller countries may not have the same options or choices. What is more, history matters. China and India created the initial conditions and laid the essential foundations for development during the preceding period. Countries that have not done so earlier may not be able to follow a similar path. Yet, it is possible to learn from the development experience of China and India. But such learning should seek to contextualize rather than replicate.

The implications are also clear enough. First, it is essential to recognize the importance of national development strategies. For one, this means building capabilities at a micro-level and institutions at a meso-level. For another, it means creating institutional mechanisms for blending sensible economics with feasible politics. Second, it is just as necessary to recognize the significance of the changed international context. For one, this means the use of available policy space for national development, given the international context. For another, it means some effort to create more policy space by reshaping the rules of the game in the world economy. In both spheres, the driving force is the pursuit of national development objectives.

CONCLUSIONS

This essay has sought to sketch a picture, with broad strokes on a wide canvas, of thinking about, and outcomes in, development during the second half of the twentieth century. It is difficult to sum up. But it is worth setting out some important conclusions that emerge from the discussion.

Thinking about development witnessed a complete swing of the pendulum, from the Development Consensus in the early 1950s to the Washington Consensus which evolved through the 1980s. These shifts in paradigm, which reshaped strategies of development, were strongly influenced by history and conjuncture, reinforced by the dominant political ideology of the times. However, changes in development strategies did not lead to the expected outcomes. In fact, there was a discernible mismatch between turning points in thinking and performance. During the period 1951–80, economic growth across the developing world was sustained at a respectable pace, which was a radical departure from stagnation in the colonial era, but this growth did not translate into well-being for ordinary people, which was the essential objective. During the period 1981–2005, economic growth across the developing world, except for China and India, was much slower and more volatile than in the preceding three decades, while poverty persisted and economic inequalities between countries and people registered a significant increase.

The dramatic changes in perceptions about China and India, from role models in the early 1950s to disaster stories in the mid-1970s and star performers in the early 2000s, almost coincided in time with the swings in doctrines about development. In both countries, economic growth was more than respectable during the period 1951–80, indeed impressive in comparison with the preceding 50 years, and even better during the period 1981–2005, although there were shortcomings and failures in other aspects of development throughout. But it would be a mistake to attribute cause-and-effect simply to the temporal sequence. For development strategies in China and India did not conform to the caricature versions associated with doctrinal swings in thinking. In fact, both countries used unorthodox or heterodox policies for orthodox objectives. And, their impressive economic performance during the period 1981–2005 was, in significant part, attributable to the initial conditions that were created and the essential foundations that were laid during the period 1951–80.

In retrospect, it would seem that development outcomes in the period 1951–80 were not bad, even if these were not in conformity with expectations about economic growth in countries and living conditions of people. The advocates of the Development Consensus sought to introduce correctives for past mistakes, to ameliorate poverty and stress human development, without rethinking strategies. The critics sought fundamental changes in economic policies for faster growth and greater efficiency. This culminated in the Washington Consensus which was implemented almost everywhere. But development outcomes in the period 1981–2005 belied expectations, even about economic growth. This unfolding reality, which revealed a mismatch between regime change and economic performance, has so far not persuaded orthodoxy to contemplate correctives let alone rethink strategies. Of course, experience of the past 50 years did lead to some rethinking about development. This learning from experience, however, was selective. And it differed across schools of thought. For it was shaped only in part by outcomes. It was also significantly influenced by priors in thinking and ideology in perspectives. Thus, attempts to unlearn from development, which questioned beliefs or changed priors embedded in ideologies, were few and far between. China and India are perhaps different, insofar as changes in strategies were shaped more by their own development experience than by swings in development doctrines. And when the mismatch between expectations and realities persisted over time, long held belief-systems were subjected to question, so that there was some attempt, even if lagged and limited, to unlearn from experience.

References

Akyuz, Y. (ed.) (1999), *East Asian Development: New Perspectives*, Frank Cass, London.

Amsden, A.H. (1989), *Asia's Next Giant: South Korea and Late Industrialization*, Oxford University Press, New York.

Amsden, A.H., J. Kochanowicz, and L. Taylor (eds) (1994), *The Market Meets its Match: Restructuring the Economies of Eastern Europe*, Harvard University Press, Cambridge.

Atkinson, A.B. (2003), 'Income Inequalities in OECD Countries: Notes and Explanations', *mimeo*, Oxford.

Baster, N. (1972), 'Development Indicators', *Journal of Development Studies*, Vol. 8, No. 3, pp. 1–20.

Bhaduri, A. and D. Nayyar (1996), *The Intelligent Person's Guide to Liberalization*, Penguin Books, New Delhi.

Bhagwati, J. and P. Desai (1970), *India: Planning for Industrialization*, Oxford University Press, London.

Bourguignon, F. and C. Morrison (2002), 'Inequality among World Citizens, 1820–1992', *American Economic Review*, Vol. 92, No. 4, pp. 727–44.

Chang, H.J. (1996), *The Political Economy of Industrial Policy*, Macmillan, London.

——— (2002), *Kicking Away the Ladder: Development Strategy in Historical Perspective*, Anthem Press, London.

——— (2003), 'The East Asian Development Experience', in H.J. Chang (ed.), *Rethinking Development Economics*, Anthem Press, London.

Cornia, G.A. and S. Kiiski (2001), 'Trends in Income Distribution in the Post World War II Period: Evidence and Interpretation', WIDER Discussion Paper No. 89, UNU-WIDER, Helsinki.

Cornia, G.A. and V. Popov (eds) (2001), *Transition and Institutions*, Oxford University Press, Oxford.

Diaz-Alejandro, C.F. (1975), 'Trade Policies and Economic Development', in P.B. Kenen (ed.), *International Trade and Finance*, Cambridge University Press, Cambridge.

Easterly, W. (2001), *The Elusive Quest for Growth*, The MIT Press, Cambridge.

Haq, M. (1995), *Reflections on Human Development*, Oxford University Press, New York.

Hausmann, R., L. Pritchett, and D. Rodrik (2004), 'Growth Accelerations', NBER Working Paper No. 10566, National Bureau of Economic Research, New York.

Krueger, A.O. (1978), *Foreign Trade Regimes and Economic Development: Liberalization Attempts and Consequences*, National Bureau of Economic Research, New York.

Lal, D. (1998), *Unfinished Business: India in the World Economy*, Oxford Univesity Press, New York.

Lall, S. (1990), *Building Industrial Competitiveness in Developing Countries*, OECD Development Centre, Paris.

——— (1997), 'Imperfect Markets and Fallible Governments: The Role of the State in Industrial Development', in D. Nayyar (ed.) *Trade and Industrialization*, Oxford University Press, New Delhi.

Lee, E. (ed.) (1981), *Export-led Industrialization and Development*, International Labour Organization, Geneva.

Little, I.M.D., T. Scitovsky, and M. Scott (1970), *Industry and Trade in Some Developing Countries: A Comparative Study*, Oxford University Press, London.

Maddison, A. (1989), *The World Economy in the Twentieth Century*, OECD Development Centre, Paris.

——— (2003), *The World Economy: Historical Statistics*, OECD, Paris.

Milanovic, B. (2005), *Worlds Apart: Measuring International and Global Inequality*, Princeton University Press, Princeton.

Morris, M.D. (1979), 'Measuring the Conditions of the World's Poor', Pergamon Press, Oxford.

Nayyar, D. (1997), 'Themes in Trade and Industrialization', in D. Nayyar (ed.), *Trade and Industrialization*, Oxford University Press, New Delhi.

——— (1998), 'Economic Development and Political Democracy: The Interaction of Economics and Politics in Independent India', *Economic and Political Weekly*, Vol. 33, No. 49, pp. 3121–31.

_____ (2004), 'Economic Reforms in India: Understanding the Process and Learning from Experience', *International Journal of Development Issues*, Vol. 3, No. 2, pp. 31–55.

_____ (2006a), 'Globalization, History and Development: A Tale of Two Centuries', *Cambridge Journal of Economics*, Vol. 30, No. 1, pp. 137–59.

_____ (2006b), 'India's Unfinished Journey: Transforming Growth into Development', *Modern Asian Studies*, Vol. 40, No. 3, pp. 797–832.

_____ (2007), 'Development through Globalization?', in G. Mavrotas and A. Shorrocks (eds), *Advancing Development: Core Themes in Global Economics*, Palgrave, London.

Nolan, P. (2004), *Transforming China: Globalization, Transition and Development*, Anthem Press, London.

Ocampo, J.A. and M. Parra (2005), 'The Dual Divergence: Growth Successes and Collapses in the Developing World', DESA Working Paper No. 24, United Nations, New York.

Rodrik, D. (ed.) (2003), *In Search of Prosperity: Analytic Narratives on Economic Growth*, Princeton: Princeton University Press.

_____ (2005), Rethinking Growth Strategies, WIDER Annual Lecture 8, UNU-WIDER, Helsinki.

Rodrik, D. and A. Subramanian (2004), 'From Hindu Growth to Productivity Surge: The Mystery of the Indian Growth Transition', IMF Working Paper WP/04/77, International Monetary Fund, Washington, DC.

Seers, D. (1972), 'What are We Trying to Measure?', *Journal of Development Studies*, Vol. 8, No. 3, pp. 21–36.

Sen, A. (1989), 'Development as Capability Expansion', *Journal of Development Planning*, No. 19, pp. 41–58.

Singh, A. (1994), 'Openness and Market-Friendly Approach to Development: Learning the Right Lessons from Development Experience', *World Development*, Vol. 22, No. 12, pp. 1811–24.

Stewart, F. (1985), *Planning to Meet Basic Needs*, Macmillan, London.

Streeten, P. (1981), *First Things First: Meeting Basic Human Needs in Developing Countries*, Oxford University Press, Oxford.

Stiglitz, J.E. (1998), 'More Instruments and Broader Goals: Moving Toward the Post-Washington Consensus', WIDER Annual Lecture 2, UNU-WIDER, Helsinki.

_____ (2002), *Globalization and its Discontents*, Allen Lane, London.

Taylor, L. (2007), 'Development Questions for 25 Years', in G. Mavrotas and A. Shorrocks (eds), *Advancing Development: Core Themes in Global Economics*, Palgrave, London.

Toye, J. (2003), 'Changing Perspectives in Development Economics', in H.J. Chang (ed.), *Rethinking Development Economics*, Anthem Press, London.

United Nations (2006a), *Diverging Growth and Development, World Economic and Social Survey 2006*, United Nations, New York.

___ (2006b), *National Accounts Main Aggregates Database*, Department of Economic and Social Affairs, New York, available at *http://unstats.un.org/unsd/snaama/introduction.asp*

___ (2006c), *Demographic Yearbook System*, Department of Economic and Social Affairs, New York, available at *http://unstats.un.org/unsd/demographic/products/dyb/dyb2.htm*

Wade, R. (1990), *Governing the Market: Economic Theory and the Role of the Government in East Asian Industrialization*, Princeton University Press, Princeton.

Williamson, J. (ed.) (1994), *The Political Economy of Policy Reform*, Institute of International Economics, Washington, DC.

Wilson, D. and R. Purushothaman (2003), 'Dreaming with BRICS: The Path to 2050', Global Economics Paper No. 99, Goldman Sachs, New York.

World Bank (1993), *The East Asian Miracle*, Oxford University Press, New York.

Chapter 6

SHORT-TERMISM, PUBLIC POLICIES, AND ECONOMIC DEVELOPMENT*

THE CONTEXT

The second half of the twentieth century witnessed a complete swing of the pendulum in thinking about public policies and economic development. In the post-colonial era, which began soon after the end of the Second World War, most underdeveloped countries adopted strategies of development that provided a sharp contrast with their past during the first half of the twentieth century. For one, there was a conscious attempt to limit the degree of openness and of integration with the world economy, in pursuit of a more autonomous, if not self-reliant, development. For another, the State was assigned a strategic role in development because the market, by itself, was not perceived as sufficient for meeting the aspirations of these latecomers to industrialization. Both represented points of departure from the colonial era which was characterized by open economies and unregulated markets. But this approach also represented a consensus in thinking about the most appropriate strategy for industrialization. It was, in fact, the Development Consensus at the time. It is more than 50 years since then. And it would seem that, in terms of perceptions about development, we have arrived at the polar opposite. Most countries in the developing world, as also in the erstwhile socialist bloc, are reshaping their domestic economic policies so as to integrate much more with the world economy and to enlarge the role of the market *vis-à-vis* the State. This is partly a consequence of the collapse of planned economies and excessive or inappropriate State intervention in market economies. It is also significantly influenced by the profound transformation in the world political situation. The widespread acceptance of this approach represents a new consensus in thinking about development. It has come to be known as the Washington Consensus.

*I owe an intellectual debt to Amit Bhaduri for helpful discussion on the theme of this paper and constructive comments on an earlier draft which clarified my ideas on the subject. I would also like to thank Mritiunjoy Mohanty for useful suggestions.

This shift of paradigm has been associated with a profound change in the concerns of public policies for development. The old-fashioned development economics was formulated in the context of poor countries where the prime concerns were the eradication of poverty and bringing about an improvement in living conditions of the people. The emphasis, then, was on savings, investment, and growth. But equity was an important objective. The time horizon was the long-term. It is no longer so. In developing countries, many of which have run into debt crisis or other forms of macroeconomic turbulence, public policies have come to be preoccupied with macro-management in the short-run and restructuring of economies in the medium-term. The former is driven by the quest for stabilization. The focus is on fiscal, monetary and exchange rate policies as a means of stabilizing the balance of payments and controlling inflation. The latter is prompted by the quest for efficiency. The essential concern is the management of incentives and the supply side. Such a policy stance has been particularly pronounced in countries that have been guided by IMF programmes of stabilization and World Bank programmes of structural adjustment. But other countries, too, have adopted similar economic policies in conformity with the new orthodoxy embodied in the Washington Consensus. The time horizon now is the short-run and, at most, the medium-term.

The object of this essay is to explore the implications of this short-termism in public policies for economic development. The first section analyses how economic policies implemented with a short-term objective and designed in a medium-term perspective may have adverse consequences for the performance of the economy in the long-term. The second section discusses how a preoccupation with the short-term leads to a neglect of long-term development objectives, which could also have serious implications.

Some Long-Term Consequences of Short-Termism

The essence of the Washington Consensus is more openness *vis-à-vis* the world economy and less intervention by the government in the market. The bottom line is to *get prices right*. Thus, structural reform seeks to shift resources through the price mechanism: (a) from the non-traded goods sector to the traded goods sector and, within the latter, from import competing activities to export activities; and (b) from the government sector to the private sector. Apart from such resource allocation, structural reform seeks to improve resource utilization by: (a) by increasing the degree of openness of an economy; and (b) changing the structure of incentives and institutions which would reduce the role of the State to rely more on market forces. The restructuring of economies, however, is easier said than done. And problems of transition are a reality that cannot be wished away, for change is neither smooth nor automatic.[1]

The process of adjustment is not smooth. Getting prices right may not have the desired effect in terms of resource allocation for a long time. The speed of adjustment on the supply side is inevitably slow because resources are not perfectly mobile across sectors or substitutable in uses. Moreover, prices, particularly of factors such as labour, cannot be completely flexible. These structural rigidities constrain the supply response to structural reforms. Hence, it is important to recognize structural rigidities where they exist instead of assuming structural flexibilities where they do not exist.

The process of adjustment is not automatic either. The introduction of competition through deregulation and openness may be necessary but is not sufficient to improve resource utilization. The management of incentives, motivated by the object of minimizing cost and maximizing efficiency at a micro-level, is based on a set of policies that is intended to increase competition between firms in the market place. Domestic competition is sought to be provided through deregulation in investment decisions, in the financial sector, and in labour markets. Foreign competition is sought to be provided through openness in trade, investment, and technology flows. It must, however, be recognized that these policies which seek to enhance competition may be necessary but are not sufficient, for there is nothing automatic about competition. Policy regimes can only allow things to happen but cannot cause things to happen. The reliance on the price mechanism to enhance competition and enforce efficiency may be misplaced because such change is a time consuming process. But the change in prices may be abrupt. This creates the illusion that these problems have short-term solutions. Reality often turns out to be different.

The problems associated with short-termism, as also its consequences in the long-term, are best illustrated with the example of trade liberalization. The object is to reduce the protection available to domestic industry through a substantial reduction in tariffs, and to bring domestic prices closer to world prices through a substantial depreciation in the exchange rate. The consequent change in relative prices is often large, if not drastic. The presumption is that it would shift resources from the production of non-traded goods to the production of traded goods while exposure to international competition will force domestic firms to become more efficient.

The process of adjustment is neither as smooth nor as automatic as orthodox economics suggests. What is more, the emphasis on trade liberalization, which

---

[1]For a discussion on problems of transition, see Nayyar (1996). See also, Taylor (1988).

assumes that international competition will force domestic firms to become more efficient, makes an elementary but commonplace theoretical error in the design of policies. It confuses *comparison* (of equilibrium positions) with *change* (from one equilibrium position to another). In the real world, economic policy must be concerned not merely with comparison but with how to direct the process of change. Thus, even if a reduction in protection can, in principle, lead to a more cost-efficient economy, the transition path is by no means clear. In the process of transition, however, things can go wrong. But this is simply not recognized in a world characterized by short-termism. Indeed, the temporal dimension of change is altogether neglected.[2] So much so, it would seem, that time does not matter. Such short-termism in public policies may have an adverse effect on the performance of the economy, as also its growth potential, in the long-term.

In the real world, rapid trade liberalization may enforce not only efficiency but also closures at the micro-level during periods of transition. The firms which are not competitive at the new set of relative prices would have to close down. This is not simply a temporary exit. In the presence of *hysteresis* effects, it could change the industrial landscape in a quasi-permanent manner. We know that capacity utilization and technological learning are neither automatic nor costless for firms.[3] And widespread exits reduce the flexibility of economies to make corrections as also the ability of economies to change course after a time. Consider a situation where rapid trade liberalization leads to the exit of firms from some segments in the industrial sector. Imported goods may replace home-produced goods, or foreign firms may displace domestic firms. After a time, even if a substantial devaluation seeks to improve the profitability of producing importables at home in a more competitive milieu, domestic firms may not be able to exploit the opportunities in the changed circumstances.[4] The reason is simple. Exit is easy but re-entry is difficult. The past influences the present, just as the present shapes the future, if economic policies have consequences which are irreversible after a time lag. Such *hysteresis* means that

---

[2]The analytical difficulties associated with understanding the process of economic change over time are enormous. But these must be recognized rather than ignored. This limitation of mainstream economics is stressed by Bhaduri (1996) in a paper which seeks to address the problem. He provides a formal model which examines the interaction between the public and private sectors in the process of transformation from a command economy to a market system.

[3]The literature on this subject is now considerable. See, for example, Pack and Westphal (1986), Evenson and Westphal (1995), and Lall (1997).

[4]Mohanty (1996). For an interesting discussion of similar problems attributable to *hysteresis*, in the context of the North American Free Trade Agreement, see McLaren (1997).

trade liberalization which leads to the exit of domestic firms on a significant scale ultimately affects the capacity of an economy to respond to changes in relative prices. Therefore, it affects the performance of the economy in the long-term.

Similar consequences may follow, through *hysteresis,* when capital inflows such as portfolio investment become an important source of financing current account deficits in the balance of payments. This is attributable, in part, to trade liberalization which may widen the trade deficit in the short-run. But financial liberalization in the external sector is also an essential part of the Washington Consensus. And there are other pressures for a rapid integration into international financial markets. The economy then needs a high interest rate and strong exchange rate regime to sustain such inflows in terms of profitability and confidence. This erodes the competitiveness of exports in the world market and of import-substitutes in the domestic market. Trade deficits become larger. Yet, governments keep the exchange rate pegged to ensure that the confidence of portfolio investors is not disturbed. The persistent, if not mounting, overvaluation means that domestic firms are exposed to competition from foreign goods through imports and from foreign firms through entry.[5] Many domestic firms may be forced to close down and, in some sectors, such exit may be widespread. Over time, larger current account deficits require larger portfolio investment flows which, beyond a point, undermine confidence and create adverse expectations even if the government resists a devaluation. And, ultimately, an exchange rate depreciation is inevitable. However, by the time this adjustment takes place and the overvaluation is undone, hysteresis effects could be strong. This means that re-entry becomes difficult, for domestic firms must create new capacities to capture the opportunities created by the changed set of relative prices.

The change in policy regimes can influence the investment behaviour of firms in the long-term. Trade liberalization, industrial deregulation, and financial liberalization bring about far-reaching changes in the rules of the game. These structural reforms are usually combined with a sharp adjustment in relative prices. This increases both uncertainty and risk. The uncertainty

---

[5]Such an overvaluation, with similar consequences, may be attributable to monetary contraction or fiscal expansion, as in the United States during the first half of the 1980s. And there was a literature that examined the *hysteresis* effects of the persistent overvaluation of the US dollar. The upshot of this literature was that overvaluation leads to an accumulation of adverse trade effects which ultimately need to be remedied through an overdepreciation. The reason is that, in the presence of *hysteresis,* a period of sustained undervaluation is needed to bring forth the required investment. For a discussion, see Dornbusch (1987).

increases for two reasons. First, if the prices are volatile,[6] firms find it difficult to form hypotheses about price behaviour on which to base investment decisions. Second, if the credibility of the government is not high, firms may believe that the reforms are neither sustainable nor irreversible and thus decide to wait until the rules of the game are seen to be established. The decision to wait-and-see may lead firms to defer investment decisions. Investment hold-ups mean output forgone.[7] More important, such perceptions or expectations dampen investment in the long-term. But that is not all. The increase in the degree of openness in the form of trade flows, investment flows, and technology flows, may change both the perception and the reality of risk. Domestic firms would see investment decisions as distinctly more risky than earlier. And some risk-averse firms may even prefer investing in a portfolio of financial assets rather than in physical capital.[8] The end result, once again, would be a dampening of investment in the long-term.

It is clear that investment may be squeezed through the large-scale exit of firms at a micro-level. But the problem may be accentuated on the demand side at a macro-level through an acceleration-type effect. The initial fall in investment would reduce aggregate demand, leading to a reduction in the size of the domestic market through the multiplier and consequently a further fall in investment.

The process of contraction in domestic demand is set in motion not only by investment (expenditure) but also by consumption (expenditure). Import liberalization switches domestic demand away from home-produced goods to foreign goods. The adverse effect on output, and hence on employment, would not end there. It would be magnified through the multiplier effect.[9] As inefficient firms exit, the initial contraction in employment would multiply through the consequent decline in purchasing power, reducing output and employment elsewhere in the economy, even in industries which are not so inefficient, through successive rounds of the same multiplier mechanism. Thus, the contractionary effect would be a multiple of the initial increase in

---

[6]In situations where sectors or markets are differentiated by structural characteristics— say some are flex-price while others are fix-price—their response to shocks would be different, thus adding volatility to the inflationary process. For a discussion on the complications that may arise under such circumstances, see Taylor (1988) and Nayyar (1996).

[7]Uncertainty may lead to investment hold-ups even when prices are right (Bernanke 1983).

[8]This argument is developed by Mohanty (1996).

[9]Bhaduri and Nayyar (1996). See also Bhaduri and Skarstein (1996), who formulate a similar argument to analyse the macroeconomic consequences of aid-financed imports in a foreign-exchange-constraint situation.

imports. Insofar as the demand for capital goods is a derived demand, a contraction in the demand for output would reduce the size of the market and dampen investment.

Structural reform simply seeks to improve the expected profitability of private investment. This is necessary but cannot be sufficient. It must be associated with animal spirits of entrepreneurs and an increase in investment by firms. The excessive concern with the productivity of investment is disproportionate. It can turn into a serious problem if, as a result, we lose sight of the level of investment (in real terms) at a micro-level and the rate of investment (as a proportion of national income) at a macro-level. The reason is clear enough. Economic growth can come, in part, from an increase in the productivity of investment. But only in part. Ultimately, sustained economic growth also requires an increase in the rate of investment. And if the rate of investment is much lower than before, it would require a corresponding increase in the productivity of investment just to maintain the earlier rate of economic growth.[10] This is simple arithmetic. It must also be recognized that the level and productivity of investment are interdependent variables that tend to move together. Consider a situation in which there is a fall in the level of investment. This would reduce aggregate demand. It would, in turn, lower capacity utilization. The capital–output ratio would rise as a consequence. The average rate of profit would decline.[11] And a fall in investment may follow. It is clear that a drop in investment will also dampen productivity growth. This can only harm the prospects of economic growth in the future.

Short-termism, then, may exercise an important influence on the growth potential of an economy in the long-term. The examples of trade liberalization and financial liberalization in the external sector illustrate how it may stifle the capabilities of domestic firms through *hysteresis* effects. Similarly, trade liberalization, together with structural reforms, may adversely effect the investment behaviour of firms through an increase in uncertainty and risk. But that is not all. It may dampen investment at a macro-level through an interaction of the multiplier mechanism and the acceleration principle. This could also dampen productivity growth.

[10]For a discussion, see Nayyar (1996).

[11]The causation outlined here is analysed by Bhaduri and Marglin (1990). It is set out in the form of an equation: $r = R/K = (R/Y)(Y/Y^*)(Y^*/K)$, where R denotes profit, K is the book value of capital, Y is the actual output, and Y^* is the full capacity output. It shows that the average rate of profit (r) depends definitionally on the profit margin/share (R/Y) and the degree of capacity utilization (Y/Y*) where the output–capital ratio at full capacity (Y*/K) is assumed as given in the short period.

The Neglect of Long-Term Objectives

The process of economic reform is either strategy-based or crisis-driven. There are relatively few examples of strategy-based reform except for the success stories among the East Asian countries. Crisis-driven reform is much more common : a crisis in the economy mostly on account of external debt provided the impetus in Latin America, sub-Saharan Africa, and South Asia, while a collapse of the political system gave the push in Eastern Europe. The probability of success or failure is strongly influenced by the economic or political origins of the reform process. Economic reform that represents a natural transition in the strategy of development can both sustain and succeed in part because it creates a capacity to manage problems of transition. Economic reform which is crisis-driven, irrespective of whether the crisis is an external shock or an internal convulsion, is more difficult to sustain and less likely to succeed. The reasons are manifold and complex.[12] But there is one which merits attention in the context of this essay.

The preoccupation with stabilization in the short-term and adjustment or reform in the medium-term, which is natural for multilateral financial institutions (the IMF and the World Bank, respectively), leads to confusion between tactics and strategies or means and ends in the minds of governments. This often leads to a neglect of long-term development objectives. There are two reasons for this. First, such objectives cannot be defined in terms of performance criteria, in the sphere of economics, laid down by the multilateral financial institutions. Second, such objectives do not bring tangible gains, in the realm of politics, which can be exploited by governments within one term as they seek to renew their mandate in the next elections. Yet, economic development cannot do without a longer time horizon. In a long-term perspective, the development of human resources and the acquisition of technological capabilities are examples of such objectives, the neglect of which could turn out to be most problematic.

Short-termism almost inevitably means a neglect of education and human resource development because there are no visible economic returns or obvious political constituencies. Indeed, stabilization and adjustment programmes almost always lead to a contraction in the real value of resources provided for education. Unless an economy invests enough in human beings, productivity increases may not follow structural reform and in the absence of sufficiently developed human resources the benefits of integrating with the world economy

---

[12]These reasons are discussed, at some length, in Nayyar (1996).

will simply elude it. The spread of education in society was, in a sense, crucial for the economic development of late industrializers, particularly the success stories of East Asia that are now perceived as role models. But the significance of the lessons which emerge from this experience is lost in a world of short time horizons. Such neglect, however, has implications and consequences that are serious. For human resource development is both a means and an end. It is a means of raising levels of productivity and mobilizing labour, the most abundant resource, for the purpose of development. It is an end insofar as it makes a basic contribution to an improvement in the quality of life for people as individuals and for society at large. Education, then, is not simply a part of the social infrastructure or social consumption. It is a priority, not only for the present but also for the future. The relative importance of its components may change over time in conformity with the stage of development: from primary education and adult literacy through vocational education to higher education, technical education or professional education. But investing in human beings is always important at every stage of development. The returns to society may accrue after a time lag but are always high.

The acquisition of technological capabilities at a micro-level and the development of technologies at a macro-level are fundamental in the process of industrialization. The former shapes efficiency of production by firms in the manufacturing sector, while the latter influences growth of productivity in industry and in the economy as a whole. These dimensions of industrialization, however, do not figure in the Washington Consensus which treats technology as a non-issue or a black box. The inherent short-termism also leads to a neglect of such development objectives the realisation of which takes a long time.

At the micro-level, the strong emphasis on allocative efficiency in the Washington Consensus is matched by a conspicuous silence on technical efficiency. It is forgotten that low levels of productivity in most developing countries are attributable more to technical inefficiency than to allocative inefficiency. And intra-country differences, as also intra-firm differences, in technical efficiency are explained, in large part, by differences in technological (and managerial) capabilities at a micro-level. These capabilities determine not just efficiency in the short-run but also competitiveness in the long-run. But given the nature of the learning process, such capabilities are both firm-specific and path-dependent.[13] The new orthodoxy simply ignores this critical dimension on the supply side. In contrast, the heterodox literature places the acquisition and development of technological capabilities at the centre stage

---

[13]Rosenberg (1994).

in the story of success at industrialization.[14] It also shows that the presumed relationship between trade liberalization and technical efficiency is dubious in terms of both theory and evidence.[15]

At the macro-level, the Washington Consensus simply stresses that there must be a liberal access to imports of technology. This is important. But an industrializing economy must be able to make a transition from importation through absorption and adaptation to diffusion and innovation, at least in some sectors, so that the acquisition of technology through imports is, after a time, followed by the development of domestic technological capabilities.[16] An open regime for the import of technology cannot suffice, for the discipline of the market cannot restrain the recurrence of such imports by domestic firms time after time. Such firms are much like the school boy who can always find someone else to write his examinations for him year after year and thus never learns. Domestic technological capabilities may not emerge either because there is no incentive to learn (imports are possible) or because they are stifled (imports are better). The problem may be accentuated in sectors where technical progress is rapid and obsolescence is high. The new orthodoxy forgets that the role of the government is crucial in planning technological development across sectors and over time. This means planning for the acquisition of technology where it is to be imported, setting aside resources for technology where it is to be produced at home, or even deciding to opt out of a technology where it is not needed. For this purpose, it is necessary to formulate a policy regime for the import of technology, allocate resources for R&D and evolve government procurement policies.

In the long-term, the spread of education in society, the acquisition of technological (and managerial) capabilities at a micro-level, and the development of technology at a macro-level are the essential foundations of international competitiveness. Indeed, there is no country that has succeeded at industrialization without attaining these objectives. And, it is one of the unambiguous lessons of recent economic history that the role of the government is critical in each of these pursuits. What is more, strategic forms of State intervention

[14]See, for example, Lall (1997). See also Bell and Pavitt (1993) and Pack and Westphal (1986).

[15]In an essay which analyses the relationship between trade policy and technical efficiency, based on theory and experience, Rodrik (1992, p. 172) reaches the following conclusion : 'If truth-in-advertising were to apply to policy advice, each prescription for trade liberalization would be accompanied with a disclaimer : Warning! Trade liberalization cannot be shown to enhance technical efficiency; nor has it been empirically demonstrated to do so'.

[16]Nayyar (1997).

interlinked across sectors and over time are necessary to attain such long-term objectives of development.[17] Their neglect represents the danger of short-termism in public policies.

REFERENCES

Bell, M. and K. Pavitt (1993), 'Accumulating Technological Capability in Developing Countries', *Proceedings of the World Bank Annual Conference on Development Economics 1992,* pp. 257–81, World Bank, Washington, DC.

Bernanke, B. (1983), 'Irreversibility, Uncertainty and Cyclical Investment', *Quarterly Journal of Economics,* Vol. 98, pp. 85–106.

Bhaduri, A. (1996), 'Dynamic Patterns in Transformation', *Structural Change and Economic Dynamics,* Vol. 7, pp. 281–97.

Bhaduri, A. and S. Marglin (1990), 'Unemployment and the Real Wage: The Economic Basis for Contesting Political Ideologies', *Cambridge Journal of Economics,* Vol. 14, pp. 375–93.

Bhaduri, A. and D. Nayyar (1996), *The Intelligent Person's Guide to Liberalization,* Penguin Books, New Delhi.

Bhaduri, A. and R. Skarstein (1996), 'Short-Period Macroeconomic Aspects of Foreign Aid', *Cambridge Journal of Economics,* Vol. 20, pp. 195–206.

Dornbusch, R. (1987), 'Exchange Rate Economics', *Economic Journal,* Vol. 97, pp. 1–18.

Evenson, R.E. and L. Westphal (1995), 'Technological Change and Technological Strategy', in J. Behrman and T.N. Srinivasan (eds), *Handbook of Development Economics,* Vol. 3, North-Holland, Amsterdam.

Lall, S. (1997), 'Imperfect Markets and Fallible Governments: The Role of the State in Industrial Development', in D. Nayyar (ed.), *Trade and Industrialization,* Oxford University Press, New Delhi.

McLaren, J. (1997), 'Size, Sunk Costs and Judge Bowker's Objection to Free Trade', *American Economic Review,* Vol. 87, pp. 400–20.

Mohanty, M. (1996), 'Restructuring of an Economy: The Mexican Experience after the 1982 Debt Crisis', unpublished PhD dissertation, Centre for Economic Studies and Planning, Jawaharlal Nehru University, New Delhi.

Nayyar, D. (1996), *Economic Liberalization in India: Analytics, Experience and Lessons,* Orient Longman, Calcutta.

——(1997), 'Themes in Trade and Industrialization', in D. Nayyar (ed.), *Trade and Industrialization,* Oxford University Press, New Delhi.

Pack, H. and L. Westphal (1986), 'Industrial Strategy and Technological Change: Theory versus Reality', *Journal of Development Economics,* Vol. 22, pp. 87–128.

---

[17]For a discussion on the role of the State, in particular strategic intervention, to attain long-term objectives of development, see Nayyar (1997).

Rodrik, D. (1992), 'Closing the Productivity Gap: Does Trade Liberalization Really Help?', in G.K. Helleiner (ed.), *Trade Policy, Industrialization and Development,* Clarendon Press, Oxford.

Rosenberg, N. (1994), *Exploring the Black Box: Technology, Economics and History,* Cambridge University Press, Cambridge.

Taylor, L. (1988), *Varieties of Stabilization Experience: Towards Sensible Macroeconomics in the Third World,* Clarendon Press, Oxford.

Chapter 7

WORK, LIVELIHOODS, AND RIGHTS*

The world changed almost beyond recognition during the last quarter of the twentieth century, not only in the sphere of economics but also in the realm of politics. For one, national economies became ever more closely integrated through cross-border flows of trade, investment, and finance. For another, there was a profound change in the political situation, as communism collapsed and capitalism emerged triumphant. In both domains, the 1990s were particularly eventful. And the consequences for the life and work of people have been far-reaching.

The object of this essay is to analyse the implications of the changed national context, characterized by a growing enthusiasm for liberalization, and the changed international context, shaped by the gathering momentum of globalization, for work, livelihoods, and rights, from a development perspective. The structure of the chapter is as follows. The first section explores the changes in the world of work. The second section discusses the response of trade unions to these changes. The third section examines why such changes are reshaping livelihoods. The fourth section analyses how markets exclude people, the impact of which may extend beyond an economic exclusion from livelihood. The fifth section considers the profound change in thinking about rights, from a narrow legal perspective to a much wider canvas of social ethics. The sixth section argues that this is not just consistent with, but reflects important changes in thinking about development. The last section concludes.

WORK

The world of work is diverse. Every person works in one way or another. But not everyone is employed. A significant proportion of this work, however, is not sufficiently recognized or adequately rewarded. There are many who work hard for a living. There are a few who hardly work and yet lead a comfortable

*I would like to thank Padmanabha Gopinath and John Harriss for helpful suggestions.

life. There are some who work very hard but do not earn enough for a living. There are others who work but are not paid for their labour. The reality is complex indeed. Its complexity is not captured even by the perceptive statement that 'the world is full of over-worked and unemployed people.'[1]

It is not surprising that analysis of work is characterized by abstractions where the focus is on the parts and not on the whole. The domain of concern is often restricted to narrower groups, such as workers in the organized sector, which leaves out the unorganized sector. The perspective is not always so narrow. But even when all wage workers are considered, the home-workers and the self-employed are left out. And, even if all people actively engaged in work are considered, the unemployed are left out.[2] Such abstractions, on the part of analysts, are understandable. For the concerns and interests differ across groups.

This cannot be a substitute for a comprehensive approach. The totality can only be understood through a universal coverage. The world of work includes *all* workers wherever they are and whatever they do: not just workers in the organized sector, but also workers in the unorganized sector and the informal sector; not only wage workers but also the home-workers and the self-employed. The objective of securing decent work for people everywhere, articulated by the International Labour Organization (ILO) not so long ago, is about the world of work in its totality.[3]

The reality, however, is also changing. The increasing importance of markets in the national context and the gathering momentum of globalization in the international context are exercising a profound influence on the world of work.

It is beginning to change the nature of work in industrial societies. High rates of unemployment have come to be accepted as a natural state of being. These are attributed to the nature of technical progress, which is replacing several unskilled workers with a few skilled workers, and the impact of macroeconomic policies, which have sought to maintain price stability at the expense of full employment. This is reinforced by the belief system that markets know best. The modes of adjustment in response to this reality differ across countries. In some, there is a work-sharing implicit in a reduction of working hours per day or working days per week. In others, there is a casualization of the workforce, as permanent employees in the workplace turn into contract workers at home who are engaged for limited durations or specified purposes,

---

[1]ILO (1999, pp. 3–4).

[2]For a discussion, see Sen (2000, pp. 120–1).

[3]In its conceptualization of decent work, the ILO is concerned with all workers (ILO 1999).

so that work no longer means what it did. For such people, there is no security of employment. As a corollary, superannuation benefits or health care benefits provided by the employer also cease.

It is creating sharper divides, as also greater disparities, between categories of work in poor countries. There are the privileged few, mostly professionals, at the top of the ladder of skills. Globalization has made them as mobile as capital. Indeed, we can think of them as globalized people who are employable almost anywhere in the world.[4] The world is their oyster. And their prosperity is almost unbound. It is, in a sense, a secession of the successful. At the same time, there is an erosion of rights at work, or security of employment, for wage labour in the organized sector. Orthodox economics describes it, almost innocently, as the introduction of flexibility in labour markets. This may affect only a small proportion of the total workforce. Even so, a change in the nature of its work exercises an important influence on the nature of work in the unorganized sector. In fact, it leads to a sharp dichotomization of, and dualism in, labour markets. Consequently, instead of integration, there is a further marginalization of workers, whether urban or rural, in the informal sector.

It is obvious that the world of work has become more complex and diverse with the passage of time. There is a growing recognition of this change. And the characterization of work is much more complete in its coverage. Consequently, there is an explicit shift in the focus from labour to work. It is also possible to discern a change in the nature of work. This change, which began on a modest note in the mid-1970s, gathered momentum in the late 1990s. But it is not sufficiently recognized. Nevertheless, there is an implicit shift in emphasis from workers as a class to workers as individuals. The inclusive characterization of work is an important step forward. But the much narrower characterization of workers is problematic because the microcosm cannot be a substitute for the macrocosm. There is no associated conception of social organization, or social dialogue, even if it needs to change. This outcome has been facilitated by the decline and fall of trade unions.

Trade Unions

The process of globalization has strengthened capital and weakened labour. It would be no exaggeration to suggest that the response of the trade union movement to the globalization of the world economy has simply been inadequate. In this context, it is important to make a distinction between trade unions in the advanced capitalist countries and those in the developing world. The trade union movement in the former was always much wider and

---

[4]This argument is developed, at some length, in Nayyar (2002a).

stronger than in the latter. But it seems that trade unions have experienced an erosion of their political significance and economic strength in both parts of the world.

Trade unions in the industrialized countries have, for the moment, lost the battle in the arena of both politics and economics. In the realm of politics, it began with the retreat of social democratic parties as State power was captured by conservative political parties. The same social democratic parties, after a time lag, adapted themselves to the changed reality with an ideological shift that could be described as right-of-centre in the political spectrum. But that is not all. The world of competing ideologies—capitalism versus communism—has now given way to a world with a single dominant ideology where capitalism is triumphant. Politics has then come to accept that markets know best. This outcome has been reinforced by three developments in the sphere of economics.

First, the trade union movement, based on its experience during the quarter century that followed the Second World War, came to think of full employment as a natural state of being. Consequently, it sought to bargain for the protection of, or increase in, real wages rather than concern itself with employment levels.

Second, the trade union movement made no attempt to change either its strategy or its tactics as most governments rejected the Keynesian world view and accepted the monetarist doctrine in the macro-management of economies. Margaret Thatcher and Ronald Reagan politicized the proposition that there is a trade-off between inflation and unemployment. Following the experience of the oil-shocks, which induced price increases, western societies opted for lower rates of inflation even if it meant higher levels of unemployment. This conservative economics found political acceptance even among trade unions.

Third, the trade union movement could not quite cope with the nature and the pace of technical progress which followed the microchip revolution. It displaced much labour at low-skill levels in existing activities but created little employment at high-skill levels in new activities.

It is clear that trade union responses to political and economic developments in the advanced capitalist countries, which led the process of globalization, were inadequate and confused. It is hardly surprising that trade unions in the developing countries, which were never comparable in terms of their base or their strength, fared no better.

It is ironical that the worsening employment situation has not led to any strengthening of the trade union movement in the developing countries or transitional economies. If anything, the trade union movement is weaker. The story is almost as true for democratic regimes as it is for authoritarian ones. Therefore, the explanation of this paradoxical situation lies not in any political repression of the trade union movement but in a political ideology which has gained widespread acceptance among the literati and the influential so as to marginalize trade unions as an economic and social force.

Trade unions have also not helped their own cause, for they have not recognized the significance of changed realities. For one, there is a discernible conflict of interests between workers in industrialized countries and in the developing world. For another, business is global while unions are national. What is more, the shift in the focus from labour to work has meant that unions are confined only to one segment of space in the world of work.

LIVELIHOODS

The changes in the nature of work mean that livelihoods no longer depend upon employment alone. And it is clear that work is necessary but not sufficient to ensure a livelihood. The quantity and the quality of work matter. For they must yield an income that is enough to meet basic needs or ensure material well-being. Therefore, livelihoods are shaped by incomes. Incomes are determined by the duration of work and the earnings from such work. Both can, and do, vary over time. Consequently, there is a discernible change in the sources of livelihoods everywhere.

In industrialized countries, the nature of technical progress which uses skilled labour and displaces unskilled labour, combined with the objective of macroeconomic policies to restrain inflation, has made employment creation and income opportunities curiously asymmetrical. For one, employment creation is limited. Even if it is at significantly higher wages, it constitutes a small proportion of the total workforce or the increases therein. It benefits only a few. For another, income opportunities for a large proportion of the workforce, including the unemployed, are provided through insecure employment or casual employment in low-wage occupations, essentially in the services sector.[5] This is the fate of many.

In developing countries, structural reforms associated with liberalization and globalization have important implications for employment creation and income opportunities. For one, insofar as such reforms increase the average productivity of labour, through the use of capital-intensive or labour-saving technologies or through a restructuring of firms which increases efficiency, they reduce the contribution of any given rate of economic growth to employment growth. For another, insofar as trade liberalization enforces closures rather than efficiency at a micro-level, or switches domestic demand away from home-

[5]The most obvious examples are fast-food chains or retail stores. Such employment in the provision of consumer services is often casual, always insecure, and mostly at low wages.

produced goods to foreign goods at a macro-level, it has an adverse effect on output, and hence employment, which is magnified through the multiplier effect. This has important consequences in the medium-term. There is a contraction of employment in some sectors without a compensatory expansion of employment in other sectors. And, as employment elasticities of output decline, employment creation slows down. For any given level of employment, the globalization of prices without a globalization of incomes also threatens livelihoods.[6] The poor, at the margin, are the most vulnerable. But the non-rich workers are not immune.

The living conditions of people are determined in large part by private consumption but also in part by social consumption. Private consumption, in turn, depends upon work for individuals and incomes of households. Social consumption, in turn, depends on public expenditure by the government in social sectors such as education, health care, or housing. The gathering momentum of liberalization and globalization has shifted the emphasis from equity to efficiency and from development to growth. In such a milieu, employment is no longer a means to the end, let alone an end in itself. This has obviously affected private consumption possibilities through its impact on livelihoods. It has also squeezed social consumption possibilities through cuts in public expenditure on social sectors. Such cuts begin life as an integral part of stabilization and adjustment programmes but become systemic because of the retreat of the State from the economy.

EXCLUSION

Joan Robinson once said: 'There is only one thing that is worse than being exploited by capitalists. And that is not being exploited by capitalists.' Much the same can be said for markets and globalization, which may not ensure prosperity for everyone but may, in fact, exclude a significant proportion of people.

The term *exclusion* has become a part of the lexicon of economists recently, although it has been in the jargon of sociology and the vocabulary of politics in Europe for somewhat longer. The phrase *social exclusion* is used to describe a situation, as also to focus on a process, which excludes individuals or groups from livelihoods and rights, thus depriving them of sources of well-being that have been assumed, if not taken for granted, in industrial countries.[7] The

[6]The implications of the globalization of prices without a globalization of incomes are considered elsewhere by the author. See Nayyar (2001).

[7]See Commission of the European Communities (1993). For an extensive discussion on social exclusion, ranging from conceptual issues through country studies to policy issues, see Rodgers et al. (1995).

essential point is that economic stratification is inevitable in market economies and societies, which systematically integrate some and marginalize others to distribute the benefits of economic growth in ways which include some and exclude others. Exclusion, then, is in the logic of markets.

Markets exclude people as consumers or buyers if they do not have any incomes, or sufficient incomes, which can be translated into purchasing power. Such people are excluded from the consumption of goods and services which are sold in the market. This exclusion is attributable to a lack of *entitlements*.[8] But they may also be excluded from the consumption of public goods and services if they live in clusters such as urban slums, or rural settlements, where drinking water, sanitation facilities, roads, electricity, or even street lights are not provided. It is, then, the location of the poor (and not their income) which deprives them of access to public services which may be (almost) free elsewhere.

Markets exclude people as producers or sellers if they have neither *assets* nor *capabilities*. People experience such exclusion if they do not have assets, physical or financial, which can be used (or sold) to yield an income in the form of rent, interest, or profits.[9] Even those without assets could enter the market as producers or sellers, using their labour, if they have some capabilities.[10] Such capabilities which are acquired through education, training, or experience are different from abilities which are endowed. But the distribution of capabilities may be just as unequal if not more so. It is these capabilities which can, in turn, yield an income in the form of wages. Hence, people without capabilities, the poor who cannot find employment, are excluded. In fact, even people with capabilities may be excluded from employment if there is no demand for their

[8]This term was first used by Sen (1981) in his work on poverty and famines.

[9]The rural poor in the developing world, who are landless, experience such exclusion. The landless are deprived not only of a source of livelihood but also of a status in society. Exclusion, then, is both economic and social.

[10]In this essay, I use the word *capabilities* to characterize the mix of natural talents, skills acquired through training, learning from experience, and abilities or expertise based on education, embodied in a person, that enable him or her to use these (capabilities as a producer or a worker) for which there is not only a price but also a demand in the market. It follows that even persons with capabilities may be excluded from employment if there is no demand for their capabilities in the (labour) market. It is essential to note that the same word, *capabilities*, has been used in a very different sense by Amartya Sen, who argues that the well-being of a person depends on what the person succeeds in *doing* with the commodities (and their characteristics) at his command. For example: food can provide nutrition to a healthy person but not to a person with a parasitic disease; or, a bicycle can provide transportation to an able-bodied person but not to a disabled person. Thus, for Sen (1985), *capabilities* characterize the combination of functionings a person can achieve, given his personal features (conversion of characteristics into functionings) and his command over commodities (entitlements).

capabilities in the (labour) market.[11] And, in the ultimate analysis, such capabilities are defined by the market. That is the problem.

An economic exclusion from livelihood often creates or accentuates a political exclusion from rights. Thus, for the poor in a democracy, the right to vote may exist in principle, but in practice it may be taken away by coercion or coaxed away by material incentives at the time of elections. Similarly, the very poor are vulnerable to exploitation or oppression because their civil rights or equality before the law exist in principle but are difficult to protect or preserve in practice. The reason is simple. They do not have the resources to claim or the power to assert their rights.

Exclusion extends beyond the economic and the political spheres to the social sphere. The social manifestations of exclusion can be powerful. This is best illustrated with an example from India where the underprivileged in society, such as the lower castes, are poor because they have little in the form of entitlements, assets, or capabilities, but even where they are better endowed in terms of these attributes, their exclusion from markets, particularly from the markets for land and labour in rural India, persists for social rather than economic reasons. At the same time, economic exclusion accentuates social exclusion, while social exclusion accentuates political exclusion.

It must be said that the nature of inclusion or exclusion matters.[12] Coercive inclusion by markets, whether child labour, tribal populations, or immigrant workers can be exploitative. The employment of women as wage labour on terms inferior to those of men, or the employment of migrants from rural areas in the unorganized urban sector, at wages lower than those of workers in the organized sector, provide other examples. The basic point is that inclusion which is coercive or on inferior terms is not desirable. For similar reasons, coercive exclusion from markets is bad. The denial of access to the labour market, for bonded labour, is much worse than exploitative. The denial of access to product markets, for tenants or share-croppers is also exploitative. In such situations, the freedom to enter markets and to participate in economic inter-change can itself be a significant contribution,[13] even if markets themselves are characterized by exclusion.

---

[11]Open unemployment means simply exclusion from the labour market. But there is also exclusion within the labour market experienced by those who are underemployed in the agricultural sector and by those who are self-employed or in casual employment in the urban informal sector. The segmented labour market means that access to good jobs which are secure and well-paid is exceedingly difficult whereas access to bad jobs which are insecure and poorly paid is easier.

[12]The preceding analysis of exclusion draws upon earlier work of the author (Nayyar 2003).

[13]For a more detailed discussion, see Sen (1999).

It is only the State that can, and should, introduce correctives to pre-empt exclusion or interventions to limit the adverse effects of exclusion. The reason is simple. Governments are accountable to their people, whereas markets are not. Yet, the dominant ideology of our times, driven by an enthusiasm for markets and globalization, seeks to roll back the government wherever possible so that it approximates to the ideal of a minimalist State. The irony of the situation is striking.

RIGHTS

The conventional view about rights at work is limited. Its domain and perspective is essentially legal. More often than not, it is confined to the existing labour legislation. At best, its scope is enlarged to include the possibilities of establishing more legal rights through new legislation. Rights-based thinking, however, extends much beyond the recognition of rights of workers. It begins from the premise that some basic rights are an integral part of a decent society, irrespective of whether or not there is supportive legislation.[14] Such rights are thus seen as a prior to legal recognition. And their realization requires public action in the economic, social, or political spheres, for the enactment of laws, even if necessary, cannot be sufficient. This shift in emphasis from the limited domain of a legal perspective to a much broader arena of social ethics is an essential part of the ILO Declaration on Rights at Work and the evolving approach of the United Nations on human rights. But that is not all. It also reflects the change in thinking about development.

Is there, then, a conflict between the traditional view, which is based on legal rights and socially accepted principles of justice, on the one hand, and rights-based reasoning which stresses goal-based formulations of social ethics, on the other? For example, it is possible that there is a conflict between the legal priority of individual rights and the ethical primacy of social objectives. Some legal theorists believe that there is, indeed, some tension, if not conflict between these two perspectives.[15] Amartya Sen thinks not and argues that, even if there is, the conflict does not run deep. There could be a real impasse if we want to make the fulfilment of each right a matter of absolute adherence, as some liberatarians would, with no room for acceptable trade-offs. If we do

---

[14]This is reflected in the *ILO Declaration on Fundamental Principles and Rights at Work* (1998). For the text of the Declaration, see *International Labour Review*, Vol. 137, No. 2, pp. 253–7.

[15]See, for example, Dworkin (1977).

not live in an either–or world, so that trade-offs are allowed, it should be possible to value the realization of legal rights and the fulfilment of social goals.[16]

Another question arises. Can such rights exist without corresponding obligations? For philosophers and lawyers, there can be no rights without duties. It is true that the realization of rights is easier in a world where there are co-specified obligations. That is, in fact, the logic of legal systems. But rights-based reasoning has a different, wider perspective. In this world view, human rights are a prior. It is possible that such rights remain unrealized. But the non-fulfilment of these rights cannot be a reason for a denial of rights just because there are no corresponding obligations.

The debate around these two questions is not so much about words as it is about substance. Amartya Sen believes that the use of the word 'rights' in a political or moral discourse is simply not the same as the use of the word 'rights' in a legal system. Therefore, he concludes that ... 'the idea of rights is neither in tension with a broadly goal-based ethical framework, nor ruled out by some presumed necessity of perfect obligations allegedly needed to make sense of the idea of rights'.[17]

This emerging concern with rights is perhaps part of an increasing consciousness about human rights, where workers' rights constitute an important subset. There are important underlying reasons that are not in the realm of jurisprudence and philosophy. For one, new communications technologies, which have provided a momentum to globalization, have also increased access to information about abuses or denials of rights. Until not so long ago, this was easily hidden behind national borders. For another, even as trade unions have declined, civil society in general and non-government organizations in particular, are increasingly proactive. These actors have capabilities in the form of *advocacy* and *protest* which seems to have replaced *representation* and *bargaining* by trade unions.

The change in thinking about rights has also been shaped by the change in thinking about development. If human well-being is the purpose of development, meeting basic human needs for all and ensuring decent work for people must be fundamental objectives. Rights-based reasoning is consistent with, and could be seen as a part of, this perspective. It is not surprising that there is a rethinking about rights in the context of work. The traditional view

[16]In support of this argument, Sen cites an interesting example. The rights of those at work can be considered along with, and not instead of, the interests of the unemployed. For a lucid discussion of the possible conflicts or trade-offs between rights and goals, see Sen (2000).

[17]Sen (2000, p.125).

was concerned with the legal assertion of rights. The emerging view is concerned with the realization of rights in a wider economic, social, and political context. Until recently, rights at work were simply a juridical issue. But rights at work are a part of the development agenda now. The ILO *Declaration on Fundamental Principles and Rights at Work* is a major step in this direction. The traditional perspective of the ILO was about legal rights of labour at the workplace.[18] Interestingly enough, even this bastion of conventional thinking on labour has shifted its emphasis to *workers* and *development*.

DEVELOPMENT

There is a vast literature on economic development which is rich in terms of range and depth. Yet, there is not enough clarity about the meaning of development. There are many different views. And perceptions have changed over time. There is, however, an irreducible minimum which may be construed as the essential meaning. Development must bring about an improvement in the living conditions of people. It should, therefore, ensure the provision of basic human needs for all: not just food and clothing but also shelter, health care, and education. This simple but powerful proposition is often forgotten in the pursuit of material wealth and the conventional concerns of economics. The early literature on development emphasized economic growth and capital accumulation at a macro level. The contemporary literature on development emphasizes economic efficiency and productivity increases at a micro level. Industrialization has always been seen as an essential attribute of development. The emphasis has simply shifted from the pace of industrialization to the efficiency of industrialization. The underlying presumption is that economic growth and economic efficiency are not only necessary but are also sufficient for bringing about an improvement in the living conditions of people. From time to time, dissenting voices questioned the conventional wisdom about economic growth, or increases in per capita income, as a measure of development, to suggest other indicators of development, such as a reduction in poverty, inequality, and unemployment, that would capture changes in the quality of life.[19] But these aspects of development were largely ignored by mainstream economics. For it did not make a distinction between means and ends.

---

[18]In keeping with its origins, the ILO always paid most attention to the needs of wage workers, the majority of them men, in formal enterprises in the organized sector. The concept of *decent work* articulated by the ILO represents a fundamental departure because its concerns extend much beyond the formal labour market to workers in the unorganized sector, the self-employed, and the home workers. See ILO (1999).

[19]See, for example, Seers (1972).

Economic growth and economic efficiency, or for that matter industrialization, are means. It is development which is an end. Thus, growth and efficiency need to be combined with full employment, poverty eradication, reduced inequality, human development, and a sustainable environment, to attain development. The purpose of development, after all, is to create a milieu that enables people, ordinary people, to lead a good life.

In conventional terms, the world has made enormous economic progress during the second half of the twentieth century. At the same time, economic disparities between regions and between people within countries have registered an increase. In other words, many parts of the world and a significant proportion of its people have been largely excluded from development. This may be attributable to the logic of markets, which give to those who have and take away from those who have not, as the process of cumulative causation leads to market-driven virtuous and vicious circles. This may be the outcome of patterns of development where economic growth is uneven between regions and the distribution of its benefits is unequal between people, so that there is growing affluence for some combined with persistent poverty for many. This may be the consequence of strategies of development, as a similar economic performance in the aggregate could lead to egalitarian development in one situation, and growth which bypasses the majority of people in another situation.

Uneven development is not without consequences for people. Poverty, inequality, and deprivation persist. And there is poverty everywhere, not only in the developing world or in transitional economies, but also in industrial societies. Economic inequalities have increased during the last quarter of a century as the income gap between rich and poor countries, between rich and poor people within countries, as also between the rich and the poor in the world's population has widened.[20]

The exclusion of countries and of people from development has become much less acceptable with the passage of time. The proposition that economic growth, or economic efficiency, will ultimately improve the lot of the people is, obviously, far less credible now than it was in 1950. The democratization of polities, even if it is much slower than the marketization of economies, has enhanced the importance of time in the quest for development. For almost three-fourth of the world's people now live in pluralistic societies with democratic regimes. And even authoritarian regimes need more legitimacy from their people. Poverty or austerity now for prosperity later is no longer an acceptable trade-off, for people who want development here and now.

[20]For a discussion, as also sources of evidence, see Nayyar (2000).

This reality, perhaps, provides the essential foundations of the emerging literature on the right to development.[21] It also finds an elegant statement in Amartya Sen's conception of development as freedom.[22] There are strong interconnections between political freedoms, social opportunities, and economic capabilities. The removal of fetters on freedoms, or the expansion of freedoms that people enjoy, is constitutive of development. More freedom for people, in this world view, is both the primary end and the principal means of development. It would seem that the change in thinking about rights mirrors the change in thinking about development.

CONCLUSION

The world of work has become complex and diverse. The characterization of work is more complete, so that there is an explicit shift in the focus from labour to work. It is also possible to discern a change in the nature of work. And there is an implicit shift in emphasis from workers as a class to workers as individuals. This outcome has been facilitated by the decline and fall of trade unions, which are now simply confined to one segment of space in the world of work because of their failure to recognize the significance of changed realities.

The changes in the nature of work also mean that livelihoods no longer depend upon employment alone. Even work is necessary but not sufficient. What matters is the income it yields. There is a threat to livelihoods everywhere. Levels of unemployment are much higher. And employment creation has slowed down. Income opportunities are provided by insecure or casual employment. The poor, at the margin, are the most vulnerable. The problem is compounded by exclusion which is in the logic of markets. Markets exclude people as producers or sellers if they have neither assets nor capabilities. An economic exclusion from livelihood often creates or accentuates a political exclusion from rights.

There is a significant change in thinking about rights, from a narrow legal perspective to a much wider canvas of social ethics. The traditional view was concerned with the legal assertion of rights, so that rights at work was simply a juridical issue. The emerging view is concerned with the realization of rights in a wider economic, social, and political context, so that rights at work are a part of the development agenda. The change in thinking about rights reflects the change in thinking about development. And, even if development has

[21]For a comprehensive survey of the literature on the right to development, see Sengupta (2002).

[22]See Sen (1999).

not brought about an improvement in the living conditions of ordinary people, it is increasingly recognized that the welfare of humankind is the essence of development.

It would seem that markets and globalization are transforming the nature of work. In this world, workers are individuals rather than a class. Trade unions are marginalized. Livelihoods are at risk. Income opportunities are provided by insecure or casual employment. At the same time, the limited legal perspective of rights at work is being replaced by a concern about the rights of people in the wider context of development in the much broader arena of social ethics. The mismatch between the emerging reality and the emerging thinking is striking. It is possible to bridge this gap only through correctives and interventions in national development strategies.[23] That would make for a more egalitarian development, which can only be introduced by the State because, unlike markets, governments are accountable to their people. The realization of rights as a part of the development agenda would also reshape the world of work and of livelihoods.

REFERENCES

Commission of the European Communities (1993), *Towards a Europe of Solidarity: Intensifying the Fight against Social Exclusion and Fostering Integration*, EC, Brussels.

Dworkin, Ronald (1977), *Taking Rights Seriously*, Duckworth, London.

ILO (1999), *Decent Work*, Report of the Director General, International Labour Conference, 87th Session, International Labour Office, Geneva.

Nayyar, Deepak (2000), 'Globalization and Development Strategies', High-Level Roundtable on Trade and Development at UNCTAD X. TD X/RT.1/4, United Nations, New York and Geneva.

_____ (2001), 'Globalization: What Does it Mean for Development?', in KS Jomo and S. Nagaraj (eds), *Globalization versus Development*, Palgrave, London.

_____ (2002a), 'Cross-Border Movements of People', in Deepak Nayyar (ed.), *Governing Globalization: Issues and Institutions*, Oxford University Press, Oxford.

_____ (2003), 'On Exclusion and Inclusion: Democracy, Markets and People', in Amitava Krishna Dutt and Jaime Ros (eds), *Development Economics and Structuralist Macroeconomics*, Edward Elgar, Cheltenham.

Rodgers, G., C. Gore, and J. Figueiredo (1995), *Social Exclusion: Rhetoric, Reality, Responses*, International Labour Organization, Geneva.

Seers, Dudley (1972), 'What are We Trying to Measure?', in N. Baster (ed.), *Measuring Development*, Frank Cass, London.

Sengupta, Arjun (2002), 'On the Theory and Practice of the Right to Development', *Human Rights Quarterly*, Vol. 24, No. 4, pp. 837–89.

---

[23]For an analysis of such correctives and interventions, see Nayyar (2000).

Sen, Amartya (1981), *Poverty and Famines: An Essay on Entitlement and Deprivation*, Clarendon Press, Oxford.

_____ (1985), *Commodities and Capabilities*, North-Holland, Amsterdam.

_____ (1999), *Development as Freedom*, Oxford University Press, Oxford.

_____ (2000), 'Work and Rights', *International Labour Review*, Vol. 139, No. 2, pp. 119–28.

UNDP (1999), *Human Development Report 1999*, Oxford University Press, New York.

PART 3
INDUSTRIALIZATION

Chapter 8

INTERNATIONAL RELOCATION OF PRODUCTION AND INDUSTRIALIZATION IN LESS DEVELOPED COUNTRIES*

INTRODUCTION

The internationalization of production is nothing new, nor is the participation of poor countries in the process. Indeed, since the turn of the century, large firms from metropolitan countries have sought to integrate the less developed countries into their production activities. The nature of this involvement has, of course, changed over time.

It might be useful to place the transition in historical perspective. The first stage of foreign investment in the Third World was one of resource exploitation, in which less developed countries provided raw materials and primary commodities to the industrialized countries. The next stage witnessed a shift of foreign investment into manufacturing for import substitution, the purpose of which was to secure the protected markets of less developed countries and to pre-empt potential competition. In the third stage—which relates directly to the subject of this essay—domestic resources or markets of poor countries have little significance, and the participation of transnational firms in *manufacturing for export* represents the incorporation of labour from less developed countries into an integrated corporate structure of manufacturing production which is spread across the world economy.

Thus, American firms employ a very large number of workers outside the US, British firms outside the UK, West German firms outside the Federal Republic, and Japanese firms outside Japan. To begin with, such relocation of production might have been confined to the advanced capitalist countries. However, during the period 1960–80, it has been extended to less developed countries in Latin America, Asia and, more recently, Africa. In fact, the ownership of capital and the location of production in the contemporary

*For critical comments and helpful suggestions on an earlier draft, which led to several improvements, I would like to thank Amiya Bagchi, Nirmal Chandra, Sushil Khanna, N. Krishnaji, Hans Singer, John Spraos, and Paul Streeten.

world has gone so far beyond national boundaries that it is sometimes difficult to identify the country of origin for a firm.

It has been argued, *albeit* for different reasons, that the first two phases—of resource exploitation and import substitution—were not conducive to industrialization and development in poor countries. On the other hand, the international division of labour emerging from the third phase, in which transnational corporations play a crucial role, is seen by some as a step towards the resolution of development problems. Briefly stated, the argument runs as follows.

Outward-looking policies which seek to promote industrial exports, frequently through foreign capital, remove the constraints imposed by the small size of the domestic market and lead to the adoption of technologies more suited to the needs of underdeveloped economies. Moreover, the pursuit of these policies means that production and trade in less developed countries is determined by comparative advantage, which not only leads to rapid economic growth but also represents an efficient utilization of resources on a world scale.

This recipe of outward-looking policies and export-led industrialization is not entirely new in the realm of economics.[1] In recent years, however, it has become more persuasive, as also fashionable, following the development experience of a small group of East Asian countries since the mid-1960s. The much cited success stories are Hong Kong, Singapore, South Korea, and Taiwan which not only achieved a phenomenal expansion in manufactured exports and attained very high, almost unprecedented, rates of economic growth, but also succeeded in bringing about an impressive structural transformation in their economies within a span of two decades. Similar export-led industrialization, in which labour-intensive exports and transnational corporations might play an important role, is now being advocated as a strategy of industrialization that would succeed across the board in poor countries.[2] In my view, such policy prescriptions are open to serious question simply because it might not be feasible to emulate and replicate this industrialization experience in a global context. I shall elaborate some of the reasons for my view later in the essay.

At the outset, it must be stressed that the debate on trade policies and economic development cuts across a wide range of controversial issues. A

[1]Indeed, the basic hypothesis can be traced back to the days of classical political economy. In the contemporary literature on development economies, a clear statement of this position can be found in Keesing (1967) and Little, Scitovsky, and Scott (1970). Of course there are numerous other contributions.

[2]See, for example, Myint (1972), ILO (1974), World Bank, *World Development Report, 1979*, Washington, DC, and Little (1981).

complete and systematic discussion of these issues, however, is beyond the scope of the present exercise. The object of this essay is a limited one. It seeks to analyse trends in the international relocation of manufacturing production during the period 1960–80 and to consider its implications for industrialization in less developed countries. To situate the discussion in its wider context, the first section attempts to provide a broad quantitative assessment of the participation by less developed countries in world industrialization and trade; it also examines the distribution of output and trade in manufactures among less developed countries. The second section narrows the focus and outlines the available evidence on the relocation of manufacturing production in less developed countries by transnational corporations. The third section explores, briefly, the economic factors underlying such international relocation of production. The fourth section discusses the possibilities and prospects of replicating or generalizing the East Asian experience of export-led industrialization in other less developed countries. The last section tentatively examines the wider implications for less developed countries which might traverse a similar path on the road to industrialization.[3]

WORLD TRADE AND OUTPUT OF MANUFACTURES: DIMENSIONS OF PARTICIPATION BY LESS DEVELOPED COUNTRIES

The world economy experienced an unprecedented rate of industrial growth and a remarkable expansion in international trade for a quarter of a century in the post-war era. It is important to recognize that much of this growth in the output of, and trade in, manufactures was confined to the industrialized countries which, taken together, accounted for a little more than 90 per cent of world value-added in manufacturing and a slightly higher proportion of world trade in manufactures throughout this period. Available evidence highlights the imbalances and inequities associated with the distribution of population, income, and industrial production among the countries in the world. At the end of the 1970s, for example, 71.4 per cent of the world population lived in the less developed countries, while the share of less developed countries in world income was 17.1 per cent and their share in manufacturing value-added was a mere 10.7 per cent.[4] This unequal distribution has characterized the position of the less developed countries in the world economy for a long time.

---

[3]This essay, published in 1983, seeks to focus on the period 1960–80 in terms of both evidence and analysis. It is reprinted in this volume without any changes except for some minor editing.

[4]These figures relate to 1979. The share of less developed countries in world population and world income has been calculated from the data in the *World Bank Atlas 1981*.

Table 8.1: Share of Less Developed Countries in
World Manufacturing Value-added

Year	Percentage Share	Year	Percentage Share
1960	8.2	1971	9.1
1961	8.4	1972	9.3
1962	8.2	1973	9.4
1963	8.1	1974	9.8
1964	8.3	1975	10.3
1965	8.2	1976	10.3
1966	8.2	1977	10.4
1967	8.2	1978	10.5
1968	8.3	1979	10.7
1969	8.4	1980	10.9
1970	8.8		

Note: The shares are estimated at constant 1975 prices.
Source: UNIDO (1981).

The international relocation of manufacturing production in the less developed world should, in the ultimate analysis, be reflected in the participation of the less developed countries in world industrialization and trade. As a first step, therefore, it is necessary to examine the evidence on the share of less developed countries in world industrial production and world trade in manufactures, and also to trace the changes in these shares over time. Such a global perspective is rather important, but it might conceal the uneven distribution of output and trade in manufactures among less developed countries. Thus the next step should be to consider the evidence at a disaggregated level and to highlight the relative importance of the more industrialized economies among the less developed countries.

The share of less developed countries in world manufacturing value-added, over the period from 1960 to 1980, is outlined in Table 8.1. This share was stable at a little over 8 per cent throughout the 1960s, which suggests that industrialization in less developed countries kept pace with the rapid industrial growth in the rest of the world. In contrast, during the 1970s, this share registered a slow but steady increase, from 8.8. per cent in 1970 to 10.9 per cent in 1980, which is attributable to the sustained pace of industrialization in the less developed countries combined with a discernible slowdown in the rates of growth in the industrialized world.[5]

. [5]For a discussion on this point, see UNIDO (1979).

Table 8.2: Share of Less Developed Countries in
World Manufactured Exports

	(*in US $billion at current prices*)		
Year	*Manufactured Exports from LDCs*	*Manufactured Exports from World*	*Percentage Share of LDCs*
1955	1.8	42.2	4.3
1960	2.5	65.6	3.8
1965	4.5	103.0	4.4
1970	9.7	190.2	5.1
1971	11.3	216.2	5.2
1972	14.8	258.9	5.7
1973	23.1	346.9	6.7
1974	31.1	458.3	6.8
1975	32.1	500.7	6.4
1976	41.9	564.1	7.4
1977	49.9	647.0	7.7
1978	63.0	783.6	8.0
1979	83.4	942.1	8.9
1980	100.6	1091.3	9.2

Notes: (a) Manufactures are defined as SITC categories 5 to 8 less 68. (b) Figures are rounded off to the nearest tenth of a billion. (c) The data for 1980 are obtained from the UN *Monthly Bulletin of Statistics*, May 1982. (d) LDCs stands for less developed countries.
Source: UNCTAD Handbook of International Trade and Development Statistics 1979, Supplement 1980, and Supplement 1981.

Table 8.2 outlines the trend in the export of manufactures from less developed countries and reveals a remarkable rate of growth which accelerated after the mid-1960s. A comparison with total manufactured exports from the world shows that the share of less developed countries, which averaged a little over 4 per cent in the period 1955 to 1965, increased steadily thereafter and attained a level of about 9 per cent in 1980—more than double what it was 15 years earlier. This rapid growth in manufactured exports also led to a structural change in the composition of exports from the underdeveloped world. The share of manufactures in total exports from less developed countries rose from 12 per cent in 1965 to 18 per cent in 1980; if we exclude fuels from the total exports of less developed countries, we find that this proportion rose from 18 per cent to 47 per cent.[6]

[6]The percentages have been calculated from international trade statistics published by the United Nations.

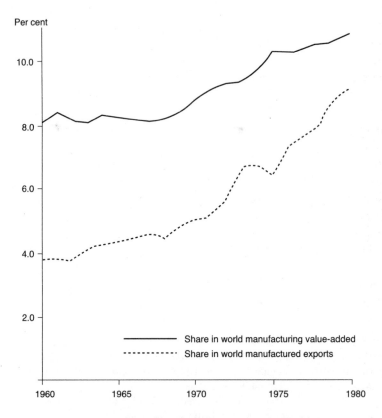

Figure 8.1: Share of Less Developed Countries in World Output and
Exports of Manufactures

Yet, a comparison of the data in Tables 8.1 and 8.2 shows that the
participation of less developed countries in world manufactured exports was
even more peripheral than their contribution to world industrial production;
the former was less than the latter throughout the period under review. In
1960, for instance, the share of less developed countries in world manufactured
exports was 3.8 per cent, whereas their share in world manufacturing value-
added was 8.2 per cent. By 1980, the gap had closed to a considerable extent
and these proportions were 9.2 per cent and 10.9 per cent, respectively. To
facilitate the comparison between these trends, the changes in shares are traced
in Figure 8.1, which confirms a narrowing of the gap, beginning in the early
1970s. It seems that the rapid pace of industrialization in the Third World,
during the 1970s, might have enabled less developed countries to increase
their contribution to the world trade in manufactures such that it now matches

their contribution to the world output of manufactures more closely. But it was not industrialization alone. Between 1965 and 1980, the volume of manufactured exports from less developed countries increased at a rate of 12.6 per cent per annum, whereas value-added in manufacturing at constant prices increased at a rate of 6.5 per cent per annum.[7] Hence it appears that manufacturing for export to external markets became an important element of industrialization in less developed countries during the 1970s, in contrast to the earlier stress on manufacturing for the domestic market through import substitution.

On the surface, the changes described above seem to suggest the beginning of a transition towards industrialization in less developed countries in which exports might perform an increasingly important role. However aggregate statistics for less developed countries as a whole in the world economy conceal the fact that industrial production and manufactured exports are concentrated in a very small number of less developed countries. It is worth considering the evidence available on this issue before we arrive at any conclusions.

There are substantial disparities in the level of industrialization both within and among the three continents of the underdeveloped world. In 1980, for instance, the share of Africa in world manufacturing value-added was just 1 per cent, whereas the share of Latin America was 6.1 per cent, and that of Asia was 3.8 per cent. The share of Africa was roughly constant over the two decades from 1960 to 1980, and the increased share of less developed countries during the 1970s was attributable to industrialization in Latin America and Asia.[8] However, even such a disaggregation at the level of regions is not sufficient; the industrialization process is concentrated among a few countries in Latin America and Asia.

In order to highlight this fact, Table 8.3 presents data on value-added in the manufacturing sector of 10 selected less developed countries which were among the more industrialized economies of the Third World. It shows that Argentina, Brazil, Hong Kong, India, Malaysia, Mexico, Pakistan, South Korea, Singapore, and Thailand, taken together, accounted for more than 60 per cent of manufacturing value-added in less developed countries throughout the period from 1965 to 1980. If anything, there was a slight increase in the degree of concentration as these countries were responsible for two-thirds of the total increase in manufacturing value-added in less developed countries between 1965 and 1980.

---

[7]Calculated as point-to-point compound growth rates from the figures in Table 8.3 and from data on the volume index numbers of manufactured exports from less developed countries which are published in the UN *Monthly Bulletin of Statistics*.

[8]UNIDO (1981, p. 31).

Table 8.3: Value-added in Manufacturing Sector for
Ten Selected Less Developed Countries

(*US $ million at constant 1975 prices*)

Country	1965	1970	1975	1980
Argentina	13,190.2	17,079.2	21,741.4	22,125.8
Brazil	12,646.2	20,715.5	35,894.3	50,829.8
Hong Kong	900.9	1760.1	2194.2	3198.6
India	9820.4	11,833.3	13,830.9	18,543.2
Malaysia	689.8	1045.3	1638.4	3080.6
Mexico	8935.2	13,551.0	18,174.7	24,346.8
Pakistan	1412.3	1934.2	2202.9	3083.6
Singapore	354.8	850.6	1386.3	2321.9
South Korea	902.3	2391.5	5450.8	10,008.2
Thailand	906.1	1481.0	2667.1	4505.4
(A) Total above	49,758.2	72,641.7	105,181.0	142,143.9
(B) All LDCs	82,274.1	118,723.6	167,933.2	224,198.8
(A) as a percentage of (B)	60.5	61.2	62.6	63.4

Note: LDCs stands for less developed countries.
Source: Data compiled by the UNIDO Secretariat from National Accounts Statistics.

It is not surprising, therefore, that manufactured exports from less developed countries were also concentrated among the same set of countries. Table 8.4 outlines the trends in the exports of manufactures from the ten selected less developed countries, and reveals roughly the same orders of magnitude in terms of the degree of concentration.

A careful comparison of Tables 8.3 and 8.4 reveals a striking asymmetry between the distribution of industrial production, on the one hand, and the distribution of manufactured exports, on the other, within this group of 10 selected less developed countries. To illustrate the point, these countries are divided further into three groups: (a) Group A, constituted by Argentina, Brazil, Mexico, and India, the large economies in which industrialization is based largely on the domestic market; (b) Group B, constituted by Hong Kong, Singapore, and South Korea, the small open economies in which industrialization is based on the world market; and (c) Group C, constituted by Malaysia, Pakistan, and Thailand, the remaining three countries, which are among the more industrialized less developed countries in Asia.

Table 8.5 sets out the compiled figures on the share of each of these groups in manufacturing value-added in less developed countries and

Table 8.4: Exports of Manufactures from Ten Selected
Less Developed Countries

(US $ million at current prices)

Country	1965	1970	1975	1980
Argentina	82	249	722	1935
Brazil	124	369	2192	7492
Hong Kong	989	2330	5590	17,951
India	809	1052	1961	4920
Malaysia	65	151	665	2418
Mexico	166	391	930	1720
Pakistan	190	425	571	1277
Singapore	300	428	2,232	9048
South Korea	104	640	4137	15,661
Thailand	12	39	332	1214
(A) Total above	2842	6074	19,332	63,636
(B) All LDCs	4480	9740	32,120	100,610
(A) as a percentage of (B)	63.4	62.4	60.2	63.3

Notes: (a) Manufactures are defined as SITC categories 5 to 8 less 68. (b) LDCs stands
for less developed countries.
Source: United Nations, *Yearbooks of International Trade Statistics*, and 'Commodity Trade
Statistics', *Statistical Papers, Series D*.

manufactured exports from less developed countries, and highlights the
asymmetry. For example, in 1980, the large semi-industrialized countries in
Group A accounted for more than half of industrial production but less than
one-sixth of manufactured exports from less developed countries. In sharp
contrast, the small East Asian countries in Group B, which were responsible
for 42 per cent of manufactured exports contributed a mere 7 per cent of
industrial production in less developed countries. But that is not all. The
disproportionality appears to have risen over time insofar as the share of
Group A countries in manufactured exports from less developed countries
declined continuously from 26 per cent in 1965 to 15 per cent in 1980, even
though their share of manufacturing value-added in less developed countries
was relatively stable at a little more than 50 per cent over the same period. Of
course, the share of Group B countries in manufactured exports did not
even remotely resemble their share in manufacturing value-added at any stage,
whereas there was a fairly close correspondence between the two shares for
the Group C countries.

Table 8.5: Distribution of Output and Trade in
Manufactures among Less Developed Countries

(percentage)

Country-groups	\multicolumn{8}{c}{Percentage Share of Selected LDCs}
	\multicolumn{4}{c}{*Manufacturing Value-added in LDCs*}	\multicolumn{4}{c}{*Manufactured Exports from LDCs*}
	1965	*1970*	*1975*	*1980*	*1965*	*1970*	*1975*	*1980*
Group A Argentina Brazil Mexico India	54.2	53.2	53.4	51.7	26.4	21.2	18.1	16.0
Group B Hong Kong Singapore South Korea	2.6	4.2	5.4	7.0	31.1	34.9	37.2	42.4
Group C Malaysia Pakistan Thailand	3.7	3.8	3.8	4.7	5.9	6.3	4.9	4.9
Total above	60.5	61.2	62.6	63.4	63.4	62.4	60.2	63.3
Other LDCs	39.5	38.8	37.4	36.6	36.6	37.6	39.8	36.7
All LDCs	100.0	100.0	100.0	100.0	100.0	100.0	100.0	100.0

Note: LDCs stands for less developed countries.
Source: Tables 8.3 and 8.4.

The asymmetry would be accentuated if Taiwan were included in the group of Esat Asian NICs. Unfortunately, however, statistics published by the United Nations do not report data on the economy of Taiwan. Using alternative sources, I have estimated that in 1975, Hong Kong, Singapore, South Korea, and Taiwan, taken together, accounted for only 9.5 per cent of manufacturing value-added in less developed countries but were responsible for 45 per cent of manufactured exports from less developed countries;[9] it is worth noting that, in the same year, just about 2 per cent of the total population of less developed countries lived in these four countries.[10]

[9]The share of the four East Asian countries in manufacturing value-added in less developed countries, at 1970 prices, has been calculated from the data in *World Development Report, 1979*, pp. 136–7; the value of manufactured exports for Taiwan has also been obtained from the same source.

[10]Estimated from the *World Bank Atlas*, 1977.

The evidence presented here suggests that there has been an acceleration in the process of industrialization in less developed countries during the period 1960–80. Yet it also reveals the glaring inequalities between them when we consider the distribution of output and trade in manufactures among less developed countries. Indeed, the international relocation of manufacturing production in the Third World is confined to a very small number of countries, while trade in manufactures is concentrated in even fewer economies.

RELOCATION OF MANUFACTURING PRODUCTION IN LESS DEVELOPED COUNTRIES

In the period from 1960 to 1980, the emergence of large transnational corporations in the world economy has led to the reorganization of production and trade within the nexus of these firms on a global basis. In recent years, transnational enterprises have become adept at shifting manufacturing production across national boundaries by moving capital, technology managers, and marketing skills to suitable locations dictated by economic factors—be it cheap labour, proximity to markets, or product and process innovations embodied in technical change. While production might be relocated outside the industrialized world, the output is sold primarily in the markets of industrialized economies.

There is a presumption in the existing literature that such international relocation of manufacturing production is a phenomenon of increasing importance in underdeveloped countries.[11] But there is relatively little systematic information on the subject. To some extent, of course, such a hypothesis is quite plausible, at least on surface, for two reasons: First, a substantial and growing proportion of world trade in manufactures is now recognized as intra-firm trade; second, transnational participation in the export of manufactures from less developed countries is also significant and, according to some scholars, on the increase. It is important, nevertheless, to provide a quantitative assessment of the available evidence.

Before we consider the empirical evidence, it is essential to define international production in a concrete sense. Towards that end, it is important to distinguish between transnational corporations which are manufacturing enterprises and those that are buying groups. The former are, in general, parts of vertically integrated global organizations which are involved in the process of production as well as export, including the marketing of goods abroad. Sometimes, the complete production process is located in underdeveloped countries. But this is not always the case. During the period 1960–80, manufacturing for export

[11]See, for example, Frobel et al. (1980).

by transnationals in less developed countries has also taken the form of producing components and offshore processing or of mere assembly operations. International buying groups, on the other hand, leave production to domestic entrepreneurs or firms but buy from them on a contractual basis and sell these goods in overseas markets. Such buying groups, in turn, may be constituted by large retailing firms from the industrialized countries or by trading houses that act as intermediaries between producers in the poor countries and sellers in the rich countries. Transnational buyers, however large, perform the task of marketing and distribution but are not directly engaged in manufacturing. Yet, in a fundamental sense, their activities represent one form of the relocation of production across countries.[12] For our purpose, therefore, internationalization of production refers to the activities of transnational firms which relocate the entire production process, or parts thereof, in underdeveloped economies, with the explicit intention of exporting the output, primarily to the markets of industrialized countries.

It is very difficult to estimate the share of transnational manufacturing firms and buying groups in manufactured exports from less developed countries, *inter alia*, because trade statistics compiled by governments are not sufficiently disaggregated, even though customs authorities frequently record international transactions according to the firm of origin. All the same, the evidence available across countries, which I have examined at length elsewhere, does enable us to arrive at approximate orders of magnitude. It appears that the share of transnational manufacturing firms in exports of manufactures from less developed countries is smaller than widely believed; it was probably not much greater than 15 per cent *circa* 1974.[13] Given the scant nature of the data, however, this conclusion can only be treated as tentative.

In a situation where direct quantitative evidence is extremely hard to find, it is worth considering the evidence available from the United States. The US government has published a considerable amount of information on the activities of transnational corporations and their impact on world trade. There are two principal sources: first, the US Department of Commerce, which has published fairly detailed statistics on the exports by majority-owned affiliates of US companies abroad; second, the US Tariff Commission, and now the US International Trade Commission, which have compiled data on US imports from less developed countries under the special tariff provisions

---

[12]Unfortunately, very little is known about transnational buying firms and primary research alone would enable us to determine their impact on the trade flows of less developed countries. For a valuable discussion on the *Sago Shoshas* from Japan, see Eddy Lee (ed.) (1981, Chapter 7).

[13]Nayyar (1978).

for offshore assembly, constituted largely by trade originating in the international subcontracting industries. The particularly useful feature of both these sources is that they have data on a time series basis, which might make it possible to comment on the changing role of transnational corporations over time. In terms of coverage also, the data are significant because, in the late 1960s and the mid-1970s, about half the total stock of direct foreign investment in less developed countries originated from the United States.[14] What is more, during the period 1966–80, the US market absorbed 25 to 30 per cent of total manufactured exports from less developed countries.[15] Therefore, I consider each of the two sources in turn.

Export by Affiliates of US Companies in Less Developed Countries

Studies carried out by the US Department of Commerce a few years ago provide estimates of exports by majority-owned affiliates of US companies classified by country of location and industry of affiliate.[16] For the less developed countries, however, the information is available only on a regional basis. Using this source material, together with international trade statistics, in an earlier paper I estimated the share of majority-owned affiliates of US companies in manufactured exports from less developed countries for the period 1966–74. The results of the exercise are reproduced in Table 8.6 which shows that the share of subsidiaries of US transnational firms in manufactured goods sold abroad by less developed countries was roughly constant until 1970, and declined a little thereafter; the average share for all less developed countries taken together, during the period 1966–74, was 9.2 per cent. This share was 8.1 per cent in 1975 and 7.6 per cent in 1976.[17] Unfortunately, such data are not readily available for subsequent years. I shall not enter into a discussion about the factors underlying the variations across regions and the changes over time as that has been done in Nayyar (1978). But it is worth noting that the participation of American firms in the trade of underdeveloped economies was distinctly smaller than their participation in the trade of industrialized countries. For instance, in 1970, US based transnational firms accounted for 11 per cent of total manufactured exports from less developed countries, whereas, in the same year, they were responsible

[14]United Nations (1973 and 1978).

[15]Calculated from the matrix on world trade by commodity classes and regions published in UN *Monthly Bulletin of Statistics*.

[16]See 'Sales by Majority-owned Foreign Affiliates of US Companies', *Survey of Current Business*, August 1975 and May 1976, US Government Printing Office, Washington, DC.

[17]These figures have been estimated from the same sources as Table 8.6.

Table 8.6: Share of Majority-owned Affiliates of US Companies in
Manufactured Exports from Less Developed Countries

(*percentage*)

Year	Latin America	Africa	Middle East	Other Asia	All LDCs
1966	37.8	–	1.3	7.0	10.6
1967	40.0	2.6	1.1	7.7	11.5
1968	33.0	5.7	0.9	8.2	11.0
1969	29.4	6.0	1.0	6.5	9.2
1970	22.3	6.4	0.9	8.8	10.8
1971	23.7	6.3	1.1	6.0	9.5
1972	22.1	7.2	2.0	4.9	8.5
1973	19.2	5.6	2.2	5.4	8.1
1974	19.2	6.1	2.8	5.8	8.7

Note: LDCs stands for less developed countries.
Source: Nayyar (1978).

for 21 per cent of manufactured exports from OECD countries and 19 per cent of such exports in the world economy.[18]

US Imports from Less Developed Countries under the Special Tariff Provisions for Offshore Assembly

An alternative source of information on the international relocation of manufacturing production by the American transnational firms is the data on US imports from less developed countries under items 807.00 and 806.30 of the Tariff schedules.[19] Under these items, import duties are levied only on the value-added abroad, if the manufactured inputs originate in the United States. Item 807.00 relates to offshore processing and assembly operations in general, and item 806.30 relates to metal processing. More than 90 per cent of these imports are in the former category. Such offshore processing and assembly operations are concentrated in clothing, consumer electronics, office machine parts, semi-conductors, electrical appliances, automobile parts, electrical machinery, and so on, where unskilled labour-intensive parts of the production process are relocated in less developed countries by transnational firms.[20]

[18]See US Tariff Commission (1973, pp. 280 and 283).

[19]To begin with, this information was compiled and published by the US Tariff Commission. The compilation is now done by the Statistical Services Division of the US International Trade Commission and is available in mimeographed form. I am grateful to Donald Keesing for sending me the data from Washington, DC.

[20]For a detailed discussion of this phenomenon, see Helleiner (1973), and Sharpston (1975). Both authors provide a wide range of examples. To cite a few: garments, gloves, and

This provision for offshore assembly in the American tariff law has played a crucial role in the phenomenal expansion of international subcontracting. The organization of relocated manufacturing activities and the consequent trade inevitably requires management by transnational corporations: it might be offshore processing, component manufacture, or mere assembly operations carried out within vertically integrated transnational manufacturing firms on the one hand, or it might be subcontracted to domestic firms in LDCs through trading houses and buying firms, on the other.

For our purpose, it is necessary to review the statistical evidence on trade arising out of the relocation of manufacturing production through such international subcontracting. Table 8.7 outlines the trend in imports of manufactures from less developed countries, by the United States, under these special tariff provisions for the period 1966–80.[21] Apart from the phenomenal growth which is apparent from a mere glance at the table, there is another feature of this trade that is worth noting; the gross value of imports is not a good index of foreign exchange earnings derived by less developed countries from such trade, because approximately half that value is attributable to inputs first manufactured in the US, which sum, in turn, is exempted from import duties in the US. However, the growth in the dutiable value of these imports, the equivalent of value-added in less developed countries, was equally impressive.

The expansion in absolute values of trade at current prices might be deceptive. To assess its relative importance, therefore, I have compared it with time-series data on manufactured exports from less developed countries to (i) the United States and (ii) the world.

The results of the exercise are interesting. We find that the share of offshore assembly imports in total US imports of manufactures from less developed countries registered a remarkable increase between 1966 and 1975, but declined a little thereafter and stabilized at a lower level, whether we consider gross value or dutiable value. In terms of gross value, this proportion rose

---

leather baggage are sewn together in less developed countries for American and Japanese firms; data are flown to less developed countries for punching upon tape by low-wage, key-punch operators; automobile parts are manufactured for transnational firms in a wide variety of countries: piston rings in South Korea, auto lamps in Mexico, braking equipment in India, batteries in Thailand, and so on.

[21] It is essential to point out that these figures are not comparable with the data on exports by majority-owned affiliates of US companies discussed above. This is so for three reasons: (a) it is not known what proportion of imports under tariff items 807.00 and 806.36 are attributable to large international firms; (b) these import statistics include not only manufacturing firms engaged in production but also retailing firms involved primarily in distribution; and (c) foreign firms in the US also qualify for the benefit of such special tariff provisions.

Table 8.7: US Imports from Less Developed Countries under
the Special Tariff Provisions for Offshore Assembly

Year	US Imports from LDCs under Tariff Items 807.00 and 806.30 (in $ million)		As Percentage of Manufactured Exports from LDCs to the US		As Percentage of Manufactured Exports from LDCs to the World	
	(1)	(2)	(3)	(4)	(5)	(6)
	Gross Value	Dutiable Value	Gross Value	Dutiable Value	Gross Value	Dutiable Value
1966	60.7	31.4	5.1	2.6	1.2	0.6
1967	99.0	42.8	7.0	3.0	1.7	0.7
1968	221.7	97.7	11.7	5.2	3.2	1.4
1969	394.8	177.3	16.2	7.3	4.7	2.1
1970	541.5	245.9	19.5	8.9	5.6	2.5
1971	652.5	314.1	18.4	8.8	5.8	2.8
1972	1031.7	531.2	22.2	11.4	7.0	3.6
1973	1522.9	827.0	22.7	12.3	6.6	3.6
1974	2328.8	1289.4	28.8	16.0	7.5	4.1
1975	2261.7	1238.7	30.3	16.6	7.0	3.9
1976	2807.0	1548.6	24.5	13.5	6.7	3.7
1977	3306.8	1721.4	23.7	12.3	6.6	3.4
1978	4277.8	2168.2	23.1	11.7	6.8	3.4
1979	5308.4	2670.7	25.1	12.6	6.4	3.2
1980	6337.0	3173.9	26.1	13.1	6.3	3.2

Notes: (a) Manufactured exports in columns (3) to (6) are defined as SITC categories 5 to 8 less 68.

(b) The percentages in columns (3) and (4) have been calculated from data on manufactured exports by developing market economics to the United States; these figures, in turn, were compiled from the matrix of world trade by commodity classes and regions, published in the UN *Monthly Bulletin of Statistics*.

(c) The percentages in columns (5) and (6) have been calculated on the basis of data in Table 8.2.

(d) LDCs stands for less developed countries.

Source: For columns (1) and (2), US Tariff Commission and US International Trade Commission.

from 5 per cent in 1966 to 30 per cent in 1975, and fluctuated around a level of 25 per cent in the late 1970s. A similar trend emerges from a comparison of US manufactured imports under tariff items 807.00 and 806.30, with total manufactured exports from less developed countries to the world. In terms of gross value, the share rose from 1 per cent in 1966 to 7.5 per cent in 1974 and remained in the range 6–7 per cent during the subsequent years. However, in terms of dutiable value, which is the more appropriate index of value-added in less developed countries, this share was far smaller and increased from 0.6 per cent in 1966 to a peak of 4.1 per cent in 1974, also declining thereafter.

The implication of these trends is clear enough. The relative importance of the trade arising out of the international relocation of manufacturing production, through international subcontracting by US transnational firms in less developed countries, increased steadily from the mid-1960s to the mid-1970s, but it diminished somewhat in the late 1970s.

It would be natural to ask, how US imports of manufactures under the special tariff provision for offshore assembly were distributed between the less developed countries, on the one hand, and the industrialized countries, on the other. In terms of gross value, the share of less developed countries in these imports rose from 6 per cent in 1966 to 25 per cent in 1970, 44 per cent in 1975, stabilized thereafter, and was 45 per cent in 1980. In terms of dutiable value, these shares were 4 per cent, 15 per cent, 32 per cent, and 31 per cent, respectively.[22] The latter shares were significantly smaller because the value-added component of such imports from the industrialized economies was much higher. Offshore assembly in the industrialized countries accounted for more than half this trade in terms of gross value, and more than two-thirds this trade in terms of dutiable value, even as late as 1980.

It is worth pointing out, too, that US imports from less developed countries under tariff items 807.00 and 806.30 were concentrated in a very small number of countries and that is borne out by the data in Table 8.8. It would appear that five countries—Mexico, Hong Kong, Singapore, South Korea, and Taiwan—accounted for almost nine-tenths of American imports under the special tariff provisions for offshore assembly until the mid-1970s. However, their combined share dropped to a little over 70 per cent in the late 1970s. Mexico retained its overwhelming share, while that of Singapore and, to a lesser extent, South Korea registered an increase. On the other hand, the relative importance of Hong Kong and Taiwan declined steeply; and this was attributable partly to the relocation of such manufacturing production in Malaysia and the Philippines. During the period 1976–80, the average annual share of Malaysia in US offshore assembly imports from less developed countries was 11.3 per cent and that of the Philippines was 4.6 per cent.[23]

[22]These percentage figures have been calculated from the data compiled by the US International Trade Commission.

[23]Unfortunately data on Malaysia and the Philippines are not readily available for earlier years; the share of these countries during the period 1976–80 has been calculated from US International Trade Commission statistics.

Table 8.8: Country Composition of US Imports
from Less Developed Countries under
Tariff Items 807.00 and 806.30

Country	(average annual shares in percentages)		
	1966–9	1970–4	1976–80
Mexico	32.4	42.8	37.4
Hong Kong	32.2	12.2	6.5
Taiwan	17.6	17.0	9.7
South Korea	4.8	5.6	6.2
Singapore	1.5	10.4	10.7
Total above	88.5	88.0	70.8
Total LDCs	100.0	100.0	100.0

Notes: (a) These percentages are based on the gross value of US imports and have been calculated from the data which provide a country-wise break-down of imports under 807.00 and 806.30. (b) LDCs stands for less developed countries.
Source: US Tariff Commission and US International Trade Commission.

Similar tariff provision for offshore assembly exist in Western Europe. While these provisions vary from country to country, tariffs on imports of manufactures are levied only on the value-added abroad, provided that the inputs originate in the country of importation. Unfortunately, however, comparable data on a time series basis are not published by most industrialized countries. The Netherlands and West Germany are the only exception, but for these countries also data are not readily available for the period since 1972. And, until then, imports from less developed countries in this category were very small indeed.[24]

The evidence presented here is by no means comprehensive or adequate. For one thing, it provides no information on the dimensions of relocation of manufacturing production in less developed countries by transnational firms which originate in Western Europe and Japan. For another, it probably conceals important variations between industries in the category of manufacturing. Further research on primary sources is essential in order to determine the extent of internationalization of production by industries, sectors, and countries.

[24]In 1972, for example, offshore assembly imports from less developed countries were $156 million in West Germany (of which $139 million were from Yugoslavia), and a mere $16 million in the Netherlands compared to $1032 million in the US. For available evidence on the Netherlands and West Germany, see Finger (1975).

Given the paucity of information, however, for the moment we must rely on the evidence that is available. On balance, it would be reasonable to infer that this international relocation of production is a relatively modest phenomenon in the context of less developed countries: whether we consider its existing scale or its growth during the period 1960–80. It is striking that, in spite of the rapid pace of industrialization in less developed countries and the phenomenal expansion in manufactured exports during the 1970s, the share of less developed countries in world exports of manufactures was smaller than their share in world manufacturing value-added, even as late as in 1980. The share of the majority-owned affiliates of US firms in manufactured exports from less developed countries declined a little in the 1970s. What is more, the relocation of manufacturing production in less developed countries by US transnational firms, under offshore assembly provisions, which registered a dramatic increase during the period 1966–74, also slowed down in the late 1970s. Most important, perhaps, it is worth stressing that an overwhelming proportion of the international relocation of manufacturing production is concentrated in 10, or even fewer, less developed countries. There can be little doubt that the process of internationalization of production is far more important as between rich capitalist countries. Within the industrialized world, the relocation of production has probably been concentrated in the immediate geographical periphery of the most developed economies. Thus, in Western Europe, countries such as Ireland, Spain, Portugal, and Greece are locations used by transnational corporations to manufacture for export, and even some East European countries such as Yugoslavia and Hungary have been drawn into the process.[25]

FACTORS UNDERLYING THE PROCESS

Assessing the dimensions of the phenomenon is only the first step. In order to analyse the new internationalization of production, and to examine its implications for industrialization in less developed countries, it is also necessary to explore the factors underlying the process and to consider the determinants of its spread across industries and countries.

The reasons for the international relocation of production by transnational enterprises are fairly well known and have been examined, at some length, in the literature.[26] Factors such as transport costs, tariff policies in industrialized countries, export incentives implicit in fiscal or trade polices adopted by less

[25]Bienefeld, Godfrey, and Schmitz (1977).
[26]See Helleiner (1973) and Sharpston (1975).

developed countries, and the risks involved are obviously important determinants of the location decision.[27]

It is widely accepted, however, that labour costs are the major determinant. The absolute differences in wage rates between rich countries and poor, for workers engaged in the manufacturing sector, are indeed phenomenal. It is not unusual to find that wages in less developed countries are less than one-tenth the level prevalent in industrialized countries.[28] At the same time, differences in labour productivity, particularly for manufacturing export industries relocated in less developed countries, are not very significant.[29] Therefore, wage costs per unit of output are markedly lower in underdeveloped economies.[30] These differences, in average unit labour costs of production, are nothing new, of course, but the international relocation of production and the corresponding participation of transnational firms in manufacturing for export is a relatively recent development. The timing of this phenomenon can be explained in terms of two basic factors: competition *among* advanced capitalist countries, and conflict between capital and labour *within* the industrial economies.[31]

The first explanation stresses competition for markets among industrialized countries as the motive of export-oriented investments in less developed countries. To start with, US-based firms sought to preserve their markets for manufactured goods by investing in Europe and Japan. Economies of scale in production and in marketing enabled them to retain an oligopolistic hold on these markets. Over time, however, European and Japanese firms surmounted the disadvantages arising from the technological gap, and the latter in particular acquired a competitive edge over US firms on account of the low wages in Japan. For American firms, not only did this mean a loss of overseas markets but their home market was also no longer secure. The response of US firms was to move to low wage locations in Asia. Transnational firms from Europe and Japan followed in the same path to establish low-cost bases for export.

It is worth pointing out that this explanation conforms to the product cycle theory of trade, wherein relocation is possible once the mature product

[27]To avoid repetition, I shall not elaborate as these points have been discussed elsewhere. See Helleiner (1973, pp. 35–40).

[28]Helleiner (1973, p. 45) and Sharpston (1975, p. 103). See also UNCTAD (1975).

[29]See US Tariff Commission (1973, p. 118).

[30]For evidence on this point see US Tariff Commission (1973), and US Tariff Commission (1970).

[31]The following discussion in this section of the essay draws upon my earlier work: see Nayyar (1978, pp. 72–8).

becomes standardized. Typically, in such cases, it is the complete production process which is relocated.

At the same time, certain other forces, stemming from conflicts between capital and labour in the industrialized countries, provided a push in the same direction. Industrial workers in the developed world were increasingly reluctant to perform certain unpleasant or monotonous tasks, for example, assembly line operations. What is more, trade unions became more militant and, therefore, less willing to accept reductions in real wages or employment in a crisis. The industrial disputes which arose as a result clearly affected productivity in the advanced capitalist countries. As such, where possible, transnational firms tended to relocate parts of the production process in less developed countries. Given the levels of unemployment and poverty, the monotony or unpleasant nature of the work does not matter. On the other hand, the industrial workforce in poor countries is frequently not organized, or it is systematically repressed, so that transnational corporations can eliminate industrial disputes and need not worry about cutting back on employment in times of recession.

This analysis should not, of course, be taken to imply that the internationalization of production is a consequence of conflict and contradiction alone. It is as much an outcome of opportunities as it is of challenge. Transnational firms do, in fact, have positive reasons for expansion: the rapid growth of markets abroad where exports are not always possible and the existence of cheaper labour which makes it profitable to produce abroad. Nevertheless, it cannot be denied that it is competitive pressure rather than foresight which guides international capital to expand. It is possible to cite a historical example in support: US firms did not invest significantly in Europe or Japan during the late 1940s or early 1950s, when American political influence was very substantial. It was only after the formation of the EEC and the emergence of serious competition from Japan that US firms acquired an international outlook.

The international relocation of manufacturing is not spread evenly across products or countries. It is concentrated in some products and processes. What is more, only a few less developed countries have been developed as bases for export. Given the limit on space, it is not possible to discuss the reasons underlying choice of products and choice of countries in the relocation of production. Instead, I shall simply summarize my views, based upon earlier work, on the two issues.[32]

---

[32]For a more detailed discussion, see Nayyar (1978), see also Helleiner (1973), and Adam (1975).

Generalizations are no doubt difficult, but it would seem that large international firms have developed manufacturing for export in less developed countries, in three sets of industries.

1. Capital- or technology-intensive goods, such as chemicals, iron and steel, light engineering goods, machinery, and transport equipment: most such industries were first set up in less developed countries largely for purposes of import substitution, and they have over time also entered into export markets. Recently, however, international firms have established a few technology-intensive industries, which manufacture products such as cameras, scientific instruments, or automobiles, primarily for export; in these cases, the entire production process, often in the form of a complete plant, is relocated in less developed countries.

2. Simple labour-intensive products, such as clothing, sports goods, toys, travel goods, plastic products, and so on: although production is largely in the hands of domestic entrepreneurs or firms, transnational buying groups perform a crucial role in the export of these from less developed countries. The absence of foreign participation in manufacturing stands to reason, as most of these products are standardized, technologically simple, and require few overheads. Yet they are consumer goods destined for highly brand-conscious markets where designing, advertising, and market channels are necessary attributes of a successful export effort.

3. Products of footloose industries: the electronics industry is by far the most important in this sphere; semi-conductors, tuners, valves, and related components are manufactured, sometimes assembled, in Mexico or South Korea for re-export to parent electronic firms in the United States or Japan. There are numerous other examples of these footloose industries in less developed countries. The evolution of extremely specialized labour-intensive processes for manufacturing components and undertaking assembly operations has led to a significant relocation of industrial production in less developed countries which, in turn, generates manufactured exports. Our earlier discussion about US imports from less developed countries under the special tariff provisions for offshore assembly bears testimony to the remarkable growth in such export trade. Taken as a whole, these industries are highly capital as well as technology-intensive and far from being standardized in outputs, frequently embody the latest technological developments. The point to note is that it is the unskilled-labour-intensive parts of the production process which are separated and relocated in poor countries to take advantage of cheap labour.

The other question relates to the choice of countries and to the factors that might influence the location or sourcing decisions of transnational corporations. A large proportion of the few less developed countries that are an integral part of the international relocation of production have their own special attractions for international firms seeking to develop low cost bases for export. Brazil offers liberal tax incentives, an attitude of welcome, and an industrial infrastructure to investors from abroad, all of which might have been a strong attraction to American, European, and Japanese firms seeking to relocate complete production processes for the export of technology-intensive goods. Mexico, of course, has a very special advantage for footloose industries in terms of its proximity to the United States. The small East Asian countries have extremely close political ties with the home countries of transnational firms; while Hong Kong is a British colony, Taiwan, South Korea, and Singapore are completely dependent on the US for military and political support in the international sphere.

It would be superficial to treat these countries as special cases. Analysis requires identification of common features. Relatively cheap labour is an obviously important factor, but it cannot explain the location of export-oriented investments in particular less developed countries when there are so many others with the same characteristic. In my view, *inter alia*, there are two basic factors which influence the choice of transnational firms as between low wage countries: political stability and labour docility. The first implies that the risks of nationalization or confiscation of assets are reduced to a minimum. On the other hand, a docile labour force reduces the possibility of industrial disputes, enables firms to dismiss workers for the purpose of maintaining discipline, and allows a cut-back in employment during recessions. In this context, it is easy to see why economies such as Hong Kong, Taiwan, South Korea, Singapore, Malaysia, and even Brazil are attractive locations. They provide not only the necessary political stability but also a strict control over trade unions, frequently through internal repression.[33] In addition, the political dependence of the small East Asian countries gives transnational firms considerable leverage over government policies, and this is used to promote their own interests.

POSSIBILITIES OF EXPORT-LED GROWTH IN LESS DEVELOPED COUNTRIES

The international relocation of manufacturing production has, perhaps, contributed to a rapid growth in manufactured exports and an acceleration

---

[33]The following examples can be cited as evidence in support: (a) Singapore offers a strike holiday to multinational corporations for a number of years; (b) countries such as Singapore, Malaysia, and Indonesia advertise their repressive labour legislation; (c) in South Korea a special labour law rules out industrial disputes with foreign firms. For details and sources of this evidence, see Nayyar (1978, p. 77).

in the pace of industrialization for a few countries in the Third World. For analysts and policymakers, however, it has become fashionable to focus on the recent development experience of Hong Kong, Singapore, South Korea, and Taiwan which not only achieved a phenomenal expansion in manufactured exports and attained almost unprecedented rates of economic growth, but also succeeded in bringing about an impressive structural transformation in their economies. A characterization of the East Asian experience as export-led industrialization implies: 'first, that the production of manufactured exports was the leading sector in the growth process and, second, that this pattern of growth constituted genuine industrialization'.[34]

Both these propositions are open to question and we shall leave them aside for the moment. The discussion in this section is limited to a critical evaluation of the view that similar export-led industrialziation associated with outward-looking policies, in which labour-intensive manufactured exports play a central role, is a strategy of development that would succeed across the board in the Third World.[35] Towards that object, I shall attempt to answer two questions. First, is it possible to generalize the East Asian experience of economic growth led by manufactured exports for all less developed countries? If not, would it be possible at least for a few less developed countries to replicate the East Asian model in the 1980s? Let me consider these questions in turn.

It would not be possible to generalize the East Asian model of export-led growth across countries in the Third World, simply because such a prescription suffers from the fallacy of aggregation. While it might be possible for one, two, or a few small economies to pursue export-oriented policies without worrying about the impact it might have on world trade, the adoption of this strategy on a global basis is an altogether different matter.

Consider what would happen if less developed countries, in general, became as successful exporters of manufactured goods as the four East Asian economies. In 1975, for example, the weighted average value of manufactured exports per capita in Hong Kong, Singapore, South Korea, and Taiwan was $281; if Argentina, Brazil, Mexico, India, Malaysia, Pakistan, and Thailand attained the same level, the value of manufactured exports from these eleven less developed countries alone would have been 8.5 times the actual manufactured exports from all less developed countries in that year, and would have constituted a little more than half of world manufactured exports in 1975.[36]

[34]Lee (1981), p. 13.
[35]Kessing (1967), Little et al. (1970); see also Hughes (1980).
[36]The calculation is based on the data in Table 8.9. For 1980, the corresponding figures work out at 10 times the actual value of manufactured exports from all less developed

The dimensions would be even larger if other less developed countries were included in the computation. It is not surprising that such an exercise produces almost absurd results, given the massive population of India at one end of the spectrum and the tiny populations of Hong Kong or Singapore at the other end. The futility of the comparison is illustrated further by the fact that, even as early as in 1975, the level of per capita manufactured exports in Hong Kong and Singapore was significantly higher than that in the US, the UK, France, and Japan.[37]

It might be more appropriate therefore to use a method which is not unduly influenced by the enormous variations in the size of population less developed countries. There are two alternative possibilities. We can compare the ratio of (a) manufactured exports per capita to manufacturing value-added per capita, or (b) manufactured exports to GDP, in the East Asian countries with that in other less developed countries.

1. Table 8.9 presents data on the value of manufactured exports per capita and value-added in the manufacturing sector per capita, in 1975, for the selected less developed countries which were among the more industrialized economies in the Third World. To facilitate comparison, it also provides corresponding figures for five selected industrialized economies. The choice of year was dictated by available information. The evidence reveals significant differences between countries in the ratio of manufactured exports to manufacturing value-added per capita; these figures are set out in the last column of the table. In Hong Kong, Singapore, South Korea, and Taiwan, this ratio was abnormally high: the weighted average ratio for the four economies was 1.10, which implies that the gross value of manufactured exports exceeded value-added in the manufacturing sector. Among the other selected less developed countries, the same ratio varied from as low as 0.03 in Argentina to as high as 0.40 in Malaysia. The range in the industrialized economies was also considerable, from 0.20 in the US to 0.61 in the UK, while the average for the five selected countries was 0.34.

Clearly, it would be extreme to postulate a situation where this ratio attained the East Asian level of 1.10 in all less developed countries. We have made two alternative assumptions—that this ratio might be 0.50 or 1.00—and estimated the required expansion in manufactured exports from the selected, as also other, less developed countries.

---

countries and more than 90 per cent of world manufactured exports; this latter calculation is based on the level of per capita manufactured exports from Hong Kong, Singapore, and South Korea in 1980 ($ 933.50), as data for Taiwan were not available.

[37]See Table 8.9. The same was true in 1979.

Table 8.9: Per Capita Manufactured Exports and
Manufacturing Value-added for Selected Countries, 1975

Country	(1) Population Mid-1975 (millions)	(2) Manufactured Exports Per Capita in 1975 (US$)	(3) Manufacturing Value-added Per Capita in 1975 (US$)	(4) Ratio of (B) to (C)
Hong Kong	4.4	1270.45	498.68	2.55
Singapore	2.2	1014.55	630.14	1.61
South Korea	35.3	117.20	154.41	0.76
Taiwan	16.0	268.94	358.12	0.75
Argentina	25.4	28.43	855.96	0.03
Brazil	106.2	20.64	357.99	0.06
Mexico	60.1	15.47	302.41	0.05
India	600.8	3.26	23.02	0.14
Malaysia	11.9	55.88	137.68	0.40
Pakistan	70.3	8.12	31.34	0.26
Thailand	41.9	7.92	63.65	0.12
France	52.7	739.58	1753.61	0.42
Japan	111.6	471.58	1344.71	0.35
United Kingdom	55.9	630.60	1025.76	0.61
United States	213.6	331.05	1627.18	0.20
West Germany	61.8	1264.27	2517.39	0.50

Note: The figures in Columns (2) to (4) have been rounded off to the second decimal place.
Sources: (a) For column (1), United Nations (1981), *Statistical Yearbook 1979–80*, New York.
(b) For the less developed countries in columns (2) and (3), Tables 8.3 and 8.4, in conjunction with the population figures in column (2).
(c) For data on manufactured exports from the five industrialized countries, used in column (2), UN *Yearbook of International Trade Statistics, 1978*.
(d) For data on manufacturing value-added in the five industrialized countries, used in column (3), World Bank, *World Development Report, 1979* and *1981*.
(e) For data on Taiwan, in columns (1) to (3), *Taiwan Statistical Data Book*.

The results of the hypothetical exercise are set out in Table 8.10. It shows that, in 1975, for example, if the norm ratio was 0.50, exports of manufactures from Mexico would have been 10 times their actual value. For the seven selected less developed countries—Argentina, Brazil, Mexico, India, Malaysia, Pakistan, and Thailand—the same ratio yields a multiple of 6.25 as the expansion factor. For all less developed countries, taken together, we find that if the ratio of manufactured exports to manufacturing value-added per capita is assumed to be 0.50, total exports of manufactures from less developed countries would have been 2.8 times their actual value, and would

Table 8.10: Ratio of Manufactured Exports to Manufacturing
Value-added for Selected Less Developed Countries in 1975
and Hypothesized Expansion Factors

Country	(1) Actual Ratio of Manufactured Exports to Manufacturing Value-added Per Capita in 1975	Required Expansion in the Value of Manufactured Exports	
		(2) If the Ratio is Assumed to be 0.50	(3) If the Ratio is Assumed to be 1.00
Argentina	0.03	16.67	33.33
Brazil	0.06	8.33	16.67
Mexico	0.05	10.00	20.00
India	0.14	3.57	7.14
Malaysia	0.40	1.25	2.50
Pakistan	0.26	1.92	3.84
Thailand	0.12	4.17	8.33
Total above	0.08	6.25	12.50
Other LDCs	0.20	2.50	5.00
Hong Kong, Singapore, and South Korea	1.32	(1.00)*	(1.00)*
All LDCs	0.19	2.84	5.32

Notes: (a) Hong Kong, Singapore, and South Korea are excluded from the category of
'other LDCs', but are included in the total for 'all LDCs'. It is assumed that manufactured
exports from these East Asian countries remain at their *actual* level rather than the lower
level implicit in the norms hypothesized for all other LDCs. Hence the expansion factors
in columns (2) and (3) are kept at 1.00.
(b) Taiwan is excluded from the above exercise since comparable data required from
Table 8.3 and 8.4 are not available.
(c) All figures are rounded off to the second decimal place.
(d) LDCs stands for less developed countries.
Source: For column (1) and for the last row, Tables 8.3, 8.4, and 8.9. The proportions in
columns (2) and (3) have been calculated by dividing 0.50 and 1.00 respectively by the
ratios in column (1).

have constituted 18 per cent of the actual world exports of manufactures in
1975.[38] If the ratio is assumed to be 1.00, the corresponding figures work
out at 5.3 times their actual value and 34 per cent of world manufactured

[38]The expansion factors for all less developed countries, taken together, are estimated
on the assumption that manufactured exports from Hong Kong, Singapore, and South Korea
remain at their *actual* level rather than the level hypothesized in the norm for other less
developed countries.

exports.[39] In contrast, it is worth noting that, in 1975, the actual share of less developed countries in world manufactured exports was just 6.4 per cent. Given this reality, it is obvious that the expansion in manufactured exports from less developed countries, implicit in any attempt to generalize the East Asian model, would have far exceeded the absorptive capacity of the world market.[40]

2. A similar, but somewhat more sophisticated, exercise has recently been published by Cline.[41] He estimates that, in 1976, the value of manufactured exports from less developed countries would have been 7.5 times their actual value, if all less developed countries experienced the same intersity of exports in their economies as the four East Asian countries, measured by the percentage share of manufactured exports in GDP after adjustment for normal inter-country differences associated with size and level of development. If the analysis is confined to seven countries—Argentina, Brazil, Colombia, Mexico, Indonesia, Israel, and Malaysia—those more likely to follow in East Asian footsteps, the expansion factor works out to 4.2. In both cases, the estimated ratios of import penetration by less developed countries in the markets of industrialized economies would far exceed the threshold of tolerance. A seven-fold increase in exports of manufactures from less developed countries would mean that their share in manufactured imports by the industrialized countries would have to jump from the actual 16.7 per cent to a required 60.6 per cent. Cline concludes that the flood of less developed country exports which would follow any attempt to generalize the East Asian model would almost certainly provoke a response in terms of widespread protection by the rich countries.

The exercises outlined above are neither meaningful projections nor predictions of reality. They suffer from all the limitations of comparative statics. Yet they constitute a sort of litmus test, which makes it plausible to argue that, if everybody pursued the East Asian strategy, there would be a marked resurgence of protectionism in the world economy. Or, as Cline puts it aptly: 'Elevator salesmen must attach a warning label that their product is safe only if not

[39]The figures of 18 and 34 per cent, respectively are calculated from the expansion factors for all less developed countries in Table 8.10 and the data on actual manufactured exports in Table 8.2.

[40]The required expansion in exports of manufactures from less developed countries would also be inconsistent with the degree of industrialization in less developed countries. After all, in 1975, the share of less developed countries in world manufacturing value-added was only 10.3 per cent.

[41]See Cline (1982).

overloaded by too many passengers at one time; advocates of the East Asian export model would do well to attach a similar caveat to their prescription'.[42]

The recent rise of protectionism in the industrialized countries and the experience of the Tokyo Round of multilateral trade negotiations only confirm that any substantial increase in manufactured exports from less developed countries would lead to a further imposition of trade barriers in the developed world.

The argument, however, cannot be in terms of the fallacy of aggregation alone, because there would be a corresponding increase in import demand from less developed countries. But such a dynamic formulation of the problem cannot escape from the difficulties associated with the structural adjustment that would be required in the Western countries.[43] In fact, the 1970s have witnessed an upsurge in protectionism, despite the rapid growth in imports of manufactures by less developed countries from the West. The resistance to trade liberalization probably stems from the fact that the implicit change in the composition of international trade would require a restructuring and relocation of production on a world scale, both of which are likely to impose serious economic and political costs on the industrialized nations.

Clearly, the East Asian model can not be generalized among less developed countries. It would be natural to ask: is it possible even for a few less developed countries to follow in the footsteps of the four East Asian economies and replicate their experience? In my view it would be ahistorical to expect replication, for two reasons.

First, there has been a dramatic change in the state of the world economy in the early 1980s. The East Asian countries achieved a remarkable expansion in manufactured exports during a period when there was a boom in world trade which, in turn, was associated with a phase of rapid and sustained growth in the industrialized countries. This prolonged buoyancy came to an end in a world economy characterized by stagflation; economic growth in industrialized countries slowed down, almost to a halt, while protectionism registered an increase.[44]

Second, prescriptions which advocate a replication of the East Asian model tend to ignore the characteristics of these economies which were specific in terms of both time and space. Their success stories were based not simply on appropriate exchange rates and outward-looking policies, as is often made

---

[42]Cline (1982, p. 89).

[43]Cline (1982, p. 88).

[44]For evidence on this point, see World Bank, *World Development Report, 1982*, Chapter 2.

out, but also on more long-term factors. In South Korea, for example, such factors were the successful land reform, a history of industrialization based on import substitution, the development of entrepreneurial skills over a long period, and a high degree of State intervention which sought to promote capitalist development.[45] The role of the State and a redistributive land reform were important in Taiwan, while in Hong Kong it was the accumulation of industrial experience and entrepreneurial skills combined with *laissez-faire* policies. Singapore, by contrast, relied on foreign capital and skills much more than the others.[46] It would involve too much of a digression to enter into a discussion of these complex issues here. Suffice it to say that generalized prescriptions distilled from the development experience of East Asian countries tend to ignore the complexities of the growth process. In sum, therefore, exact replicas are most unlikely simply because times have changed and economic conditions are so different across countries.

In spite of the changed parameters, however, it might be possible for a few more less developed countries to increase their exports of manufactures as part of the international relocation of manufacturing production. The option might not be entirely with the less developed countries themselves; to a significant extent, it would depend on the choice of location by transnational corporations for their offshore manufacturing activities. Obviously, there would be competition among aspiring less developed countries not only over a share in slowly growing markets but also over the relocation of production. It is perfectly possible that, in an attempt to attract transnational firms, less developed countries might offer concessions and incentives to outbid each other and thereby worsen the distribution of gains from the trade arising out of international subcontracting. In this context, it is also worth noting that there are certain limits to the international relocation of manufacturing production by transnational corporations in the contemporary world economy.

1. The number of countries which might follow in the footsteps of the East Asian economies would depend on the success of the latter in making a transition from labour-intensive to skill and capital-intensive exports, and on the speed at which they vacate their position in the world trade matrix for less developed countries behind them. The transition may turn out to be difficult.[47]

2. There are technological limits to the international relocation of production in terms of the number and range of processes that can be relocated,

[45]See Datta-Chaudhuri (1981).
[46]For a careful analysis and detailed discussion, see Lee (ed.) (1981).
[47]Lee (ed.) (1981, pp. 20–1), and Park (1981).

either in divisible parts or as a whole. Indeed, unskilled, simple, and repetitive operations are most likely to be automated or mechanized with technical progress. There is some evidence to suggest that the emergence of the microprocessors might reduce labour costs to such an extent that activities relocated in less developed countries during the 1970s might be shifted back to the industrialized countries.[48]

3. At the same time, there are political limits to the export of capital from metropolitan countries, for the relocation of manufacturing production in less developed countries is often at the expense of employment in the industrialized economies which, beyond a point, is likely to be opposed by the workers. Given the present levels of unemployment, organized labour is bound to resist the trend towards any substantial relocation of production in less developed countries, as its effects on employment at home become increasingly discernible. Thus, it is hardly surprising that the trade unions are a major lobby for protectionism in the rich countries.[49] Ironically enough, the conflict between capital and labour within industrialized economies, which was one of the factors responsible for the international relocation of production being extended to less developed countries, might also constrain its further development.

NATURE OF INDUSTRIALIZATION AND IMPLICATIONS FOR LESS DEVELOPED COUNTRIES

It would be somewhat difficult to summarize the sequence of developments and the range of issues outlined in the preceding discussion. Instead, I shall attempt to conclude the essay with some observations about the implications of the international relocation of production for the industrialization process in less developed countries. This might enable us to situate the problem in its wider context.

Quite apart from the rapid export-led growth, in terms of most conventional indicators of development, the economic performance of the four East Asian countries during the period 1960–80 has been quite extraordinary. Real incomes per capita have registered a rapid and continuous increase, while mass poverty has been largely eradicated, and the massive absorption of labour into the industrial sector has created near full-employment.[50] Such achievements have eluded most less developed countries. In this context, it is worth reflecting on the nature of the industrialization process in the four economies of East Asia and asking whether their experience is worthy of emulation.

[48]J. Rada (1980).
[49]This hypothesis is developed, at some length, by Helleiner (1977).
[50]For evidence and discussion, see Lee (ed.) (1981).

Clearly, it is not possible to discuss such fundamental issues which, in themselves, constitute a vast subject and lie beyond the scope of this essay. In any case, the points at issue cannot be resolved on the basis of the available evidence. I shall simply outline a few ideas on the wider implications for development of less developed countries which might traverse a similar path on the road to industrialization.

It is obvious that lessons from the experience of Hong Kong and Singapore—which are city-states without a rural hinterland and thus without the problem of rural poverty—are bound to be of very limited relevance to most less developed countries. However, it has been argued that the industrialization experience of South Korea and Taiwan might serve as a model of development for other less developed countries. But this view is also open to question. For instance, in an essay which provides an overview of the process of export-led industrialization in East Asia, based on a number of country-studies, Eddy Lee observes:

... nagging doubts remain on whether the type of growth path traversed by these economies represents the most desirable escape route from underdevelopment. The objection on this score is perhaps best exemplified in the feeling that the industrial growth that has occurred has been shallow. More graphically these economies are sometimes regarded as gigantic sweatshops turning out cheap labour-intensive products and components within an iniquitous international division of labour. The concentration on labour-intensive products and on exporting is held to retard the capacity for autonomous industrial development. Inter-industry linkages within the manufacturing sector are low and no indigenous capital goods sector or technology generating capacity can grow. In addition, there are the well-known objections over the repressive political and economic policies that were used to push through the strategy of rapid export growth. This detracts considerably from the attractiveness of the experience of these countries.[51]

The proponents of the East Asian model might of course think that this, in turn, constitutes a short-term view. After all, the advocates of free trade, ever since the days of classical political economy, have pointed to the 'learning' or 'educational' effects of international trade over time: the openness of economies, it is said, stimulates wants, widens the horizons of producers, develops the skills of workers, and encourages innovation, thus increasing productivity and promoting economic growth.[52] There can be little doubt

[51]Lee (ed.) (1981, p. 21).
[52]Mill (1904).

that the cumulative development of skills and technology is essential to any strategy of industrialization in the Third World. At the same time, less developed countries must capture the benefits of externalities and promote linkages in the domestic economy, both of which are so crucial in the process of development. Therefore, the international relocation of production by transnational corporations would be consistent with the long-term objectives of industrialization in less developed countries if it gives rise to linkages in the domestic industrial sector and to externalities in the form of 'learning by doing'.

The evidence on these issues is clearly insufficient, and the need for detailed empirical research has been rightly stressed by several scholars.[53] However, it would be perfectly plausible to argue, though impossible to prove, that the 'linkage' and 'learning' effects arising from the relocation of manufacturing production in less developed countries (for the purpose of exports to the industrialized world) are not likely to be very significant.

The reasons are fairly obvious. In the footloose industries, for example, an international relocation of production would create minimal linkage effects, simply because transnational enterprises tend to use nothing other than the unskilled labour and the infrastructure available in less developed countries; an overwhelming proportion of the other inputs are imported while the bulk of the output is exported. Given the global outlook of these firms, the only linkages which matter are those that relate to their own international production and marketing nexus. Learning effects also cannot amount to much, either in terms of technology transfer if only parts of the production process are located in less developed countries, which is often the case, or in terms of marketing skills if overseas sales are entirely under the control of transnational buying groups. The manufacture of capital- or technology-intensive goods for export where the complete production process is located in poor countries is, perhaps, the only exception. Much would depend on the extent to which such plants use local inputs or components. In such a context, it would not be surprising if the prospects for innovation or indigenous technological development are considerably reduced.

While the effects in terms of linkages, learning, and technical progress might not be significant, the new internationalization of production absorbs scarce domestic infrastructural inputs which might have other priority uses in the industrialization programme of less developed countries. It also reduces the ability of governments in less developed countries to influence the long-term pattern of industrial investment or production and to mobilize or allocate

[53]See for example, Lee (ed.) (1981) and Lall (1978).

resources in accordance with the needs of development. The integration of manufacturing production with the activities of large international firms links industrialization in less developed countries to the world economy in a manner which is somewhat more vulnerable than usual. This is so because the activities of footloose industries and international buying groups give rise to manufacturing production for which there are no outlets other than transnational firms. Indeed, most of these goods cannot be sold in the world market by less developed countries on their own. The situation is rather different from primary commodities where, in spite of the predominant role of international firms, poor countries can always market their exportables at some price. What is more, there is a real danger that less developed countries might get 'locked' into such a pattern of production and trade, with relatively little room for manoeuvre, either in terms of domestic economic policy or in terms of bargaining at an international level, in much the same way as primary production for export.[54]

The international relocation of production in less developed countries might increase the proportion of manufactures in total exports, or in total output, but in a rudimentary, perhaps exaggerated, sense the 'enclave' nature of development remains: the mines and plantations are now replaced by branchplants in export processing zones. Manufacturing activities relocated in less developed countries by transnational firms tend to be concentrated in simple labour-intensive products or footloose industries. In either case, R&D, technology, management, control, and sophisticated production are centralized in the industrialized countries, whereas simple decisions, uncomplicated production, or mere unskilled-labour-intensive parts of the production process are located in less developed countries. More than 200 years ago, Adam Smith wrote the following passage about the division of labour among men. Seen in the present international context, it is not entirely inappropriate and is worth citing *à propos* the division of labour between nations:

In the progress of the division of labour, the employment of the far greater part of those who live by labour ... comes to be confined to a few very simple operations .... But the understandings of the greater part of men are necessarily formed by their ordinary employments. The man whose life is spent in performing a few simple operations, of which the effects too are, perhaps, always the same, or very nearly the same, has no occasion to exert his understanding, or to exercise his invention in finding out expedients for removing difficulties which never occur. He naturally loses, therefore,

[54]Helleiner (1976).

the habit of such exertion, and generally becomes as stupid and ignorant as it is possible for a human being to become.[55]

REFERENCES

Adam, G. (1975), 'Multinational Corporations and Worldwide Sourcing', in H. Radice (ed.), *International Firms and Modern Imperialism*, Penguin Books, Harmondsworth.

Bienefeld, M., M. Godfrey, and H. Schmitz (1977), 'Trade Unions and the New Internationalisation of Production', *Development and Change*, No. 8, pp. 417–39.

Cline, William R. (1982), 'Can the East Asian Model of Development be Generalised?', *World Develpment*, Vol. 10, No. 2, pp. 81–90.

Datta-Chaudhuri, M. (1981), 'Industrialisation and Foreign Trade: The Development Experiences of South Korea and the Philippines', in Eddy Lee (ed.) (1981).

Finger, J.M. (1975), 'Tariff Provisions for Offshore Assembly and the Exports of Developing Countries', *Economic Journal*, Vol. 85, No. 2, pp. 365–71.

Frobel, Folker, Jurgen Heinrichs, and Otto Kreye (1980), *The New International Division of Labour*, Cambridge University Press, Cambridge.

Helleiner, G.K. (1973), 'Manufactured Exports from LDCs and Multinational Firms', *Economic Journal*, Vol. 83, No. 1, pp. 21–47.

＿＿ (1976), 'Transnational Enterprise, Manufactured Exports and Employment in LDCs', *Economic and Political Weekly*, Annual No., February.

＿＿ (1977), 'Transnational Enterprises and the New Political Economy of US Trade Policy', *Oxford Economic Papers*, Vol. 29, No. 1, pp. 102–16.

Hughes, Helen (1980), 'Achievements and Objectives of Industrialisation', in J. Cody, H. Hughes, and D. Wall (eds), *Policies for Industrial Progress in Developing Countries*, Oxford University Press, New York.

ILO (1974), *Sharing in Development*, International Labour Organization, Geneva.

Keesing, D.B. (1967), 'Outward-Looking Policies and Economic Development', *Economic Journal*, Vol. 77, No. 2, pp. 303–20.

Lall, Sanjaya (1978), 'Transnationals, Domestic Enterprises and Industrial Structure in Host LDCs: A Survey', *Oxford Economic Papers*, Vol. 30, No. 2, pp. 217–48.

Lee, Eddy (ed.) (1981), *Export-Led Industrialization and Development*, Asian Employment Programme, ILO, Geneva.

Little, I.M.D. (1981), 'The Experience and Causes of Rapid Labour-Intensive Development in Korea, Taiwan, Hong Kong and Singapore', in Eddy Lee (ed.), *Export-Led Industrialisation and Development*, Asian Employment Programme, ILO, Geneva.

[55]Smith (1976), pp. 781–2.

Little, I.M.D., T. Scitovsky, and M. Scott (1970), *Industry and Trade in Some Developing Countries*, Oxford University Press, London.

Mill, J.S. (1904), *Principles of Political Economy*, Longmans, Book III, Chapter XVII, London.

Myint, H. (1972), *South East Asia's Economy*, Penguin Books, Harmondsworth.

Nayyar, Deepak (1978), 'Transnational Corporations and Manufactured Exports from Poor Countries', *Economic Journal*, Vol. 88, No. 1, pp. 59–84.

Park, Yung Chul (1981), 'Export-Led Development: The Korean Experience 1960–78', in Eddy Lee (ed.) (1981).

Rada, J. (1980), *The Impact of Micro-Electronics: A Tentative Assessment of Information Technology*, ILO, Geneva.

Sharpston, M. (1975), 'International Sub-contracting', *Oxford Economic Papers*, Vol. 27, No. 1, March, pp. 94–135.

Smith, Adam (1976), *The Wealth of Nations*, Book V, Chapter 1, R.H. Campbell and A.S. Skinner (eds), Clarendon Press, Oxford.

UNCTAD (1975), *International Subcontracting Arrangements in Electronics*, UN, New York, p. 19.

UNIDO (1979), *World Industry since 1960: Progress and Prospects*, United Nations, New York, pp. 33–43.

——— (1981), *World Industry in 1980*, United Nations, New York.

United Nations (1973), *Multinational Corporations in World Development*, UN, New York.

——— (1978), *Transnational Corporations in World Development: A Re-examination*, UN, New York.

US Tariff Commission (1970), *Economic Factors Affecting the Use of Items 807.00 and 806.30 of the Tariff Schedules of the United States*, US Government Printing Office, Washington, DC, pp. 115 and 172–3.

——— (1973), *Implications of Multinational Firms for World Trade and Investment and for US Trade and Labour*, US Government Printing Office, Washington, DC.

World Bank, *World Bank Atlas*, various years.

Chapter 9

THEMES IN TRADE AND INDUSTRIALIZATION*

INTRODUCTION

In the post-colonial era, which began soon after the end of the Second World War, most underdeveloped countries adopted strategies of development that provided a sharp contrast with their past during the first half of the twentieth century. For one, there was a conscious attempt to limit the degree of openness and of integration with the world economy, in pursuit of a more autonomous, if not self-reliant, development. For another, the State was assigned a strategic role in development because the market, by itself, was not perceived as sufficient to meet the aspirations of latecomers to industrialization. Both represented points of departure from the colonial era which was characterized by open economies and unregulated markets. But this approach also represented a consensus in thinking about the most appropriate strategy for industrialization. It was, in fact, the Development Consensus at the time.

It is more than 50 years since then. And it would seem that, in terms of perceptions about development, we have arrived at the polar opposite. Most countries in the developing world, as also in the erstwhile socialist bloc, are reshaping their domestic economic policies so as to integrate much more with the world economy and to enlarge the role of the market *vis-à-vis* the State. This is partly a consequence of internal crisis situations in economy, polity, or society. It is also significantly influenced by the profound transformation in the world economic and political situation. The widespread acceptance of this approach represents a new consensus in thinking about development. It has come to be known as the Washington Consensus.

This dramatic change in thinking is significant enough to be characterized as a shift of paradigm. The change, however, is not confined to the domain

*I am indebted to Amit Bhaduri for helpful discussion. I would also like to thank Satish Jain, Mritiunjoy Mohanty, Anjan Mukherji, and Abhijit Sen for useful suggestions.

of thinking. It extends to reality. For the process of globalization is changing the character of the world economy. Yet, the theme of trade and industrialization has remained central to the debate throughout this period. It was then. It is now.

This essay seeks to explore themes in trade and industrialization which have not received sufficient attention in mainstream literature. The discussion, therefore, is selective rather than exhaustive. It does, however, widen the canvas to consider the implications of globalization for trade and industrialization.

The first section begins with the underlying economic theory. It sets out the logic of the free trade argument and explains the rationale of exceptions to this rule. The second section examines the evolution of thinking about the degree of openness (in the sphere of trade) and the degree of intervention (by the State in the market) in the process of industrialization, to provide a critical assessment of the consensus: old and new. The third section explores the neglected themes in the literature on the subject. It situates trade in a macroeconomic perspective, highlights the importance of the demand side, outlines the implications of demand–supply linkages, and states the problems associated with missing out on the technology factor. The fourth section sketches the broad contours of globalization in the contemporary world economy, which has changed the international context, to discuss what it means for trade and industrialization in the developing world. The fifth section analyses the role of the State in countries that are latecomers to industrialization. In particular, it attempts to redefine the role of the State *vis-à-vis* the market, with reference to the present conjuncture, when globalization has increased the degree of openness of economies but reduced the degrees of freedom for nation states.

ECONOMIC THEORY AND THE FREE TRADE DOCTRINE

It is necessary, as also appropriate, to begin by outlining the logic of the free trade doctrine, which has received so much emphasis in economic theory, and by explaining the rationale of departures from free trade, which have been central to the debate on trade and industrialization over the past two centuries.[1]

The analytical foundations of the orthodox theory of international trade, as it now exists, were laid in the era of classical political economy by Adam Smith, David Ricardo, and John Stuart Mill. Smith (1776) enunciated the principle of absolute advantage to demonstrate that there were gains from trade, by extending his concept of the division of labour between men to a

[1] For a detailed discussion, see Nayyar (1996a)

division of labour between countries. Ricardo (1812) formulated the theory of comparative advantage to develop an explicit argument against protection and an implicit argument for free trade. At the same time, Smith and Ricardo endeavoured to provide a rationale, as also to analyse the conditions, for a transition from the prevalent feudalism to a prospective capitalism. Thus, for Adam Smith, free trade was simply one dimension of the case for *laissez faire* which confirmed his belief in the magic of the invisible hand. Similarly, for David Ricardo, the formulation of comparative advantage was not simply about the pattern of trade or the gains from trade, as contemporary textbooks would have us believe. It was as much, if not more, about the impact of international trade on income distribution, capital accumulation, and economic growth. The repeal of the Corn Laws and the adoption of free trade was advocated by Ricardo in the belief that it would redistribute incomes away from the reactionary landed gentry, who would at worst not save and at best invest in agriculture which promised diminishing returns, in favour of a progressive industrial capitalist class, who would earn more profits (given a lower corn wage) through cheap imports of wheat, and invest in manufacturing which promised increasing returns. The moral of the story was that, consequent upon the removal of restrictions on trade, an increase in profits would lead to an increase in the rate of accumulation which in turn would lead to a growth in employment, income, and wealth.

Subsequent economic theorizing about international trade, beginning in the late nineteenth century, became much narrower in perspective.[2] The neoclassical paradigm, as it emerged, emphasized the gains from trade. The economic logic underlying the proposition was indeed simple. In the most elementary sense, there are gains to be derived from trade if it is cheaper for an economy to import a good than to produce it at home, in terms of domestic resources used, and pay for it by exporting another. The gains are attributable in part to international exchange when costs or prices differ among countries before trade is introduced, and in part to international specialization in production after trade commences. In a world where countries enter into international trade on a voluntary basis, each partner must derive some benefit to be in the game. The very existence of trade, then, becomes proof of its mutual benefit, irrespective of how the gains from trade are distributed between countries. Orthodox theory combined the economic logic of the gains from trade proposition with the assumption of perfect competition to establish

[2]This process started with Alfred Marshall and Francis Edgeworth in the late nineteenth century. It was taken to its logical conclusion by Heckscher (1919), Ohlin (1933), and Samuelson (1939) during the first half of the twentieth century.

that free trade will enable an economy to operate with technical efficiency in production, in terms of resource allocation, and to optimize consumption through trade, in terms of utility maximization. The neat conclusion derived from this theorizing is that free trade ensures efficiency for a country and for the world as a whole.

The belief in free trade is almost a sacred tenet in the world of orthodox economics. Yet, from time to time, the profession of economics has recognized that there are reasons—orthodox and unorthodox—which may justify departures from free trade.[3] Economic theory has analysed these exceptions to the rule, mostly in response to developments in the real world which have questioned the free trade doctrine.

In the era of classical political economy, even before the doctrine gained widespread acceptance, it was recognized that there are two critical assumptions underlying the strong prescription of free trade: first, that market prices reflect social costs and, second, that a country's trade in a good is not large enough to influence world prices. If these assumptions do not hold, free trade cannot ensure an efficient outcome. Market failure provides the basis of the infant industry argument, recognizing that free trade may prevent an economy from realizing its comparative advantage in manufacturing activities. Monopoly power provides the basis of the optimum tariff argument recognizing that restricting the volume of trade may enable an economy to increase its real income at the expense of the rest of the world. These arguments were accepted as valid exceptions to the rule by Mill (1848), thus providing the analytical foundation for legitimate departures from free trade. It must be recognized that this thinking was prompted largely by the concerns of late industrializes such as the United States and Germany who wished to follow in the footsteps of England and France.[4] It was also motivated by the pursuit of economic interests rather than economic efficiency on the part of nation states.

More than a century later, at the beginning of the post-colonial era, the aspirations of underdeveloped countries were similar for they were latecomers to industrialization and wanted to accelerate the catching-up process. In the realm of politics, of course, the strong sentiment against free trade stemmed from the perceived association between openness and underdevelopment during the colonial era. In the sphere of economics, however, the argument against

---

[3]The challenges to free trade are discussed, at some length, by Irwin (1991) and Bhagwati (1994). See also Nayyar (1996a).

[4]The origin of the infant industry argument is associated with Alexander Hamilton whose *Report on Manufactures* was published in the United States in 1791 and Friedrich List whose *Das Nationale System der Politischen Okonomie* was published in Germany in 1841.

free trade was based on market failure. It had two dimensions. First, it was argued that there were significant positive externalities in any process of industrialization which were difficult to identify, let alone capture. Second, it was argued that imperfections in factor markets, both labour and capital, would pre-empt the realization of potential comparative advantages in manufacturing. The infant industry argument was, thus, generalized into the infant-manufacturing sector argument.[5] The industrial sector was protected from foreign competition and the pursuit of industrialization in most developing countries came to be based on the strategy of import substitution.

The response of modern neoclassical economics was two-fold. At one level, it accepted the infant industry argument, or the optimum tariff argument, as the basis of justifiable departures from free trade but reduced the validity of such arguments to a very demanding set of conditions.[6] At another level, it argued that if market prices did not measure social costs, whether on account of a divergence arising out of market failure or on account of a distortion arising out of government intervention, the optimum policy intervention is one which is applied at the point at which the divergence or the distortion arises; the simple solution which followed from this complex discussion was that, as a rule, intervention in the form of trade policies would be sub-optimal.[7] In sum, such theoretical analyses sought to strengthen the case for fee trade by accepting that there is market failure and by arguing that protection is not the best corrective.

Developments in the theory of international trade which have relaxed the assumptions of constant returns to scale and perfect competition, to model scale economic and market structures, have, once again, questioned the free trade argument.[8] This literature on strategic trade policy, which surfaced in the industrialized countries during the 1980s, developed a theoretical case for

[5]This generalization is attributable, among others, to Myrdal (1956). It was also in keeping with List's conception of an infant economy argument.

[6]See, for example, Corden (1974) who provides a meticulous analysis of the conditions under which the infant industry argument and the optimum tariff argument constitute valid arguments for protection.

[7]Bhagwati and Ramaswami (1963) and Corden (1974). In this context, there are two points that are worth noting. First, an appropriately chosen trade policy intervention, even if it is second-best or third-best, may result in a level of welfare higher than would be attainable under free trade. Second, the tax-cum-subsidy alternative may not be first-best if the taxes levied involve large collection costs or impose sizeable distortions elsewhere and if the disbursement costs of subsides are significant.

[8]For an overview of new theories of international trade, see Dixit and Norman (1980), Helpman and Krugman (1985), and Krugman (1986).

government intervention in trade on the basis of assumptions which are different from those in orthodox theory but conform more to observed reality.[9] In terms of positive economics, the new theories suggest that trade flows are driven by increasing returns rather than comparative advantage in international markets which are characterized by imperfect competition. This has led to the formulation of two arguments against free trade in the sphere of normative economics.[10] The first is the strategic trade policy argument which states that appropriate forms of government intervention can deter entry by foreign firms into lucrative markets and thus manipulate the terms of oligopolistic competition to ensure that excess returns are captured by domestic firms. The idea is that, in a market which has a small number of competitors, strategic support for domestic firms in international competition can raise national welfare at the expense of other countries. The second is an old argument in a new incarnation which states that governments should encourage activities that yield positive externalities. In a world of increasing returns and imperfect competition, such externalities are easier to identify in industries where R&D expenditures are large and firms cannot entirely appropriate the benefits from investment in technology and learning.

It should come as no surprise that the new trade theories received an asymmetrical response from economists: ready acceptance of the positive aspects and strong criticism of the normative aspects. Orthodox economics sets out three criticisms: (a) it is difficult to model imperfect markets and thus impossible to formulate appropriate policies for intervention; (b) potential gains from intervention would be dissipated by the entry of rent-seeking firms; and (c) in a general equilibrium world, the benefits from explicit promotion of one sector may be less than the cost of implicit discrimination against other sectors. These criticisms may weaken the arguments against free trade but cannot eliminate them. Yet, the new theorizing has withdrawn in the face of criticism on the basis of what is described as wider considerations of political economy. The explanation runs as follows. For one, it is possible that successful intervention

[9]It is no coincidence, however, that such theorizing has coincided with the resurgence of protectionism in the industrialized world. The analytical foundations of the new trade theories can be traced to the work of Edward Chamberlin and Joan Robinson who explored the world of market structures other than perfect competition or pure monopoly. It became clear that, under conditions of imperfect competition, market prices did not reflect social costs. This undermined the basis of the free trade argument. But the question was not even posed. The ability of the new trade theories to question the optimality of free trade is, perhaps, attributable to the juncture in time.

[10]For a lucid exposition of these arguments, which are associated with the work of several economists who have worked on the new trade theories, see Krugman (1987).

would have a beggar-thy-neighbour impact, which could lead to retaliation by trading partners making everybody worse-off. For another, governments are not Plato's guardians who act in the national interest, and intervention may simply be manipulated by vested interests who can influence the State to appropriate economic gains. This strategic withdrawal leads Paul Krugman (1987, p. 143) to a revealing conclusion:

> The economic cautions about the difficulty of formulating useful interventions and the political economy concerns that interventionism may go astray combine into a new case for free trade. This is not the old argument that free trade is optimal because markets are efficient. Instead, it is a sadder but wiser argument for free trade as a rule of thumb in a world whose politics is as imperfect as its markets .... It is possible, then, both to believe that comparative advantage is an incomplete model of trade and to believe that free trade is nevertheless the right policy. In fact, this is the position taken by most of the new trade theorists themselves. So free trade is not passè—but it is not what it once was.

The preceding discussion suggests that economic theory has, from time to time, thrown up serious questions about free trade. The response of orthodoxy has been predictable. It has endeavoured to reduce the validity of the widely accepted arguments for protection to a set of stringent conditions. It has attempted to dilute the arguments against free trade, in the context of industrialization and development, by arguing that domestic economic policies provide the first-best corrective. It has coaxed the new trade theorists into an acceptance of free trade as the best policy by invoking the real world of politics. The exceptions, it would seem, have been explored to establish the rule.

Yet, these exceptions have provided the rationale for departures from free trade in the real world of policy choices. The infant industry argument, sometimes generalized into the infant manufacturing sector argument, has shaped the strategies of most countries that were, or are, latecomers to industrialization, at least in the earlier stages of their development. It has, therefore, been the focus of an extensive literature and an intensive debate on trade and industrialization, particularly with reference to the experience of the developing world during the second half of the twentieth century.

In recent years, the new trade theories have revived the same issues and similar concerns by exploring the linkages between trade, industrialization, and growth in a dynamic context. For one, these theories have emphasized, once again, the importance of externalities, scale, or learning, and recognized, for the first time, the significance of market structures. For another, these theories have pointed to the inequalizing effects of trade (Krugman 1981), given the importance of initial conditions, so that even if trade is good, more trade is not always better. Thus, unmindful of the conclusions reached by orthodoxy, economic theory has lent new dimensions to the discussion on openness and industrialization.

OPENNESS, INTERVENTION, AND INDUSTRIALIZATION

The theme of trade and industrialization, situated in the wider context of development, has aroused considerable interest and stimulated much debate among economists during the period from the 1950s to the 1990s. It is striking that, throughout this period, the degree of openness *vis-à-vis* the world economy and the degree of intervention by the State in the market remained the critical issues, despite the shift in paradigm from the Development Consensus of the early 1950s to the Washington Consensus of the early 1990s.

At the beginning of the post-colonial era, there was a clear consensus in thinking about development. It was widely accepted that underdeveloped countries must industrialize and that their industrialization must be based on import substitution in the manufacturing sector combined with a leading role for the State in the process of economic development. This consensus was dominant until the early 1970s.

It was the actual industrialization experience of economies in Asia, Africa, and Latin America, during the quarter century which follower the Second World War, that led to questions. Research on the subject which attempted to describe, analyse, and evaluate this experience suggested that industrialization in developing countries was characterized by success stories in a few, muddling-through in some, and near-failure in others. Such uneven development, over time and across space, should not have come as a surprise. For those who questioned conventional wisdom, however, the post-mortem of failures led to a diagnosis while the analysis of successes led to prescriptions. These lessons drawn from the experience of particular countries were sought to be generalized and transplanted elsewhere. Such an approach tended to ignore not only the complexities of the growth process but also the characteristics of economies which are specific in time and space.

Yet, this approach came to exercise a profound influence on thinking about development. Its origins can be traced to the work of Little, Scitovsky, and Scott (1970), which attempted a systematic evaluation of the industrialization experience in selected developing countries to question the Development Consensus. Among the country studies, India's industrialization experience was examined by Bhagwati and Desai (1970). This set of studies was followed by those of Bhagwati (1978) and Krueger (1978) some years later, in which

Bhagwati and Srinivasan (1975) studied the Indian experience. These studies were among the first to provide an elaborate critique of the industrialization experience until then, from a neoclassical perspective, suggesting that the policy framework led to economic inefficiency and resource misallocation while the cumulative effect of these policies became an obstacle to growth. The basic object of these studies was an evaluation of import-substitution strategies and the economic efficiency of industrialization. The main conclusion was that industrialization policies, which protected domestic industries from foreign competition and led to excessive or inappropriate State intervention in the market, were responsible for the high cost and the low growth in these economies. Inward-looking policies, particularly in the sphere of trade, were seen as the prime culprit. The prescription followed from the critique. More openness and less intervention would impart both efficiency and dynamism to the growth process. And outward-looking policies, particularly in the sphere of trade, were seen as the prime saviour. Thus, trade policies were perceived as critical in the process of industrialization and development.

It needs to be said that this approach to trade and industrialization was narrow in its focus. For it was not recognized that there is more to trade policies than the distinction between import substitution and export promotion or inward and outward orientation, just as there is much more to industrialization than simply trade policies.[11] Even more important, perhaps, this approach was selective in its use of theory and history. For one, there was a striking asymmetry between the unqualified enthusiasm of policy prescriptions advocating free(r) trade, unmindful of the distinction between statics and dynamics or irrespective of time and place, and the formal exposition of the free trade argument in economic theory with its careful assumptions, proofs, and exceptions.[12] For another, the characterization of the success stories as economies which approximated to free trade and *laissez-faire* was partial if not caricature history, for their export orientation was not the equivalent of free trade just as the visible hand of the State was more in evidence than the invisible hand of the market.[13]

[11]Helleiner (1992).

[12]In an essay on the debate about trade and industrialization, this proposition was set out most succinctly by Diaz-Alejandro (1975, p. 96): 'In the trade and development literature, there has existed for a long time, going back at least to John Stuart Mill, a striking difference between the rigour of formal proofs on the static advantages of free trade, typically involving careful assumptions and caveats, and the impetuous enthusiasm with which most of the professional mainstream advocates free or freer trade policies, on both static and dynamic grounds, for all times and places.'

[13]In the literature on the development experience of the East Asian success stories—Hong Kong, Korea, Singapore, and Taiwan—Lee (1981), was among the first to emphasize this limitation. It has come to be recognized far more widely with the subsequent work of Amsden (1989) and Wade (1991). See also, Singh (1994).

In spite of these limitations, however, the neoclassical critique continued to gather momentum through the 1980s. The policy prescriptions derived from it became increasingly influential as these were adopted by the World Bank, to begin with in its research agenda and subsequently in its policy menu.[14] The process was reinforced by the reality that unfolded. The earlier success stories—Korea, Hong Kong, Taiwan, and Singapore—turned into the East Asian miracle which spread to China, Malaysia, Thailand, and even Indonesia. The debt-crisis which surfaced in Latin America, moved to sub-Saharan Africa and ultimately caught up with South Asia. The collapse of the political system in East Europe, particularly in the former Soviet Union, represented the failure of planned economies. The disillusionment with the Development Consensus was complete. And, by the early 1990s, the Washington Consensus acquired a near-hegemonic status in thinking about development.

Economic policies and development strategies in much of the developing world and the erstwhile socialist bloc are now shaped by the Washington Consensus, in part because it provides the basis of policy reform advocated by the IMF and the World Bank in their stabilization and structural adjustment programmes. In content, these adjustment and reform programmes are more elaborate than the earlier incarnation based on the neoclassical critique, but the logic is similar if not the same. The bottom line is more openness and less intervention. There is, however, more to openness than trade. It extends to investment flows, technology flows, and financial flows. Similarly, reduced State intervention extends beyond deregulation and liberalization. It suggests rolling back the government in every sphere. Structural reform seeks to shift resources: (a) from the non-traded goods sector to the traded goods sector and within the latter from import-competing activities to export activities; and (b) from the government sector to the private sector. Apart from such resource allocation, structural reform seeks to improve resource utilization: (a) by increasing the degree of openness of an economy; and (b) by changing the structure of incentives and institutions which would reduce the role of the State to rely more on market forces and wind up the public sector to rely on the private sector.

It would mean too much of a digression to enter into a detailed discussion on the industrialization experience, its neoclassical critique, and the neo-liberal prescription. There is an extensive literature on the subject, which is characterized by a diversity of views that range from the orthodox through the

---

[14]The research publications of the World Bank provide ample confirmation. See, for example, *World Development Report 1987* and World Bank (1993).

heterodox to the unorthodox. I would simply like to highlight some of the analytical limitations of the new orthodoxy on trade and industrialization.

First, it is a simple fallacy in logic to claim that if something (State intervention or protection) does not work, its opposite (the free market or free trade) must work. This is true only in a dichotomous world of two alternatives. In the world of economic policies, where there are always more than two alternatives, such a view is obviously false. Thus, if A is wrong, it does not mean that the opposite of A (say B) must necessarily be right. If there are other alternatives, say C, D, E, or F, one of these rather than B may be right.

Second, the emphasis on trade liberalization, which assumes that international competition will force domestic firms to become more efficient, makes an elementary but commonplace error in the design of policies. It confuses *comparison* (of equilibrium positions) with *change* (from one equilibrium position to another). In the real world, economic policy must be concerned not merely with comparison but with how to direct the process of change. Thus, even if a reduction in protection can, in principle, lead to a more cost-efficient economy, the transition path is by no means clear. And the process of change should not be confused with the ultimate destination of an economy that is competitive in the world market.

Third, the analytical construct is narrow. Success at industrialization is not only about resource allocation and resource utilization at a micro-level. It is as much, if not more about resource mobilization and resource creation at a macro-level. The excessive concern with resource allocation, in terms of static allocative efficiency criteria, is perhaps misplaced, while the strong emphasis on resource utilization, in terms of competition through deregulation and openness, is important but disproportionate. Significant new developments in the neoclassical tradition, whether in industrial economics or in trade theory, are almost ignored when such analysis is applied to problems of industrialization and development. Hence this approach, which is static rather than dynamic in conception, tends to ignore inter-temporal considerations and does not quite incorporate increasing returns, market structures, externalities, or learning which are inherent in any process of industrialization.

Fourth, there is a presumption that what is necessary is also sufficient. The management of incentives, motivated by the object of minimizing cost and maximizing efficiency at a micro-level, is based on a set of policies that is intended to increase competition between firms in the market place. Domestic competition is sought to be provided through deregulation in investment decisions, in the financial sector, and in labour markets. Foreign competition is sought to be provided through openness in trade, investment, and technology flows. It must, however, be recognized that policies may be necessary but not sufficient, for there is nothing automatic about competition. Policy regimes can allow things to happen but cannot cause things to happen. The creation of competitive markets that enforce efficiency may, in fact, require strategic intervention through industrial policy, trade policy, and financial policy.[15]

Fifth, the strong emphasis on allocative efficiency is matched by a conspicuous silence on technical efficiency. It is forgotten that low levels of productivity in most developing countries are attributable more to technical inefficiency than to allocative inefficiency. And inter-country differences, as also inter-firm differences, in technical efficiency are explained, in large part, by differences in technological (and managerial) capabilities at a micro-level. These capabilities determine not just efficiency in the short-run but also competitiveness in the long-run. But, given the nature of the learning process, such capabilities are both firm-specific and path-dependent.[16] The new orthodoxy simply ignores this critical dimension on the supply side. In contrast, the heterodox literature places the acquisition and development of technological capabilities centre-stage in the story of success at industrialization.[17] It also shows that the presumed relationship between trade liberalization and technical efficiency is dubious in terms of both theory and evidence.[18]

THE NEGLECTED THEMES

The preceding discussion suggests that the orthodox literature on trade and industrialization is narrow and selective in its focus. In view of its widespread influence, however, it has set the terms of reference for the debate. Much of the discussion in the literature, therefore, centres on what has been said in the neoclassical critique or the neo-liberal prescription. Little attention is paid to what has not been said. But the unsaid is important even if it is neglected. Insofar as orthodoxy is micro-theoretic in its analytical foundations, it lacks a macroeconomic perspective. Insofar as orthodoxy emphasizes the supply side, it neglects the demand side. Consequently, the interaction between supply

---

[15]This issue is discussed, at some length, later in the essay in the section on the role of the State.

[16]Rosenberg (1994).

[17]See Bell and Pavitt (1993), Dahlman et al. (1987), and Pack and Westphal (1986).

[18]In an essay which analyses the relationship between trade policy and technical efficiency, based on theory and experience, Rodrik (1992, p. 172) reaches the following conclusion. 'If truth-in-advertising were to apply to policy advice, each prescription for trade liberalization would be accompanied with a disclaimer: Warning! Trade liberalization cannot be shown to enhance technical efficiency; nor has it been empirically demonstrated to do so.'

and demand which has important implications and consequences for industrialization has not entered the picture. Similarly, technology is another missing dimension because it is treated almost as a non-issue, subsumed in resource allocation, embodied in production functions or, at best, thought of as available 'off-the-shelf'. It is important to highlight, albeit briefly, these somewhat neglected themes in trade and industrialization.

Trade in a Macroeconomic Perspective

In the realm of orthodox economics, the ideal world is one where resource allocation follows revealed comparative advantage, to choose industries in accordance with relative international prices, so that industrialization everywhere is part of an optimal division of labour between countries in the world economy. This provides the essential logic for trade liberalization. The presumption is that it will shift resources from the production of non-traded goods to the production of traded goods, while exposure to international competition will force domestic firms to become more efficient. But trade, or trade liberalization, is not situated in a macroeconomic perspective. This omission means that analysis and understanding are both incomplete.

In a macroeconomic context, at the simplest level, the role of trade is to bridge the gap between aggregate demand and aggregate supply as also to match the composition of demand with the composition of supply. Hence, exports and imports help maintain an equilibrium between demand and supply in an open economy. But the role of trade extends beyond this equilibrating mechanism. For one, it has a direct macroeconomic impact on output. For another, its interaction with other macroeconomic variables may lead to an indirect impact on output.

Let me begin with the short-run. In an open economy, exports mean an addition to, while imports mean a deduction from, the level of aggregate demand. The multiplier in an open economy is, in principle, similar to that in a closed economy. An increase in exports is the equivalent of an increase in investment, if we assume that the additional employment and income in the export sector create a demand for goods that is met entirely by domestic production. In any case, increased exports would increase effective demand even if some part of the increased demand spills over into imports. On the other hand, an increase in imports is the equivalent of an increase in savings, for it decreases effective demand for domestic goods. Thus, exports increase the size of the multiplicand whereas imports reduce the size of the multiplier. It follows that any increase in exports, attributable to trade liberalization, would have as stimulating effect on output and employment. Contrariwise, any increase in imports, attributable to trade liberalization, would have a dampening effect on output and employment. For one, if it increases the marginal propensity to import, it would reduce the size of the foreign trade multiplier. For another, if import liberalization shifts domestic demand from home-produced goods to imports, it would reduce output by a much larger amount (because the contractionary effect would be a multiple of the initial increase in imports), for any given size of the foreign trade multiplier.

Consider next, the medium-term or the long-run. There is a possible important nexus between exports and investment at a macro-level. Exports provide an external market on the demand side and enforce a cost discipline on the supply side, whereas investment creates a domestic market on the demand side and transforms the industrial structure on the supply side. Hence, there is a possible cumulative causation that arises from the interaction between the effects of the foreign trade multiplier and of capacity creation combined with industrial cost efficiency. On the demand side, high investment and high exports together induce market expansion and may be conducive to high growth. On the supply side, a high or rising proportion of investment in national income may provide flexibility through more rapid supply side adjustment, while a high or rising proportion of exports in national income may provide discipline by enforcing cost efficiency. Such a virtuous circle of cumulative macroeconomic causation would be associated with a rapid growth in manufactured exports, industrial output, and national income.

To begin with, if investment exceeds domestic savings there would be a corresponding excess of imports over exports which would need to be financed by foreign capital inflows. So long as these inflows are used to supplement domestic savings, and augment investment, even borrowing is sustainable. After a period, however, higher rates of investment must be supported by higher rates of domestic saving. This is possible when investment creates profits which become a source of savings that are used for capital accumulation. The cumulative causation outlined here may lead to a virtuous circle if an increase in investment coincides with an increase in exports, while there is no neutralizing change in the capital–output ratio and higher rates of investment are, ultimately, sustained by higher rates of domestic saving.[19] The East Asian

[19]This cumulative macroeconomic causation and its relevance to the Indian development experience is analysed in Nayyar (1994a). It is, of course, possible that an increase in investment does not coincide with an increase in exports, or there is a compensating increase in the capital–output ratio, *and* external resources become a substitute for domestic resources, used to support consumption rather than investment. In such a situation, a vicious circle, rather than a virtuous circle, is the likely outcome. The South Asian economies, which ran into debt crises, provide an example of this vicious circle.

economies provide an example of this virtuous circle. But such an understanding is not possible unless trade is situated in the wider macroeconomic context.

The Demand Side

In the context of open economies, orthodox economics simply assumes away the demand side by making the small country assumption. The elasticity of demand for exports is assumed to be infinite so that the country can sell as much as it wants to at world prices, while the elasticity of supply of imports is assumed to be infinite so that a country can buy as much as it wants to at world prices. Understanding industrialization requires a recognition of supply factors, but it does not call for a neglect of demand factors. It does not, for example, serve much purpose to consider a high marginal capital–output ratio or a slow factor productivity increase as performance criteria if capital or capacities are underutilized. Unfavourable values for these variables follow as a statistical result. The emergence or existence of widespread excess capacity in many sectors of the economy cannot always be explained in terms of resource misallocation or cost inefficiencies. In such a context, it would be a mistake to neglect demand factors, particularly for large industrializing economies such as India, on the presumption that inadequacy of demand is not a real problem, given the existence of a virtual unlimited demand for exports. The level of demand and the composition of demand both matter.[20]

The relative importance of the internal market and of external markets in the process of industrialization must obviously depend, among other things, on the size of the country. In large countries, where the domestic market is overwhelmingly important, sustained industrialization can only be based on the growth of the home market. On the other hand, in small countries, the possibilities of industrialization may be limited by the size of the domestic market. It must be stressed, however, that these possibilities are not mutually exclusive. It is simply a matter of natural emphasis and temporal sequence. In the ultimate analysis, large economies must seek to externalize internal markets whereas small economies must endeavour to internalize external markets. Therefore, industrialization may stress manufacturing for the domestic market through import substitution or manufacturing for export to external markets. The emphasis would depend on the size of an economy

[20]The importance of the level and the composition of demand for industrialization in India is discussed, at greater length, in Nayyar (1994b); see, in particular, the essays by K.N. Raj, Sukhamoy Chakravarty, Deepak Nayyar, and C. Rangarajan. See also, Bagchi (1970) and Chakravarty (1987). For a theoretical analysis of the significance of the demand factor in open economies, see Bhaduri and Marglin (1990).

and the stage of its development. Unfortunately, this basic issue has been reduced to a debate about trade policies for industrialization or a choice between import substitution and export promotion. It is essential to get out of this false dilemma and examine the home market question in its wider context. In terms of an appropriate strategy for industrialization, striking a balance between import substitution and export promotion is equivalent of walking on two legs. The timing and the pace of the transition in shifting emphasis from one to the other clearly matters. However, success or failure depends not so much on the choice between inward-looking and outward-looking policies as it does on the setting in which these are introduced. An environment that produces a spectacular export performance is also conducive to efficient import substitution and rapid economic growth.

It is also worth considering the composition of demand to analyse the possibilities of expansion in the size of the market. Let us start from the national income accounting identity. On the expenditure side, GDP can be disaggregated into its principal components: (a) private consumption; (b) private investment; (c) government consumption and investment taken together; and (d) trade surplus (excess of exports over imports). From this accounting definition, it follows that aggregate demand or the size of the market can be expanded in four ways that are analytically distinct from each other even if they are difficult to separate in real world situations.

First, it is possible to conceive of private-consumption-led expansion which would require a redistribution of incomes, if not assets, in favour of the poor who, it is reasonable to presume, have a higher propensity to consume. There is a diluted version, or another variant of this theme, which may be described as consumer-durable-led expansion, where incomes are redistributed in favour of a small elite or larger middle class which has a high propensity to consume. The former postulates an egalitarian strategy of development which may be constrained by political factors. The latter may give rise to an economic constraint manifest in the balance of payments or a social constraint in the form of income inequalities, but its capacity to alleviate the demand constraint on industrialization would depend upon the size of the elite or the middle class as a proportion of the total population. The second possibility is private-investment-led expansion. This can happen only if there is an improvement in the expected profitability of investment. Such profitability, however, is necessary but not sufficient, unless it is associated with animal spirits and managerial capabilities of entrepreneurs. There is now a variation around this theme which regards profitability as both necessary and sufficient, on the assumption that inflows of direct foreign investment would, at least in the first instance, provide the entrepreneurship for industrialization.[21]

The third analytically distinct way is government-expenditure-led expansion. Such an expansion can be based either on public investment or on public expenditure. The multiplier effect of the former may be larger if it is directed to the creation of a physical or human infrastructure for development. The fourth possibility is export-surplus-led expansion. Unlike the other three components, in this case it is the external market instead of the internal market, which is critical in increasing the size of the market to sustain the industrialization process. In principle, however, import substitution should have an identical effect on aggregate demand insofar as one dollar of imports saved generates the same trade surplus as one dollar of exports. While there is an obvious accounting similarity, there is an important analytical difference. A dollar saved through import substitution may decrease the propensity to import and hence increase the size of the foreign trade multiplier. A dollar earned through exports would increase the level of exports and hence enlarge the base on which the foreign trade multiplier operates.

Supply–Demand Linkages

Industrialization is associated with economic growth and structural change. The process of economic growth is characterized by a dynamic interaction between demand factors and supply factors, so that a mismatch between aggregate demand and aggregate supply, as also disproportionalities between and within sectors, which surface overtime, affect either the price level or the balance of payments or both. The process of structural change reflects differences in the rates of expansion or contraction of output, employment, or investment in different sectors, where the underlying factors are changes in the structure of final demand and changes in the technology of productive activities in the national context juxtaposed with changes in comparative advantage in the international context. Studies on the industrialization experience of developing countries focus on the supply side, or on the demand side, and do not pay adequate attention to the interaction between the forces of demand and supply in a macroeconomic perspective.

---

[21]The structural reforms and policy changes introduced in India during he early 1990s, focus on these two methods of increasing aggregate demand: to create a demand for consumer goods on the part of the middle class and to create an environment where private investment, both domestic and foreign, would be profitable.

On the demand side, the size of the market is an important determinant of industrialization prospects. The relative importance of the internal market and the external market then assumes significance. On the supply side, the level of resource mobilization, the pattern of resource allocation, the mode of resource utilization, and the potential for resource creation, taken together, shape the possibilities of industrialization. The contribution of internal resources as compared with external resources obviously influences the nature of industrialization. It follows that, whether we consider markets on the demand side or resources on the supply side, the mix between the internal and the external is crucial in any process of industrialization. The relative importance depends on the size of a country or the stage of its development. In general, countries can exercise greater control or influence over internal markets and domestic resources as compared to external markets and foreign resources. Nevertheless, a recognition and utilization of markets and resources beyond national boundaries can foster industrialization in terms of both pace and quality. This is an important lesson that emerges from the East Asian development experience.

The process of industrialization and growth in an economy may be associated with supply–demand balances or supply–demand imbalances that emerge over time at a macro-level. In either case, interaction between the forces of supply and demand, in a dynamic setting, has important implications for the process of economic growth. *Ceteris paribus*, balances may serve as catalysts to growth while imbalances may operate as constraints on growth.

Consider first, a situation where industrialization is associated with a balanced growth in demand and supply over time. An increase in market size facilitates the realization of scale-economies, thus bringing about a cost-reduction, just as a reduction in costs, hence prices, induces a demand expansion. In an industrializing economy, a rapid increase in the share of manufacturing in total output may then be associated with a steady decline in average costs over time. The underlying factors would be dynamic scale-economies, which are function of cumulative past output or cumulative production experience, and increase in labour productivity. The cost-reduction, passed on to consumers in the form of lower prices, would stimulate demand expansion in domestic, as also foreign markets. This cumulative causation, which is complex but virtuous, is often termed the 'Kaldor–Verdoorn Law'.

Consider next, a situation where industrialization is associated with the emergence over time of imbalances between supply and demand. More often than not, this is a short-term problem but it can persist in the medium-term. If there emerges a gap between demand and supply, it can be bridged either through imports or by allowing prices to rise. Industrialization and growth may then be disrupted by a balance of payments crisis or mounting inflation. The problem of imbalances may be exacerbated by an asymmetry, or a mismatch, between the speeds of adjustment on the demand side and on the supply side. The responsiveness of aggregate demand, through some of its principal components, is relatively fast and macroeconomic policies can be deployed to adjust domestic demand expansion. Supply adjustment, on the other hand, takes longer even if all the price incentives of a market economy can be brought to perfect function. In other words, the reallocation of resources from one industry to another, one sector to another, or one activity to another is a relatively slow process, for resources are neither so mobile nor so substitutable as neoclassical economics suggests. In some economies, supply may adjust particularly slowly due to problems such as the nature of agrarian relations or very inadequate infrastructural facilities, so that State intervention may be essential to coax a response on the supply side. The fast dynamics of demand and the slow dynamics of supply have two important macroeconomic implications. For one, growth in aggregate demand and aggregate supply often diverge. For another, insofar as the composition of demand, guided by income elasticities, and the composition of supply, guided by relative profitabilities, do not match, sectoral problems of excess demand or excess supply often emerge. These imbalances affect both the price level and relative prices. Insofar as economies have tolerance limits in terms of an acceptable rate of inflation or a manageable current account deficit in the balance of payments, beyond a point, the persistence of supply–demand imbalances can only operate as a constraint on growth and disrupt industrialization.

The Technology Factor

The acquisition of technological capabilities at a micro-level and the development of technologies at a macro-level is fundamental in the process of industrialization. The former shapes efficiency of production by firms in the manufacturing sector, while the latter influences growth of productivity in industry and in the economy as a whole. These dimensions of industrialization, however, do not figure in the Washington Consensus which treats technology as a non-issue or a black-box. The heterodox literature does, of course, focus on technical efficiency and technological capabilities at a micro-level as an integral part of success at industrialization. Thus, I shall explore, briefly, problems of technology development at a macro-level.

The industrialization experience of developing countries in the sphere of technology is mixed. In most countries, other than the newly industrializing economies which are characterized as the success stories, the level of technological development is just not adequate by international standards. The Indian experience is illustrative. There are distressing examples of situations where technologies were imported for particular sectors at a point of time but the import of such technologies has been followed by stagnation rather than adaptation, diffusion, and innovation at home. At the same time, in many cases, indigenous development of technology has not led to widespread diffusion, let alone technological upgradation. Although the underlying reasons are complex, it is clear that market structures and government policies have not combined to provide an environment that would encourage the absorption of imported technology and speed up the development of indigenous technology, or create a milieu that would be conducive to diffusion and innovation. It is seldom mentioned that the record of the private sector in terms of R&D effort has been dismal in this sphere. There is, however, a curious asymmetry in the lessons that the orthodoxy has drawn, or not drawn, from this experience.[22] It deserves elaboration.

The lesson that has been learnt is that there must be a liberal access to imports of technology. It is an important lesson. But an industrializing economy must be able to make a transition from importation through absorption and adaptation to diffusion and innovation, at least in some sectors, so that the acquisition of technology through imports is, after a time, followed by the development of domestic technological capabilities. An open regime for the import of technology cannot suffice, for the discipline of the market cannot restrain the recurrence of such imports by domestic firms time after time. Such firms are much like the school boy who can always find someone else to write his examinations for him year after year and thus never learns. Domestic technological capabilities may not emerge either because there is no incentive to learn (imports are possible) or because they are stifled (imports are better). The problem may be accentuated in sectors where technical progress is rapid and obsolescence is high.

The lesson that has not been learnt is that the role of the government is crucial for planning technological development across sectors and over time. This means planning for the acquisition of technology where it is to be imported, setting aside resources for technology where it is to be produced at home, or even deciding to opt out of a technology where it is not needed. For this purpose, it is necessary to formulate a policy regime for the import of technology, allocate resources for R&D, and evolve government procurement

---

[22]Bhaduri and Nayyar (1996).

policies. In the absence of such strategic intervention by the government, Japan would never have produced automobiles or optical instruments that could compete with their European or American counterparts, Europe would never have produced the Airbus that could compete with Being aircraft, and Korea would never have produced consumer electronics that could compete with established Japanese brand names. Let it also be remembered that, despite heavy initial investment, Japan decided to pull out of aircraft production when things did not come up to the mark. Industrial policy must mean both carrot and stick: reward for international success through unstinted government support but punishment for failure through withdrawal of government support. For industrial policy, it is not the market alone but also the government that must be active in this game of reward and punishment.

It is one of the unambiguous lessons of recent economic history that the guiding and supportive role of the State at a macro-level is a necessary condition for the development of technology in countries that are latecomers to industrialization. And, there is no country that has succeeded at industrialization without developing such technological capabilities in firms at a micro-level. In the long-term, technological development at a macro-level and technological capabilities at a micro-level are the essential foundation on which international competitiveness is built.

GLOBALIZATION: THE CHANGED CONTEXT

The significance of the neglected themes, considered here, suggests that the literature on trade and industrialization is incomplete in some important aspects. But that is not all. Subsequent developments in the world economy, manifest in globalization, have led to far-reaching changes in the reality. The debate on trade and industrialization must now be situated in this changed international context if it is to retain its relevance.

Globalization means different things to different people. It can be defined simply as the expansion of economic activities across political boundaries of nation states. More important, perhaps, it refers to a process of increasing economic openness, growing economic interdependence, and deepening economic integration between countries in the world economy. It is associated not only with a phenomenal spread and volume of cross-border economic transactions but also with an organization of economic activities which straddles national boundaries. This process is driven by the lure of profit and the threat of competition in the market.

The word *globalization* is used in two ways, which is a source of confusion and a cause of controversy. It is used in a *positive* sense to *describe* a process of increasing integration into the world economy: the characterization of this process is by no means uniform. It is used in a *normative* sense to *prescribe* a strategy of development based on a rapid integration with the world economy: some see this as salvation while others see it as damnation.

The world economy has experienced a progressive international economic integration since 1950. However, there has been a marked acceleration in this process of globalization during the last quarter of the twentieth century. The fundamental attribute of globalization is the increasing degree of openness in most countries. There are three dimensions of this phenomenon: international trade, international investment, and international finance. It needs to be said that openness is not simply confined to trade flows, investment flows, and financial flows. It also extends to flows of services, technology, information, and ideas across national boundaries. But the cross-border movement of people is closely regulated and highly restricted. And, there can be no doubt that trade, investment, and finance constitute the cutting edge of globalization.

The gathering momentum of globalization has already brought about profound changes in the world economy. It is worth highlighting the broad contours of these changes.[23] An increasing proportion of world output is entering into world trade, while an increasing proportion of world trade is made up of intra-firm trade (across national boundaries but between affiliates of the same firm). Between the early 1970s and the early 1990s, the share of world exports in world GDP rose from one-eighth to one-sixth, while the share of intra-firm trade in world trade rose from one-fifth to one-third. The significance of international investment flows has also registered a rapid increase. Between 1980 and 1992, the stock of direct foreign investment in the world as a proportion of world output rose from 4.8 per cent to 8.4 per cent, while world direct foreign investment flows as a proportion of world gross fixed capital formation rose from 2 per cent to 3.7 per cent. The growth in international finance has been explosive. So much so that in terms of magnitudes, trade and investment are now dwarfed by finance. The expansion of international banking is phenomenal. Between 1980 and 1991, net international bank loans increased from 51.1 per cent to 131.4 per cent of gross fixed domestic investment in the world economy. The international market for financial assets has experienced a similar growth. Between 1980 and 1993, gross sales and purchases of bonds and equities transacted between domestic and foreign residents rose from less than 10 per cent of GDP to more than 100 per cent of GDP in the major industrialized countries. Government debt has also become tradeable. Between 1980 and 1992, the proportion of government

---

[23]The figures cited in this paragraph draw upon earlier work by the author. For sources and details, see Nayyar (1995).

bonds held by foreigners rose from less than 10 per cent to more than 25 per cent in many industrialized countries. Global foreign exchange transactions have soared from $60 billion per day in 1983 to $900 billion per day in 1992. The size of international foreign exchange markets is staggering. This is apparent from the fact that, in 1992, world GDP was $64 billion per day and world exports were $10 billion per day, while the reserves of central banks put together were $693 billion.

The politics of hegemony or dominance is conducive to the economics of globalization. The process of globalization, beginning in the early 1970s, has coincided with the political dominance of the United States as the superpower. This political dominance has grown stronger with the collapse of communism and with the triumph of capitalism. And the political conjuncture has transformed the concept of globalization into a 'virtual ideology' of our times. Dominance in the realm of politics is associated with an important attribute in the sphere of economics. For globalization requires a dominant economic power with a national currency which is accepted as the equivalent of international money: as a unit of account, a medium of exchange, and a store of value. In the late twentieth century, this role was performed by the US dollar, ironically enough after the collapse of the Bretton Woods system when its statutory role as a reserve currency came to an end.

Economic theorizing often follows in the footsteps of political reality. It should come as no surprise, then, that recent years have witnessed the formulation of an intellectual rationale for globalization that is almost prescriptive. It is perceived as a means of ensuring not only efficiency and equity but also growth and development in the world economy. The analytical foundations of this world view are provided by the neo-liberal model. And it builds on the infrastructure of the Washington Consensus. Orthodox neoclassical economics suggests that intervention in markets is inefficient. Neo-liberal political economy argues that governments are incapable of intervening efficiently. The essence of the neo-liberal model, then, can be stated as follows. First, the government should be rolled back wherever possible so that it approximates to the ideal of a minimalist State. Second, the market is not only a substitute for the State but also the preferred alternative because it performs better. Third, resource allocation and resource utilization must be based on market prices which should conform as closely as possible to international prices. Fourth, national political objectives, domestic economic concerns, or even national boundaries should not act as constraints.[24] In conformity with this world view, governments

---

[24]In this world, domestic economic concerns mesh with, and are substumed in, the maximization of international economic welfare, and national political objectives melt away in the bargain.

everywhere, particularly in the developing countries and the former communist countries, are being urged or pushed into a comprehensive agenda of privatization (to minimize the role of the State) and liberalization (of trade flows, capital flows, and financial flows). It is suggested that such policy regimes would provide the foundations for a global economic system characterized by free trade, unrestricted capital mobility, open markets, and harmonized institutions. And the ideologues believe that such globalization promises economic prosperity for countries that join the system and economic deprivation for countries that do not.[25]

It needs to be stressed that this normative and prescriptive view of globalization is driven in part by ideology and in part by hope. It is not validated by history. The process of globalization during the period from 1870 to 1914, which provides a remarkable historical parallel, did not reproduce or replicate Britain everywhere.[26] Indeed, some of the most open economies in this earlier phase of globalization, such as India, China, and Indonesia, experienced de-industrialization and underdevelopment. The process of globalization was uneven then. It is so even now. There are less than a dozen developing countries which are an integral part of globalization in the late twentieth century: Argentina, Brazil, and Mexico in Latin America and Korea, Hong Kong, Taiwan, Singapore, China, Indonesia, Malaysia, and Thailand in Asia.[27] It would seem that globalization is most uneven in its spread. And, there is an exclusion in the process. Sub-Saharan Africa, West Asia, Central Asia, and South Asia are simply not in the picture, apart from many countries in Latin America, Asia, and the Pacific which are left out altogether. It is, then, plausible to suggest that globalization may lead to uneven development in the late twentieth century just as it did in the late nineteenth century.[28] But there can be no doubt that this process of globalization has profound implications for trade and industrialization everywhere in the developing world.

The process of globalization has placed new players centre stage. There are two main sets of economic players in this game: transnational corporations which dominate investment, production, and trade in the world economy,

[25]See, for example, Sachs and Warner (1995).

[26]For an analysis of this historical parallel, between globalization in the late nineteenth century and in the late twentieth century, see Nayyar (1995).

[27]These eleven countries accounted for 66 per cent of total exports from developing countries in 1992. The same countries, excluding Korea, were also the main recipients of direct foreign investment in the developing world, accounting for 66 per cent of the average annual inflows during the period 1981–91 (Nayyar 1995).

[28]This argument is developed, at some length, in Nayyar (1995).

and international banks or financial intermediaries which control the world of finance. It would seem that the present conjuncture represents the final frontier in the global reach of capitalism to organize production, trade, investment, and finance on a world scale without any fetters except, of course, for tight controls on labour mobility. Transnational corporations and international banks or financial intermediaries wish to set new rules of the game which would enable them to manage the risks associated with globalization. In this task, the nation states of the industrialized world provide the much needed political clout and support. The multilateral framework of the WTO, the IMF, and the World Bank is, perhaps, the most important medium.

The rules of the game for the international trading system are being progressively set in the WTO. It would seem that this institutional framework for globalization is characterized by a striking asymmetry.[29] National boundaries should not matter for trade flows and capital flows but should be clearly demarcated for technology flows and labour flows. It follows that the developing countries would provide access to their markets without a corresponding access to technology and would accept capital mobility without a corresponding provision for labour mobility. This asymmetry, particularly that between the free movement of capital and the unfree movement of labour across national boundaries, lies at the heart of the inequality in the rules of the game for globalization in the late twentieth century. These new rules, which serve the interests of transnational corporations as capital-exporters and technology leaders in the world economy, are explicit as an integral part of a multilateral regime of discipline.

The rules of the game, which would serve the interests of the international banks of financial intermediaries in the process of globalization, are in part implicit and in part unwritten. Even here, there is an asymmetry as there are rules for some but not for others. There are no rules for surplus countries or even deficit countries in the industrialized world, which do not borrow from the multilateral financial institutions. But the IMF and the World Bank set rules for borrowers in the developing world and the erstwhile socialist bloc. The conditionality is meant in principle to ensure repayment but in practice it imposes conditions to serve the interests of international banks which lend to the same countries. The Bretton Woods institutions, then, act as watchdogs for moneylenders in international capital markets. This has been so for some time. But there is more to it now. IMF programmes of stabilization and World

---

[29]The asymmetry in the rules of the game for the international trading system, outlined here, is examined in Nayyar (1996a).

Bank programmes of structural adjustment in developing countries and in the erstwhile communist countries, impose conditions that stipulate structural reform of policy regimes. The object is to increase the degree of openness of these economies and to reduce the role of the State, so that market forces shape economic decisions. In this manner, the Bretton Woods institutions seek to harmonize policies and institutions across counties which is in consonance with the needs of globalization.

In a world of unequal partners it is not surprising that the rules of the game are asymmetrical, if not inequitable. But the process of globalization, combined with these rules, is bound to significantly reduce the autonomy of developing countries in the formulation of economic policies in their pursuit of industrialization and development. This is attributable, in part, to the asymmetrical rules and, in part, to the economic implications of globalization.

The existing (and prospective) rules of the WTO regime allow few exceptions and provide little flexibility to countries that are latecomers to industrialization. There was more room for manouevre in the erstwhile GATT, *inter alia*, because of special and differential treatment for developing countries. The new regime is much stricter is terms of the law and the implementation. The rules on market access, tariff binding, quantitative restrictions, subsidies, and so on will make the selective protection or strategic promotion of domestic firms *vis-à-vis* foreign competition much more difficult. The tight system for the protection of intellectual property rights might pre-empt or stifle the development of domestic technological capabilities. The possible multilateral framework for investment, when it materializes, will almost certainly reduce the possibilities of strategic bargaining with transnational firms. Similarly, commitments on structural reform, an integral part of stabilization and adjustment programmes with the IMF and the World Bank, inevitably prescribe industrial deregulation, privatization, trade liberalization, and financial deregulation. Taken together, such rules and conditions are bound to curb the use of industrial policy, technology policy, trade policy, and financial policy as strategic forms of intervention to foster industrialization.

The constraints implicit in the economics of globalization are most easily explained with an example. Consider the vulnerability associated with rapid integration into international financial markets which often begins with a reliance on portfolio investment to finance current account deficits in the balance of payments. An economy needs high interest rates together with a strong exchange rate regime to sustain portfolio investment flows in terms of both profitability and confidence. This erodes the competitiveness of exports over time and enlarges the trade deficit. It is important to recognize the macroeconomic implications. Larger trade deficits and current account deficits require larger portfolio investment inflows which, beyond a point, undermine confidence and create adverse expectations even if the government keeps the exchange rate pegged. But when a stifling of exports does ultimately force an exchange rate depreciation, confidence may simply collapse and lead to capital flight. These problems have indeed surfaced in several Latin American economies.

The problem is, in fact, much deeper and larger. Exchange rates can no longer be used as a strategic device to provide an entry into the world market for manufactured goods, just as interest rates can no longer be used as a strategic instrument for guiding the allocation of scarce investible resources in a market economy. What is more, countries which are integrated into the world monetary system are constrained in using an autonomous management of demand to maintain levels of output and employment. Expansionary fiscal and monetary policies—large government deficits to stimulate aggregate demand or low interest rates to encourage domestic investment—can no longer be used because of an overwhelming fear that such measures could lead to speculative capital flight and a run on the national currency.

It is not surprising that the advent of international capital associated with globalization, has meant significant political adjustments in the contemporary world. It has induced a strategic withdrawal on the part of the nation state in some important spheres. They remain the main political players but are no longer the main economic players. We live in an era where the old fashioned autonomy of the nation state is being eroded by international industrial capital and international finance capital everywhere, both in the industrialized world and in the developing world. It needs to be stressed, however, that there is a qualitative difference in the relationship between international capital and the nation state when we compare the industrialized world with the developing world. The nation state in the former has far more room for manouevre than the nation state in the latter. In the industrialized countries, the political interests of the nation state often coincide with the economic interests of international capital. This is not so for developing countries from which very few transnational corporations or international banks originate. In spite of the profound changes unleashed by the present phase of globalization, however, it would be naive to write off the nation state, for it remains a crucial player in political and strategic terms. Even today, only nation states have the authority to set rules of the game. The nation states in the industrialized world provide international capital with the means to set new rules for the game of globalization. The nation states in the developing world provide these countries and their people with the means of finding degrees of freedom *vis-à-vis* international capital in the pursuit of development.

THE ROLE OF THE STATE

The second half of the twentieth century witnessed a complete swing of the pendulum in thinking about the role of the State in industrialization and development. There was a move from a widespread belief prevalent in the 1950s that the State could do nothing wrong to a conviction, fashionable in the 1990s, that the State could do nothing right. These are caricatures of perceptions, but the disillusionment with the role of the State now extends much beyond the profession of economics. It needs to be said that such rethinking began life, on a modest note, in the literature on trade and industrialization. But the dramatic change in thinking since then can be attributed in part to ideology and in part to reality. The world of competing ideologies, capitalism versus communism, has given way to a world with a single dominant political ideology. Communism has collapsed and capitalism has emerged triumphant. The reality that we observe around us has also made its contribution. The market economies of East Asia epitomize success. The erstwhile planned economies of East Europe, in particular the former Soviet Union, represent failure. The success of the market shines when juxtaposed with the failure of the State. However, this is an oversimplified perception. The reality is more complex. For market failure is also a fact of life. In fact, the term *market failure*[30] has been in the jargon of economists for quite some time. It is the term *government failure*[31] that has entered their lexicon relatively recently.

---

[30]It is obvious that the word failure is used to describe outcomes that are inefficient or undesirable with reference to some idealized state of economy. Most text books in economics elaborate on such failures. For a simple exposition, see Bhaduri and Nayyar (1996, pp. 129–32). See also, Stiglitz (1989a).

[31]Government failure takes many forms and is attributable to many factors. Sometimes, governments make mistakes because they do not have adequate information about a problem. Often, governments do not quite understand the nature of the problem. Without adquate information and necessary understanding, governments are neither able to predict nor able to control the consequences of their actions. Hence, government intervention may not resolve the problem it intends to. Instead, it may lead to unwanted adverse effects that are unintended. There is, also, a divergence between the conception and design of intervention by the government. The divergence between the design and implementation of policies, is, perhaps, even greater. For a critical analysis of government failure in the context of development, from the perspective of orthodox economics, see Krueger (1990).

It is important to recognize that the juxtaposition of government failure and market failure, or judgements about which is worse, as if there is a choice to be made, is misleading because it diverts us into a false debate. Both market failure and government failure are facts of life. For neither markets nor governments are, or can ever be, perfect. Indeed, markets are invariably imperfect and governments are without exception fallible. The important thing is to introduce corrective devices against both market failure and government failure. These failures are seldom absolute. A reasonable degree of correction is possible in either case.

There can be no doubt, however, that it is necessary to redefine the economic role of the State *vis-à-vis* the market at the present juncture. Such a redefinition, I believe, should be based on two basic propositions.[32] First, the State and the market cannot be substitutes for each other but must complement each other. Second, the relationship between the State and the market cannot be specified once and for all in any dogmatic manner, for the two institutions must adapt to one another in a cooperative manner over time. I also believe that these propositions explain the difference between success and failure. Successful economic development is observed mostly in countries where the Sate and the market complement one another and adapt to one another in response to changing circumstances. This proposition is borne out both by the history of capitalism among the early industrializers during the nineteenth century and by the more recent experience of the late industrializers in the twentieth century.

Economic historians tracing the evolutionary course of the market under early capitalism noted repeatedly that the market could become the organizing principle of capitalism only when it was embedded in the regulatory mechanism of the nation state.[33] The very extension of the scope of the free market necessitated, at each stage, the imposition of new regulations by the State to ensure further growth of the market. Thus, any characterization of the State and the market in opposition to one another is a misreading of history. Instead, it is more useful to think of the relationship as being governed by a kind of adaptive principle in which neither the State nor the market becomes destructively dominant to cripple the other institution.

From this perspective, it is instructive to consider the experience of the late industrializers. The belief that markets know best is associated with an

---

[32]Bhaduri and Nayyar (1996).

[33]See, for instance, Polyani (1944), who examined the complex interaction between State regulation and the growth of the market as an institution.

unstated presumption that State intervention is not needed or is counterproductive in the process of industrialization. This is ahistorical. Experience from the second half of the twentieth century suggests that the guiding and supportive role of the State has been the very foundation of successful development in countries which are latecomers to industrialization. Even among the East Asian countries, which are often cited as success stories that depict the magic of the market place, the visible hand of the State is as much in evidence as the invisible hand of the market. This is the unavoidable inference if we consider, for example, the development of industrial capitalism in Japan after the Meiji Restoration in 1868, or the emergence of market socialism in China after the modernization and reform programme was launched in 1978. The economic role of the State has been almost as crucial in Korea, Taiwan, and even Singapore.[34]

In the earlier stages of industrialization, State intervention creates the conditions for the development of industrial capitalism. It creates a physical infrastructure through government investment in energy, transport, and communication, which reduces the cost of inputs used by the private sector or increases the demand for goods produced by the private sector. It develops human resources through education, which raises private profitability as it lowers the private cost of training workers. It facilitates institutional change through agrarian reform, which increases productivity and incomes in the agricultural sector to foster industrialization through supply–demand linkages. I must emphasize that institutional reform in the agricultural sector, the spread of education in society and, above all, the role of State intervention have been crucial for development among late industrializers, particularly the success stories in East Asia that are now perceived as role models.[35]

[34]See Amsden (1989) and Wade (1991).

[35]An important illustration of the economic role of the State in the early stages of development, among late industrializing countries, is provided by the protection of infant industries through tariffs (or other means). The State protects emerging domestic entrepreneurs in the private sector from international competition in the domestic market. Thus, the State and the market complement one another. If the objective is to be realized, the State must, after a time, progressively reduce its protection so that infant industries grow up as healthy adults ultimately capable of competing in the world market. Thus, the respective roles of the State and the market must undergo an adaptive change. However, in several developing countries, of which India is a frequently cited example, the objective has not been realized. There are infant industires that grow up as problem adolescents, or go from a first childhood to a second childhood without passing through the stage of adulthood. Such infant industries need protection forever, in part because the role of the State does not change adaptively over time. This example of the infant industry argument illustrates that the difference between success and failure depends upon the adaptive response of the State and the market to one another as circumstances and times change.

In the later stages of industrialization, it is not just the *degree* but also the *nature* of State intervention that must change. The role of the State, then, is neither that of a promoter nor that of a catalyst. The role of intervention by the State in the market can be classified conveniently as *functional, institutional,* or *strategic.*

Functional intervention by the State seeks to correct for market failures insofar as prices give the wrong signals. It can be specific or general. That depends on the nature of the failure of the price mechanism. Although, in principle, there is a case for government intervention whenever the price mechanism fails grossly, the reality is far more complex. The debate, in such cases, centres on the availability of alternative market-based solutions or the ability of governments to design and implement correct solutions on the basis of adequate information. Nevertheless, the logic of this form of intervention is, analytically, not difficult to comprehend.

Institutional intervention by the State seeks to govern the market. It does so by setting the rules of the game for players in the market. In particular, it creates frameworks for regulating markets and creates institutions to monitor the functioning of markets. Some examples would highlight the significance of this form of intervention. A market economy needs rules of the game to ensure a level playing field and to pre-empt a free-for-all at the same time. Thus, trade policy reform which ushers in import liberalization must be matched by a comprehensive system of anti-dumping laws for domestic firms to invoke wherever necessary. Industrial deregulation requires corresponding anti-trust laws. Financial liberalization requires matching regulatory laws. Consumer protection requires laws that curb restrictive trade practices, ensure quality control, and check misinformation in advertising. A market economy needs these institutions to facilitate the function of markets.

Strategic intervention by the State seeks to guide the market. It is interlinked across activities or sectors in an attempt to attain broader, long-term objectives of development. It is possible to cite several different types of examples. Exchange rate policy is not simply a tactical matter of getting prices right but may turn out to be a strategic matter. Deliberately undervalued exchange rates, maintained over a period of time, have been known to provide an entry into the world market for differentiated manufactured goods. This is especially true where quality is perceived in terms of established brands but lower prices of unknown brands allow initial access to markets. Thus a strategically undervalued domestic currency makes the price of domestic manufactured exports cheaper for foreigners to buy, and gradually creates their reputation in competition with established brands. Japanese cars and cameras in an earlier period or Korean consumer electronics and cars may illustrate this strategy. The structure of interest rates is not just about allowing market forces to determine the scarcity price of borrowing finance, as economists are fond of saying. The structure of interest rates, short-term and long-term, may be a strategic instrument for guiding the allocation of scarce investible resources and credit in a market economy, in accordance with a long-term perspective of comparative advantage or national priorities. Restrictions on the use of foreign brand names is not symptomatic of an inward-looking attitude, if it is perceived as a strategic means of buying time to develop brand names that become acceptable in world markets after a time lag, but could never have surfaced in competition with established foreign brands. In this manner, State intervention may constitute an integral part of any strategy of industrialization that endeavours to strengthen capabilities and develop institutions rather than rely on incentives and markets alone. In these instances, strategic intervention complements rather than thwarts the initiative of domestic industrialists. This is perhaps the most important lesson that emerges from the experience of Japan and the Republic of Korea in particular, and from East Asia in general. Both Japan and Korea put exchange rate policy to such strategic use, manipulated interest rates as a strategic price to influence private investment decisions and, in effect, banned the use of foreign brand names for a period of time as a strategic means of developing their own brand names. Strategic intervention by the State, particularly in the realm of industrial policy and technology policy, but also in the sphere of trade policy, rather than a blind reliance on market forces alone, has been a crucial factor underlying efficiency and dynamism in the later stages of industrialization, which enabled Japan, and then Korea, to join the league of the industrialized nations.[36]

In many developing countries, particularly India, just as much as in Eastern Europe, perceptions have been so strongly influenced by the counterproductive role of State intervention that we have not yet recognized the possibilities of a creative interaction between the State and the market. And scepticism about the State runs deep. In theory, it may be possible to remedy market failure by State intervention. In practice, governments may lack the ability or the willingness to intervene efficiently. The wrong kind of State intervention can induce rent-seeking unproductive activities, but so can unregulated markets. The right kind of State intervention can channel rents created in the process of industrialization, through market forces into productive uses. It is the nature

---

[36]The preceding discussion on the role of the State in countries that are latecomers to industrialization draws upon Nayyar (1996b) and Bhaduri and Nayyar (1996).

and the form of State intervention that matters.[37] The experience of excessive State intervention associated with government failures, however, should not lead to the conclusion that minimal State intervention is best or that market failures do not matter. The crux of the problem is to assess the costs of government failure and market failure, at critical points of time, so as to minimize the cost to economy and society. And those who never tire of emphasizing the costs of State intervention must also recognize the costs of State inaction at such critical points. In the present context, therefore, we need to reformulate the questions about the economic role of the State. The real question is no longer about the size of the State (how big?) or the degree of State intervention (how much?). The question is now about the nature of State intervention (what sort?) and the quality of the performance of the State (how good?). The reality remains. In a world of uneven development characterized by rapid technical progress, ever-changing comparative advantage, and imperfect market structures, the role of governments in the industrialization process remains vital and could account for the difference between success and failure. For industrialization is not only about getting-prices-right. Industrialization is also about getting-State-intervention-right.[38]

The reality of globalization has reduced the autonomy of the nation state in the economic sphere. But there remain some degrees of freedom which must be exploited in the pursuit of industrialization and development. The ideology of globalization seeks to harmonize not only policy regimes but also institutions, including the economic role of the State, across the world. This is a mistake because the role of the State in an economy depends on its level of income and its stage of development. What is more, the State is the only institution that can create room for introducing correctives. The irony is that, at the present juncture, when the disillusionment with the State is so widespread its role is more critical than ever before.

The pursuit of the development in the context of globalization necessitates a role for the nation state in the domestic economic sphere and in economic or political interaction with the outside world. In the national context, the

---

[37]The experience of India illustrates that it is possible for State intervention to create an oligopolistic situation in a competitive environment, just as the experience of the Republic of Korea illustrates that it is possible for State intervention to create a competitive situation in an oligopolistic environment and this had far-reaching implications for industrialization in both countries. It is essential, therefore, to analyse the conditions under which the right kind of State intervention is possible.

[38]See Shapiro and Taylor (1990) and Lall (1990). For a discussion on the economic role of the State, see also Stiglitz (1989b) and Killick (1990).

State must endeavour to create the preconditions for more equitable development and bargain with international capital to improve the distribution of gains from cross-border economic transactions. In the international context, the State should attempt to reduce the asymmetries and the inequalities in the rules of the game. It is worth considering these possibilities in turn but it is important to stress that the discussion is meant to be illustrative rather than exhaustive.

Let me begin with the national context. First, in the earlier stages of industrialization, the State must create conditions for the development of industrial capitalism, such as building a physical infrastructure, developing human resources, and catalyzing institutional change. It must be emphasized that the benefits of integration with the world economy through globalization would accrue only to those countries which have laid such requisite foundations for industrialization and development. Similarly, economic development would be more equitable and social development would be more broadbased in countries which have created these preconditions. Both propositions are borne out by the East Asian development experience.

Second, the State must bargain with large international firms not only to improve the distribution of gains from economic transactions with them but also to ensure that their activities are conducive to development. The reason is simple. Transnational corporations are in the business of profit while governments are in the business of development. Unilateral trade liberalization which reduces tariffs across the board opens up the market for foreign goods. Uniform investment liberalization, irrespective of country-of-origin or sector-of-destination, opens up the economy to foreign firms. This is obviously in the interest of large international firms. But it may not be in the interest of developing countries. Transnational corporations want access to domestic markets of large countries such as India and China or access to natural resources in countries with such endowments. Governments in these host countries should, therefore, drive a bargain on a reciprocal basis: to improve terms of trade, to obtain market access for exports, to facilitate transfer to technology, or to establish manufacturing capacities in ancillaries, components, or downstream activities. Such examples can be multiplied. This means strategic negotiations in the sphere of trade and investment, which can only be done by governments and not by individuals or firms. Hence, governments must possess the minimal determination to negotiate, rather than to surrender from a perceived position of weakness or to give concessions without reciprocity in keeping with the rhetoric of unilateral liberalization.

In the international context, nation states must endeavour to influence the rules of the game so that the playing field is less uneven, even if it is not level, and the outcome is more equitable. There is a need for greater symmetry in the rules of the international trading system. If developing countries provide access to their markets, it should be matched with a corresponding access to technology. This, in turn, requires that the regime for the protection of intellectual property rights should recognize that the interest of technology-followers and technology-importers is just as important as the interest of technology-leaders and technology-exporters. Similarly, if there is almost complete freedom for capital mobility across national boundaries, the draconian restrictions on labour mobility across national boundaries should at least be reduced if not eliminated. It needs to be recognized that any provisions for commercial presence of corporate entities (capital) should correspond to provisions for temporary migration for workers (labour), just as the right-of-establishment for corporate entities (capital) has an analogue in the right-of-residence for persons (labour).[39] The need for symmetry extends beyond the rules of the international trading system. There is need to influence and reshape the rules of the multilateral financial institutions, in particular the IMF and the World Bank. Stabilization programmes and structural adjustment programmes need to be flexible in terms of conditionalities particularly where these are not consistent with national development objectives in the long-term. It is possible to cite many examples. The fetish about reducing fiscal deficits might reduce the benefits of integration through globalization if it reduces public investment in infastructure or public expenditure on social sectors. The insistence on high interest rates might squeeze domestic investment and constrain growth. Import liberalization supported by portfolio investment inflows may simply not be sustainable. Liberal entry for foreign firms and easy access to foreign technology might stifle the development of domestic managerial and technological capabilities. It is inevitable that moneylenders have their rates, but the imposition on borrowers of a standardized package of policies, which is inflexible, creates many difficulties.

In sum, there is need to reduce asymmetries and inequalities in the rules of the game. How is this to be done? In the multilateral institutions, whether the WTO, the IMF, or the World Bank, developing countries and transitional economies must ensure that their voices are heard. This is easier said than done, but groups of countries with mutual interests are more likely to be heard than single countries by themselves. For this purpose, it is essential to find common causes in a world where there are many conflicts and contradictions. There are two means of creating such country-groupings: regional and sub-regional

---

[39]For a further discussion of this issue, see Nayyar (1989).

economic initiatives (such as ASEAN in South East Asia) or strategic alliances between countries across regions (say, China, India, Iran, South Africa, and Brazil). Such arrangements can succeed and sustain only if member countries recognize that trade-offs are a necessary condition. In other words, there must be a willingness and an ability to accept some compromise in respect of national political sovereignty, within the grouping, to acquire greater economic influence or stronger bargaining power in the international context. The more discerning and farsighted might even be willing to accept some erosion of national autonomy in the short-term to improve economic performance in the medium-term on the premise that, ultimately, it is economic strength which provides nation states with political clout in the international community.

Regional arrangements or strategic alliances may also straddle countries at different levels of development. We have a concrete example of the former in NAFTA and a potential example of the latter in APEC. The dynamics of economic competition and political rivalry between nation states may lead to the formation of trade blocs as strategic alliances or strategic responses. But there might be more to it than meets the eye. For a wide range of reasons, nation states in the industrialized world may also wish to create economic space or degrees of freedom *vis-à-vis* international capital. The European Community, after all, is not simply a counterpoint to the United States as an economic or political bloc. Globalization, particularly in the realm of finance, has almost certainly eroded the ability of governments everywhere to tax, or print money, and to borrow. Monetary and fiscal policy are blunted. Macroeconomic management in the pursuit of internal and external balance is that much more difficult. International financial markets are much too powerful for governments that may wish to maintain an exchange rate. Governments are concerned about the high levels of unemployment in the industrialized world, even if it is not part of the objective function that large international firms seek to maximize, because governments need legitimacy and support in domestic political constituencies. There may thus be some willingness on the part of nation states in the industrialized world to set rules that introduce a modicum of discipline on the forces of globalization.

It is essential to stress that these strategic alliances, whether among developing countries, among industrialized countries or between developing countries and industrialized countries, must be based on a coincidence of mutual interests. Unless they constitute an integral part of the pursuit of national interest, such alliances or arrangements cannot sustain themselves, let alone provide a real solution. The impetus can only come from material interests in the sphere of economics and national interests in the realm of politics. There will always be conflict and contradiction. But there would be areas where it is possible to find common cause and accept trade-offs.

CONCLUSION

This essay explores selected themes in trade and industrialization situated in the wider context of development. The stage is set by explaining the rationale of departures from free trade in economic theory and by setting out the orthodox critique of the experience with industrialization in developing countries. The latter highlights the sins of import substitution and State intervention to stress the virtues of openness and markets. However, the policy prescriptions derived are strong generalizations, which do not match orthodox trade theory in terms of rigour and do not recognize recent theoretical developments in terms of insights. What is more, the neoclassical critique and the neo-liberal prescription are both characterized by analytical limitations. The discussion also reveals that the mainstream literature on trade and industrialization is narrow in its focus just as it is selective in its use of theory and experience. The significance of the neglected themes suggests that its analysis and understanding are both incomplete in some important aspects. For an understanding of industrialization, it is essential to situate trade in a macroeconomic perspective, recognize the importance of the demand side, and consider why demand–supply linkages matter.

It is worth emphasizing an important conclusion that emerges. In spite of the shift in paradigm from the Development Consensus of the 1950s to the Washington Consensus of the 1990s, the degree of openness *vis-à-vis* the world economy and the degree of intervention by the State in the market remain critical issues in the debate on industrialization. However, the second half of the twentieth century witnessed a complete swing of the pendulum in thinking about the two issues. But the complexity of reality is not captured by either consensus: old or new.

The changed international context, attributable to globalization, has important implications for trade and industrialization in the developing world which must be recognized. An increase in the degree of openness of economies is inevitable, while the degrees of freedom for nation states are bound to be fewer. But it would be a mistake to consider this necessity as a virtue. Simplified prescriptions, which emphasize more openness and less intervention to advocate a rapid integration with the world economy combined with a minimalist State that vacates space for the market, are not validated either by theory or by history. Economic theory recognizes and economic history reveals the complexities of the industrialization process. The degree of openness and the nature of intervention are strategic choices in the pursuit of industrialization, which cannot be defined (and should not be prescribed) once-and-for-all for they depend upon the stage of development and must change over time. And there can be no magic recipes in a world where economies are characterized by specificities in time and space. The irony is that, at a time, when the disillusionment with the State is so widespread, given the reality of globalization, its role in the pursuit of industrialization and development is more critical than ever before. However, this does not mean, nor should it suggest, more of the same. Correcting for mistakes and learning from experience is vital. It is, therefore essential to redefine the economic role of the State *vis-à-vis* the market, so that the two institutions complement each other and adapt to one another as circumstances or times change. That is what success at industrialization is about.

REFERENCES

Amsden, A.H. (1989), *Asia's Next Giant: South Korea and Late Industrialization*, Oxford University Press, New York.

Bagchi, A.K. (1970), 'Long-Term Constraints on India's Industrial Growth', in E.A.G. Robinson and M. Kidron (eds), *Economic Development in South Asia*, Macmillan, London.

Bell, M. and K. Pavitt (1993), 'Accumulating Technological Capability in Developing Countries', *Proceedings of the World Bank Annual Caonference on Development Economics 1992*, pp. 257–81.

Bhaduri, A. and S. Marglin (1990), 'Unemployment and the Real Wage: The Economic Basis for Contesting Political Ideologies', *Cambridge Journal of Economics*, Vol. 14, pp. 375–93.

Bhaduri, A. and D. Nayyar (1996), *The Intelligent Person's Guide to Liberalization*, Penguin Books, New Delhi.

Bhagwati, J. (1978), *Foreign Trade Regimes and Economic Development: Anatomy and Consequences of Exchange Control*, Ballinger, Mass.

—— (1994), 'Free Trade: Old and New Challenges', *Economic Journal*, Vol. 104, No. 2, pp. 231–45.

Bhagwati, J. and V.K. Ramaswami (1963), 'Domestic Distortions, Tariffs and the Theory of Optimum Subsidy', *Journal of Political Economy*, Vol. 71, No. 1, pp. 44–50.

Bhagwati, J. and P. Desai (1970), *India: Planning for Industrialization*, Oxford University Press, London.

Bhagwati, J. and T.N. Srinivasan (1975), *Foreign Trade Regimes and Economic Development: India*, Columbia University Press, New York.

Chakravarty, S. (1987), *Development Planning: The Indian Experience*, Clarendon Press, Oxford.

Corden, W.M. (1974), *Trade Policy and Economic Welfare*, Clarendon Press, Oxford.

Dahlman, C., B. Ross-Larson, and L. Westphal (1987), 'Managing Technological

Development: Lessons from the Newly Industrializing Countries', *World Development*, Vol. 15, No. 6, pp. 759–75.

Diaz-Alejandro, C.F. (1975), 'Trade Policies and Economic Development', in P.B. Kenen (ed.), *International Trade and Finance: Frontiers for Research*, Cambridge University Press, Cambridge.

Dixit, A.K. and V. Norman (1980), *International Trade*, Cambridge University Press, Cambridge.

Heckscher, E.F. (1919), 'The Effect of Foreign Trade on the Distribution of Income', *Economisk Tidskrift*, pp. 495–512.

Helleiner, G.K. (1992), *Trade Policy, Industrialization and Development*, Clarendon Press, Oxford.

Helpman, E. and P. Krugman (1985), *Market Structure and Foreign Trade: Increasing Returns, Imperfect Competition and the International Economy*, The MIT Press, Cambridge.

Irwin, D. (1991), 'Challenges to Free Trade', *Journal of Economic Perspectives*, Vol. 5, No. 2, pp. 201–8.

Killick, T. (1990), *A Reaction Too Far: Economic Theory and the Role of the State in Developing Countries*, Overseas Development Institute, London.

Krueger, A.O. (1978), *Foreign Trade Regimes and Economic Development: Liberalization Attempts and Consequences*, National Bureau of Economic Research, New York.

—— (1990), 'Government Failures in Development', *Journal of Economic Perspectives*, Vol. 4, No. 3, pp. 9–23.

Krugman, P. (1981), 'Trade, Accumulation and Uneven Development', *Journal of Development Economics*, Vol. 8, No. 2, pp. 149–61.

—— (1986), (ed.), *Strategic Trade Policy and the New International Economics*, The MIT Press, Cambridge.

—— (1987), 'Is Free Trade Passè'?, *Journal of Economic Perspectives*, Vol. 1, No. 2, pp. 131–44.

Lall, S. (1990), *Building Industrial Competitiveness in Developing Countries*, OECD Development Centre, Paris.

Lee, E. (ed.) (1981), *Export-Led Industrialization and Development*, International Labour Organization, Geneva.

Little, I.M.D., T. Scitovsky, and M. Scott (1970), *Industry and Trade in Some Developing Countries: A Comparative Study*, Oxford University Press, London.

Mill, J.S. (1848), *Principles of Political Economy*, with an introduction by W.J. Ashley, Longmans, London.

Myrdal, G. (1956), *An International Economy: Problems and Prospects*, Routledge and Kegan Paul, London.

Nayyar, D. (1989), 'Towards a Possible Multilateral Framework for Trade in Services: Some Issues and Concepts', in *Technology, Trade Policy and the Uruguay Round*, United Nations, New York.

—— (1994a), 'The Foreign Trade Sector, Planning and Industrialization in India', in T.J. Byres (ed.), *The State and Development Planning in India*, Oxford University Press, New Delhi.

_____ (ed.) (1994b), *Industrial Growth and Stagnation: The Debate in India*, Oxford University Press, Bombay.

_____ (1995), 'Globalization: The Past in Our Present', Presidential Address to the Indian Economic Association, 1995, reprinted in *Indian Economic Journal*, January 1996, Vol. 44, No. 1, pp. 1–18.

_____ (1996a), 'Free Trade: Why, When and for Whom?', *Banca Nazionale del Lavoro Quarterly Review*, Vol. 49, No. 198, pp. 333–50.

_____ (1996b), *Economic Liberalization in India: Analytics, Experience and Lessons*, Orient Longman, Calcutta.

Ohlin, B. (1933), *Interregional and International Trade*, Harvard University Press, Cambridge.

Pack, H. and L. Westphal (1986), 'Industrial Strategy and Technological Change: Theory versus Reality', *Journal of Development Economics*, Vol. 12, No. 1, pp. 87–128.

Polyani, K. (1944), *The Great Transformation*, Holt, Rinehart and Winston, New York.

Ricardo, D. (1812), *Principles of Political Economy and Taxation*, with an introduction by Donald Winch, Dent, London.

Rodrik, D. (1992), 'Closing the Productivity Gap: Does Trade Liberalization Really Help?', in G.K. Helleiner (ed.), *Trade Policy, Industrialization and Development*, Clarendon Press, Oxford.

Rosenberg, N. (1994), *Exploring the Black Box: Technology, Economics and History*, Cambridge University Press, Cambridge.

Sachs, J. and Warner, A. (1995), 'Economic Reform and the Process of Global Integration', *Brookings Paper on Economic Activity*, No. 1, pp. 1–118.

Samuelson, P. (1939), 'The Gains from International Trade', *Canadian Journal of Economics and Political Science*, pp. 195–205.

Shapiro, H. and L. Taylor (1990), 'The State and Industrial Strategy', *World Development*, Vol. 18, No. 6, pp. 861–78.

Singh, A. (1994), 'Openness and the Market Friendly Approach to Development: Learning the Right Lessons from Development Experience', *World Development*, Vol. 22, No. 12, pp. 1811–24.

Smith, A. (1776), *The Wealth of Nations*, with an introduction by Andrew Skinner, Pelican Books, Harmondsworth.

Stiglitz, J.E. (1989a), 'Markets, Market Failures and Development', *American Economics Review, Papers and Proceedings*, Vol. 79, No. 2, pp. 197–202.

_____ (1989b), 'Economic Role of the State: Efficiency and Effectiveness', in A. Heertje (ed.), *The Economic Role of the State*, Basil Blackwell, Oxford.

Wade, R. (1991), *Governing the Market: Economic Theory and the Role of Government in East Asian Industrialization*, Princeton University Press, Princeton.

World Bank (1993), *The East Asian Miracle: Economic Growth and Policy*, World Bank, Washington, DC.

Chapter 10

INDUSTRIAL DEVELOPMENT IN INDIA

*Growth or Stagnation?**

INTRODUCTION

In the quarter century from 1950 to 1975, at first sight, the record of industrial growth in India appears impressive. Industrial production more than quadrupled. What is more, this growth was accompanied by a marked diversification of the industrial structure which came to be reflected in the wide range and complexity of goods manufactured in India. However, a mere glance at the aggregate data reveals that the pace of industrial development was somewhat uneven over time. In the period 1951–65 industrial production increased at an average rate of 7.7 per cent per annum. This rate dropped rather sharply to 3.6 per cent per annum during the decade 1965–75.

In retrospect, it is clear that the poor performance, which became discernible in the middle and late 1960s, was neither an aberration nor a temporary deviation from the trend, but the beginning of a long-term structural problem. The sluggishness of industrial growth, which persisted for more than ten years, cannot be attributed to short-term problems and obviously needs systematic analysis. While the problem area is vast, the object of this paper is a limited one. It seeks to analyse the factors underlying the marked deceleration in the rate of industrial growth which transformed a scenario of rapid industrialization into a situation of persistent quasi-stagnation.

The first section examines the trends in industrial production and establishes the fact of deceleration in growth. The second section provides a critical review of the alternative explanations for stagnation in the industrial

*This essay, published in 1978, was an important contribution to the lively debate on growth and stagnation in the industrial sector at the time. It is reprinted in this volume without any changes, except for some minor editing. The context has changed but the issues considered retain their analytical relevance.

sector. The third section attempts to focus attention on factors which have, in a relative sense, been neglected by the literature on the subject, and explores the relationship between income distribution, the demand factor, and industrial growth. The fourth section is directed towards developing a unified hypothesis about the sluggishness of growth in India's industrial sector from the mid-1960s to the mid-1970s.

TRENDS IN INDUSTRIAL PRODUCTION

It is rather difficult to outline the trends in industrialization because there is no complete time series on the index numbers of industrial production which spans the entire period. In fact, changes in base years make intertemporal comparisons problematic. All the same, there is overwhelming evidence in support of the proposition that the mid-1960s witnessed a dramatic decline in the rate of industrial growth: the average annual rate during the decade beginning 1965 turned out to be less than half of what it was in the preceding 15 years. However, it might be argued that starting from a small base all growth rates appear unusually large and, therefore, one might be overstating the degree of deceleration in growth. In an attempt to circumvent this legitimate problem the present essay considers 1955 as the base year for all comparisons. While such a method might not eliminate the bias altogether it should certainly reduce the magnitude.

Table 10.1 sets out the available data on the indices of production in the industrial sector. A slackening of growth is discernible from a cursory study of the table and is confirmed by a few simple computations. During the decade 1955–65 total industrial production increased at an average annual rate of 7.8 per cent while manufacturing output increased at 7.6 per cent. In the following decade, 1965–75, the rates dropped to 3.6 per cent and 3.1 per cent, respectively. These are point-to-point compound growth rates. In order to take account of all the observations in the two periods we fitted a semilog trend to the indices for both total industrial production and manufacturing (Series B) only to find that the results were remarkably similar.

The reader would notice that the above exercise on growth rates ignores 1976, a year in which industrial production registered an unprecedented increase of 10 per cent over the preceding year. This omission is deliberate because the revival of 1976 was more apparent than real. It was the outcome of a phenomenal bumper harvest and the unusual political circumstances of the time. The government stepped up public sector production irrespective of whether the output could be utilized, so that there was a rapid accumulation of stocks in intermediate goods such as steel and coal. A higher level of output and improved capacity utilization followed from the government's policy

Table 10.1: Index Numbers of Industrial Production

| Year | Series A: 1956=100 | | Series B: 1960=100 | | Series C: 1970=100 | |
	General Index	Manufact- turing	General Index	Manufac- turing	General Index	Manufac- turing
1955	91.9	91.6	(72.7)	(73.8)		
1956	100.0	100.0	(78.4)	(79.6)		
1957	104.2	103.3	(82.7)	(83.4)		
1958	107.7	106.2	(84.4)	(84.8)		
1959	116.8	114.9	(90.3)	(90.5)		
1960	130.2	127.9	100.0	100.0		
1961	141.0	137.9	109.2	109.2		
1962	152.9	149.2	119.8	119.6		
1963	167.3	162.9	129.7	129.1		
1964	177.8	173.6	140.8	141.2		
1965	187.7	182.3	153.8	154.0		
1966	192.6	186.0	153.2	151.7		
1967			152.6	149.6		
1968			163.0	158.7		
1969			175.3	170.6		
1970			184.3	178.9	100.0	100.0
1971			186.1	178.9	104.2	104.2
1972			199.4	191.4	110.2	110.1
1973			200.7	193.4	112.0	112.2
1974			(210.7)	(202.2)	114.3	113.0
1975			(219.9)	(207.7)	119.3	116.1
1976					131.6	127.7

Note: For Series B the figures given in brackets are derived from Series A and C, respectively. Those relating to the period 1955–9 are based on 1960 weights and have been taken from *Commerce*, Annual Number, Bombay, 1968, p. 287. The figures for 1974–5, however, are unweighted and calculated simply by using the ratio of the 1970 index in Series B to that in C as the conversion factor.
Source: CSO *Statistical Abstract, India*, annual issues.

towards its work force, the Emergency laws being used extensively to eliminate strikes and all other forms of industrial disputes.[1] But these policies did not transform the industrial scene in the private sector. Indeed, private corporate

[1]Statements originating in official sources provide confirmation. For instance, the government's *Economic Survey* for 1975–6 stressed the fact that the number of man-days lost through industrial disputes fell from 6 million in July–September 1974 to 1.5 million

investment during 1976–7 was, in absolute terms, significantly lower than it had been in 1975–6.[2] Given this context, it has been convincingly argued by Patnaik and Rao (1977) that the industrial performance in 1976 did not mark the beginning of the end of stagnation. Nor did it mean a return to the trend rate witnessed earlier, quite simply because the factors which propped up growth in 1976 were not sustainable in the long-run. As such, it is hardly surprising that industrial output in 1977 was just about 4 per cent higher than the previous year.

From the above it seems obvious that 1976 was an abnormal year which cannot serve as a point of reference or comparison. In the following discussion, therefore, we shall focus attention on the trends in industrial production until 1975. Our choice of terminal year is perfectly justifiable, particularly as the primary purpose of this paper is to analyse the long-term shifts in the pace of industrialization.

In order to pinpoint changes in the rate of industrial growth, for the period 1955–75, we fitted the equation $\text{Log } Y = a + bt + ct^2$ to the data in Table 10.1, Series B where 'Y' is either the general index of industrial production (I_{ip}) or the index of manufacturing (I_m), and 't' is the time period. The following results were obtained from the exercise:

$$\text{Log } I_{ip} = -4.6440 + 0.2387t - 0.0014t^2 \quad R^2 = 0.99; \text{ D.W.} = 1.03$$
$$(0.0338) \quad (0.00026)$$
$$\text{Log } I_m = -4.8486 + 0.2480t - 0.0015t^2 \quad R^2 = 0.99; \text{ D.W.} = 0.95$$
$$(0.0371) \quad (0.00029)$$

In both cases, the estimated values of 'c' turned out to be negative, and significant at the 1 per cent level of probability, thereby providing definitive evidence of a deceleration in the rate of growth.

The picture of deceleration is substantiated further if we examine data at a disaggregated level. Table 10.2 outlines the trends in output starting from the two-digit level of the Central Statistical Organization (CSO) industrial classification. While the composition of industrial production certainly changed over time, the ten manufacturing industry groups selected for the table, taken together, contributed approximately 90 per cent of the total output in

---

in July–September 1975. It also emphasized the progressive decline in work time lost since July 1975 as a possible factor underlying the spurt in industrial output.

[2]It has been estimated that net capital formation in the private industrial sector during 1976–7 was Rs 537 crores as compared to Rs 848 crores in 1975–6; see *The Economic Times*, New Delhi, 1 January 1978, p. 1. These figures, it is worth noting, are in terms of current prices.

Table 10.2: Composition and Time Profile
of Industrial Growth in India, 1955–75

Industry Group	Weights (1960= 100)	Index Number of Production (1960=100)			Average Growth Rate (per cent per annum)	
		1955	1965	1975	1955–65	1965–75
Food products	12.09	75.9	122.2	171.2	4.9	3.4
Beverages and tobacco	2.22	61.7	147.6	200.9	9.1	3.1
Textiles	27.06	94.1	114.8	112.0	2.0	–0.5
Chemical and chemical products	7.26	60.1	152.6	306.9	9.8	7.2
Non-metallic mineral products	3.85	53.7	149.1	243.3	10.8	5.0
Basic metals	7.38	53.3	180.9	242.3	13.0	3.0
Metal products	2.51	54.1	205.6	310.0	14.3	4.2
Machinery: non electrical	3.38	35.5	320.9	623.6	24.6	6.9
Electrical machinery and appliances	3.05	49.0	208.2	443.8	15.6	8.0
Transport equipment	7.77	99.2	205.3	149.4	7.6	–3.2
All Manufacturing	84.91	73.8	154.0	207.7	7.6	3.1
Mining and Quarrying	9.72	74.6	131.7	189.8	5.9	3.7
Electricity	5.37	51.5	190.9	461.8	14.0	9.2
Total Industrial Production	100.00	72.7	153.8	219.9	7.8	3.6

Note: The figures in the last two columns of the table have been computed as point-to-point compound growth rates.

Sources: CSO (a) For the 1960 weights and for 1965 index numbers, *Statistical Abstract, India, 1974*, pp. 127–31.

(b) For 1955 index numbers, *Commerce*, Annual Number, Bombay, 1968, pp. 287–90. These figures are derived from the 1956 series using 1960 weights, and have also been compiled by the CSO; *Basic Statistics Relating to the Indian Economy, 1950–51 to 1974–75*, New Delhi, 1976, p. 46.

(c) The index numbers for 1975 have been calculated from the 1970 base series, as reported in the CSO, *Monthly Abstract of Statistics*, July, 1977, pp. 27–30. To convert them to 1960 base we have used the relevant ratio of the 1970 index in the two series, for each industry group, as the conversion factor.

Table 10.3: Deceleration of Growth in the Industrial Sector, 1960–75

		(average annual percentage increase in production)		
Industry Group	Weights (1960 = 100)	(1) 1960–5	(2) 1965–70	(3) 1970–5
Basic Industries	25.11	10.4	6.2	5.2
Capital Goods Industries	11.76	19.5	–1.7	5.1
Intermediate Goods Industries	25.88	7.0	2.5	2.6
Consumer Goods Industries	37.25	5.0	3.9	1.6
(a) Durable Goods	(5.68)	10.7	8.4	2.4
(b) Non-durable Goods	(31.57)	3.8	2.7	1.5
Total Industrial Production	100.00	9.0	3.3	3.6

Notes: (a) The figures in the table have been calculated from the index numbers of industrial production as point-to-point compound growth rates.
(b) Columns (1) and (2) are derived from the series on index numbers of industrial production with 1960 as base year, whereas column (3) is derived from the new series with 1970 as base year.
Source: RBI, *Report on Currency and Finance, 1974–75*, Vol. II, p. 26 and *1975–76*, Vol. II, p. 28.

manufacturing throughout the period under review.[3] A comparison of the average annual growth rates in the period 1955–65 with the corresponding ones in 1965–75 conclusively shows that the slow-down in growth occurred across the board in the industrial sector, though it might have been more pronounced in some industries than in others.

The mid-1960s were obviously the turning point. This is brought out even more clearly in Table 10.3 which is based on an alternative industrial classification but the source of primary data is the same. From the viewpoint of a macroeconomic analysis, a use-based classification is certainly more interesting; unfortunately, however, data in this series do not extend back beyond 1960. Nevertheless, the available statistics do highlight the dramatic deceleration in growth of the capital goods sector. The table also shows that the fate of intermediate goods industries was roughly similar, although the drop in the growth rate was not as steep. The basic industries group (constituted by electricity, mining, fertilizers, heavy chemicals, cement, and basic metals), on the other hand, fared a little better insofar as the rate of growth remained at a reasonable level even after the deceleration set in. It is worth noting that growth in the consumer goods industries was always significantly below the average for the

[3]The share of manufacturing in total industrial production, however, declined a little over time, from 88.85 per cent in 1956 to 84.91 per cent in 1960 and 81.08 per cent in 1970.

industrial sector. In the 1960s it was sustained at a respectable level by a rapid expansion in the output of consumer durables. However, even the modest growth disappeared in the 1970s as the pace of expansion in the durable goods industries slackened markedly.

It needs to be stressed that the evidence presented so far relates only to the organized factory sector. Given the paucity of published data it is almost impossible to assess how the performance of the small-scale sector would influence the overall trends in industrial production. Available information suggests that small-scale industries account for roughly 15 per cent of the total value of industrial production.[4] Thus, it would seem that the statistical evidence outlined in the preceding pages is a reasonable indicator of the trends in industrial output. In any case, the performance of the small-scale sector should be reflected in the level of industrial production (originating in registered large-scale units) insofar as it provides inputs to, or purchases them from, the factory sector.

As a starting point for our discussion it might be useful at this stage to recapitulate the salient features of the pattern of industrial development in India since the time of independence until the mid-1970s. In the years following independence, infrastructural developments and import substitution in the consumer goods sector stimulated industrial production. After that phase, in the late 1950s and early 1960s, the high rate of industrial growth was sustained by investment in the capital goods sector and in basic intermediate goods industries. Starting around 1965 there was a marked deceleration in the rate of growth which led to a near stagnation of industrial output in the early 1970s. The little growth that did take place in the period 1965–70 was largely attributable to infrastructural basic industries and to consumer durables. However, the expansion in luxury goods industries also came to an end thereafter. The ostensible revival in 1976 was a consequence of special circumstances and did not mean a return to the trend growth rate of earlier years.

ALTERNATIVE EXPLANATIONS OF DECELERATION AND STAGNATION

Several explanations were advanced to account for the sluggishness of industrial growth from the mid-1960s to the mid-1970s. Of these, in my view at least, two sets are clearly inadequate essentially because they do not get to the core

[4]The latest census of small-scale industries estimates the gross value of their output at Rs 2603 crores in 1972 (GoI 1977, p. 2). Unfortunately, data for the corresponding period are not available in case of the factory sector because the usual annual survey of industries was not carried out in 1972. But we do know that in 1971–2 the gross value of output in the registered manufacturing units was Rs 14,980 crores (GoI 1976, p. 103). Thus, the share of the small-scale sector in the gross value of *total* industrial output works out at 14.8 per cent. While this figure might not be entirely accurate it is a reasonable approximation.

of the problem. On the other hand, there are explanations which are perfectly plausible and merit careful discussion. Before we move on to such a critical review, however, a brief sketch of the inadequate hypotheses about industrial stagnation might be worthwhile.

Soon after the slowdown in growth became discernible, the problems of the industrial sector were frequently attributed to exogenous factors or random occurrences. While this view is not widely held, its adherents have not disappeared altogether. The emphasis has varied but, *inter alia*, short-term analysts draw attention to the following (a) the wars of 1962, 1965, and 1971 which diverted potential public investment into unproductive uses; (b) the successive droughts of 1965–6 and 1966–7, and later 1971–2 and 1972–3, which restricted the supply of raw materials and the demand for industrial goods from the agricultural sector; (c) supply constraints which became more pronounced in the late 1960s in the form of infrastructural bottlenecks (power and transport) or shortages of intermediate goods; (d) the oil crisis of 1973 which led to considerable industrial dislocation and severe balance of payments difficulties.

It is hardly surprising that in the early stages policymakers in the government and economists outside stressed the importance of these occurrences (Government of India 1968–9). Bagchi (1970) has critically evaluated this view. Even now it would be naive to deny that such occurrences had a significant impact on the level of industrial production at the time. With the benefit of hindsight, however, it seems fairly obvious that the aforesaid random factors cannot account for the persistence of stagnation simply because the economy should have returned to even keel after the event, which it did not. In retrospect it is clear that the disappearance of the short-term problems did not mean a revival of industrial growth.

There is a second, more long-term, view of industrialization in India, which does not concern itself with the problem of deceleration in growth, but stresses the difficulties arising from the industrial policies pursued by the government. The volumes by Bhagwati and Desai (1970) and Bhagwati and Srinivasan (1975) provide an elaborate exposition of this view. It is argued that the complex bureaucratic system of licensing, restrictions, and controls led not only to inefficiencies but also to misallocation of resources. What is more, the cumulative effect of these policies became an obstacle to growth. Thus, Bhagwati and Srinivasan conclude that, 'India's foreign trade regime, in conjunction with domestic licensing policies in the industrial sector, led to economic inefficiencies and impaired her economic performance.... The policy framework was detrimental, on balance, to the growth of the economy by adversely influencing export performance, by wasteful inter-industrial and inter-firm allocation of resources, by permitting and encouraging expansion of excess capacity and by blunting competition and hence the incentives for cost-consciousness and quality improvement'[5] (1975, p. 245).

Such an analysis, however, does not throw much light on the problem posed in this essay. One can, after all, ask: (a) Why did the industrial sector perform satisfactorily until 1965 in spite of these policies, and why did it not respond to liberalization thereafter? (b) Why did other economies, operating in a framework similar to that of India, achieve significantly higher rates of industrial growth? These questions are seldom raised, let alone answered, primarily because the authors are interested in a completely different set of issues.

Much of the literature cited here is preoccupied with an evaluation of import substitution strategies and the economic efficiency of industrialization. It is hardly surprising, therefore, that relatively little attention is paid to the process of growth. In any case, neoclassical writing on the subject is essentially static in conception and largely ignores intertemporal considerations. Even the limited analysis of growth effects is often derived from static allocative efficiency criteria (Bhagwati and Srinivasan 1975, Chapter 13, p. 175).

Other hypotheses about the deceleration of industrial growth in the past decade, with a few exceptions, hinge on two basic themes: the performance of the agricultural sector and the level of investment in the economy. Detailed discussion of these contributions to the literature is a task outside the scope of this essay. For our purpose, it would be sufficient to provide a critical review of the more important contributions with a focus on salient features, and to examine the extent to which they provide satisfactory explanations.

Performance of the Agricultural Sector

For an economy such as India the importance of the agricultural sector arises, in principle, from its overwhelming share in production and consumption. Quite apart from that, however, its performance has a direct impact on the pace of industrialization through the following mechanism: a slow increase in agricultural production would act as a brake on industrial growth if, (a) a surplus of wage goods and/or investible resources is not forthcoming; (b) the

---

[5]Bhagwati and Desai (1970, p. 499) are more elaborate in discussion but less definite in conclusion. Their final chapter begins as follows: 'It seems to us manifest, even though policy analysis in economic questions can rarely be as definitive as in the natural sciences, that Indian planning for industrialization suffered from excessive attention to targets down to product level, and a wasteful physical approach to setting and implementation thereof, along with a generally inefficient framework of economic policies designed to regulate he growth of industrialization.'

supply of agricultural raw materials is restricted; or (c) the demand for industrial goods is constrained. On the other hand, a rapid expansion in agricultural output would, through the same linkages, provide a sustained stimulus to growth in the industrial sector.

It is only to be expected that different authors would emphasize different factors and outline different mechanisms through which such linkages operate. Following this general line of argument, however, a number of scholars, notably Chakravarty (1974), Raj (1976), and Vaidyanathan (1977), sought to explain the sluggish growth of industrial output since the mid-1960s in terms of the meagre growth in agricultural production. It is possible to argue about the numbers and debate about the trends, as indeed a few economists have (see Srinivasan and Narayana 1977 and Vaidyanathan 1977), but it is difficult to dispute the basis of such a fundamentalist explanation. Once the fact of deceleration in the growth of agricultural output is accepted, there remains the question of factors responsible for it, which, in turn, have been discussed at length in the literature—they range from technological factors, on the one hand, to the institutional framework and property relations in agriculture, on the other. It would involve too much of a digression to enter into a discussion of these issues here. For the sake of analysis, therefore, let us grant the proposition that there has been a slackening of growth in the agricultural sector and that this may have had an adverse effect on industrialization in the recent past. Available evidence, on the balance, probably lends support to such a hypothesis.

Nevertheless, it is important to pose the simple question: is this a sufficient explanation for the persistence of industrial stagnation? For if it were, a resumption of steady growth in agriculture would revive and stimulate industrial production. In my view, however, the explanation is only partial, on account of the reasons set out below. Thus, while agricultural expansion might be a necessary condition for sustained industrial growth it is by no means a sufficient condition in the Indian context.

Technical change, improved inputs, more resources, or even successive bumper harvests would increase agricultural production. If there is a balanced growth in crop output it would almost certainly increase the marketed surplus of raw materials and food, but these surpluses might not be available on the terms necessary to revive industrial growth. Past experience suggests that a secular movement in the intersectoral terms of trade in favour of the agricultural sector, operating through a squeeze on profits, might have held back industrial expansion. Chakravarty (1974) notes this point in his analysis but ascribes the shift in relative prices to the deceleration in growth of agricultural output. However, it is likely that the landlord class, through political influence, manipulated the intersectoral terms of trade in its favour (Mitra 1977) and might well do so in the future. Under such circumstances an improved performance in agriculture would not ensure industrial growth. An increase in agricultural production may not be sufficient on other counts either. While it would lead to an increase in the total income of the farm sector there can be little doubt that the bulk of increments in income would be appropriated by those who own the means of production—landlords and rich farmers. But unless incomes accrue to the poor the demand for industrial wage goods from the rural majority cannot revive. We shall return to this issue later in the chapter.

The Level of Investment

During the decade 1955–65, real investment in the economy increased rapidly but the pace of expansion slackened markedly thereafter, notably in the public sector (see Raj 1976 and Srinivasan and Narayana 1977). The share of gross domestic capital formation in GDP which attained a peak level of 19.7 per cent in 1966–7, declined a little in subsequent years and fluctuated around an average level of 17 per cent in the period 1967–8 to 1974–5 (GoI 1976, pp. 30–1). The trend was much the same for gross fixed capital formation in the public sector. Thus some economists have attempted to explain the slowdown in industrial growth in terms of the stagnation in investment. There are two rather different variants of this hypothesis.

Consider first the paper by Srinivasan and Narayana (1977). They start from two sets of observations for the period since the mid-1960s: (a) a slackening of real investment, particularly in the public sector and (b) a deceleration in the rate of industrial growth. It is stressed that these developments constituted a marked departure from the trends established in the first three Five Year Plans. The authors go on to argue that the stagnation of real investment, especially public investment, is among the principal causes of sluggish industrial development, and if the economy is to surmount its present crisis there should be a vigorous expansion of public investment. Towards that end, they believe, recourse to deficit financing is perfectly possible given the enormous reserves of food and foreign exchange.

The thesis is somewhat simplistic. It does not even attempt to analyse the factors underlying the slowdown in public investment, nor does it trace the reasons why this failure of the public sector restrained industrial growth. Reading between the lines, one can discern an implicit view that large net inflows of foreign aid until 1965 sustained high levels of public investment, which, in turn, had complementarities with private investment. Problems arose once the sources of aid began to dry up, ultimately leading to stagnation.

Such an analysis is open to criticism on two counts. First, it assumes that aid supports investment alone and not, even in part, consumption. As a matter of fact, substantial aid inflows in the period 1955–65 might have provided the government with a soft option, preventing it from mobilizing domestic resources to the extent it should have. Second, net aid inflows rose very sharply in the 1970s, from their lowest ever level of Rs 159 crores in 1972–3 to Rs 1153 crores in 1975–6, around which level they remained (GoI 1976–7) but public investment failed to pick up.

Patnaik and Rao (1977) put forward a much more perceptive and interesting hypothesis about industrial stagnation. They advanced an explanation in terms of the circumstances leading to (a) a decrease in public investment, and (b) a loss of stimulus for private investment; both these occurrences, it was suggested, were a natural consequence of the earlier growth process. The impressive industrial growth until 1965 followed from a rapid expansion of public investment on the one hand and public expenditure on the other. While the former ensured the supply of basic industrial inputs, the latter generated a demand for goods manufactured in the private sector. At the same time, the strategy of import substitution, implemented through protection, virtually guaranteed a market for domestic producers, thereby providing a steady stimulus for private investment. This process of growth was not sustained for two reasons. In the first place, import substitution was nothing but a transient stimulus which lasted so long as the local markets remained uncaptured. Second, and possibly more important, there was a marked deceleration in the growth of public investment and expenditure. During the period 1960–1 to 1964–5 gross fixed capital formation in the public sector increased at 9.1 per cent per annum whereas the total expenditure of the government increased even faster at 13.2 per cent per annum, both expressed in terms of constant prices. In the following years, 1964–5 to 1973–4, these rates dropped to 0.7 per cent and 2.0 per cent, respectively (Patnaik and Rao 1977, p. 126). As a result, basic inputs manufactured in the public sector became scarce, while the demand for several outputs manufactured in the private sector tapered off. In this manner the deceleration in investment led to a deceleration in industrial growth. The authors are careful to tie up the loose ends in the argument. They explain that the level of investment stagnated primarily because the government failed to mobilize resources for the public sector. On the other hand, the private sector, which appropriated the increments in the economic surplus and was, therefore, capable of investment, channelled resources into speculation, luxury goods, construction, and the like.

In the framework set out above, stepping up the rate of investment in the public sector should provide an obvious solution to the problem of industrial stagnation. However, Patnaik and Rao believe that there are limits to the expansions of public investment. In the short-run, given the reserves of food and foreign exchange, deficit financing might appear simple enough, but it does imply a serious threat of inflation which would restrict the room for manoeuvre.[6] Anyway, in the long-run, a sustainable increase in public investment must be backed by a mobilization of domestic resources or, in effect, a major shift of the economic surplus form the private sector to the public sector.

The basic thrust of this hypothesis is perfectly acceptable but, as an explanation and prescription, it remains incomplete. First, the failure on the part of the private sector to invest its accumulating resources productively cannot be attributed to the stagnation in public investment alone. Surely, the profitability of private investment is a relevant consideration which depends, among other things, on the pattern of consumer expenditure and demand in the overwhelmingly important home market. Second, even if we assume that resources could *somehow* be mobilized to step up public investment, would it revive industrial growth on its own? Possibly not. Public investment may have made for rapid industrial growth until the mid-1960s and its decline may have been responsible for the stagnation thereafter. It does not, however, follow that public investment by itself would do the trick now, simply because the nature of the problem is different. Let me elaborate. In the early stages of industrialization, outlets for public investment posed no problem and resources were used to develop basic industries. But, at the present juncture, the avenues for public investment in the industrial sector are not unlimited. There already exist substantial underutilized capacities in the capital goods and intermediate goods industries. More public investment along the same lines would only create further excess capacity and compound difficulties, unless there is a growth in the final goods sector which absorbs these capacities. In other words, the supply of investible resources in the hands of the government is not the only constraint on public investment. A demand for such investment is as crucial—for public investment is not something autonomous which can be stepped up irrespective of appropriate outlets, nor can it create its own demand. It is

[6]According to Patnaik and Rao (1977), the danger of inflation arises once we allow for speculation. Corresponding to the 18 million tonnes of foodstocks and Rs 3800 crores of foreign exchange reserves there is an enormous amount of liquidity in the economy. In this context, deficit financing might generate inflationary expectations which, in turn, might induce people holding these liquid resources to switch from money into commodities, thereby pushing up prices.

worth stressing, however, that the composition of public investment does provide the government with a policy variable insofar as it determines the extent of direct and indirect employment creation which, in turn, would determine the growth in consumer demand. Hence, the investment mix in the public sector would matter as much as the rate of investment.

To recapitulate, it would appear that the best of the hypotheses about sluggish industrial growth, outlined so far, are partial and somewhat incomplete. If this were not the case stagnation should have disappeared. After all, there were no exogenous shocks after the oil crisis in 1973; licensing, controls, and trade policies were liberalized; the constraints imposed by agricultural production were significantly relaxed by a succession of good monsoons; the limit on public investment was not as rigid any more, what with the reserves of food and foreign exchange. Thus it is imperative that we probe further and work towards a coherent and unified hypothesis.

INCOME DISTRIBUTION AND THE DEMAND FACTOR

It is my contention that a satisfactory explanation of stagnation cannot afford to ignore the relationship between income distribution, the demand factor, and industrial growth. So far relatively little attention has been paid to this aspect of the problem. The only exceptions are a paper by Bagchi (1970), parts of a recent book by Mitra (1977), and, to some extent, an article by Raj (1976). In this section, therefore, I shall attempt to sketch a preliminary hypothesis which concentrates attention on consumer demand and income distribution as possible factors underlying the persistent sluggishness of growth in the industrial sector. *Prima facie*, demand factors might appear somewhat unusual, even Keynesian, as an explanation of low levels of industrial output in an economy such as India, but they might well be very significant at the present stage of development.

Given the overwhelming importance of the agricultural sector, private consumer expenditure obviously depends, to a large extent, on farm incomes. It follows that slow growth in agriculture could restrain the demand for manufactured goods and, consequently, hold back industrial expansion. This point is stressed by Raj (1976), who notes that regions characterized by moderately high and stable rates of agricultural growth have also experienced high growth rates in industry,[7] although there were a few exceptions (to this rule). Looking at aggregate demand, however, might be slightly misleading,

---

[7]Apart from the demand factor, Raj also specifies other linkages between agricultural and industrial growth. For an interesting, but different, analysis of how a shortage of agricultural wage goods would affect the demand for industrial goods, see Patnaik (1972).

and it is important to consider it in the context of income distribution. The reason for this is simple. In an economy where the bulk of the consumption, production, and investment decisions are made through the market mechanism, it is income distribution which determines the pattern of consumer expenditure as well as demand and, hence, the composition of industrial output.

The Bagchi (1970) thesis, which derives from this basic proposition, is as follows. The unequal income distribution (that exists) is reinforced by the process of growth for it is the private sector which owns the means of production and, as such, appropriates the increments in income. The government is unable to exercise effective control over the allocation of resources between: (a) consumption and saving, reflected in the failure to mobilize domestic resources for investment, and (b) 'essential' and 'non-essential' consumption— as revealed by the excessive importance of luxury goods in industrial production. Therefore, it is not possible for the government to maintain a high rate of investment irrespective of the unequal income distribution and the demand pattern generated by it. In this analysis Bagchi considered the period 1951–68, towards the end of which the slowdown in growth was just about discernible. The primary object of his paper was to highlight the problems which arose in the execution of the Mahalanobis strategy, and to pinpoint the reasons for its failure to generate a balanced and sustained industrial growth.

Given the fact of persistent quasi-stagnation for a decade, we can take the argument further. Up to a point, it is possible to bring about rapid industrialization through import replacement in the consumer goods sector and through investment in the creation of a capital and intermediate goods sector. Ultimately, however, the pace of industrialization can only be sustained if there is a growth in the domestic market, because the production capacities created in the investment goods sector must be absorbed by final consumer demand. But, in a market economy where the distribution of income is unequal, the demand base might be very narrow in terms of population spread. That was, and indeed is, the case in India. For the year 1964–5, using National Sample Survey data, it has been estimated that in the rural sector the richest 10 per cent of the population was responsible for 32.2 per cent of the total consumption of industrial goods, whereas the poorest 50 per cent accounted for only 22 per cent of the total. Consumption inequalities were even more pronounced in the urban sector, where the top decile purchased 39.3 per cent of the industrial goods and the bottom five deciles absorbed just 19.9 per cent of the total.[8]

[8]Sau (1974); the richest 20 per cent accounted for 48.4 per cent of the total consumption of industrial goods in rural India, and 55 per cent of the same in urban India.

Clearly, a large proportion of the demand for industrial products originates from a narrow segment of the population. However, sale of manufactured goods to the relatively few rich can use up only so much and no more of the capacity in the intermediate and the capital goods sector. Only a broad-based demand for mass consumption goods can lead to a full utilization of capacity (and generate sustainable increases in output), but that in turn requires incomes for the poor. Thus an unequal income distribution, operating through the demand factor, might well restrict the prospects of sustained industrial growth. As an aside, let me stress that one does not have to be an under-consumptionist to hold this view. What has just been described is not uncommon to crises in capitalist economies. From time to time it is possible that inadequate demand might constrain growth. While higher wages for workers might improve the situation they would lead to a squeeze on profits and investment. In other words, solving one problem exacerbates the other.

The hypothesis outlined here can only be tested through careful empirical work and further research. Of course, the assimilation of direct, quantitative evidence on the relationship between income distribution and industrial growth might turn out to be an elusive pursuit. Indeed, for this particular issue one might have to rely on indirect evidence. But even that would require another paper: a task we shall set aside for the future. For the present, it is sufficient that the hypothesis is plausible and, given available information, cannot be rejected out of hand. Mitra (1977) posits a mechanism through which a worsening income distribution might have retarded industrialization in India. A statistical analysis by Ranjit Sau, though somewhat out of date, provides limited evidence in support. The persistent sluggishness of industrial growth, over a decade otherwise characterized by plenty, further points to income distribution and the demand factor as important elements in a complete explanation of stagnation.

It has been argued by Mitra (1977) that the redistribution of income attempted in the country via the manipulation of relative prices in favour of agriculture and against industry is a major factor responsible for the deceleration in industrial growth since the mid-1960s. He suggests that 'the shifting terms of trade have been instrumental in eroding the level of real incomes of the majority of the population in both urban areas and the countryside'. The causation is straightforward enough. An increase in foodgrain prices, which accompanied the change in intersectoral relative prices, squeezed the non-food expenditure of the urban as well as the rural poor, because there was no corresponding increase in their incomes and food remained a preponderant item in their budget.[9] After a time, higher prices of agricultural commodities, operating through an escalation of raw material and wage costs, led to an across-the-board increase in industrial prices, so that the demand for manufactured products was squeezed further. The end result was that the demand for mass consumer goods in the economy levelled off.

In principle, the industrial sector could have been compensated for this loss by an expansion in demand on the part of the rich, who appropriated the bulk of the growth in incomes. But this did not happen because their avenues for further consumption were limited. For them, luxury consumer goods industries were the only outlet, apart from speculation, trade, and construction. The point relates clearly to the urban industrial bourgeoisie and the large affluent farmers. In this context, however, the rich peasantry in the countryside remains a puzzle, for it is unlikely that their consumption of basic industrial goods reached saturation point so quickly.

Available evidence on intersectoral resource flows reveals some interesting trends in demand. On the basis of data drawn from the NSS, Sau (1974)[10] has shown that the percentage of per capita consumer expenditure spent on industrial goods declined over the period 1952–3 to 1964–5, rather sharply in rural India but less markedly in the urban sector. More important, he found that the decline was far more pronounced in the case of the poorer sections of the population, particularly the bottom five deciles. From these findings Sau concludes that the market for industrial consumption goods was shrinking over the years, which is, in a sense, correct. But it is worth noting that these trends did not disrupt the process of industrialization. Indeed, this was also a period of rapid industrial growth. One can only presume that the industrial expansion occurred in spite of the constraints imposed by income distribution and consumer demand. I shall return to this issue towards the end of the essay.

From our viewpoint it would be far more interesting to examine the changing pattern of consumer expenditure and the trends in demand during the period 1965–75. While such an exercise is not possible here, a rough calculation from the CSO *National Accounts Statistics* does suggest that an increase in relative food prices did squeeze the demand for manufactured goods

[9]Patnaik (1972). It is assumed, of course, that the absolute level of food consumption is maintained; in fact, it might also be cut back if the erosion of real incomes is large enough.

[10]Mundle (1975) questions the methodology adopted by Sau, but his alternative method confirms the findings cited in the text.

after 1965. In terms of current prices, the proportion of private final consumption expenditure in the economy devoted to cereals and cereal substitutes rose from 27.4 per cent in 1965–6 to 32.7 per cent in 1974–5, whereas the proportion spent on industrial goods fell from 23.1 per cent to 19.3 per cent.[11] This points to the importance of the demand factor in industrial performance.

Unless incomes are created for the poor, either in the urban sector or in the rural sector, there is no new demand for manufactured wage goods which could sustain industrial growth. Consider, for a moment, the rural poor. Successive bumper harvests might have increased incomes in the agricultural sector. But whose incomes? There can be little doubt that much of the benefit has accrued to large landowners and rich peasants; not to the rural poor. Even in the heyday of the Green Revolution, therefore, stagnation in the industrial sector was not transformed into growth. As for the urban poor, among whom it is possible to identify the industrial working class, the situation probably deteriorated during the Emergency. A stringent incomes policy coupled with the Compulsory Deposit Scheme and the legislation on bonus payments effectively squeezed the real income of this group.

While the government has done almost nothing towards raising the incomes of the poor, a large number of recent policies have been directed towards stimulating consumption of the higher income groups and encouraging investment in the private corporate sector. The policies introduced to meet these objectives are: reduction of indirect taxes on luxury goods, a substantial cutback in income taxes payable by the rich, a delicensing of industries, and an open-door policy towards multinational corporations. However, the response of the economy has been slow and investment in the industrial sector has not revived. Consequently, the government is rather puzzled by the fact that investment has failed to pick up in spite of policies designed to remove all possible constraints and to create an environment conducive to industrial growth.[12] But the static level of investment is not surprising in the context of our hypothesis. After all, an increased production of consumer goods destined for the richer sections of the population can utilize the existing

[11]The proportion devoted to food (excluding edible oils, sugar, and salt which are also manufactured) increased, as the same time, from 51.3 per cent to 55.2 per cent. These percentages have been computed from the data in (GoI 1976, pp. 26–7). In our calculation, the category of industrial goods includes *pan*, tobacoo, intoxicants, clothing, footwear, fuel, power, furniture, furnishings, household equipment, and miscellaneous goods.

[12]See, for example, a statement by H.M. Patel, the Finance Minister: 'We have in fact removed all constraints on investment. We have not put any fresh hurdles to investment. If it does not pick up, the reasons are somewhat deeper to seek. I frankly confess I have not found an answer to my satisfaction.' *The Times of India*, New Delhi, 10 February 1978, p. 1.

production capacities only to a limited extent; it cannot bring about a sustained increase in industrial output.

The argument presented so far has one important lacuna. Critics might well ask if it is possible for India to circumvent the demand problem at home and repeat the Brazilian experience of 'successful' capitalist development. Given an underutilized intermediate and capital goods sector, a declining rate of investment, and a luxury goods sector that has run out of steam, the Brazilian model must appear as a rather attractive option to policymakers. Such a path of development, *inter alia*, has three essential ingredients: (a) external markets—which are necessary to get around the domestic demand bottleneck; (b) foreign capital—which provides resources as well as technology; and (c) a dominant class of industrial capitalists—in whose interest state power is exercised; their consumption forms the basis of the home market and they also provide the savings for investment. We shall consider each in turn.

Export-led growth is a curiously naive prescription for the problems faced by the Indian economy, and is not a feasible proposition. The reasons underlying my view have been developed, at length, elsewhere (Nayyar 1976). Suffice it to say that the problem of Indian exports is a problem of production. In the ultimate analysis, exports can be increased on a sustainable basis only if there is a growth in real national income. Therefore, export performance is likely to be determined by economic growth rather than the other way round. There is also very little evidence to suggest that foreign capital would flow into India in large amounts. This is because transnational corporations are extremely cautious about their decision to relocate production where it affects global operations, as in export-oriented manufacturing. The same international firms are far less worried bout choosing sites for a horizontal spread, and setting up production units in India to cater for local markets. The essential point is that the internationalization of production is limited to a finite number of countries, of which Brazil is one, but it will be some time before it spreads to India. In the Indian context, however, the most important problem is the difficulties that will arise in the fostering of an urban industrial elite at the expense of the rest of the population. It would mean a rupture of the ruling class alliance and a dumping of the rural oligarchy somewhere along the line. Recent policies such as the subsidy on fertilizers, priority in public investment to irrigation, and high procurement prices, all point to the continued existence of the rural oligarchy as a potent force in the Indian polity (Mitra 1977). Unless there is a change in the class character of the Indian State, and the government opts squarely for industrial capitalists, the Brazilian model is unlikely to materialize in the subcontinent.

The moral of the story, if one emerges, is that 'in an economy such as India, where the domestic market is overwhelmingly important, steady and continuous industrial growth requires a broad-based and increasing mass consumer demand. In a fundamental sense, therefore, sustained industrialization can only be based on a growth of the internal market'.

TOWARDS A POSSIBLE HYPOTHESIS

The preceding discussion has sought to focus attention on income distribution and the demand factor simply to compensate for the relative neglect in the existing literature. The intention was not to minimize the importance of other factors. Indeed, no explanation for the uneven pace of industrial development in the Indian context, can be logically complete without reference to both public investment and the agricultural sector. Therefore, it would be useful to recapitulate and draw together the stands of the different arguments outlined so far. Such an approach, to the extent it provides a macroeconomic view of the growth process should, hopefully, facilitate our understanding of the problem and might even suggest policy prescriptions. Towards this end, I shall attempt to formulate a unified, albeit tentative, hypothesis about the factors responsible for the transition from rapid industrial growth to the point of quasi-stagnation, and for the persistent sluggishness of growth in the industrial sector from the mid-1960s to the mid-1970s.

The impressive expansion of industrial output in the period 1950–65 can be explained as follows. Large doses of public investment created an infrastructure and set up intermediate goods industries so as to ensure a supply of inputs to the private sector. In doing so, it carried out a task the domestic capitalists could not have done on their own (Chakravarty 1974). At the same time, an ever increasing level of public expenditure gave rise to a demand for outputs manufactured in the corporate sector. As an aside, it is worth noting that this *modus operandi* of fostering industrialization was not different from the tactics of State capitalism elsewhere in the world, though it might have been at a later stage in history. But that was not all. The policies of import substitution, implemented through protection, reinforced the demand stimulus. Local capitalists were not only guaranteed existing markets but were also ensured a future insofar as the excess demand attributable to import restrictions would continue to provide markets, at least in the medium-term. Given this background, the sequence of industrial development is hardly surprising. In the years following independence, infrastructural developments and import substitution in the consumer goods sector stimulated industrial production. Thereafter, the high rate of industrial growth in the late 1950s and early 1960s was sustained by investment on the part of the government in the capital goods sector and is basic intermediate goods industries. During this phase of rapid development a reasonable rate of expansion of agricultural output ensured the *supply* of food—the basic wage good—and raw materials, thereby allowing industrialization to be sustained at a moderate pace which was, against the backdrop of colonial history, unprecedented. However, it should be stressed that the growth in industrial production was more directly attributable to public investment and protection.

In retrospect, the negative impact of agricultural performance on industrial development turned out to be far more significant. Starting around the mid-1960s, growth in the agricultural sector began to slow down, for reasons that have been discussed at length in the literature. Food prices began to rise and raw materials became scarce, so that the indirect support provided by agriculture to industrialization diminished markedly. As the intersectoral terms of trade shifted in favour of the agricultural sector, even the reduced support was now available to the industrial sector on less favourable terms. Difficulties were compounded by the fact that the principal sources of industrial growth in the first phase also waned in their impact. There was a dramatic deceleration in the growth of real public expenditure and investment (Patnaik 1972). The proximate causes of this occurrence might appear to lie in the wars which diverted investment to unproductive uses, or the successive droughts of the mid-1960s, which generated unforeseen consumption needs, but, in the ultimate analysis, it was a direct consequence of the government's failure to mobilize domestic resources.

A question immediately springs to mind: is it possible that accelerated investment in the private corporate sector could have sustained growth? Under the circumstances the answer is a definite no. In the first place, the complementarities between public and private investment in India have always been rather important. Moreover, the market stimulus provided by import substitution also disappeared. It was, almost by definition, a transient stimulus which could last only so long as the existing markets were uncaptured and excess demand remained. Once these opportunities were taken up, a growth of the domestic market was essential. Even after import substitution ran out of steam, investment could be sustained for a while by expansion in the capital goods sector and in basic industries, as indeed, it was during 1960–5. But it was not possible to continue with the creation of capacities in these sectors, for, ultimately, even their existence depends upon demand in the final goods sector.

It would be perfectly legitimate to ask why industrial growth came up against the demand barrier since 1965 and not earlier for, after all, income distribution was unequal right at the start, so that the majority of the Indian population was not in the market for industrial products.[13] The answer is relatively straightforward. Irrespective of the income distribution at the time, there was an assured domestic market, the size of which was determined by the level of imports and the state of excess demand for importables. This guaranteed source of demand was exhausted once import substitution in consumer goods was virtually complete, and the capacities created in the capital goods and the intermediate goods sector transcended the prevalent needs of the final goods sector. The demand for industrial goods generated by the elite did, to some extent, support the process of growth in the 1960s, but it was only a limited and temporary solution—limited because it could use only so much and no more of the capacity in the capital and intermediate goods sector; temporary because the demand for luxury goods on the part of a small fraction of the population is likely to reach saturation point. The alternative of export-led growth, we have noted earlier, is not feasible in the Indian case. Therefore, both the utilization of excess capacity and sustained industrial growth require a demand for mass consumption goods. In this context it is worth stressing that creating incomes for the poor is not a simple matter of redistribution through taxes and subsidies, for in a market economy such as India the distribution of incomes is closely related to, and cannot be divorced from, ownership of the means of production.

The demand factor needs to be singled out not only because it has received little attention so far, but also because it does explain, in part, the present crisis in the economy and the persistent sluggishness of industrial growth. Moreover, it has obvious policy implications. Successive bumper harvests, the unprecedented stockpile of food, and massive foreign exchange reserves have, at least for the time being, removed the supply constraints. Yet there is little evidence of a return to the earlier trend rate or of sustained industrial growth. Why? *Inter alia*, it is because the lack of a mass domestic demand for industrial goods has surfaced as a problem.

Given the political aspects of the situation a radical redistribution of income might be unattainable. What about stepping up the rate of investment which is frequently thought of as a possible solution? Such a strategy is clearly difficult in the case of private investment because investment decisions in the corporate industrial sector follow signals provided by the market mechanism;

---

[13]Even in 1952–3, the richest 10 per cent of the population was responsible for 32.7 per cent of the total consumption of industrial goods in the rural sector and 36.8 per cent of the total in the urban sector. The shares of the poorest 50 per cent were 23.6 per cent and 19.7 per cent, respectively; see Sau (1974).

hence, they depend on the state of demand, the pattern of consumer expenditure and, ultimately, the existing income distribution. On the other hand, in terms of policy, public investment does provide some room for manoeuvre. In the long-run, however, the rate of public investment itself depends on the ability of the government to mobilize domestic resources, for otherwise a serious threat of inflation remains; the reserves of food and foreign exchange do not entirely solve this problem once speculation enters the picture. What is more, even if the rate of investment in the public sector could be stepped up it would not suffice unless adequate attention is paid to the composition of investment, so that it leads to employment creation and incomes for the poor, if not directly at least as a second order effect.

For sustained industrial growth it is essential not only to mobilize the savings of the rich for investment but also to channel increments in income to the poor, which, in turn, would generate a broad-based demand for industrial goods. Stepping up of public investment, supported by an inflow of foreign resources, can only be a temporary and partial solution. It cannot generate a process of sustained industrialization in India.

REFERENCES

Bagchi, A.K. (1970), 'Long-term Constraints on India's Industrial Growth, 1951–1968', in E.A.G. Robinson and M. Kidron (eds), *Economic Development in South Asia*, Macmillan, London.

Bhagwati, J. and P. Desai (1970), *India: Planning for Industrialization*, Oxford University Press, London.

Bhagwati, J. and T.N. Srinivasan (1975), *Foreign Trade Regimes and Economic Development: India*, National Bureau of Economic Research, New York.

Chakravarty, S. (1974), *Reflections on the Growth Process in the Indian Economy*, Hyderabad.

Chattopadhyay, P. (1970), 'State Capitalism in India', *Monthly Review*, March.

Government of India (GoI) (1968–9), *Economic Survey, 1968–69*, Ministry of Finance, Government of India, New Delhi.

——— (1976–7), *Economic Survey, 1976–77*, Ministry of Finance, Government of India, New Delhi.

——— (1976), *National Accounts Statistics: 1960/1–1974/5*, CSO, Ministry of Planning, Government of India, New Delhi.

——— (1977), *Report on the Census of Small Scale Industrial Units*, Development Commissioner, Small-Scale Industries, Government of India, New Delhi.

Mitra, A. (1977), *Terms of Trade and Class Relations*, Frank Cass, London.

Mundle, S. (1975), 'Intersectoral Flow of Consumer Goods: Some Preliminary Results', *Economic and Political Weekly*, Annual Number, February, pp. 165–74.

Nayyar, D. (1976), *India's Exports and Export Policies in the 1960s*, Cambridge University Press, Cambridge.

Patnaik, P. (1972), 'Disproportionality Crisis and Cyclical Growth', *Economic and Political Weekly*, Annual Number, February, pp. 329–36.

Patnaik, P. and S.K. Rao (1977), '1975–76: Beginning of the End of Stagnation?', *Social Scientist*, January–February, pp. 120–38.

Raj, K.N. (1976), 'Growth and Stagnation in India's Industrial Development', *Economic and Political Weekly*, Annual Number, February, pp. 223–36.

Sau, R. (1974), 'Some Aspects of Inter-sectoral Resource Flows', *Economic and Political Weekly*, Special Number, August, pp. 1277–84.

Srinivasan, T.N. (1977), 'Constraints on Growth and Policy Options: A Comment', *Economic and Political Weekly*, 26 November, pp. 1987–9.

Srinivasan, T.N. and N.S.S. Narayana (1977), 'Economic Performance Since the Third Plan and its Implications for Policy', *Economic and Political Weekly*, Annual Number, February, pp. 225–39.

Vaidyanathan, A. (1977), 'Constraints on Growth and Policy Options', *Economic and Political Weekly*, 17 September, pp. 1643–50 and 17 December, pp. 2105–9.

Chapter 11

THE FOREIGN TRADE SECTOR, PLANNING, AND INDUSTRIALIZATION IN INDIA

INTRODUCTION

The role of the external sector, in general, and the foreign trade sector, in particular, has been at the centre of the debate about the strategy of industrialization and development in India from time to time: to begin with, during the mid-1950s in the controversy around the Mahalanobis model; once again, during the late 1960s following the devaluation of the rupee; and, more recently, during the mid-1980s as part of the package of new economic policies. However, it is possible to discern a qualitative change in the significance attached to the foreign trade sector from the late 1980s.

There is an extensive literature on the subject which analyses export performance or evaluates import substitution in the process of industrialization and development.[1] The contours of the debate around these issues are now so familiar that yet another essay on the same theme would serve little purpose. This essay makes a modest attempt to steer away from the beaten track. It seeks to situate the foreign trade sector in the wider context of planning for industrialization, develop a macroeconomic overview, and analyses the interaction between foreign trade and the national economy since the inception of economic planning in 1950 until the late 1980s.

The first section outlines the changes in the perceptions about foreign trade in the planning process, from the 1950s through the 1980s and discusses the underlying factors. The second section develops a simple analytical framework on the macroeconomics of the external sector. The third section examines the possible impact of the foreign trade sector on the economy as a whole and on the process of industrialization. The fourth section considers the other side of the coin, and explores the implications and consequences of developments

---

[1]See, for example, Singh (1964), Bhagwati and Desai (1970), Nayyar (1976), Bhagwati and Srinivasan (1976), and Wolf (1982).

in the national economy for the foreign trade sector. In conclusion, the fifth section situates foreign trade in the larger context of strategic issues in planning for industrialization.

FOREIGN TRADE AND THE PLANNING PROCESS

Economic planning in India began *circa* 1950. The period since then, until the mid-1980s, witnessed significant changes in the planners' view of foreign trade in the process of industrialization and development. It is difficult to outline any sequence of events and developments which span a long period of time. All the same, it is important to sketch the contours if only to highlight the salient features or the turning points. The discussion that follows attempts to pinpoint the major changes in the planners' outlook on exports and imports. It is worth noting that the changes are explicitly stated in the first three Five Year Plans, but there is some need to read between the lines in the subsequent plan documents.

Given the relatively comfortable position of foreign exchange reserves in the late 1940s, boosted further by the Korean War boom in commodity prices, the First Plan was largely indifferent to exports and liberal in imports.[2] The Second Five Year Plan provided a sharp contrast. It assumed that no significant increase in export earnings was possible.[3] This pessimism was based on two factors. In the first place, it sprang from the widespread belief that exports of primary products and raw materials were faced with unfavourable prospects in the world market. Second, it was felt that non-traditional manufactures, which constituted a tiny proportion of the country's exports at the time, had little prospect of securing sizeable export markets until industrialization was well under way.[4] The natural consequence of such export pessimism was a conviction that, in the long-run, industrialization could be consistent with a viable balance of payments position only if it was based on a programme which minimized imports. The Mahalanobis model, which provided the theoretical framework for the Second Plan, stressing the importance of the rate and the composition of investment in a closed economy, also provided indirect support to the rationale for replacing imports to further the objective of industrialization. Thus, import substitution became the keystone of the development strategy in the late 1950s. Consequently, exports were neglected by the government while imports were subjected to strict control.

---

[2]For example, it was stated that 'in periods of relatively easy foreign exchange supplies, the need for export promotion would be less evident', see Planning Commission (1951, p. 453).

[3]See Planning Commission (1956, pp. 96–9).

[4]Planning Commission (1956, p. 99).

As it happened, the concentration in import-saving investment did not lead to all the desired results. It was discovered that the process of import substitution in the capital goods sector and the intermediate goods sector turned out to be far more difficult than import substitution in the consumer goods sector. What is more, it did not lead to the expected reduction in pressure on the balance of payments. In fact, increasing investment in the capital goods sector compounded import needs rapidly. Thus, in spite of the general sense of fatalism about exports and the actual stagnation of export earnings, there was a gradual realization that if the Indian economy was ever to attain its objective of self-reliance, it was necessary that an increasing proportion of the external resources required to finance economic development be met out of foreign exchange receipts derived from exports. In other words, exports had to be increased simply to reduce the dependence on foreign aid. From being a neglected issue, this is how export growth came to be an imperative in Indian economic planning.

Consequently, the Third Five Year Plan showed a distinct change in the attitude of planners towards exports, when it argued that 'one of the main drawbacks in the past has been that the programme for exports has not been regarded as an integral part of the country's development effort under the five year plans'.[5] And so it was finally recognized that export promotion is just as important as import substitution in the process of development. Exports were, therefore, given a high priority in the Plan, and export promotion was envisaged as a major plank of economic policy.[6] This radical shift in the role assigned to exports was followed by the introduction of export promotion measures on a wide scale. The subsidization implicit in these measures was gradually escalated. However, export promotion policies during the Third Plan were, at least in principle, designed to offset the bias against exports which was implicit in the overvalued exchange rate and the prevalent level of import restrictions.[7]

Throughout the period of the first three plans, from 1951–2 to 1965–6, trade policies and the balance of payments were an integral part of the wider planning perspective. This does not mean that there were no errors of strategy or tactics during this phase. Indeed, there were: positive discrimination against the export sector and inefficient import substitution in the 1950s; or inappropriate, sometimes excessive, subsidization of exports in the 1960s. Nevertheless, the relative shift in emphasis from import substitution to export

[5]Planning Commission (1961, p. 137).
[6]Planning Commission (1961, pp. 138–41).
[7]For a detailed discussion, Nayyar (1976).

promotion was a part of the planners' long-term view and was introduced as a corrective for past mistakes. It did not represent a change in the strategy of industrialization or development.

As we know, the poor harvests and the successive droughts of the mid-1960s led the government to abandon planning for an interregnum of three years. But, the spirit of economic planning in India never revived to its earlier level thereafter, despite the resumption of the Five Year Plans. In retrospect, it is clear that the role of planning was slowly but steadily eroded by administrative fiat. The formulation of economic policies in general, and trade policies in particular, came to be based on short-term crisis management rather than long-term planning. It is always difficult to draw temporal lines, but it would appear that this phase of crisis management stayed with us from the mid-1960s to the mid-1970s. This was particularly true of policies towards the external sector; whether it was aid for food imports in 1966–7, the attempted rationalization of trade policies following the devaluation of the rupee in June 1966, or managing the balance of payments crisis in 1974–5.[8] It is striking that, during this period, the foreign trade sector and trade policies received little, if any, systematic attention from the planners. Indeed, apart from projections about imports and exports, the Fourth Plan and the Fifth Plan documents barely discussed the foreign trade sector in the context of the planning process.[9]

The story does not end with the phase of crisis management described above. Beginning in the late 1970s, it is possible to discern a change in perceptions about foreign trade and an associated shift of emphasis in trade policies. As the balance of payments situation became comfortable in 1976–7 and 1977–8, the government introduced a dose of import liberalization. For the first time, perhaps, the stress on import substitution was also diluted a little. At the same time, there was a stress on export promotion which went beyond the need to offset the bias implicit in import substitution policies: so much so that there was a perceptible change in the outlook of policymakers who began to see the export sector as a potential leading sector in industrialization and development. This perception was probably reinforced

[8]Nayyar (1986, pp. 134–67).

[9]In the *Fourth Five Year Plan* (Planning Commission 1969), for example, there is no chapter on foreign trade or the balance of payments; there is a very brief discussion on the role of exports in the context of external resources for the financing of the plan (pp. 92–4). Similarly, the *Fifth Five Year Plan* (Planning Commission 1976) has no chapter on foreign trade or trade policies. There is a short section on the balance of payments in the chapter on financial resources (pp. 49–50), the policy content of which is minimal.

by the unprecedented export growth in India over the preceding quinquennium, as also by the rapid export growth witnessed in the NICs. These shifts in emphasis were not an integral part of the planning process, but there were implicit suggestions in the Fifth Plan document.[10]

There has been a more explicit discussion of these issues in the 1980s, which is, to some extent, reflected in the Sixth Plan and the Seventh Plan documents.[11] It is recognized that export promotion and import substitution are neither mutually exclusive nor alternative strategies of development. In principle, therefore, trade polices are sought to be formulated in such a manner that the policy-mix strikes a balance between export promotion on the one hand and import substitution on the other. Yet, it is stressed that exports would have to become increasingly important as a means of financing the balance of payments deficit, if the levels of external debt and the burden of debt servicing are to be kept within manageable proportions. Important as exports are, it is believed that import substitution must also remain an integral part of the quest for self-reliance.[12] In the view of the planners, however, the past emphasis on import substitution *per se* should be replaced by an emphasis on efficient import substitution.[13]

It is also possible to discern the beginning of a new long-term perspective about trade policies and industrialization, which provides a contrast with the approach of the earlier planning era.[14] It is stressed that foreign trade cannot be separated from the national economy, just as trade policies cannot be separated from economic policies. Such a perspective recognizes that developments in the foreign trade sector and developments in the economy are interdependent, but the interdependence is not analysed further. The objectives of export promotion and import substitution, it is suggested, are realized in the performance of the economy as a whole rather than the external sector alone. Similarly, there is an emerging perception that the rate of export expansion and the pace of import substitution are not determined by the framework of trade policies alone, for there is a clear nexus between trade policies, industrial

[10]The *Fifth Five Year Plan*, for example, stated that 'the objective of export growth should be to further strengthen the 'leading' sectors of growth', Planning Commission (1976, p. 49).

[11]See *Sixth Five Year Plan*, Planning Commission (1981, pp. 71–2 and 84–5) and *Seventh Five Year Plan*, Planning Commission (1985, pp. 66–7 and 75–8).

[12]The views outlined in this paragraph are developed in Government of India (1984).

[13]Government of India (1984). See also, Planning Commission (1981, p. 72), which argues that 'it will be counter productive to pursue a policy of indiscriminate import substitution; the emphasis has to be on efficient import substitution which improves both our balance of payments and national income'.

[14]Planning Commission (1985, pp. 76–7) and Government of India (1984, pp. 1–7).

policies, and other economic policies in the monetary and fiscal spheres. A co-ordinated set of policies, it is argued, would be conducive both for rational export promotion and for efficient import substitution. Thus, it would seem that trade policies are now situated in the wider context, even though the macroeconomics of the foreign trade sector has not been subjected to any systematic analysis by planners or policymakers.

It is difficult to summarize the complex sequence of developments outlined in the preceding paragraphs. Nevertheless, it is possible to discern the following changes in the perceptions of planners. From the late 1940s until the mid-1950s, foreign trade was regarded as marginal if not irrelevant. For two decades thereafter, until the mid-1970s, the foreign trade sector was seen as a constraint on growth. Beginning in the late 1970s, for a short period, foreign trade was thought of as a leading sector in development, but by the early 1980s the foreign trade sector was envisaged as a catalyst in industrialization. In retrospect, it appears that there were three factors underlying the shifts in emphasis or the changes in direction: the balance of payments situation, the strategy of industrialization, and the perceived role of foreign trade in the process of development. Taken together, these determinants also explain the direction and the timing of changes in trade policies.

It is clear that the indifference towards exports and the liberal attitude towards imports during the first half of the 1950s, the First Plan period, was significantly attributable to a comfortable balance of payments situation and to a perception that the role of foreign trade was marginal at that stage of development.

The fundamental change in the sphere of import policies came in the mid-1950s, when there was a sudden transition to a strict regime of import controls, which was a consequence of the deterioration in the balance of payments situation and the strategy of industrialization adopted in the Second Plan. These considerations remained the basic determinants of import policies for more than two decades. The next turning point, in the late 1970s, coincided with a comfortable balance of payments situation and a discernible shift in the industrialization strategy which diluted the strong emphasis on import substitution.

The indifference towards exports implicit in the First Plan was followed by a pessimism about exports during the Second Plan which, taken together, meant that the export sector was neglected, indeed discriminated against, during the 1950s. The Third Plan provided the basic point of departure in the early 1960s as export promotion policies were introduced on a wide scale, at least in part to combat the pressure on the balance of payments which mounted further despite, perhaps even because of, import substitution. Ever since then, the need to finance deficits in the balance of payments has remained an important determinant of export policies. There was, however, in the late 1970s, a further emphasis on export promotion associated with a slight change in industrialization strategy which perceived the export sector as a potential leading sector, but this perception did not last long.

The 1980s witnessed a departure from the earlier asymmetrical emphasis either on import substitution or on export promotion, as policymakers endeavoured to strike a balance between the two objectives. The balance of payments factor, however, no longer provided a consistent explanation. The stress on exports continued because of, while the import liberalization was sustained in spite of, the difficult payments situation. It would seem that, at the time, the strategy of industrialization and the perceived role of foreign trade in the development process constituted the important determinants of trade policies. Indeed, the importance attached to the foreign trade sector in the national economy, provided a sharp contrast with the 1950s. However, the dictates of the balance of payments situation could, once again, exercise an important influence on the shape of things to come.

MACROECONOMICS OF THE EXTERNAL SECTOR

Economic planning and policy formulation in India tend to consider the external sector, particularly foreign trade, in isolation from the rest of the economy. Such an approach, often characteristic of large continental countries, is not appropriate in terms of either theory or policy. For meaningful analysis, a macroeconomic perspective is essential because developments in the external sector and developments in the economy as a whole are interdependent. It is not sufficiently recognized that the causation runs in both directions. What happens in the sphere of foreign trade affects the economy, just as what happens in the economy affects the foreign trade sector.

Consider, first, the impact of foreign trade on the national economy. Exports are a source of demand to realize the vent for surplus and a means of transforming domestic resources into foreign resources which are necessary to finance the process of development. Imports, so financed by exports, are essential to sustain desired levels of consumption, investment, and production in the economy which, in turn, generate multiplier effects. This is both recognized and emphasized by the planners. But it does not complete the picture. In open economies, the external sector exercises an influence on national income through the foreign trade multiplier. In the Indian context, this macroeconomic impact may be limited by two factors. First, insofar as exports and imports are a relatively small proportion of national income, the impact of the foreign trade multiplier cannot be large particularly in terms of its base but also in terms of its size. Second, insofar as there are binding supply constraints, the foreign trade multiplier may work with respect to money income rather than real income.

Consider, now, the impact of the national economy on the foreign trade sector. The performance of the economy as a whole affects both exports and imports through the forces of supply and demand. For exports, on the supply side, the output of exportables and its cost of production both depend on the size of the home market, as exports are the end, rather than the beginning, of the typical market expansion path for firms in India;[15] on the demand side, the relative profitability of the home market in conjunction with the pressure of domestic demand is a crucial determinant of export performance, as a large proportion of India's exports, whether consumer goods or intermediate goods, are exportables which enter into domestic consumption or use.[16] For imports, on the supply side, the domestic production of importables is a vital factor insofar as imports are a residual (which is the case for most bulk imports);[17] on the demand side, the level of investment and the choice of technology in the economy are basic determinants of imports whether we consider capital goods, manufactured intermediates, or raw materials. But that is not all. At a macro level, an excess of imports over exports corresponds to an excess of investment over savings in the economy; even if savings exceed investment in the private sector, a larger fiscal deficit in the government sector would mean an excess of imports over exports for the economy. In this macroeconomic sense, the balance of trade deficit, or the current account deficit, simply represents a situation where absorption exceeds output or expenditure exceeds income for the economy as a whole;[18] it is

---

[15]There are important exceptions. For exports such as gems and jewellery, marine products, iron ore, manganese ore, mica, and cashew kernels, the entire output or an overwhelming proportion of the output is exported. For exports such as garments, carpets, and handicrafts, production for the export market is, for all practical purposes, separated from production for the home market.

[16]This argument is developed with supporting evidence, in Nayyar (1976).

[17]In India, imports of foodgrains, edible oils, fertilizers, crude oil and petroleum products, iron and steel, non-ferrous metals, newsprint, and cement are described as 'bulk imports'. There are two characteristics of such imports which account for more than 50 per cent of the total import bill. First, these are essential imports which are necessary to support levels of consumption and production in the economy. Second, these imports are the monopoly of state trading organizations, so that the decision about the volume of imports is made by the government based on the estimated difference between domestic production and domestic consumption.

[18]In other words, the state of the balance of payments depends not simply on its components, or the changes therein, but also on aggregate income and aggregate expenditure.

possible that the excess of expenditure over income may be attributable, in large part, to the fiscal deficit of the government.

Starting from this perspective, where the focus is on the short-run, it is worth outlining a simple analytical framework towards a macroeconomics of the external sector, where the focus shifts to the medium-term or long-run.[19] This highlights some key issues that have received scant attention from planners in India or even the academic literature on the subject. There is an important nexus between exports and investment at a macro-level. Exports provide an external market on the demand side and enforce a cost discipline on the supply side, whereas investment creates a domestic market on the demand side and transforms the industrial structure on the supply side. Hence, there is a possible cumulative causation that arises from the interaction between the effects of the foreign trade multiplier and of capacity creation combined with industrial cost-efficiency. On the demand side, high investment and high exports together induce market expansion and may be conducive to high growth. On the supply side, a high or rising proportion of investment in GDP may provide flexibility through more rapid supply side adjustment, while a high or rising proportion of exports in GDP may provide discipline by enforcing cost-efficiency. It would be too much of a digression to enter into a discussion of what determines or drives investment and exports. For our purpose here, it is sufficient to note that such a virtuous circle of cumulative macroeconomic causation would be associated with a rapid growth in GDP, industrial output, and manufactured exports.

An increase in the degree of openness in trade, associated with a high or rising export–GDP ratio and investment–GDP ratio, has another dimension. Over time, particularly in the medium-term, imports may rise faster than exports as a proportion of GDP. At a macro level, this is because investment rises faster than domestic savings. The excess of imports over exports, which corresponds to the excess of investment over savings, would need to be financed by foreign capital inflows. An increase in external indebtedness would be a natural consequence, and the process can be sustained only if an economy has the capacity to meet its debt obligations in terms of amortization and interest payments. Concessional aid flows apart, the capacity of an economy to manage its debt problem would depend upon its ability to curb the increase

---

In terms of Keynesian macroeconomic analysis, the absorption approach suggests that the current account deficit is nothing but the difference between income and expenditure (absorption) for the economy as a whole, that is, $B = Y - A$ where $B = X - M$ and $A = C + I + G$.

[19]I am indebted to Amit Bhaduri for helpful discussion and valuable suggestions in the formulation of this analytical framework.

in the import–GDP ratio which would raise the value of the foreign trade multiplier, and to sustain a high investment–GDP ratio combined with a high export–GDP ratio, by raising domestic savings, which would increase the base on which the foreign trade multiplier operates.

The cumulative causation outlined here may lead to a virtuous circle if the increase in investment coincides with an increase in exports, while there is no neutralizing change in the capital–output ratio, and if external resources are an addition to, rather than a substitute for, domestic resources and are used to support investment rather than consumption. Where the situation is reversed, so that the increase in investment does not coincide with an increase in exports, or there is a compensating rise in the capital–output ratio, *and* external resources become a substitute for domestic resources, used to support consumption rather than investment, a vicious circle may be the likely outcome. It would be reasonable to ask: what underlies a virtuous circle or a vicious circle? The question is too complex for a simple answer. *Inter alia*, obviously, technological choice and the investment mix have a direct impact on the capital–output ratio, just as the fiscal regime and government decisions exercise an indirect influence on the use of external resources. The factors that determine investment and exports are manifold and complex. It needs to be stressed, however, that the nature of State intervention, both at the macro-level and at the micro-level, is crucial as a determinant of the outcome.

FOREIGN TRADE, THE ECONOMY, AND INDUSTRIALIZATION

In the wider context of the national economy, the foreign trade sector in India has never been important in quantitative terms. This should not be surprising for a continental country with a diverse resource base and an enormous size reflected in its population and area if not income. Yet, the foreign trade sector has always been significant in qualitative terms. What, then, has been its impact on the economy as a whole and the process of industrialization? The discussion that follows explores this question in retrospect and prospect.

To start with, it is worth comparing the size of the foreign trade sector with a macroeconomic aggregate such as national income. Table 11.1 sets out the share of exports, imports, and total foreign trade in GDP during the four decades since the advent of planning in 1950. In order to reduce the volume of data to manageable proportions, the figures are presented as annual averages for five-year periods. The share of foreign trade in national income declined from an average level of 13 per cent during the first half of the 1950s to an average level of less than 10 per cent during the first half of the 1970s; it recovered to an average level of more than 13 per cent in the decade that

Table 11.1: Exports, Imports, and Investment in the National Economy

Period	Exports	Imports	Foreign Trade	Investment	Investment plus Exports
	(as a percentage of GDP at market prices: annual averages)				
1951–2 to 1955–6	6.0	7.0	13.0	10.8	16.8
1956–7 to 1960–1	4.8	7.2	12.0	15.3	20.1
1961–2 to 1965–6	3.8	6.3	10.1	16.7	20.5
1966–7 to 1970–1	3.9	5.5	9.4	17.3	21.2
1971–2 to 1975–6	4.5	5.3	9.8	18.9	23.4
1976–7 to 1980–1	5.9	7.7	13.6	22.9	28.8
1981–2 to 1985–6	5.1	8.4	13.5	24.2	29.3
1986–7 to 1988–9	4.8	6.9	11.7	23.9	28.7

Note: For the period 1951–2 to 1985–6, data on gross domestic capital formation and GDP at current prices are obtained from the 1970–1 series of *National Accounts Statistics*; for the period 1986–7 to 1988–9, these figures are obtained from the recently introduced new series of *National Accounts Statistics* and are not strictly comparable with those for the earlier period.

Sources: (a) For data on the values of exports and imports: DGCIS, Calcutta; (b) For data on gross domestic capital formation (investment) and GDP at market prices: CSO, *National Accounts Statistics*.

followed and dropped, once again, thereafter. These data reveal the trends but conceal the turning points. As a substitute for a time-series, therefore, Figure 11.1 outlines the change in the share of exports and of imports in GDP over the period under review. We find that the share of exports in GDP declined steadily from the mid-1950s until the early 1970s, registered a rapid increase for a relatively short period of five years and declined, albeit slowly, during the next decade. On the other hand, the share of imports in GDP fluctuated through the 1950s, declined slowly until the early 1970s, rose sharply during the remaining years of that decade, and declined again thereafter. It is worth noting that, as a proportion of GDP, imports always exceeded exports by a large margin except for two short periods during the early 1950s and the mid-1970s. These trends and turning points are consistent with, and to some extent even explain, the changes in the perceptions of planners about the foreign trade sector which were discussed earlier in the essay.

It is plausible to argue that the impact of the external sector on national income in India, through the foreign trade multiplier, was not very significant. The low export–GDP ratio, even when it was rising for a short period, could not have increased the base on which the foreign trade multiplier operates so much as to have an appreciable effect on the growth in national income. Similarly, the import–GDP ratio, though somewhat higher, was not high enough to exercise a significant influence on the size of the foreign trade multiplier, for most of the period under review; it is, of course, possible that the dramatic increase in the share of imports from 4.1 per cent of GDP in 1970–1 to 9.8 per cent of GDP in 1980–1 (three-fifths of which was attributable to the increased volume and prices of oil imports),[20] did lead to a discernible reduction in the size of the foreign trade multiplier.[21]

In terms of macroeconomic causation, the nexus between exports and investment could not have materialized as a virtuous circle leading to a rapid growth of national income in India. The reason is clear enough. During the four decades, an increase in the investment–GDP ratio did not quite coincide with an increase in the export–GDP ratio. This is confirmed by the data in Table 11.1, which also show that the sum of investment–GDP and export–GDP ratios rose significantly only twice: once in the second half of the 1950s, when the export-ratio fell, and once again in the second half of the 1970s, when the export-ratio rose. Even for the latter period, annual averages conceal that the coincidence was by no means complete; the share of exports in GDP rose from 3.7 per cent in 1971–2 to 6.4 per cent in 1976–7, whereas the share of gross domestic capital formation in GDP rose from 19.9 per cent in 1976–7 to 24.7 per cent in 1980–1.[22] Further confirmation is provided by the evidence in Table 11.3, which shows that a rapid growth in the level of investment never coincided with a rapid growth in the volume of exports during the period under review. What is more, even if a high rate of investment had been combined with a high ratio of exports to GDP in a more sustained manner, or if growth in investment and growth in exports had coincided better, the impact would have been neutralized by the compensating increase in the capital–output ratio.[23]

[20]Over the same period, the share of non-oil imports in GDP rose from 3.5 per cent to 5.7 per cent.

[21]Consider a situation in which the savings–GDP ratio is 20 per cent. If the import–GDP ratio rises from 4 per cent to 10 per cent (roughly comparable with the actual increase in the 1970s), the size of the foreign trade multiplier would be reduced from 4.2 to 3.3.

[22]These proportions have been calculated from foreign trade statistics published by DGCIS, Calcutta and *National Accounts Statistics* published by the CSO.

[23]The Planning Commission has estimated that, at 1970–1 prices, the incremental capital output ratio was 3.2 in the First Plan period (1951–2 to 1955–6), 4.1 in the Second Plan period (1956–7 to 1960–1), 5.4 in the Third Plan period (1961–2 to 1965–6), 4.9 in the Annual Plan period (1966–7 to 1968–9), 5.7 in the Fourth Plan period (1969–70 to 1973–4) and 3.9 in the Fifth Plan period (1974–5 to 1978–9); see *Sixth Five Year Plan*

So much for an analysis of the past, which suggests that the foreign trade sector did not have a significant impact on the national economy at least in quantitative terms. In the 1980s, however, there was a change in perception among planners which stressed the qualitative significance of the foreign trade sector as an important catalyst in industrialization. There were two perceptions that emerged. First, it was felt that greater participation in world trade and more interaction with the world market would facilitate modernization. Second, it was felt that a closer proximity between domestic prices and world prices would not only yield larger gains from international division of labour but also improve efficiency at home through the exploitation of comparative advantage.

In this context, it is worth noting that neither the debate nor the policies concerning liberalization in the external sector were entirely new. There was an intense debate, and a short lived liberalization in the import regime, at the time of the devaluation of the rupee in 1966.[24] The next phase of import liberalization, which began in the late 1970s, was more definite and sustained. But that was not the only difference. In the 1980s, it coincided not only with serious balance of payments difficulties but also with a near-stagnation in international trade flows and an increasing incidence of protectionism in the industrialized countries. What is more, this time around, import liberalization was associated with a perceived role of the foreign trade sector as a catalyst in the process of industrialization and development. It was argued that a more open trade regime would increase competitiveness, efficiency, and productivity in the economy as a whole. The argument was taken further to suggest that import liberalization in the sphere of products and technology would increase the competitiveness of domestic firms in the world market thus improving export performance, and would increase the degree of competition for firms in the domestic market thus facilitating cost reduction and technological upgrading. Both strands of such an argument are open to question.

Let me begin with the question of import liberalization and export performance. The available evidence, set out in Table 11.2, reveals a dramatic increase in the import intensity of export production during the period from the late-1970s to the late-1980s. Between 1977–8 and 1987–8, the average import content of Indian exports rose from 13.7 per cent to 31.5 per cent as

---

(Planning Commission 1981, p. 2). The *Seventh Five Year Plan* (Planning Commission 1985, p. 26), projects the incremental capital–output ratio at 5.0 in the Seventh Plan period (1985–6 to 1989–90) and reports that it was a little lower in the Sixth Plan period (1980–1 to 1984–5), while the trend value of the incremental capital–output ratio was 5.5.

[24]For an account of this episode of liberalization, see Bhagwati and Desai (1970), which also sets out the case for liberalization.

Table 11.2: Trends in the Import Intensity of Exports

	(import replenishment licences for exports as a percentage of value)				
	1972–3	1977–8	1980–1	1984–5	1987–8
1. Of total exports	6.9	13.7	21.2	23.5	31.5
(excluding gems and jewellery)	(4.4)	(8.3)	(15.7)	(15.3)	(18.0)
2. Of eligible exports	10.4	18.6	29.5	35.5	38.5
(excluding gems and jewellery)	(6.8)	(11.7)	(22.7)	(24.5)	(23.1)

Notes: (a) The figures on the value of import replenishment licences include all import licences issued on the basis of export performance: REP licences, Advance licences, Imprest licences, Special Imprest licences, and Additional licences. (b) It is assumed that all exports except for tea, coffee, sugar, rice, raw cotton, oil cakes, iron ore, jute manufactures, and crude oil and petroleum products are eligible for import replenishment facilities. (c) The estimated percentages in parentheses exclude gems and jewellery both from the numerator and the denominator as the import-intensity of these exports is much higher than the average for exports.

Sources: (a) For data on the value of import replenishment licences, *Report of the Committee on Trade Policies*, Ministry of Commerce, Government of India, December 1984, and RBI, *Report on Currency and Finance*, annual issues. (b) For data on the value of exports: DGCIS, Calcutta.

a proportion of total exports and from 18.6 per cent to 38.5 per cent as a proportion of exports eligible for import replenishment facilities. Even if we exclude gems and jewellery, for which the import content was very high, these proportions, albeit lower, more than doubled and registered increases that were as large.[25] In view of the fact that, apart from gems and jewellery, there was no noteworthy change in the product composition of Indian exports, it would be reasonable to infer that the rising trend in import-intensity was largely attributable to import liberalization. Yet, as I have shown elsewhere, it appears to have done little for export performance.[26] We find that until 1977–8, when the import content of exports though rising was low, the growth in exports was unprecedented. In sharp contrast, during the following decade, when the import intensity of export production rose sharply to much higher levels (Table 11.2), the growth in export was sluggish (Table 11.3). While the slowdown in exports was attributable to a range of domestic and external

[25]It must be recognized that this measure of import-intensity probably underestimtes not only the level of, but also the increase in, the import content, because it does not include imports (a) under Open General Licence by exporters in the domestic tariff area, or (b) by exporters in the export processing zones and 100 per cent export-oriented units, both of which are likely to have increased significantly since the late 1970s.

[26]Nayyar (1988).

Table 11.3: Growth in National Income, Investment, and Foreign Trade

| | | | (per cent per annum) | |
Period	GDP at Constant Market Prices	Gross Domestic Capital Formation at Constant Prices	Export Volume Index	Import Volume Index
1950–1 to 1960–1	3.9	7.6	1.5	5.0
1960–1 to 1970–1	3.7	5.0	3.6	1.0
1970–1 to 1977–8	3.4	4.8	7.8	2.9
1977–8 to 1986–7	4.5	3.7	2.4	8.4

Notes: (a) The average annual rates of growth have been calculated by fitting a semi-log linear regression equation $\log X = a + bt$, and estimating the values of b. (b) The rates of growth of GDP and gross domestic capital formation at constant prices are based on data at 1970–1 prices for the periods from 1950–1 to 1977–8, and on data at 1980–1 prices for the period 1977–8 to 1986–7. (c) The base years for the volume index numbers of exports and imports are 1953 for the period 1950–1 to 1960–1, 1958 for the period 1960–1 to 1970–1, 1968–9 for the period 1970–1 to 1977–8, and 1978–9 for the period 1977–8 to 1986–7; the series on growth rates does not extend beyond 1986–7 as that is the latest year for which data on volume index numbers of exports and imports are available.

Sources: (a) For GDP and gross domestic capital formation: CSO *National Accounts Statistics*. (b) For index numbers of exports and imports: DGCIS, Calcutta.

factors, one possible explanation for the increase in import intensity, at a macro-level, may be that progressive import liberalization simply reduced the average market premium on import replenishment licences, so that an equivalent implicit subsidy would have required a higher import content. It goes without saying that a reasonable access to imports of inputs, capital goods, and technology is essential to ensure competitiveness in the world market. Beyond such a point, however, experience shows that import liberalization is neither necessary nor sufficient for an improved export performance.

Similarly, import liberalization is neither necessary nor sufficient for stimulating competition and efficiency in the domestic economy. The experience of the Republic of Korea illustrates that it is not necessary, while the experience of Mexico demonstrates that it cannot be sufficient. The conclusion is not likely to be any different in the Indian context. The object of economic planning and policy formulation in India, at this juncture, should be to reduce the degree of monopoly and increase the degree of competition *between* firms *within* the economy, by creating an environment where producers would not only have an incentive but would also be under pressure to bring about a reduction in costs. Trade liberalization is no magic recipe for this purpose. Indeed, India cannot afford to provide such competition through the foreign trade sector for two reasons. First, at macro-level, the magnitude of foreign exchange resources required to provide effective competition through imports would be much too large to reconcile with a manageable balance of payments situation: this is borne out by the massive trade deficits and the mounting external debt in recent years. Second, structures of production, technologies in use, and levels of quality consciousness that have evolved over the decades cannot be changed at a stroke, so that unplanned or indiscriminate import liberalization may simply threaten the survival of domestic industries.

In my judgement, the import window, can, at best, be used as a sword of Damocles in a calibrated manner to squeeze monopoly profits or place an outside limit on the domestic resource cost of import competing activities. Even in this limited role, where protection in selected sectors has to be reduced over time, the optimum degree of openness of the economy is a complex question, whether we consider the sectoral mix or the temporal sequence. The transition must be planned in a phased manner and this would need a change in the nature of, rather than a reduction in the degree of, State intervention; planning at the macro-level would increase the impact of policies at the micro-level. The pursuit of such a transition in an *ad hoc* or piecemeal manner relying on market forces alone, as an article of faith, may not only lead to a precarious balance of payments situation or a rising external debt but may also set off a macroeconomic causation that has an adverse long-term impact on industrialization.

IMPLICATIONS FOR THE FOREIGN TRADE SECTOR

The preceding discussion examined the possible impact of the foreign trade sector on the economy as a whole and on the process of industrialization. It is just as important to consider the other side of the coin. Indeed, in the Indian context, it is likely that developments in the national economy exercised a more significant influence on the external sector, whether we consider exports, imports, or the balance of payments.

In my view, India's export performance has always been greatly influenced by domestic economic factors and the performance of the economy. To avoid repetition, I shall not enter into a discussion here.[27] Suffice it to say that the

---

[27]For a detailed discussion, see Nayyar (1988) and also Nayyar (1976).

pressure of domestic demand and the relative profitability of the home market on the demand side, just as much as the output of exportables and its cost of production on the supply side, have been basic determinants of export performance.

In the sphere of imports, the canalized bulk imports, particularly foodgrains, edible oils, fertilizers, crude oil, and petroleum products, have been much influenced by the domestic production of these importables on the supply side, while imports of capital goods, manufactured intermediates, or raw materials have been determined by the level of investment in the economy on the demand side.

The link between investment and imports, reflected in the level and the growth, is confirmed by available evidence. Table 11.3 sets out the average annual rates of growth, in real terms for GDP, gross domestic capital formation, exports, and imports. For this purpose, the period under review is divided into four segments: 1950–1 to 1960–1, 1960–1 to 1970–1, 1970–1 to 1977–8, and 1977–8 to 1986–7; the period of 17 years between 1970–1 and 1986–7 is divided into two sub-periods and 1977–8 is used as the mid-point not so much for reasons of symmetry but more because it constitutes a turning point in the trends for exports, imports, and investment.[28] A comparison with the data in Table 11.1 reveals that imports increased rapidly during the 1950s when the investment–GDP ratio and gross domestic capital formation both rose rapidly and, once again, during the late 1970s and the first half of the 1980s when the investment–GDP ratio climbed although gross domestic capital formation did not register a rapid growth.

At a macro-level, throughout the period under review, the excess of imports over exports corresponded with the excess of investment over savings in the economy. During the period from the mid-1950s until the late 1960s the balance of trade deficit was in the range of 2.5 per cent of GDP (Table 11.1 and Figure 11.1); over this period, the difference between gross domestic capital formation and domestic savings was in the same range.[29] There was a similar,

[28]Figure 11.1 confirms that 1977–8 was the turning point for trends in exports and imports during the period 1970–1 to 1986–7. Other evidence on the volume, the SDR value or the dollar value of exports and imports provides similar confirmation. Similarly, we find that 1977–8 marks a turning point for trends in investment, *inter alia* because public investment revived; the share of gross domestic capital formation in GDP which had been in the range of 20 per cent for several years until 1977–8 jumped to more than 24 per cent in 1978–9 and stabilized in that range for the rest of the period.

[29]The balance of trade deficit, as a proportion of GDP, was 2.4 per cent during 1956–7 to 1960–1, 2.5 per cent during 1961–2 to 1965–6 and 1.6 per cent during 1966–70 to 1970–1; in these periods, gross domestic capital formation exceeded gross domestic savings by 3 per cent, 3.4 per cent, and 1.8 per cent respectively.

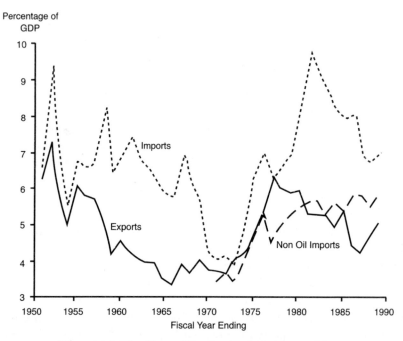

Figure 11.1: The Share of Foreign Trade in National Income

Source: DGCIS and CSO.

but not as close a, correspondence during the 1980s when the trade deficit was somewhat higher as a proportion of GDP, possibly because merchandise trade transactions did not dominate the current account as much as in the earlier phase.

The macroeconomic implications and consequences of developments or policies in the economy as a whole, for the external sector, are more obvious and striking if we consider the period from the late 1970s to the late 1980s. During this period, there was a change in the perception of planners not simply about the foreign trade sector but also about the strategy of industrialization and the macro-management of the economy. The regime of trade policies and industrial polices had a direct impact on the foreign trade sector, while the regime of fiscal policies had an indirect impact on the external sector.

The liberalization of the trade regime beginning in the late 1970s and the new regime of industrial polices introduced in the early 1980s, taken

Table 11.4: Import Intensity of Domestic Production:
Selected Indicators

(*in percentages*)

Year	Non-oil Imports as a Proportion of GDP at Market Prices	Imports of Capital Goods as a Proportion of Gross Domestic Fixed Capital Formation	Manufactured Imports (excluding Fertilizers) as a Proportion of Gross Value-added in Manufacturing	Imports of Parts and Accessories for Selected Products as a Proportion of Total Imports of Machinery and Transport Equipment
1972–3	4.0	6.8	17.1	12.9
1977–8	4.4	6.8	20.1	11.8
1980–1	5.7	7.6	26.2	9.8
1984–5	6.2	7.0	25.1	17.9
1987–8	6.5	9.3	29.5	21.9

Notes: (a) Imports of capital goods are constituted mostly by machinery and transport equipment (SITC 7) but also include metal manufactures; (b) Manufactured imports are defined as SITC categories 5 + 6 + 7 + 8, from which imports of fertilizers are excluded; (c) The data on gross value-added in manufacturing relate to the registered and unregistered sectors taken together; (d) Imports of parts and accessories for selected products in machinery and transport equipment (SITC 7) include the following eleven SITC categories 744.9: (Parts of lifting, handling, loading, and unloading equipment); 759: (parts and accessories for office machines and automatic data processing equipment); 764.9: (parts and accessories for television, radio, phonographs, sound recorders/reproducers, and telecommunication equipment); 772.2: (printed circuits and parts thereof); 776: (semi-conductor devices, electronic micro-circuits, and parts thereof); 778.19: (parts of electric accumulators); 778.29: (parts of electric filament lamps); 778.3: (electrical equipment for internal combustion engines and vehicles and parts thereof); 778.89: (electrical parts of machinery and apparatus n.e.s); 784: (parts and accessories of motor vehicles); 785.39: (parts and accessories for motor-cycles and motor scooters).

Sources: (a) For data on total imports, RBI Bombay; for data on imports of crude oil and petroleum products, DGCIS, Calcutta. (b) For data on imports of capital goods and on manufactured imports, DGCIS, Calcutta. (c) For data on GDP at market prices and on gross value-added in manufacturing, CSO *National Accounts Statistics*. (d) For data on imports of parts and accessories as also total imports of machinery and transport equipment, DGCIS, Calcutta.

together, increased the import intensity of domestic production, attributable only in part to the semi-knocked-down syndrome of industrialization which is most apparent in the automotive sector or in consumer electronics. The evidence on the rise in the import intensity of domestic production is incomplete but convincing and is presented in Table 11.4. First, there was a significant increase in non-oil imports as a proportion of GDP, which rose from 4.4 per cent in 1977–8 to 6.5 per cent in 1987–8. Second, imports of capital goods as a proportion of gross domestic fixed capital formation rose from 6.8 per cent in 1977–8 to 9.3 per cent in 1987–8. Third, the share of manufactured imports (excluding fertilizers that are meant exclusively for use in the agricultural sector) in gross value-added in manufacturing rose from 20.1 per cent in 1977–8 to 29.5 per cent in 1987–8. Fourth, imports of components or parts and accessories for selected products (mostly in the sphere of consumer electronics, electrical appliances, and the automotive sector) as a proportion of total imports of machinery and transport equipment rose from 9.8 per cent in 1980–1 to 21.9 per cent in 1987–8, although this proportion had declined in the 1970s. But that is not all. It is striking that the income elasticity of import demand for the economy as a whole registered a substantial increase beginning in the late 1970s. Table 11.3 shows that between 1977–8 and 1986–7, the volume of imports increased at a rate of 8.4 per cent per annum, whereas GDP registered a growth of 4.5 per cent per annum and investment rose at a rate of only 3.7 per cent per annum. This asymmetry provides a sharp contrast with the preceding period of almost three decades.

The implications for the foreign sector and the consequences for the external sector are not far to seek. The end of the 1970s and the beginning of the 1980s saw a sharp increase in the balance of trade deficit as a proportion of GDP, which is evident from both Figure 11.1 and Table 11.5. It is obvious that a significant part of the hump in the trade deficit was then attributable to higher oil prices and to the import bill on account of crude oil and petroleum products. But the first half of the 1980s witnessed impressive import substitution in the petroleum sector mostly because of the oil find at Bombay High, while the second half of the 1980s experienced a considerable softening of oil prices in the world market, so that the dollar value of petroleum imports declined steadily until the late 1980s.[30] Yet, as Table 11.5 shows, the balance

[30]The share of domestic production in the total supplies of crude oil increased from less than two-fifths (39.3 per cent) in 1980–1 to more than two-thirds (67.9 per cent) in 1984–5, while the average unit value for imports of crude oil and petroleum products declined from Rs 2746 (US $231) per tonne in 1984–5 to Rs 1823 (US $126) per tonne in 1988–9; these proportions and unit values have been calculated from data published by the Ministry of Finance in *Economic Survey*, various issues.

Table 11.5: External and Internal Balance in India

(as a percentage of GDP at market prices)

Year	Merchandise Trade Deficit (Surplus)	Deficit (Surplus) on Trade in Goods and Services	Current Account Deficit (Surplus)	Fiscal Deficit of Central Government	Fiscal Deficit of Central and State Governments	Private Savings minus Private Investment
1977–8	0.1	(0.6)	(1.9)	4.1	5.2	5.0
1978–9	1.9	1.2	(0.2)	5.3	6.1	6.2
1979–80	3.1	2.3	0.7	5.9	6.9	5.0
1980–1	4.7	3.8	1.3	7.0	8.6	5.7
1981–2	4.1	3.5	1.6	5.9	7.3	5.2
1982–3	3.5	2.9	1.4	6.5	7.9	5.6
1983–4	3.0	2.4	1.2	7.0	8.7	5.6
1984–5	3.1	2.5	1.3	8.3	10.4	6.9
1985–6	3.9	3.3	2.4	9.2	10.0	6.1
1986–7	3.2	2.8	2.0	9.4	10.9	6.6
1987–8	2.8	2.6	1.9	8.5	10.0	6.6

Notes: (a) The deficit or surplus on trade in goods and services is calculated by excluding investment income flows and transfer payments from transactions in the current account; (b) The table does not use the narrow definition of the budget deficit adopted by the government in India. The fiscal deficit is defined as the difference between the total revenue and the total expenditure of the government, so that it includes domestic borrowing and external assistance in addition to borrowing from the Reserve Bank of India; this has been estimated by adding capital expenditure to the revenue deficit; (c) Private savings and private investment refer to the gross domestic saving and gross domestic capital formation in the private sector at current prices. The figures for 1986–7 and 1987–8 are not strictly comparable with those for the earlier period, 1977–8 to 1985–6, as the former are obtained from the recently introduced new series of *National Accounts Statistics*.

Sources: (a) For data on the merchandise trade deficit or surplus, the balance of trade on goods and services, and the current account deficit or surplus, Reserve Bank of India, *Report on Currency and Finance*, annual issues; (b) For data on the fiscal deficit of the central and state governments, Ministry of Finance *Indian Economic Statistics: Public Finance*, 1984, 1988, and 1989; (c) For data on private savings, private investment and GDP, CSO, *National Accounts Statistics*.

of trade deficit persisted at a level of more than 3 per cent of GDP. Clearly, oil was not the only culprit. As noted above, non-oil imports as a proportion of GDP also registered a significant increase. In this context, it is worth noting that total exports which were at least as much as, and often greater than,

Table 11.6: Trade Gap, Savings Gap, and External Debt

(as a percentage of GDP at market prices)

Year	Exports	Imports (Non-oil)	Gross Domestic Saving	Gross Domestic Capital Formation	External Debt
1977–8	6.0	6.2 (4.4)	22.5	20.9	12.5
1978–9	5.7	7.6 (5.9)	24.7	24.8	12.7
1979–80	5.8	8.9 (5.9)	23.0	23.5	13.3
1980–1	5.2	9.8 (5.7)	23.0	24.7	15.3
1981–2	5.3	9.4 (5.9)	22.7	24.4	15.4
1982–3	5.5	9.0 (5.6)	22.6	24.2	16.8
1983–4	5.2	8.3 (5.8)	22.2	23.5	17.2
1984–5	5.6	8.7 (6.2)	22.9	24.4	18.4
1985–6	4.8	8.7 (6.6)	22.8	24.6	18.6
1986–7	4.5	7.7 (6.8)	21.6	24.3	19.2
1987–8	4.9	7.7 (6.5)	19.6	22.9	19.5
1988–9	5.2	8.8 (7.7)	21.0	24.4	21.2

Notes: (a) The above figures on exports, imports, and non-oil imports as a percentage of GDP are not the same as those in Table 11.1 or Figure 11.1 because of the difference between RBI and DGCIS statistics on foreign trade; the former are based on receipts or payments in foreign exchange reported to the central bank whereas the latter are based on shipments of exports or imports reported through daily trade returns at ports; (b) For the period 1977–8 to 1985–6, data on gross domestic saving, gross domestic capital formation, and GDP at current prices are obtained from the 1970–1 series of *National Accounts Statistics*. The figures for the year 1986–7, 1987–8, and 1988–9 are not strictly comparable with those for the earlier period as these are obtained from the recently introduced new series of *National Accounts Statistics*; (c) External debt is defined as the sum of: (1) external assistance on government and non-government account; (2) external commercial borrowing including supplier's credit; (3) borrowing from the IMF, and (4) repatriable deposits of non-resident Indians in commercial banks. The figures in the table are based on the rupee value of total external debt outstanding at the end of each fiscal year espressed as a percentage of GDP at current market prices for that fiscal year.

Sources: (a) For data on total exports and total imports, Reserve Bank of India, *Report on Currency and Finance*, for data on imports of crude oil and petroleum products, DGCIS Calcutta; (b) For data on gross domestic saving, gross domestic capital formation, and GDP at market prices, CSO, *National Accounts Statistics*; (c) For data on external debt, Government of India (1989); for the years 1977–8, 1978–9, and 1979–80, external debt has been estimated from data published by the Ministry of Finance in *External Assistance* and *Economic Survey*, and by the Reserve Bank of India in *Annual Reports*.

non-oil imports throughout the 1970s (Figure 11.1), were significantly less than non-oil imports during the 1980s (Table 11.6). To begin with, in the early 1980s, the current account deficit was much smaller than the balance of trade deficit as a proportion of GDP. However, during the mid-1980s, as the growth in remittances began to taper off and the burden of debt servicing mounted, the current account deficit remained in the range of two per cent of GDP and corresponded more closely with the balance of trade deficit.[31] It is necessary to stress that as the ratio of external debt to GDP rises over time, maintaining the current account deficit–GDP ratio at a constant level would require a progressive reduction in the trade deficit–GDP ratio to compensate for the increasing interest payments–GDP ratio.[32] Therefore, if the current account deficit is to be kept within manageable proportions, management of the balance of trade deficit would be critical.

At a macro-level, the emerging fiscal regime also has serious implications for the external sector, insofar as it has chosen soft options in terms of domestic resource mobilization. There has been an explicit reduction in direct taxes. At the same time, indirect taxes which already contribute the bulk of tax revenues, cannot be raised much further as that would fuel inflation, escalate costs of production across-the-board, and, of course, be regressive in incidence. Consequently, the government has relied increasingly on borrowing at home to meet its budget deficit and borrowing abroad to finance it current account deficit.

At the risk of a slight digression, it is worth pointing out that the budget deficit as reported by the government—borrowing from the Reserve Bank of India—is a deceptive number as it is only a partial measure of the fiscal imbalance. In most countries of the world, the budget deficit is defined as the difference between the total revenue and the total expenditure of the government, so that it includes domestic borrowing and external borrowing in addition to borrowing from the central bank.

It is important to recognize that the internal imbalance is closely related to the external imbalance. The budget deficit in its wider sense, say the fiscal deficit, reflects the difference between the income and the expenditure of the government, while the trade deficit, or the current account deficit, reflects

[31] For an analysis of the trend in remittances, as also other components of the current account, see Nayyar (1994).

[32] Preliminary statistics on the balance of payments, published by the Reserve Bank of India, suggest that the balance of trade deficit rose, once again, to 3.6 per cent of GDP in 1988–9 as a result of which the current account deficit reached a peak level of 2.7 per cent of GDP. These developments simply highlight the importance of managing the balance of trade situation.

the difference between the income and the expenditure of the economy as a whole.[33] The macroeconomics of the relationship between internal and external imbalance emerges clearly from a manipulation of the simple national income accounting identity. $Y = C + I + G + X - M$ can be rewritten as $I-S = M - X$ given that $Y - (C + G) = S$. In turn. $I-S$ can be rewritten as $(Ip-Sp) + (Eg - Yg)$, where Ip and Sp denote investment and saving in the private sector while Eg and Yg denote expenditure income of the government.[34] Therefore:

$$(M - X) = (Ip - Sp) + (Eg - Yg).$$

In other words, *ex post*, the current account deficit is the sum of the savings gap in the private sector and the fiscal deficit of the government.[35]

This macroeconomic relationship is borne out by the evidence on the Indian experience presented in Table 11.5. For a given excess of private savings over private investment, which was relatively stable in the range 5 to 6 per cent of GDP over the period from 1977–8 to 1987–8, there is a close correspondence between movements in the fiscal deficit (of the central and state governments taken together) and the current account deficit as a proportion of national income. We find that the transformation of a current account surplus in 1977–8 into a persistent current account deficit in the subsequent decade, and the enlargement of the merchandise trade deficit or the deficit on trade in goods and services starting from a situation of near-equilibrium, corresponds quite closely to the increase in the size of the fiscal deficit, as a proportion of GDP.

The internal imbalance in the fiscal situation and the external imbalance in the payments situation have persisted for more than a decade. These imbalances have been financed by a borrowing spree at home and abroad, without any serious attempt to introduce correctives. Indeed, it would seem that, in recent years, the strategy of macroeconomic management in India

---

[33]In the national income accounting identity, the term X–M can be equated with the trade deficit where Y represents the GDP and the current account deficit where Y represents the GNP.

[34]This is easily derived as follows. Let Ig, Sg, and Cg denote investment, saving, and consumption respectively in the government sector. Then:

$$
\begin{aligned}
(I-S) &= (Ip + Ig) - (Sp + Sg) = (Ip - Sp) + (Ig - Sg) \\
&= (Ip - Sp) + [I - (Yg - Cg)] \\
&= (Ip - Sp) + [(Ig + Cg) - Yg].
\end{aligned}
$$

[35]This follows, *ex post*, from the national income accounting identity. The *ex ante* relationship between the foreign exchange gap, the saving gap, and the fiscal gap is explored, to identify the dominant constraint for the purpose of policy formulation, in the recent literature on three-gap models. See, for exmaple, Bacha (1984, 1989); see also, Taylor (1988).

has sought to use the current account deficit as a means of maintaining an excess of investment over savings for the economy in general and an excess of expenditure over income for the government in particular. A continuous increase in external debt has been a natural consequence.

The evidence in Table 11.6 provides confirmation. During the period from 1978–9 to 1988–9, the investment–GDP ratio was stable in the range of 24 per cent, while the domestic savings–GDP ratio, always somewhat lower, declined significantly in the late 1980s, so that the savings gap registered an increase. Over the same period, the trade gap also increased. In 1977–8, the export–GDP ratio and the import–GDP ratio were almost equal at around 6 per cent. In the decade that followed, however, the export–GDP was perceptibly lower, whereas the import–GDP ratio jumped to a peak level of 9.8 per cent in 1980–1, declined a little thereafter, and remained in the range of 8 per cent in subsequent years. It is hardly surprising that the external debt–GDP ratio rose from 12.5 per cent in 1977–8 to 21.2 per cent in 1988–9.[36]

In an ideal world, it should have been possible for the government to raise the level of investment, given the level of savings, by an amount equal to the net inflow of external resources. In the 1980s, however, the fiscal regime shied away from additional domestic resource mobilization and the budget deficits mounted. Hence, it is plausible to argue that external resources, whether concessional aid flows, repatriable deposits of non-resident Indians, or commercial borrowing in international capital markets, provided a soft option. It would appear that such external resources have been used, at least in part, as a substitute for domestic resources in investment and possibly even in consumption. Apart from the cumulative causation which leads to a vicious circle of rising indebtedness, the macroeconomic consequences of this process are bound to be serious and adverse.

It is very likely that the balance of payments will turn to be the Achilles heel for the package of new economic policies and the management of the economy. Borrowing abroad, whether in international capital markets or from non-resident Indians, will only postpone the day of reckoning and lead to an unmanageable external debt. The prospective scenario of a macroeconomic squeeze, often advocated as part of a typical IMF package of policies, would not only impose excessive social costs in terms of output, income, and employment, but would also be myopic in its search for external

[36]Available estimates suggest that the external debt–GDP ratio rose further to 23.3 per cent in 1989–90. It is reported hat at the end of March 1990 India's external debt was approximately Rs 100,000 crores, while GDP (at current prices) for 1989–90 is estimated to grow by 10 per cent over the preliminary figure of Rs 391,169 crores in 1988–9.

balance at the cost of economic growth. The capacity of the economy to manage the situation, without imposing such social and economic costs, would depend upon its ability to curb the increase in the import–GDP ratio and to sustain a high investment–GDP ratio combined with a high export–GDP ratio by raising domestic savings.

CONCLUDING OBSERVATIONS

This essay would not be complete unless we situated the discussion in its wider context of economic planning and industrialization strategy. There are some issues which are recognized as fundamental or strategic in planning for industrialization: the relationship between agriculture and industry, the relative importance of the home market, the nature or the degree of State intervention, and the acquisition or development of technology. The first of these issues has received considerable attention in the literature on the subject. The other here have been recognized and discussed but not so much in relation to the foreign trade sector. Consider these issues in turn.

The first question is about the relative importance of the home market and of external markets in the process of industrialization. The answer must obviously depend, among other things, on the size of the country. In large countries such as India, where the domestic market is overwhelmingly important, sustained industrialization can only be based on the growth of the internal market. On the other hand, in small countries the possibilities of industrialization may be limited by the size of the domestic market. In the ultimate analysis, large economies must endeavour to internalize external markets. Therefore, industrialization may stress manufacturing for the domestic market through import substitution or manufacturing for export to external markets. The emphasis on, as also the quantitative or the qualitative significance of, the foreign trade sector, would depend on the size of the economy and the stage of its development. Unfortunately, this basic issue has often been reduced to a debate about trade policies for industrialization or the choice between import substitution and export promotion. It is essential to get out of this false dilemma and examine the home market question in is wider context.[37] In terms of an appropriate strategy for industrialization, striking a balance between import substitution and export promotion is the equivalent of 'walking on two legs'. The timing and the pace of transition in shifting emphasis from one to the other clearly matters. However, success or failure depends not so much on the choice between inward-looking or

---

[37]Mitra (1977), Nayyar (1978), Chakravarty (1979), and Bagchi (1981).

outward-looking polices as it does on the setting in which these are introduced. An environment that produces a spectacular export performance is also conducive to efficient import substitution and rapid economic growth. It is, therefore, necessary to analyse the factors underlying success or failure in export promotion, import substitution, or economic growth, not in terms of the policy regime but with reference to the macroeconomic context and the conjuncture of internal as also external economic factors which are responsible for the outcome.

The second issue is about the nature and the degree of State intervention in the process of industrialization. Our experience in the second half of the twentieth century suggests that the guiding and supportive role of the State has been at the foundations of successful development among the late industrializers, not only in the centrally planned economies of Eastern Europe but also in the market economies of East Asia. Even among the latter, the visible hand of the State is much more in evidence, than the invisible hand of the market, particularly at the macro-level.[38] In term of State intervention, there is not much to distinguish between import substitution and export promotion: in the former, the State protects domestic capitalists from foreign competition in the home market, whereas in the latter it protects domestic capitalists from foreign competition in the world market. It is the nature of State intervention that matters. The experience of India illustrates that it is possible for State intervention to create an oligopolistic situation in a competitive environment, just as the experience of the Republic of Korea illustrates that it is possible for State intervention to create a competitive situation in an oligopolisitc environment. Therefore, the nature and the degree of State intervention in the foreign trade sector, particularly at the macro-level, deserves serious attention in the context of planning for industrialization.

The third issue in the wider context is technology, which is strategic in the process of industrialization. The direction and the speed of technological development influences the pace of growth, the nature of structural change, and the efficiency of production in the industrial sector as also the foreign trade sector. An economy that industrializes should be able to move from importation to absorption and adaptation of technology through to the stage of innovation, at least in some sectors, on the path to sustained industrialization. In the pursuit of this objective, imports of technology and indigenous technological development need to be combined in a judicious mix. The actual experience in India suggests that there are a number of sectors

[38]See Lee (1981) and Bagchi (1987).

where the level of technological development is not adequate. It is possible to cite many examples of situations where technologies were imported for particular sectors at a point of time, and the absorption of such technologies has been followed by stagnation rather than adaptation, diffusion, and innovation. At the same time, in many cases, indigenous development of technology has not led to widespread diffusion let alone technological upgrading. The underlying reasons are complex and any discussion of these would require elaborate explanation. Suffice it to say that the existing market structure and policy framework have not combined to provide an environment which would accelerate the absorption of imported technology and foster the development of indigenous technology, or create a milieu which would be conducive to diffusion and innovation. It needs to be stressed that, at a macro-level, the role of the government is crucial in planning for technological development across sectors and over time. This means planning for the acquisition of technology where it is to be imported, setting aside resources for technology where it is to be produced at home, or even deciding to opt out of a technology where it is not needed. For this purpose, it is necessary to formulate a policy regime for the import of technology, allocate resources for R&D, and evolve state procurement policies. Such a guiding and supportive role of the State has been a necessary condition for technological development among the latecomers to industrialization.

The moral of the story outlined in the preceding pages is not that all is well. Much needs to be done in the foreign trade sector in the realm of planning for industrialization in India. The macroeconomic interconnections are crucial. But the solutions to the problems of the national economy cannot be found through the foreign trade sector or simple recipes associated with it. In my judgement, however, the problems of the foreign trade sector can be resolved to a considerable extent through an improved performance and a better management of the economy at home. In other words, the tail cannot wag the dog.

REFERENCES

Bacha, Edmar, L. (1984), 'Growth with Limited Supplies of Foreign Exchange: A Re-appraisal of the Two-Gap Model', in M. Syrquin, L. Taylor, and L. Westphal (eds), *Economic Structure and Performance: Essays in Honour of Hollis Chenery*, Oxford University Press, New York.

―――― (1989), 'A Three-Gap Model of Foreign Transfers and the GDP Growth Rate in Developing Countries', Discussion Paper No. 221, Department of Economics, Catholic University, Rio de Janeiro, April.

Bagchi, Amiya K. (1981), 'Reinforcing and Offsetting Constraints in Indian Industry', in A.K. Bagchi and Nirmala Banerjee (eds), *Change and Choice in Indian Industry*, Centre for Studies in Social Sciences, Calcutta.

_____ (1987), *Public Intervention and Industrial Restructuring in China, India and Republic of Korea*, ILO-ARTEP, New Delhi.

Bhagwati, Jagdish and T.N. Srinivasan (1976), *Foreign Trade Regimes and Economic Development: India*, National Bureau of Economic Research, New York.

Bhagwati, Jagdish and Padma Desai (1970), *India: Planning for Industrialization*, Oxford University Press, Oxford.

Chakravarty, Sukhamoy (1979), 'On the Question of the Home Market and Prospects for Indian Growth', *Economic and Political Weekly*, Special Number, August.

Government of India (1984), *Report of the Committee on Trade Policies*, Ministry of Commerce, Government of India, New Delhi.

_____ (1989), *The Current Economic Situation and Priority Areas for Action*, report of the Economic Advisory Council, New Delhi, December.

Lee, Eddy (ed.) (1981), *Export Led Industrialisation and Development*, ILO, Asian Employment Programme, Bangkok.

Mitra, Ashok (1977), *Terms of Trade and Class Relations*, Frank Cass, London.

Nayyar, Deepak (1976), *India's Exports and Export Policies*, Cambridge University Press, Cambridge.

_____ (1978), 'Industrial Development in India: Some Reflections on Growth and Stagnation', *Economic and Political Weekly*, Special Number, August.

_____ (1986), 'India's Balance of Payments', in D.K. Bose (ed.), *Review of the Indian Planning Process*, Indian Statistical Institute, Calcutta.

_____ (1988), 'India's Export Performance: 1970–85: Underlying Factors and Constraints', in Robert E.B. Lucas and Gustav F. Papanek (eds), *The Indian Economy: Recent Development and Future Prospects*, Westview Press, Colorado.

_____ (1994), *Migration, Remittances and Capital Flows: The Indian Experience*, Oxford University Press, Oxford.

Planning Commission (1951), *First Five Year Plan*, New Delhi.

_____ (1956), *Second Five Year Plan*, New Delhi.

_____ (1961), *Third Five Year Plan*, New Delhi.

_____ (1969), *Fourth Five Year Plan*, New Delhi.

_____ (1976), *Fifth Five Year Plan*, New Delhi.

_____ (1981), *Sixth Five Year Plan*, New Delhi.

_____ (1985), *Seventh Five Year Plan*, New Delhi.

Singh, Manmohan (1964), *India's Export Trends*, Oxford University Press, Oxford.

Taylor, Lance (1988), *Varieties of Stabilization Experience*, Oxford University Press, Oxford.

Wolf, Martin (1982), *India's Exports*, Oxford University Press, New York.

PART 4
LIBERALIZATION

Chapter 12

MACROECONOMIC REFORMS IN INDIA

Short-term Effects and Long-run Implications

INTRODUCTION

The external debt crisis, which surfaced in early 1991, brought India close to default in meeting its international obligations. The balance of payments situation was almost unmanageable. The fear of an acceleration in the rate of inflation loomed large. The underlying fiscal crisis was acute. It is important to recognize that the deep macroeconomic disequilibrium which plunged the economy into a crisis situation was not attributable to any endogenous shock, such as a bad monsoon, or any exogenous shock, such as a dramatic increase in world oil prices. It was the outcome of mounting macroeconomic imbalances that accumulated, and negligent macroeconomic policies that persisted, through the 1980s.[1] In response to the macroeconomic crisis, the government set in motion a process of stabilization combined with fiscal adjustment and structural reform. It needs to be said that this was nothing new. It replicated broadly the response of several developing countries in Latin America and sub-Saharan Africa, to the debt crisis in the 1980s, which was also guided by IMF programmes of stabilization and World Bank programmes of structural adjustment. The short-term compulsions were to manage the balance of payments situation and to restrain inflation. The medium-term imperative was to find a sustainable solution to the fiscal crisis, without imposing a disproportionate burden on the poor. The long-term need was to return the economy to a path of sustained growth, in part through an increase in efficiency and productivity.

The process of stabilization, adjustment, and reform was initiated in mid-1991. The period since then, less than a decade, is long enough to attempt an assessment. The object of this essay is to analyse the short-term effects,

---

[1] For a discussion on the macroeconomic origins of the fiscal crisis and the debt crisis, see Nayyar (1996) and Bhaduri and Nayyar (1996). See also Joshi and Little (1994).

the medium-term consequences, and the long-term implications of macroeconomic reforms in India. In doing so, it seeks to focus on stabilization and adjustment at a macro-level. It does not, however, attempt to evaluate structural reforms, for such an evaluation would perhaps require another essay.[2] The structure of the discussion is as follows. The first section sets out the evidence on stabilization to discuss the adjustment in the balance of payments. The second section examines the stabilization experience in terms of its record in restraining inflation. The third section analyses the nature and the quality of fiscal adjustment, to explore whether it provides a sustainable solution to the problem and what it means for the distribution of the burden of adjustment. The fourth section considers the economic impact of stabilization and adjustment at a macro-level on employment and poverty. The fifth section reflects upon some implications of the macroeconomic adjustment in India for economic growth in the long-run. The sixth section draws together the conclusions that emerge.

BALANCE OF PAYMENTS

It would seem that, in the wake of the external debt crisis, the balance of payments situation was transformed during the 1990s. The capital flight from repatriable deposits held by non-resident Indians, which was threateningly large during 1991–2, came to a stop. The exposure in terms of short-term debt, which became increasingly difficult to roll-over and could have been called in by lenders for liquidation at any time, was substantially reduced. Most important, the level of foreign exchange reserves climbed from a meagre $2.2 billion in end-March 1991, to $15.1 billion in end-March 1994, and $22.4 billion in end-March 1997. The stoppage of capital flight, the reduction in short-term debt, and the accumulation of foreign exchange reserves should be rated as a success, in terms of stabilization, provided the underlying factors are sustainable. The available evidence on the nature of balance of payments adjustment, presented in Table 12.1, suggests that, for the purpose of analysis, it is useful to distinguish between two phases in this period: 1991–2 to 1993–4 and 1994–5 to 1996–7.

The adjustment in the balance of payments, during the first phase from 1991–2 to 1993–4, was based on a substantial reduction in the balance of trade deficit not only in terms of dollar values but also as a proportion of GDP. Much of this, however, was attributable to import contraction rather than

---

[2]For an evaluation of structural reforms in India, see Nayyar (1996). See also, Bhaduri and Nayyar (1996). For a somewhat different perspective, see Joshi and Little (1996).

Table 12.1: Balance of Payments Adjustment, 1989–90 to 1996–7

(in US $ million)

	1989–90	1990–1	1991–2	1992–3	1993–4	1994–5	1995–6	1996–7
Foreign Exchange Reserves end-of-year	3368	2236	5631	6434	15,068	20,809	17,044	22,367
Exports	16,955	18,477	18,266	18,869	22,683	26,855	32,311	34,133
Imports	24,411	27,915	21,064	24,316	26,739	35,904	43,670	48,948
of which:								
Petroleum	(3768)	(6028)	(5364)	(6100)	(5753)	(5928)	(7526)	(10036)
Balance of Trade Deficit	7456	9438	2798	5447	4056	9049	11,359	14,815
Remittances	2297	2083	3798	3864	5287	8112	8539	12,435
Current Account Deficit	7269	8424	2135	3603	1158	3369	5899	4494
IMF net	–877	1214	786	1288	187	–1143	–1715	–975
Net Capital Inflows	6036	6097	4922	4057	7948	7623	8142	13,315
of which:								
External assistance (net)	1856	2210	3037	1859	1901	1526	883	1109
Commercial borrowing (net)	1777	2249	1456	–358	607	1030	1275	2848
Non-resident deposits (net)	2403	1536	290	2001	1205	172	1103	3350
Direct foreign investment		97	135	313	586	1314	2133	2696
Portfolio investment		5	4	242	3649	3581	2748	3312
External Debt (in US $ billion)	64.8	70.9	74.2	79.4	82.6	89.4	84.7	85.9
of which:								
Short-term	7.5	8.5	7.1	6.3	3.6	4.3	5.0	6.7
Medium and Long-term	57.3	62.4	67.8	73.1	79.0	85.1	79.7	79.2
(Memorandum item: Rupee debt)	(11.0)	(12.8)	(10.4)	(10.6)	(10.1)	(9.6)	(8.2)	(7.5)

(contd.)

Table 12.1 (contd.)

(as a percentge of GDP)

	1989–90	1990–1	1991–2	1992–3	1993–4	1994–5	1995–6	1996–7
Exports	6.2	6.2	7.3	7.8	8.8	8.8	9.7	9.5
Imports	8.9	9.4	8.3	10.2	10.4	11.7	13.1	13.6
(of which: petroleum)	(1.4)	(2.0)	(2.1)	(2.4)	(2.2)	(2.0)	(2.2)	(2.8)
Balance of Trade Deficit	2.7	3.2	1.0	2.4	1.6	2.9	3.4	4.1
Remittances	0.8	0.7	1.5	1.6	2.0	2.6	2.6	3.4
Current Account Deficit	2.7	3.2	0.8	2.2	0.4	1.1	1.8	1.2
Net Capital Inflows	2.2	2.0	2.0	1.8	3.1	2.5	2.5	2.4
External Debt	24.3	25.7	35.8	35.1	32.0	29.5	26.1	24.1
(Memorandum item: Rupee Debt)	(4.2)	(4.7)	(5.2)	(4.7)	(3.9)	(3.2)	(2.6)	(2.1)

Notes: (a) There is one exclusion from external debt in the table. The rouble debt (civilian and defence) to the erstwhile USSR, now denominated in rupees and repayable in exports to Rusia, is excluded. This is because it represents an accumulated debt from the past which has not changed in the period under review, but its US dollar equivalent, at current exchange rates, is set out in parentheses as a memorandum item. (b) The figures on exports, imports, balance of trade, remittances, current account deficit, net capital inflows, and external debt as a percentage of GDP have been calculated from the respective rupee values at current exchange rates and *National Accounts Statistics* on GDP at current market prices.

Source: Reserve Bank of India, *Annual Reports* and *Reports on Currency and Finance*. The data on petroleum imports are from the foreign trade statistics compiled by the Directorate General of Commercial Intelligence and Statistics, Calcutta.

export expansion. Even though the petroleum import bill did not register any significant decline, the dollar value of total imports throughout this phase remained lower than it was in 1990–1. This was juxtaposed with a surge in remittances. The total remittance inflows in this phase were as much as $12.9 billion. And, in 1993–4, remittances rose to $5.3 billion (2 per cent of GDP) as compared with $2.1 billion (0.7 per cent of GDP) in 1990–1. Consequently, the reduction in the current account deficit was greater than the reduction in the trade deficit.

The smaller current account deficits which reduced the financing need, combined with capital inflows, were responsible for the build-up of reserves. But financing was not available from the usual sources such as external assistance where net resource inflows continued to decline, or commercial borrowing where access to international capital markets was virtually closed. During this phase, from 1991–2 to 1993–4, there were three main sources of external finance.[3] The first set was constituted by borrowing from the IMF, structural adjustment loans from the World Bank or the Asian Development Bank, and special bilateral assistance from donor countries. Such exceptional financing provided $5.8 billion. The second set was made up of capital flows that originated in non-resident Indians, induced by amnesties (where no questions were asked about the sources of foreign exchange), and by special deposits (which offered more attractive terms than elsewhere or earlier). Taken together, these yielded $5.4 billion. The third set comprised private foreign capital flows which added up to $4.9 billion. Of this, direct investment was $1 billion, while portfolio investment was $3.9 billion; much of the latter came in 1993–4 alone.

It is clear that extraordinary capital flows in the form of borrowing from multilateral financial institutions or from non-residents were once-and-for-all in nature and could not provide a sustained access to external resources. What is more, much of this was in essence borrowing abroad to support the balance of payments, which led to a rapid accumulation of external debt. Consequently, between end-March 1991 and end-March 1994, the outstanding external debt (excluding short-term debt and rupee-debt) increased from $62 billion to $79 billion (and climbed further to $85 billion in end-March 1995). And, external debt rose from one-fourth of GDP at the end of 1990–91 to more than one-third of GDP throughout the first phase from 1991–2 to 1993–4.

[3]For a detailed discussion, as also for sources of evidence on the magnitudes of these capital inflows, see Nayyar (1996).

The adjustment in the balance of payments during the second phase from 1994–5 to 1996–7 was significantly different. There was a rapid growth in exports which slowed down towards the end of this phase. But the growth in imports was much faster. As a result, the balance of trade deficit registered a sharp increase to $9 billion (2.9 per cent of GDP) in 1994–5, which was almost the same as it had been in 1990–1. It rose further to $11.4 billion (3.4 per cent of GDP) in 1995–6 and $14.8 billion (4.1 per cent of GDP) in 1996–7. This would have led to a sharp deterioration in the current account deficit were it not for the continued surge in remittances, which rose to $8.1 billion (2.6 per cent of GDP) in 1994–5 and $12.4 billion (3.4 per cent of GDP) in 1996–7. As it turned out, current account deficits, although larger than those in the first phase, remained at modest levels.

The limited financing need, combined with large capital inflows, contributed to the accumulation of reserves. It is worth noting that net capital inflows in the period from 1994–5 to 1996–7 added up to $29.1 billion. This is both recognized and emphasized. But it is seldom noted that remittance inflows, which also added up to $29.1 billion over this period, were exactly the same. Although the magnitude of capital inflows in this phase was much larger, the composition of capital inflows in this phase was very different as compared with that in the first phase. In the sphere of debt-creating capital flows, net external assistance continued to decline, but there was a discernible increase in the net capital inflows attributable to commercial borrowing and non-resident deposits. The outstanding external debt registered a significant increase in 1994–5 and stabilized at a somewhat lower level thereafter. For it was non-debt-creating capital flows at $15.8 billion that contributed more than half the net capital inflows during this phase. These capital inflows, in turn, were made up of direct foreign investment which provided $6.1 billion and portfolio investment which provided $9.7 billion.

The changed composition of capital inflows may not have led to an increase in external debt but may have created a different kind of vulnerability. For problems arise when capital inflows such as portfolio investment become an important source of financing of current account deficits in the balance of payments. The economy then needs a high interest rate and a strong exchange rate regime to sustain portfolio investment inflows in terms of both profitability and confidence. This erodes the competitiveness of exports over time and enlarges the trade deficit. It is important to recognize the macroeconomic implications. Larger trade deficits and current account deficits require larger portfolio investment inflows which, beyond a point, undermine confidence and create adverse expectations even if the government keeps the exchange rate pegged. But when the stifling of exports does ultimately force an exchange rate depreciation, confidence may simply collapse and lead to capital flight. These problems have indeed surfaced in several Latin American economies, particularly Mexico, and more recently, in the South East Asian economies. This experience suggests that a reliance on portfolio investment or similar capital flows to finance current account deficits, or to build up reserves, is fraught with risk.

In this context, it is worth noting that the comfort implicit in the size of resources may be more illusory than real. These foreign currency assets are more than matched by foreign exchange liabilities which have short maturities or can be withdrawn on demand. This is the maturity mismatch problem underlying liquidity crises around the world. Consider, for example, the situation in India in March 1997.[4] The level of foreign exchange reserves was $22.4 billion. Short-term debt with a maturity of less than one year was $6.7 billion. The par value of outstanding portfolio investment, without allowing for capital gains realizable and repatriable, was $13.2 billion. These short-term liabilities in foreign exchange added up to $19.9 billion which was the equivalent of almost 90 per cent of the foreign exchange reserves. But that is not all. The outstanding stock of repatriable stocks held in India, mostly by non-residents, with a maturity of more than one year and up to three years, was as much as $11.1 billion. It must be recognized that such deposits can be withdrawn on demand and, past experience confirms, are susceptible to capital flight, should there be any crisis of confidence.[5] Thus, at the end of the fiscal year 1996–7, the total liabilities in foreign exchange, which could be called in at short notice, were $31 billion compared with reserves of $22.4 billion. Available evidence does not suggest any qualitative change in the situation during 1997–98 or thereafter.[6]

It would seem that some of the important factors underlying the transformation in the balance of payments situation are not quite sustainable. During the first phase, from 1991–2 to 1993–4, the stabilization in the balance of payments was attributable to a substantial reduction in the balance of trade

[4]The evidence cited in this paragraph is obtained from the Reserve Bank of India, *Annual Report, 1996–97*.

[5]The factors underlying the capital flight from non-resident deposits, which accentuated the balance of payment crisis in 1990–1 and 1991–2, and its macroeconomic implications are discussed, at some length, in Nayyar (1994).

[6]At the end of March 1998, the level of foreign exchange reserves was $26 billion. The short-term debt with a maturity of less than one year was $5 billion. The par value of outstanding portfolio investment was $15.2 billion, while the outstanding stock of repatriable deposits was $11.9 billion. For details, see Reserve Bank of India, *Annual Report, 1997–98*.

deficit, despite the modest export performance essentially because of the sluggish import demand. This was combined with a surge in remittances, which reduced the current account deficit further, and substantial (mostly once-and-for-all or extraordinary) capital inflows, which led to a rapid accumulation of external debt. Except for remittances, most of these underlying factors were not sustainable. During the second phase, from 1994–5 to 1996–7, there was a dramatic increase in the balance of trade deficit despite the robust export performance because of the rapid import expansion. Yet, the balance of payments situation remained comfortable, attributable, in part, to the continued surge in remittances which kept the current account deficit at a modest level and, in part, to the substantial increase in net capital inflows which led to a build-up of foreign exchange reserves. The large share of non-debt-creating capital flows in these net inflows ensured that the external debt situation did not worsen but the dependence on portfolio investment flows may have created a new kind of vulnerability. The sustained growth in remittance inflows through the 1990s made a critical contribution that is seldom recognized. However, the process of adjustment in the balance of payments would not be complete until export growth is sufficient to reduce the balance of trade deficit and would not be sustainable insofar as the build-up of reserves is based on a further accumulation of external debt or a reliance on capital inflows that are footloose or volatile in nature.

INFLATION

In India, as elsewhere, annual rates of inflation are measured in terms of the wholesale price index or the consumer price indices for different socio-economic groups such as industrial workers, urban non-manual employees, and agricultural labourers. The wholesale price index covers all commodities whereas the consumer price indices are limited to representative consumption baskets for the specified consumer-groups. Thus, the measure of inflation depends upon the price index, since the basket of commodities and the weight of each commodity differs across groups. But that is not all. It is possible to measure inflation either on a point-to-point basis or on an average-of-period basis. Point-to-point rates of inflation compare the price level on the last day of the fiscal year with the price level on the last day of the preceding fiscal year. Average-of-period rates of inflation compare the average price level during the 52 weeks of a fiscal year with the average price level during the 52 weeks of the preceding fiscal year. It is a matter of arithmetic that point-to-point rates are higher than average-of-period rates when there is an acceleration in the rate of inflation and lower when there is a deceleration in the rate of inflation.

Table 12.2: Annual Rates of Inflation, 1989–90 to 1996–7

(point-to-point)

	1989–90	1990–1	1991–2	1992–3	1993–4	1994–5	1995–6	1996–7
Wholesale Price Index	9.1	12.1	13.6	7.0	10.8	10.4	5.0	6.9
Consumer Price Index for Industrial Workers	6.6	13.6	13.9	6.1	9.9	9.7	8.9	10.0
Consumer Price Index for Urban Non-manual Employees	8.0	13.4	13.6	6.8	8.3	9.9	8.2	10.2
Consumer Price Index for Agricultural Labourers	1.0	16.6	21.9	0.7	11.6	10.6	7.4	10.5

(average-of-period)

	1989–90	1990–1	1991–2	1992–3	1993–4	1994–5	1995–6	1996–7
Wholesale Price Index	7.5	10.3	13.7	10.0	8.4	10.9	7.8	6.3
Consumer Price Index for Industrial Workers	6.6	11.2	13.5	9.9	7.3	10.3	10.0	9.4
Consumer Price Index for Urban Non-manual Employees	6.9	11.0	13.7	10.5	6.9	9.5	9.5	9.3
Consumer Price Index for Agricultural Labourers	5.4	7.6	19.3	12.4	3.5	11.9	10.8	9.1

Sources: (a) Office of the Economic Adviser, Ministry of Industry: for wholesale price index.
(b) Labour Bureau: for consumer price indices for industrial workers and agricultural labourers.
(c) Central Statistical Organization: for consumer price index for urban non-manual employees.

The evidence available for the 1990s is presented in Table 12.2. It does not suggest a real turnaround. And it would seem that inflation remained in the range of 10 per cent per annum irrespective of how we measure it. This can be described as a success only if Latin American countries are our point of reference. It is close to a failure if India's past record is the norm. Indeed, the period from 1990–1 to 1996–7 is the longest period of sustained double-digit inflation in independent India. This persistent inflation is somewhat puzzling. For one, it has coincided, for most of the time, with a concerted attempt at stabilization. For another, it has coincided, entirely, with six good monsoons in a row. What is more, the economy has not witnessed any significant exogenous shock, such as an increase in petroleum prices, during this period.

It is, therefore, necessary to explain the persistence of inflation.[7] In principle, fiscal austerity and monetary discipline, which were an integral part of the stabilization programme, should have led to a contraction of aggregate demand and thus dampened demand-pull inflation. However, the impact may have been reduced insofar as supply–demand imbalances underlying inflationary pressures persisted. Some imbalances may have worsened. For instance, credit restrictions may have squeezed the availability of working capital, particularly for small firms. Thus, supply may have been reduced in some cases even more than the contraction in demand. Monetary discipline would then have widened the gap between supply and demand in some sectors to fuel inflation. Even more important, perhaps, was the nature of fiscal adjustment enforced by the stabilization programme. It was bound to fuel cost-push inflation, when subsidies were cut as on fertilizers, administered prices were raised as for petroleum products, or user-charges were hiked by public utilities as for electricity. The tariff reform, which reduced customs duties across-the-board, was sought to be made revenue-neutral not through an increase in direct taxes that would reduce disposable incomes of the rich and dampen inflation, but through increases in indirect taxes on commodities that would fuel inflation and squeeze real incomes of the poor. The substantial depreciation of the rupee, explicit in exchange rate adjustments and implicit in the introduction of a dual exchange rate system followed by a unification of the exchange rate, obviously contributed to inflation by raising the cost of imported intermediates and the mark-ups on final goods. In the sphere of monetary policy, the higher interest rates, which were an integral part of the stabilization

---

[7]For a discussion on problems that arise in the transition from crisis to stabilization, in particular, the persistence of inflation, see Taylor (1988), Bhaduri (1992), Cooper (1992), and Nayyar (1996).

programme, probably contributed to cost-push inflation by raising the cost of borrowing for firms. However, despite the high rates of interest, liquidity was not tight enough, for the increase in money supply, defined as M3, was 17.4 per cent per annum through the first half of the 1990s, which was almost the same as the unbridled monetary expansion during the second half of the 1980s.

It is almost certain that the rate of inflation would have been higher than it was, were it not for the succession of good monsoons. The reason is simple. In the absence of exogenous shocks, the performance of the agricultural sector has always been a crucial determinant of price behaviour in India. Bad harvests fuel inflation and good harvests dampen inflation. Food prices, in particular, lead the general price level and influence inflationary expectations. In this context, it is worth noting that the bounty of the weather gods may have been neutralized, in part, by stabilization policies. The sharp reduction in fertilizer subsidies, reinforced by a politics of compromise, led to a more than compensatory increase in the procurement prices of foodgrains for producers. The objective of restraining food subsidies led to a sharp increase in the issue price of foodgrains for consumers in the public distribution system. Consequently, the procurement prices of common paddy and wheat, paid to producers, were raised by more than 50 per cent between 1990–1 and 1993–4. At the same time, issue prices in the public distribution system, charged to consumers, were raised even more, by 86 per cent for common rice and by 72 per cent for wheat between mid-1990 and early 1994. These increases exercised an important influence on market prices of foodgrains and, in turn, on inflation. The increase in procurement prices, paid to producers, continued in subsequent years. This was, probably, an important factor underlying the persistent inflation. And, in retrospect, it is clear that stabilization policies did not succeed in restraining inflation.

FISCAL ADJUSTMENT

The quality of fiscal adjustment in the government sector, which constitutes the core of the attempted macroeconomic adjustment, leaves much to be desired particularly when situated in a medium-term perspective.[8] There are three underlying reasons. First, it cannot provide a sustainable solution to the fiscal crisis. Second, it is likely to constrain economic growth. Third, it is distributing the burden of adjustment in an unequal manner. We consider each proposition in turn.

[8]The discussion that follows draws upon earlier work of the author (Nayyar 1996). Joshi and Little (1996) reach the same conclusion about the quality of fiscal adjustment.

The broad contours and dimensions of the fiscal adjustment on the part of the central government during the 1990s are set out in Table 12.3, which also compares the first half of the 1990s with the second half of the 1980s. The evidence presented suggests that there was a moderate reduction in the gross fiscal deficit of the central government, from 8.2 per cent of GDP during the period 1985–6 to 1989–90 to 6.1 per cent of GDP during the period 1991–2 to 1995–6. This was associated with a significant reduction in the monetized deficit from 2.3 per cent of GDP to 0.7 per cent of GDP and a discernible increase in the revenue deficit from 2.6 per cent of GDP to 3.1 per cent of GDP.

The almost exclusive emphasis on reducing the fiscal deficit is both inappropriate and misplaced. The macroeconomic cause for concern lies elsewhere. The more serious problem is that the revenue deficit of the central government (the excess of consumption over income supported by borrowing) is much larger than it was earlier.[9] During the second half of the 1990s, the government borrowed as much as 2.6 per cent of GDP every year, to finance its consumption expenditure. During the first half of the 1980s, however, the government borrowed even more, on an average 3.1 per cent of GDP every year, to finance its consumption expenditure. In an ideal world, there should be a revenue surplus large enough to finance capital expenditure on defence and on the social sectors, where there are no immediate or tangible returns. This would ensure that borrowing is used only to finance investment expenditure which yields a future income flow to the exchequer. So long as that income flow is greater than the burden of servicing accumulated debt, government borrowing remains sustainable. The reality in India, despite fiscal adjustment, is just the opposite. The present fiscal regime, which borrows to support consumption, is simply not sustainable over time.

It must also be stressed that the size of the fiscal deficit, or the amount of the borrowing, are the symptoms and not the disease. And there is nothing in macroeconomics which stipulates an optimum level to which the fiscal deficit must be reduced as a proportion of GDP. Indeed, it is possible that a

[9]The gross fiscal deficit measures the difference between revenue receipts plus grants and total expenditure plus net domestic lending where the latter exceeds the former. The revenue surplus or revenue deficit measures the difference between the revenue receipts (income) of the government (made up of tax revenues plus non-tax revenues) and the non-investment expenditure (consumption) of the government. The distinction between the revenue account and the capital account is most simply stated as follows: transactions which affect the income or expenditure of the central government enter into the revenue account, while transactions which affect the net wealth or debt position of the central government enter into the capital account.

Table 12.3: Government Deficits, Public Debt, and Monetary Expansion

(as a percentage of GDP at market prices)

	1985–6 to 1989–90	1990–1	1991–2	1992–3	1993–4	1994–5	1995–6	1991–2 to 1995–6	1996–7
Gross Fiscal Deficit	8.2	8.3	5.9	5.7	7.5	6.1	5.5	6.1	5.2
Revenue Deficit	2.6	3.5	2.6	2.6	4.0	3.3	2.7	3.1	2.6
Monetized Deficit	2.3	2.1	1.1	1.7	1.4	0.1	0.9	0.7	0.2
Internal Debt	50.7	52.9	51.5	50.9	53.2	51.1	50.5	51.5	48.7
Interest Payments	3.2	4.0	4.3	4.4	4.5	4.6	4.7	4.5	4.7
Money Supply (M3) percentage growth per annum	17.6	15.1	18.5	15.7	18.2	21.2	13.6	17.4	16.2

Note: The figures for 1985–6 to 1989–90 and 1991–2 to 1995–6 are average-of-period.
Source: Reserve Bank of India, *Annual Reports*.

fiscal deficit at 6 per cent of GDP is sustainable in one situation while a fiscal deficit at 4 per cent of GDP is not sustainable in another situation. The real issue is the use to which government expenditure is put in relation to the cost of borrowing by the government. Thus, government borrowing is always sustainable if it is used to finance investment and if the rate of return on such investment is greater than the interest rate payable. However, evidence available and simple macroeconomics suggest that the fiscal adjustment implemented in India cannot provide a sustainable solution to the fiscal crisis despite the reduction in the gross fiscal deficit as a proportion of GDP. For one, the cost of government borrowing has risen significantly during the 1990s. This is so for two reasons. First, the government has cut back sharply on its borrowing at low interest rates from the central bank. Second, compared with the past, the government is now borrowing much larger amounts, and at a significantly higher cost, from the commercial banking system and the domestic capital market because interest rates on government securities have been raised to market levels. For another, the use of the borrowing during the 1990s remains as unproductive as before. If anything, a much higher proportion of government borrowing is being used to finance consumption expenditure which yields no return. In this context, it needs to be stressed that the proportion of total borrowing by the central government which was used to support its consumption expenditure rose from less than one-third during the second half of the 1980s, which was a period of fiscal profligacy, to more than one-half during the first half of the 1990s, which was supposedly a period of fiscal austerity. At the same time, there is no evidence to suggest that there has been any increase in the productivity of public investment expenditure.

The evidence on the composition of fiscal adjustment by the central government during the 1990s, presented in Table 12.4, provides further confirmation that it is unsustainable. A comparison of the period 1985–6 to 1989–90 with the period 1991–2 to 1995–6 is instructive. It reveals that the revenue receipts of the central government, as a proportion of GDP, declined from 11.1 per cent to 10 per cent, essentially because tax revenue as a proportion of GDP declined from 8.3 per cent to 7.4 per cent. But revenue expenditure of the central government, as a proportion of GDP, declined somewhat less from 13.7 per cent to 13.1 per cent. Even this was possible only because expenditure on subsidies and defence, as a proportion of GDP, contracted to compensate for the significant increase in interest payments as a proportion of GDP. The increase in the revenue deficit, as a proportion of GDP, from 2.6 per cent to 3.1 per cent, was the inevitable consequence. In spite of this, the fiscal deficit, as a proportion of GDP, was reduced from 8.2 per cent to

Table 12.4: Nature and Composition of Fiscal Adjustment by the Central Government

(as a percentage of GDP at market price)

	1985–6 to 1989–90	1990–1	1991–2	1992–3	1993–4	1994–5	1995–6	1991–2 to 1995–6	1996–7
Revenue Receipts	11.1	10.3	10.7	10.5	9.3	9.6	10.0	10.0	9.9
of which:									
Tax Revenue	8.3	8.1	8.1	7.7	6.6	7.1	7.4	7.4	7.3
Non-tax-revenue	2.8	2.2	2.6	2.8	2.7	2.5	2.6	2.6	2.6
Revenue Expenditure	13.7	13.7	13.3	13.1	13.4	12.8	12.7	13.1	12.5
of which:									
Interest payments	3.2	4.0	4.3	4.4	4.5	4.6	4.7	4.5	4.7
Subsidies	2.0	2.3	2.0	1.7	1.6	1.4	1.2	1.6	1.3
Defence	2.6	2.0	1.9	1.7	1.9	1.7	1.7	1.8	1.6
Revenue deficit	2.6	3.5	2.6	2.6	4.0	3.3	2.7	3.1	2.6
Capital Expenditure	6.8	5.9	4.7	4.2	4.2	4.1	3.4	4.1	3.3
of which:									
Capital plan expenditure	4.3	3.0	2.6	2.4	2.3	2.0	1.6	2.2	1.7
Capital Receipts (excluding borrowing)	1.2	1.0	1.4	1.1	0.8	1.2	0.6	1.1	0.7
Fiscal Deficit	8.2	8.3	5.9	5.7	7.5	6.1	5.5	6.1	5.2

Note: The percentages have been calculated from the absolute values of revenues and expenditures. The figures for 1985–6 to 1989–90 and 1991–2 to 1995–6 are average-of-period.

Source: Government of India, *Union Budget* Documents and Central Statistical Organization, *National Accounts Statistics.*

6.1 per cent, essentially because capital expenditure of the central government, as a proportion of GDP, was cut back sharply from 6.8 per cent to 4.1 per cent. Some of this capital expenditure, of course, was net lending by the central government to state governments. The real cutback in capital expenditure was on investment insofar as plan expenditure, as a proportion of GDP, dropped from 4.3 per cent to 2.2 per cent.

It is obvious that the process of fiscal adjustment created a massive squeeze on public investment. And the impact on resources made available by the central government for public investment was, indeed, significant. In the *Union Budgets* from 1991–2 to 1993–4, the provision for capital expenditure in the central plan and in central plan assistance for the states—perhaps the best aggregate measure of resources allocated to public investment—remained almost unchanged in nominal terms at about the same level as 1990–1.[10] It is obvious that these budget provisions did not even compensate for inflation, let alone the substantial devaluation of the rupee, so that public investment financed by the central government declined sharply in real terms.[11] In the *Union Budgets* from 1994–5 to 1996–7, there was some increase in nominal terms but in real terms resources allocated for public investment by the central government remained almost unchanged, and even these allocations were significantly lower than in 1990–1.[12] The resource crunch was much more acute for public investment in infrastructure. Budget support provided by the central government for key infrastructure sectors—energy, transport, and communications—dropped sharply during the 1990s. It is worth noting that, between 1989–90 and 1996–7, such budget support for infrastructure declined from 8.5 per cent to 3.6 per cent of total central government expenditure, from

[10]Capital expenditure in the central plan and in central plan assistance to states and union territories was Rs 159.4 billion in 1990–1, Rs 161 billion in 1991–2, Rs 164.6 billion in 1992–3 and Rs 170.7 billion in 1993–4 (see *Union Budget* documents for respective years).

[11]It is possible to assess the implications for the level of public investment in real terms if these budget provisions for capital expenditure in the central plan and in central plan assistance to states and union territories are converted into constant prices using the GDP deflator. This calculation reveals that, at 1980–1 prices, such budget support declined from Rs 70.8 billion in 1990–1 to Rs 62.3 billion in 1991–2, Rs 58.6 billion in 1992–3 and further to Rs 56.2 billion in 1993–4. It was Rs 59.6 billion in 1994–5, Rs 51.2 billion in 1995–6, and Rs 57.7 billion in 1996–7.

[12]At current prices, capital expenditure in the central plan and in central plan assistance to states and union territories rose to Rs 198.2 billion in 1994–5, fell to Rs 182.6 billion in 1995–6 and rose again to Rs 225.3 billion in 1996–97 (see *Union Budget* documents for respective years). However, at constant 1980–81 prices, this budget support was only Rs 59.6 billion in 1994–5, Rs 51.2 billion in 1995–6 and Rs 57.7 billion in 1996–7 (calculated by using the GDP deflator obtained from *National Accounts Statistics*).

1.75 per cent to 0.57 per cent of GDP, and from Rs 39 billion to Rs 18.5 billion at constant 1980–1 prices.[13]

These cuts in public investment, particularly those for infrastructure, are bound to constrain the supply response of the economy in the medium-term and the long-run. The problem may be accentuated because available evidence in India suggests that public investment crowds in rather than crowds out private investment. Such complementarity may have dampened private investment which may have been higher if public investment had not stagnated. But that is not all. The stagnation in public investment is also a cause for concern because the level of public investment is an important determinant of the sustainability of the fiscal regime.

The distribution of the burden of fiscal adjustment has also been unequal. In a situation where inflation could not be restrained, the government should have endeavoured to protect the consumption levels of the poor by increasing public expenditure destined for them. But this did not quite happen. The evidence presented in Table 12.5, on trends in central government expenditure on programmes for employment creation and poverty alleviation in rural India during the period 1989–90 to 1996–97, provides some confirmation. It is not sufficient to examine these trends in terms of nominal values because of inflation and as a proportion of total central government expenditure because of expenditure cuts. Therefore, Table 12.5 also considers the trends in such expenditure at constant prices and as a proportion of GDP. In nominal terms and as a proportion of total expenditure, budget support declined in 1991–2, recovered somewhat in 1992–3 and rose in subsequent years until it declined once again in 1996–7. But, at constant prices or as a proportion of GDP, the expenditure on anti-poverty programmes in both 1991–2 and 1992–3 was lower than it had been in 1989–90 and 1990–1. From 1993–4 to 1995–6, this expenditure rose in real terms but remained at the 1990–1 level as a proportion of GDP. In 1996–7, however, this expenditure registered a significant decline both in real terms and as a proportion of GDP.

It may not be entirely appropriate to consider central government expenditure on poverty alleviation programmes in isolation because some part of expenditure on anti-poverty programmes is financed by state governments.

---

[13]This expenditure from the Union Budgets includes both plan expenditure and non-plan expenditure. The expenditure–GDP ratios are calculated as a percentage of GDP at market prices. Expenditure at current prices has been converted into expenditure at constant 1980–1 prices by using the deflator for GDP at factor cost. The figures cited here are calculated from data in *Union Budget* documents and *National Accounts Statistics*.

Table 12.5: Central Government Expenditure on Rural Employment
and Poverty Alleviation Programmes, 1989–90 to 1996–7

Year	In rupees million	As a percentage of total central government expenditure	As a percentage of GDP at market prices	At constant 1980–1 prices in rupees million	Employment generated in million mandays
1989–90	28,895	2.79	0.57	12,766	864.4
1990–1	24,945	2.37	0.47	11,081	874.6
1991–2	23,141	2.08	0.37	8953	809.2
1992–3	30,655	2.50	0.43	10,947	782.2
1993–4	45,952	3.24	0.57	14,994	1075.3
1994–5	55,960	3.48	0.58	16,615	1225.7
1995–6	63,889	3.58	0.57	17,531	1242.4
1996–7	59,978	2.98	0.47	15,492	803.6

Notes: (a) The expenditure–GDP ratios are calculated as a percentage of GDP at market prices. The data on GDP are from CSO *National Accounts Statistics.*

(b) Expenditure at current prices has been converted into expenditure at constant 1980–1 prices by using the deflator for GDP at factor cost. The conversion factors are obtained from CSO *National Accounts Statistics.*

Source: Government of India, Ministry of Finance, *Union Budget* documents and Ministry of Rural Development, *Annual Reports.*

But if we wish to consider the impact of fiscal adjustment, a focus on central government expenditure is unavoidable. What is more, the same conclusion is borne out by evidence available on employment generated through poverty alleviation programmes in rural India. In terms of million man-days, such employment generation declined in 1991–2 and 1992–3, recovered in 1993–4, rose significantly in 1994–5 and 1995–6, but fell sharply in 1996–7. The important fact which emerges is that the real value of resources made available for poverty alleviation programmes diminished for some time and possibly did not register the necessary increase thereafter. What is worse, the recovery was followed by another contraction. In a period of stabilization and adjustment, more real resources should have been provided to support the poor who are particularly vulnerable in such periods.[14]

Similarly, during this period, the resources provided for public expenditure on social services and in social sectors should have been increased adequately, so as to ensure that levels of social consumption for the poor were maintained, if not raised, to compensate for the possible decline in the levels of private consumption among the poor. As it turned out, however, this experience was not different from that of poverty alleviation programmes. Fiscal adjustment squeezed allocations for the social sectors—education, health, housing, water, sanitation, nutrition, and social welfare—not only in the central government but also in the state governments which were not immune from the consequences of macroeconomic reforms.[15] Thus, as a proportion of GDP, government expenditure on social sectors, for the Centre and the states taken together, experienced a stagnation or decline through the first half of the 1990s.[16]

It is clear that the fiscal adjustment should have come from a more appropriate mix of expenditure-cuts and revenue-raising instead of relying exclusively on the former. In a period when the government imposed a substantial burden on the poor through expenditure adjustment and commodity taxation, the equity principle required that the rich in particular, and the

[14]For an assessment of the impact of fiscal adjustment on resources allocated for anti-poverty programmes, as also for social services, see Guhan (1995). He concludes that: '... economic reforms have been content to treat social expenditures as a residual (which) have been "protected" in a minimal sense in the central budget(s)' (p. 1101).

[15]The implications and consequences of fiscal adjustment for government expenditure on social sectors are discussed by Guhan (1995) who considers the evidence on the central government and Prabhu (1996) who considers the evidence on the state governments.

[16]See Guhan (1995). In 1989–90, central government expenditure on social services as a proportion of GDP was 1.05 per cent. It was 0.96 per cent in 1991–2 and in 1992–3, 1.01 per cent in 1993–4, 0.97 per cent in 1994–5, 1.04 per cent in 1995–6 and 1.05 per cent in 1996–7 (calculated from *Union Budget* documents and *National Accounts Statistics*).

non-poor in general, should have shared in this burden through their contribution to direct taxes. For this, it would have been essential to broaden the base for direct taxes by bringing a larger number of people into the tax net and to deepen the structure of direct taxation by increasing the average rates of tax. The fiscal adjustment and the tax reforms implemented so far appear to have moved in the opposite direction. The underlying philosophy, it would seem, is to provide comfort for the rich even if it means hardship for the poor. It is important to stress that such patterns of adjustment, which impose a burden on the poor, are nothing new, for they have been reproduced time after time in developing countries which have embarked on stabilization and adjustment.[17]

EMPLOYMENT AND POVERTY

The data on trends in employment and unemployment during the 1990s are limited and sparse. It is only possible to put forward a plausible hypothesis about the impact of the stabilization and adjustment experience on growth in employment, supported wherever possible by available evidence.

It is reasonable to presume that growth in employment in the agricultural sector was not affected much, insofar as the increase in output was sustained entirely because of the sequence of good monsoons and, possibly, despite stabilization policies. In contrast, it is most likely that growth in employment in the industrial sector was dampened by the near-stagnation in output during the early 1990s. This plausible hypothesis is supported by available evidence. The rate of growth of employment in the organized sector of the economy, including both the public sector and the private sector, dropped from 1.7 per cent per annum in the late 1980s to 0.8 per cent per annum during the first half of the 1990s.[18] The contraction in public expenditure and the consequent reduction in aggregate demand could not but adversely affect employment in the unorganized sector, whether non-agricultural rural employment or urban informal sector employment, given the flexibility of labour markets in

[17]In periods of transition, stabilization almost always imposes a burden of adjustment that is distributed in an asymmetric manner. Without correctives, this burden is inevitably borne by the poor. For all the rhetoric about social safety nets, economies in crisis simply do not have the resources for this purpose. Adjustment with a human face is then an illusion. For evidence on the adverse impact of structural adjustment on social sectors, health, nutrition, and living standards in developing countries, see Cornia et al. (1987).

[18]The rate of growth of employment in the organized sector of the economy, including both the public sector and the private sector, was 1.7 per cent in 1989–90, 1.4 per cent in 1990–1, 1.2 per cent in 1991–2, 0.4 per cent in 1992–3, 0.7 per cent in 1993–4, 0.5 per cent in 1994–5 and 1.4 per cent in 1995–6 (see Ministry of Labour, *Annual Reports*).

such employment. It is plausible to argue, though impossible to prove, that landless labourers in the rural sector and casual wage labour in the organized sector were probably the most adversely affected by the pressure of increasing underemployment or unemployment.

In this context, it is important to recognize that the growth of the labour force in India has always been higher than the growth in employment, so that the backlog of unemployment has grown steadily over time. What is more, employment growth has not even kept pace with output growth. Evidence available suggests that the already low employment elasticities registered a significant decline between the early 1970s and the late 1980s, for the economy as a whole as also for the agricultural sector and the industrial sector. It appears that this trend continued during the period from the late 1980s to the early 1990s. The employment elasticity for the economy as a whole declined from 0.61 during the period 1972–3 to 1977–8 to 0.55 during the period 1977–8 to 1983 and 0.39 during the period 1983 to 1987–8 but remained at 0.39 during the period 1987–8 to 1993–4. The corresponding figures were 0.66, 0.49, 0.45, and 0.43, respectively for the agricultural sector, and 0.55, 0.53, 0.43, and 0.29, respectively for the manufacturing sector.[19]

In considering the longer-term prospects, it is only possible to speculate about the implications of macroeconomic reforms for employment growth.[20] In rural India, particularly in the agricultural sector, the potential for employment expansion is, in any case, limited. For one, agriculture already provides almost two-thirds of total employment in the economy although its contribution to total output is less than one-third. For another, available research suggests that beyond a certain level of development, employment creation per unit of output growth in agriculture declines. There are, of course, parts of India where agriculture is still extremely backward and agricultural growth would make a significant contribution to employment growth for some time to come but only in these areas. However, the constraint on employment creation in agriculture can be relaxed significantly through investment in agriculture, particularly in irrigation. But macroeconomic reforms which have cut fertilizer subsidies, reduced directed lending, raised interest rates, and slashed public investment, may have made this more difficult.

[19]The database for trends in employment is provided by the National Sample Survey through its quinquennial rounds. The figures on employment elasticities cited here are based on this primary source and estimated by the Planning Commission. For the periods 1972–3 to 1977–8 and 1977–8 to 1983, see Planning Commission (1990). For the periods 1983 to 1987–8 and 1987–8 to 1993–4, see Planning Commission (1998).

[20]The following discussion on this issue draws upon Bhaduri and Nayyar (1996).

The process of economic liberalization would directly affect employment growth in the industrial sector and in urban India. This impact would be positive if it leads to export expansion in labour-intensive manufacturing activities where India has a potential comparative advantage. This impact could be negative if import liberalization switches domestic demand away from home-produced goods to foreign goods, irrespective of whether it enforces efficiency or closures at a micro-level, for it would have an adverse effect on output (hence employment) at a macro-level, which would be magnified through the multiplier effect. Such a magnified contraction is most likely in the sphere of consumer goods, where import liberalization is on the cards. The consumer goods sector contributes about one-third of output and provides roughly two-thirds of employment in the manufacturing sector: much of it in the small scale sector which is that much more vulnerable. The vulnerability to import liberalization would not be confined only to the reduction in employment due to direct substitution in favour of imported goods. This contraction in employment would multiply through the consequent decline in purchasing power, reducing output and employment elsewhere in the economy through successive rounds of the same multiplier mechanism.

There is another dimension to the problem of employment in the industrial sector which is worth noting. Insofar as economic liberalization increases the average productivity of labour, through the use of capital-intensive or labour-saving foreign technologies or through a restructuring of firms which increases efficiency, it will reduce the contribution of any given rate of economic growth to employment growth. The only way out is to increase the rate of economic growth in proportion to, or more than, labour productivity growth.

The probable increase in unemployment among the vulnerable sections of the population, during the period of stabilization and adjustment, coincided with a definite increase in food prices. Existing research has established that, in India, rising food prices erode the real incomes of these vulnerable sections the most. It would, therefore, be reasonable to infer that the increase in food prices probably led to some increase in the incidence of poverty in both rural and urban India.

The database for poverty estimates is provided by National Sample Survey tables on consumer expenditure but these are now compiled only on a quinquennial basis and, during the 1990s, just one such round was conducted for 1993–4. The National Sample Survey does, however, collect data on consumer expenditure, by decile groups, on an annual basis. But this is based on thin samples. It is, therefore, not comparable with the quinquennial rounds in terms of either coverage or reliability. All the same, even such limited

Table 12.6: Incidence of Poverty in India, 1973–4 to 1993–4

			(estimates based on quinquennial rounds)		
Year	1973–4	1977–8	1983	1987–8	1993–4
Proportion below the poverty line (in percentage)					
Rural	56.4	53.1	45.7	39.1	37.3
Urban	49.0	45.2	40.8	38.2	32.4
Total	54.9	51.3	44.5	38.9	36.0
Number below the poverty line (in million)					
Rural	261.3	264.2	252.0	231.9	244.0
Urban	60.0	64.6	70.9	75.1	76.3
Total	321.3	329.0	323.0	307.0	320.4

Source: National Sample Survey and Planning Commission. These estimates are from a Press Note on Estimates of Poverty, Government of India, Planning Commission, March 1997, which are also reported in Government of India, Ministry of Finance, *Economic Survey, 1997–98*, p. 141.

information is better than mere inference or assertion. Estimates of the proportion and the number living below the poverty line, based on the quinquennial rounds are presented in Table 12.6. The table shows that the incidence of absolute poverty in both rural and urban India registered a steady and continuous decline from the early 1970s to the late 1980s. Thus, between 1973–4 and 1987–8, the proportion of the population living below the poverty line dropped from 54.9 per cent to 38.9 per cent, while the number living below the poverty line decreased from 321 million to 307 million. Evidence from the last quinquennial round conducted in 1993–4 shows that the proportion of the population living below the poverty line decreased to 36 per cent while the number living below the poverty line increased to 320 million. The quinquennial rounds, however, do not convey anything about what happened during the period between 1987–8 and 1993–4 or thereafter.

It is possible to sketch a picture of trends in poverty during the late 1980s and the first half of the 1990s by considering the evidence based on thin samples which is set out in Table 12.7. It reveals that the incidence of poverty in 1988–9 was almost the same as in 1987–8 but fell sharply in 1989–90. However, between 1989–90 and 1992–3, the proportion of the population living below the poverty line rose from 34.3 per cent to 40.7 per cent while the number of persons living below the poverty line rose from 282 million to 355

Table 12.7: Estimates of Poverty in India, 1988–9 to 1997

| | | | | | | | (based on thin samples) | |
Year	1988–9	1989–90	1990–1	1991–2	1992–3	1994–5	1995–6	1997
Proportion below the poverty line (in percentage)								
Rural	39.2	33.7	35.0	40.0	41.7	41.2	37.6	35.9
Urban	38.4	36.0	37.0	37.6	37.8	35.5	29.9	32.3
Total	39.0	34.3	35.5	39.4	40.7	39.7	35.5	34.9
Number below the poverty line (in million)								
Rural	236.7	206.7	218.4	255.6	269.0	272.9	253.5	248.6
Urban	77.8	75.1	79.5	81.6	85.8	87.3	75.5	84.9
Total	314.5	281.8	297.9	337.2	354.8	360.2	329.0	333.5

Notes: (a) These estimates of poverty are based on the methodology suggested by the Expert Group on Estimation of Proportion and Number of Poor (Planning Commission 1993).

(b) The estimates of poverty for 1988–9, 1989–90, 1990–1, 1991–2, and 1992–3 are obtained from Planning Commission (1996, p. 60).

(c) The estimates of poverty for 1994–5, 1995–6, and 1997 have been made by the author based on the all-India poverty line implicit in the methodology suggested by the Planning Commission for 1993–4, from the complete quinquennial round conducted by the National Sample Survey, was Rs 205.84 per capita per month in rural India and Rs 281.35 per capita per month in urban India. The poverty lines for 1994–5, 1995–6, and 1997 have been constructed using the Consumer Price Index for agricultural labourers for rural areas, and the Consumer Price Index for industrial workers for urban areas, as deflators. The proportion of the population living below these poverty lines has then been estimated from the National Sample Survey data on the distribution of consumer expenditure.

Source: National Sample Survey and Planning Commission.

million. The incidence of poverty rose essentially in 1991–2 and 1992–3, and the increase was far more pronounced in rural India than it was in urban India. This trend provides a sharp contrast with the steady reduction in the percentage of the population below the poverty line over the period 1973–4 to 1987–8. It also shows that the long-term trend of declining poverty, which began in 1973–4, continued beyond 1987–8. Absolute poverty declined further until 1989–90, but registered a significant increase during the early 1990s which coincided with the period of stabilization. Thus, while the incidence of absolute poverty in 1993–4 was lower than it had been in 1987–8, it was higher than that in 1989–90. Evidence available from thin samples suggests that the incidence of poverty during the mid-1990s remained about the same as it was in 1993–4. The proportion of the population living below the poverty line was 37.3 per cent in 1994–5 and 36.3 per cent in 1995–6, only slightly more than the 36 per cent in 1993–4 but discernibly higher than the 34.3 per cent in 1989–90. The evidence on the number of persons living below the poverty line is similar.

There can be little doubt that the major factor underlying the increase in poverty during the early 1990s, and the persistence of poverty despite rapid economic growth during the mid-1990s, was inflation. The sharp increase in the prices of food and necessities was probably the single most important cause.[21] The prices of foodgrains experienced double-digit inflation despite the succession of good monsoons. This was induced, perhaps, by the substantial increases in the procurement prices for producers and a more than commensurate increase in the public distribution system prices for consumers, particularly during the period 1990–1 to 1993–4. In subsequent years, from 1994–5 to 1996–7, the pressure on prices may have been accentuated, at the margin, by the trade liberalization which relaxed or removed quantitative restrictions on exports of agricultural commodities.[22]

The increase in food prices was juxtaposed with a stagnation and decline in the per capita availability of foodgrains. What is worse, over this period, there was no discernible increase in the allocation for the public distribution system while the sales through the public distribution system declined steadily as the difference between ration-shop prices and market prices narrowed to a

[21]For a detailed discussion of the argument outlined in this paragraph, as also for supporting evidence, see Nayyar (1996).

[22]For a detailed discussion on the implications and consequences of trade liberalization for the agricultural sector in India and its possible impact on domestic food prices, see Nayyar and Sen (1994).

small margin.[23] Ironically enough, there was a steady accumulation in the stock of foodgrains at the same time. It would seem that the higher procurement prices for producers, to compensate for the cut in fertilizer subsidies, enabled the government to add to its stockpile of food. But the higher issue prices for consumers, dictated by the fiscal compulsions of macroeconomic reform, meant that these inventories could not be utilized so that the public distribution system failed to serve its intended purpose. Strange though it may seem, the budget provisions for subsidies on food may have ended up in supporting the cost of carrying stocks, which increased significantly because of higher interest rates, rather than providing cheap food. The price of food, not only in the market place but also in the ration shops, was simply too high for the poor.

But that is not all. The inflation was just as high in other primary food articles (comprising cereals, pulses, fruits, vegetables, eggs, fish, meat, and spices) and manufactured food products (such as sugar, edible oils, and processed foods). Between end-March 1990 and end-March 1997, the prices of foodgrains rose by 133 per cent, the prices of primary food articles rose by 114 per cent, and the prices of manufactured food products rose by 83 per cent. Given such inflation in food and in the prices of necessities, it is not surprising that the incidence of poverty registered a significant increase in the early 1990s but did not register any notable decrease in spite of the rapid economic growth through the mid-1990s.[24] The latter provides a sharp contrast with the experience of the 1980s when similar rates of economic growth led to a sharp decline in the proportion of the population living below the poverty line.

ADJUSTMENT AND GROWTH

The short-term impact of macroeconomic adjustment on output and growth has been almost uniformly adverse across countries.[25] The stabilization

[23]For supporting evidence, see Government of India, Ministry of Finance, *Economic Survey, 1993–94*, pp. 66–7 and *Economic Survey, 1994–95*, pp. 78–82. It is worth noting that retail prices in the public distribution system were significantly higher than the central issue prices. In some states, the margin was as much as 20 per cent.

[24]In this context, it is worth noting that the purchasing power of the people, even as an arithmetic average, registered only a modest increase. Indeed, between 1990–91 and 1996–7, at constant 1980–1 prices, per capita final consumer expenditure increased by only 17 per cent, as compared with an increase of 25 per cent in per capita income and 40 per cent in national income (calculated from CSO *National Accounts Statistics*). It is, thus, plausible to suggest that inflation, which was concentrated in the prices of wage goods, probably redistributed incomes away from the poor leaving them worse off.

[25]See Taylor (1988) and Cooper (1992).

experience in India was no exception. In real terms, GDP growth dropped to 0.8 per cent in 1991–2. This provided a sharp contrast with the second half of the 1980s when growth in GDP was 6.4 per cent per annum. However, there was a recovery in 1992–3 so that the slowdown in growth lasted just two years. Beginning in 1993–4, until 1996–7, GDP growth was comparable with what it had been during the 1980s. This was, in part, attributable to the succession of good monsoons and agricultural growth. But it was also attributable to a revival of growth in the industrial sector and in the services sector.

The slowdown in growth was juxtaposed with an acceleration in inflation. It hurt the poor and led to an increase in poverty. The revival of growth, however, did not lead to a decrease in poverty. This was not in conformity with past experience. The persistence of inflation was perhaps the important underlying factor. Although public expenditure destined for the poor was squeezed by fiscal adjustment, at least for some time, the existing anti-poverty programmes did probably mitigate the adverse impact of inflation on the poor. The outcome would have been worse without these programmes and could have been better if more resources had been provided for these programmes. But the provision for basic education, health care, and social security remained grossly inadequate. It is clear that rapid economic growth is necessary but cannot be sufficient to improve the living conditions of people. It is also clear that anti-poverty programmes are essential and may need to be strengthened during difficult periods of economic transition but cannot provide a permanent solution. Ultimately, the process of economic growth must create employment and incomes for the poor. There is no other sustainable means of eradicating poverty. Hence, in the long-run, incomes for the poor, rather than transfer payments, should sustain their private consumption. But public expenditure that sustains social consumption of the poor is just as critical. For that is the only way in which economic development can create social opportunities for people at large.[26] In considering the long-run implications of macroeconomic reforms, employment creation and social opportunity need much more attention for rapid economic growth to translate into meaningful economic development.

All the same, sustained growth is critical. In retrospect, it is clear that the short-run effect of stabilization on growth in India was adverse but short-lived. And, a medium-term perspective suggests that India fared better than most

[26]This is the theme of an excellent book by Dreze and Sen (1995) which discusses this set of issues at some length.

economies in Latin America, sub-Saharan Africa, or East Europe that embarked on stabilization and adjustment. Yet, the long-run implications of macroeconomic reforms in India, for the possibilities of sustained growth, provide some cause for concern. For any given productivity of investment, the impact of adjustment on growth depends upon what happens to the *level* of investment in real terms and the *rate* of investment as a proportion of GDP. On both these counts, the Indian experience is not quite as good as it appears on surface.

In the public sector as a whole, which is made up of the central government, the state governments, and public enterprises, gross investment at constant 1980–1 prices experienced a stagnation at about Rs 200 billion during the period from 1991–2 to 1993–4 and did not even recover to the level attained in 1990–1. This was obviously attributable to the fiscal adjustment in the stabilization programme which axed public investment. In the private sector, which is made up of the household sector and the corporate sector, the trend was similar as gross domestic investment at constant 1980–1 prices fluctuated in the range of Rs 300–350 billion during the period 1991–2 to 1993–4 but did not quite return to the level reached in 1990–1. It would seem that the squeeze on public investment induced by fiscal adjustment, combined with monetary discipline, had a dampening effect on private investment. In 1994–95, the significant increase in the level of public investment (Rs 241 billion at 1980–81 prices) was perhaps an important factor underlying the substantial increase in private investment (Rs 438 billion at 1980–81 prices).[27] This experience suggests that, in India, public investment and private investment are complements rather than substitutes. And it is plausible to argue that private investment would have been higher if public investment had not stagnated. Thus, if the level of public investment continues to be constrained by the compulsion of macroeconomic reforms, it is likely to constrain the level of investment in the economy in the long-run.

The discussion on the implications of adjustment for growth cannot be complete without reference to the mode of macroeconomic adjustment in India which could have adverse consequences for economic growth in the

[27]The figures on gross domestic investment in the private sector, cited in this paragraph, are obtained from Central Statistical Organisation, *National Accounts Statistics, 1997*. There are two points that are worth noting in this context. First, there was a redistribution within the private sector as investment in the private corporate sector rose while that in the household sector fell. Second, quick (preliminary) estimates for 1995–96 suggest that public investment remained about the same at Rs 235 billion while private investment rose further to Rs 565 billion. Given the complementarity, it is plausible to argue though impossible to prove that private investment may have been higher if there had been an increase in public investment.

Table 12.8: Saving and Investment Rates in India

(as a percentage of GDP/NDP at current market prices)

	1989–90	1990–1	1991–2	1992–3	1993–4	1994–5	1995–6	1996–7
Gross Domestic Saving	24.0	24.3	22.8	22.1	23.1	24.9	25.3	26.1
Net Domestic Saving	15.7	16.1	14.0	13.1	14.4	16.7	17.0	18.0
Gross Domestic Investment	26.7	27.7	23.4	24.0	23.6	26.0	27.1	27.3
Net Domestic Investment	18.7	19.9	14.6	15.3	15.1	17.8	19.1	19.2

Note: The data for 1996–7 are provisional and based on quick estimates, reported in the CSO Press Note on National Income, February 1998.
Source: Central Statistical Organization, National Accounts Statistics, June 1997.

long-run. This is borne out by the evidence presented in Table 12.8 on the rates of investment and saving as a proportion of GDP during the period from 1989–90 to 1996–7. As a proportion of GDP, gross domestic investment registered a sharp decline during the period of stabilization, possibly because of the said complementarity between public and private investment. Insofar as investment determines aggregate demand and aggregate income, this was associated with a decline in gross domestic savings as a proportion of GDP. So much so that, between 1990–1 and 1993–4, the investment–GDP ratio dropped by more than four percentage points, from 27.7 per cent to 23.6 per cent. The decline in net domestic investment as a proportion of net domestic product (NDP), at almost five percentage points, from 19.9 per cent to 15.1 per cent, was even more pronounced. The rates of domestic investment, both gross and net as a proportion of GDP and NDP respectively, recovered in subsequent years but just about returned to 1990–1 levels only in 1995–6 and were no higher in 1996–7.

Economic growth can come, in part, from an increase in the productivity of investment. But only in part. Ultimately, sustained economic growth also requires an increase in the rate of investment. If the rate of investment was so much lower for three years, it would have required a corresponding increase in the productivity of investment just to maintain the earlier rate of economic growth. And, if the rate of investment was no higher even six years later, a return to earlier rates of growth suggests that the productivity of investment was about the same as earlier. This is simple arithmetic. It must also be recognized that the level and the productivity of investment are interdependent variables that tend to move together. Higher investments mean the realization of scale of economies and infrastructural capital formation, which raise the productivity of investment directly or indirectly. Lower levels of investment could dampen productivity growth.

It would appear that the process of macroeconomic adjustment in India has been based on an investment squeeze and insofar as investment still exceeds saving at a macro-level, the corresponding excess of imports over the exports is being financed by foreign capital inflows. This must have adverse implications for economic growth in the long-run. For, ultimately, sustained economic growth requires an increase in the rate of investment as a proportion of GDP. Thus, macroeconomic adjustment that is conducive to growth needs to raise the investment–GDP ratio. And, in an ideal world, the strategy should be to sustain higher investment rates by raising the export–GDP ratio and the domestic savings–GDP ratio and not by allowing a compensatory increase in the import–GDP ratio supported by foreign capital inflows. Some correctives at the macro-level are, therefore, necessary to sustain economic growth in the long-run.

CONCLUSION

It is time to draw together some conclusions that emerge from the preceding discussion on the experience of macroeconomic reforms in India during the 1990s. The short-term effects of stabilization present a mixed picture. The management of the balance of payments situation should not be seen as the success story it is made out to be, because some of the important factors underlying the transformation are not quite sustainable. Indeed, the process of adjustment would not be complete until export growth is sufficient to reduce the large balance of trade deficit and would not be sustainable insofar as the build-up of reserves is based on an accumulation of external debt or a reliance on capital inflows that are footloose and perhaps volatile. The record on inflation, also, does not suggest a real turnaround. The persistence of double-digit inflation for much of the period, despite the concerted attempt at stabilization, is striking. And, it is almost certain that the rate of inflation would have been higher were it not for the succession of good monsoons.

The medium-term consequences of macroeconomic reforms are worrisome. The real problem is that the quality of fiscal adjustment is poor. It cannot provide a sustainable solution to the fiscal crisis. It may only have postponed the day of reckoning. The size of the fiscal deficit is less important than the use and the cost of the borrowing. It is the revenue deficit, which requires borrowing to support the consumption expenditure of the government, that must be progressively reduced and rapidly eliminated. The fetishism about reducing the fiscal deficit despite a burgeoning revenue deficit, or eliminating the monetized deficit despite the much higher cost of borrowing, is entirely misplaced. At the same time, the burden of adjustment is being distributed in an unequal manner. Macroeconomic reforms meant that the resources made available for anti-poverty programmes, as also for the social sectors, were squeezed for some time and were not increased adequately thereafter. The persistence of inflation, particularly in the prices of food, inevitably hurt the poor. There was a significant increase in the incidence of poverty during the early 1990s which coincided with the period of stabilization and the slowdown in growth. But the rapid economic growth through the mid-1990s did not lead to any notable decrease in the incidence of poverty. In a situation where incomes are low, the consumption levels of the poor need to be protected by restraining inflation and maintaining public expenditure destined for the poor. But that is not all. The process of economic growth must also create employment and social opportunities for the people.

Clearly, India fared much better than most countries in Latin America or sub-Saharan Africa insofar as the slowdown was short-lived and the economy returned to earlier rates of growth sooner than might have been expected. Yet, the long-run implications of macroeconomic reforms for the possibilities of sustained growth are a cause of concern, primarily because the process of macroeconomic adjustment has been based on an investment squeeze. It is necessary to raise the level of investment in real terms. This, in turn, requires an increase in public investment, particularly in infrastructure where sufficient private investment, whether domestic or foreign, is not forthcoming. It is just as essential to raise the rate of investment in the economy. As far as possible, the higher investment–GDP ratio should be sustained by raising the export–GDP ratio and the domestic savings–GDP ratio rather than by allowing a compensatory increase in the import–GDP ratio. Some correctives are, therefore, necessary not only to sustain economic growth but also to avert another macroeconomic crisis.

REFERENCES

Bhaduri, A. (1992), 'Conventional Stabilization and the East European Transition', in S. Richter (ed.), *The Transition from Command to Market Economies in East-Central Europe*, Westview Press, San Francisco.

Bhaduri, A. and D. Nayyar (1996), *The Intelligent Person's Guide to Liberalization*, Penguin Books, New Delhi.

Cooper, R.N. (1992), *Economic Stabilization and Debt in Developing Countries*, The MIT Press, Cambridge.

Cornia, G.A., R. Jolly, and F. Stewart (1987), *Adjustment with a Human Face*, Clarendon Press, Oxford.

Dreze, J. and A.K. Sen (1995), *India: Economic Development and Social Opportunity*, Oxford University Press, Oxford.

Guhan, S. (1995), 'Social Expenditures in the Union Budget: 1991–1996', *Economic and Political Weekly*, Vol. XXX, Nos 18–19, pp. 1095–101.

Joshi, V. and I.M.D. Little (1994), *India: Macroeconomics and Political Economy, 1964–1991*, World Bank and Oxford University Press, Washington, DC and New Delhi.

_____ (1996), *India's Economic Reforms: 1991–2001*, Oxford University Press, New Delhi.

Nayyar, D. (1994), *Migration, Remittances and Capital Flows: The Indian Experience*, Oxford University Press, New Delhi.

_____ (1996), *Economic Liberalization in India: Analytics, Experience and Lessons*, R.C. Dutt Lectures on Political Economy, Orient Longman, Calcutta.

Nayyar, D. and A. Sen (1994), 'International Trade and the Agricultural Sector in India', in G.S. Bhalla (ed.), *Economic Liberalization and Indian Agriculture*, ISID-FAO, New Delhi.

Planning Commission (1990), *Employment: Past Trends and Prospects for the 1990s*, Government of India, New Delhi.

_____ (1993) *Report of the Expert Group on Estimation of Proportion and Number of Poor*, Government of India, New Delhi.

_____ (1996), *Draft Mid-Term Appraisal of the Eighth Five Year Plan: 1992–97*, Government of India, New Delhi, September.

_____ (1998), *Ninth Five Year Plan: 1997–2002*, Draft, Volume I, New Delhi, March.

Prabhu, K.S. (1996), 'The Impact of Structural Adjustment on Social Sector Expenditure: Evidence from Indian States', in C.H.H. Rao and H. Linneman (eds), *Economic Reforms and Poverty Alleviation in India*, Sage Publications, New Delhi.

Taylor, L. (1988), *Varieties of Stabilization Experience: Towards Sensible Macroeconomics in the Third World*, Clarendon Press, Oxford.

Chapter 13

ECONOMIC REFORMS IN INDIA

*Understanding the Process and Learning from Experience**

INTRODUCTION

Economic liberalization became a *mantra* for development everywhere in the world during the 1990s. So much so that structural reform in economies came to be seen as both a virtue and a necessity. This led countries to adapt their erstwhile models of development or to search for new models of development. The experience, since then, has been mixed. In evaluating the experience across countries, it is difficult to define, and then identify success or failure, because actual outcomes span a wide spectrum from moderate successes at one end to real disasters at the other.[1] The experience of Latin America, Eastern Europe, and sub-Saharan Africa provides cause for concern. In contrast, the experience of Asia provides reason for hope. In Asia, India and China are widely perceived as success stories.

The object of this essay, which seeks to focus on economic reforms in India, is to develop an understanding of the factors that made the reforms possible and to analyse the lessons that emerge from the experience. It does not attempt to provide an assessment or an evaluation of economic reforms. For there exists an extensive literature on the subject.[2] Instead, it endeavours to explore the context, economic and political, in which reforms began life. This provides the logical starting point to address the question: what can we learn from the experience with economic reforms in India?

*I would like to thank Andrea Cornia and T.N. Srinivasan for valuable comments on an earlier version of this paper. I am also grateful to Amit Bhaduri and Lance Taylor for helpful discussion on the subject, over the years, even though they have not read this paper.
    [1]There is an extensive literature on this subject. See, for example, Cornia et al. (1987), Taylor (1988 and 1993), Williamson (1990), and Ocampo (2004).
    [2]See, for example, Bhagwati (1993), Joshi and Little (1994 and 1996), Dreze and Sen (1995), Nayyar (1996 and 2001), and Bhaduri and Nayyar (1996).

The structure of the essay is as follows. The first section highlights the significance of the conjuncture in the national context and the international context, in which the reforms were introduced, so as to understand the process of reforms. The second section considers the lessons that have been learnt. The third section analyses the lessons that have not yet been learnt. The fourth section discusses some essentials that have been forgotten. The last section draws together some conclusions.

THE SIGNIFICANCE OF THE CONJUNCTURE

It needs to be said that the reform process, which began in the early 1990s, was not India's first experiment with economic liberalization. The first attempt was a short-lived episode of hesitant liberalization in the mid-1960s which coincided with a substantial devaluation of the rupee. The second endeavour came in the late 1970s with a focus on trade liberalization in a comfortable balance of payments situation. The third step was the package of economic policies introduced in the mid-1980s when liberalization of the trade regime gathered momentum and the process of industrial deregulation was set in motion. These liberalization episodes were perceived as correctives for an industrializing economy in transition but did not contemplate any fundamental changes in the objectives or the strategy of development.[3] In the early 1990s, however, the changes were significant enough to be characterized as a shift of paradigm.[4]

Any attempt at a broad characterization of the basic departures from the earlier strategy of development runs the obvious risk of oversimplification. Yet, it is worth highlighting three dimensions of the contrast between the past and the present. First, the objective function now is economic growth combined with economic efficiency. The earlier concern about preventing a concentration of economic power or attempting a redistribution of wealth, never more than rhetoric, has been explicitly abandoned. The object of bringing about a reduction in poverty and inequality has not been set aside but such concerns about equity have been subsumed in the pursuit of growth on the premise that it is both necessary and sufficient for an improvement in the living conditions of the people. Second, there is a conscious decision to substantively reduce the role of the State in the process of economic development

---

[3]These earlier episodes of liberalization and the factors underlying the changing emphasis in the strategy of industrialization are analysed in Nayyar (1994).

[4]The rationale for the economic reforms and the necessity of departures from the earlier strategy of development is set out, at some length, by Bhagwati and Srinivasan (1993), Bhagwati (1993), and Joshi and Little (1996).

and rely far more on the market. The government no longer seeks to guide the allocation of scarce investible resources, whether directly through industrial licensing or indirectly through intervention in the financial sector. This role is now performed largely by market forces. Third, the degree of openness of the economy has been significantly increased and at a rapid pace. The object is not simply to enforce a cost discipline on the supply side through international competition, but also to narrow the difference between domestic and world prices. Foreign capital and foreign technology are expected to perform a strategic role in the process. Every aspect of this quest for integration with the world economy provides a striking contrast with the strategy of industrialization adopted in postcolonial India.

Economic liberalization in India began on a dramatic note in mid-1991, with sudden and fundamental changes in the strategy of development. In the context of a democracy, it is essential to understand the political foundations of such economic change.[5] There are two obvious questions which spring to mind. First, why did a relatively minor crisis in the economy evoke this response while decades of persistent poverty and mounting unemployment had so little impact? Second, how were such far reaching changes introduced by what was then a minority government,[6] while predecessor governments with overwhelming majorities, such as that of Rajiv Gandhi, were unable to do so despite their stated intentions to liberalize?

These complex political questions seem to have a relatively simple economic answer. The change was dictated by the immediate economic compulsions of crisis-management. The external debt crisis which erupted in 1991 meant that the fear of default hung as the Sword of Damocles. The realization that the outside world was no longer willing to lend to India was combined with a fear that, soon, the people of India may not be willing to lend to their government. There was a sudden realization that governments can and do become insolvent even if countries do not go bankrupt. The problem was accentuated by an international compulsion that came into play at about the same time. The collapse of communism meant that competing ideologies gave way to a dominant ideology, while the collapse of the erstwhile USSR

---

[5]For a more detailed discussion of this issue, see Bhaduri and Nayyar (1996). There is also a literature on the politics of economic reforms in India. See Joshi and Little (1994), Lewis (1995), Nayyar (1998a), and Jenkins (1999).

[6]Some of these changes were announced by the government even before it had established its majority in Parliament. For example, there was a significant devaluation of the rupee in early July 1991. Similarly, major changes in industrial policy and trade policy were announced around the same time. See, for example, Government of India (1991a and b).

removed the countervailing force, an important prop for India in the past, from the international system. The success stories of East Asia, perceived by some as role models, juxtaposed with the super performance of China, also exercised an important influence on thinking at that juncture. It is not as if there were no other underlying factors. The emerging concerns about efficiency and productivity—even if not about poverty, unemployment, and inequality—had led to a debate, and some rethinking about the development strategy, through the 1980s. This had permeated vaguely through the political system in as much as the manifesto of every political party for the 1991 elections, across the ideological spectrum, talked about the need for restructuring the economy.[7] But that debate might have continued for some time to come, for many of these concerns belong to the million mutinies India lives with. And the law of inertia—the hallmark of economy and polity in India—might have prevailed. There can be little doubt that it was a combination of the reality in the national context and the conjuncture in the international context which provided the impetus for sudden change. Despite later pretensions to the contrary, the change was neither planned nor debated. Instead, the government was driven by the immediate compulsions of an impending sense of crisis in the economy. The response was driven, even dictated, by the crisis. It was not planned.

It is plausible to argue, though impossible to prove, that any other government in office in mid-1991 would have done roughly the same in terms of fire-fighting and crisis-management simply because there was little choice.[8] There was no consensus even in the ruling party, let alone across the political spectrum, about what needed to be done. It was more in the nature of a *fait accompli*. Silence meant neither consent nor acceptance. But there were two supportive factors. For one, there was a consciousness among politicians across parties, which did not necessarily mean an understanding, of the crisis in the economy. For another, the political system was somewhat tired of instability and conflict, so that opposition parties were simply not willing to bring down the government and force yet another round of elections.

Economic reforms in India should be situated in the wider international context. The experience during the last quarter of the twentieth century suggests that the process of economic reform is either strategy-based or crisis-driven. There are relatively few examples of strategy-based reform, except for the success stories among the East Asian countries. Crisis-driven reform is much more common: a crisis in the economy, mostly on account of external debt, provided

[7]The discussion that follows draws upon Bhaduri and Nayyar (1996), as also Nayyar (1996).

[8]This argument is set out, at greater length, in Bhaduri and Nayyar (1996).

the impetus in Latin America, sub-Saharan Africa, and South Asia, while the collapse of the political system gave the push in Eastern Europe. The probability of success or failure, experience suggests, is strongly influenced by the economic or political origins of the reform process.

Economic reform that represents a natural transition in the strategy of development emerges from experience and learning within countries. It is, therefore, rooted in social formations and is shaped by political processes that provide the constituencies. Such a reform process can both sustain and succeed, in part because it creates a capacity to face problems of transition. For one, the change is acceptable to polity and society. For another, the speed and the sequence of adjustment can be absorbed by the economy. Economic reform that is crisis-driven, irrespective of whether the crisis is an external shock or an internal convulsion, is more difficult to sustain and less likely to succeed. The reasons are manifold and complex. But there are some which deserve to be highlighted.

First, the preoccupation with stabilization in the short-term and adjustment or reform in the medium-term, which is natural for the multilateral financial institutions, leads to confusion between tactics and strategies or means and ends in the minds of governments. This often leads to a neglect of the long-term in terms of development objectives, particularly those that cannot be defined in terms of the so-called performance criteria in the sphere of economics or tangible gains in the realm of politics.[9] Yet, economic development in India, or elsewhere, cannot do without a longer time horizon.

Second, during such transitions, for the majority of the people the costs of the reform process surface soon while the benefits remain a distant promise. In the absence of supportive constituencies, if reform is not absorbed by the economy or is not acceptable to the polity, disillusionment sets in and even the necessary and desirable components of reform are discredited.[10] Austerity now for prosperity later, is neither credible nor acceptable to people.

Third, the political and social coalitions which support or oppose reforms determine whether the process would ultimately be sustainable. If the support comes from the rich, the literati, and the influential who are vocal and capture most of the benefits, while the opposition comes from the poor and the

[9]See Nayyar (1996). In this context, it is worth noting that short-termism in public policies has much wider implications for economic development, for the effects of short-term policies have significant long-term consequences, attributable, in part, to *hysteresis* (Nayyar 1998b).

[10]This is borne out by the electoral verdicts in country after country in Eastern Europe, where the market, it seems, met its match. See Amsden et al. (1994).

unorganized who are silent and bear most of the costs, economic liberalization accentuates social divisions and political alienation. The coalitions for and against may, of course, be more complex in their composition but it is the distribution of the benefits and costs, together with their respective size in terms of population, that determines, to a large extent, the fate of reforms. These problems appear more acute in democratic regimes but are not altogether absent in authoritarian regimes.

THE LESSONS LEARNT

The first lesson to emerge from the experience with economic reforms is that competition in the market is desirable. Such competition is essential between domestic firms, between domestic firms and foreign firms, as also between the public sector and the private sector. For it is competition between firms, in price and in quality, that creates efficiency among producers and provides a choice for consumers.

Industrial deregulation removed barriers to entry for new firms and limits on growth in the size of existing firms.[11] Investment decisions were thus no longer dependent upon government approvals or constrained by State intervention. Industrial licensing was abolished. The dismantling of the complex regime of controls, particularly in the sphere of investment decisions, was not only necessary but also desirable. For it led to competition between domestic firms.

Import liberalization rapidly dismantled the regime of import licensing. This was combined with a substantial reduction of tariffs on imports.[12] It reduced not only the nominal but also the effective protection available to domestic industry, as trade policy reform sought to bring domestic prices closer to world prices. The regime change led to competition between domestic firms and foreign firms.

Reforms in the public sector, *inter alia*, sought to reduce the number of industries reserved for the public sector.[13] It led to the recognition that there is no reason why the public sector and the private sector should not co-exist, at least in some sectors, for competition would keep both on their toes. This

[11]For details, see Government of India (1991a). The exceptions were specified industries either reserved for the public sector (Annex I, p.10) or subject to compulsory licensing (Annex II, p.11) because of security concerns or environmental considerations. Subsequent relaxations in April 1993 opened up much of the mining sector for private investment and industrial delicensing was extended to consumer durables.

[12]For evidence on, and a discussion of this issue, see Nayyar (1996).

[13]Government of India (1991a), in particular, Annex I.

is particularly important where market structures are oligopolistic because the importance of scale economies limits the number of producers, as in steel or petrochemicals. The same reasoning was extended to civil aviation where the entry of a few private airlines provided much needed competition to the public sector. The benefit accrued to consumers.

The second lesson to emerge from the experience with economic reforms is that marketization, in itself, is not always desirable. For there are two sides to a coin.

The more obvious example of this lesson comes from public sector reform, which has been long on words and short on substance. The main objectives of the government were to ease the burden on the exchequer on account of the public sector and to facilitate the closure of loss making units in the public sector.[14] The sale of government equity in the public sector was simply used to reduce the borrowing needs, hence the fiscal deficit, of the government, rather than to retire public debt, let alone restructure public enterprises. Similarly, budget support to finance losses in public sector firms was progressively withdrawn but nothing was done to ease the difficulties of these firms and closures remain in the realm of rhetoric. This approach to public sector reform which emphasized asset sales and closures represented the most rudimentary form of privatization. It was neither adjustment nor reform. It implied selling some flagships and keeping the tramp ships, or sending a few white elephants to the slaughter house, but there was no systematic attempt to address problems of efficiency and productivity.

The less obvious, but just as important, example of the second lesson comes from financial sector deregulation and liberalization. The object of financial sector reform was to improve the profitability of the State-owned commercial banking system and the functioning of the domestic capital market on the presumption that the discipline imposed by market forces would make both more efficient.[15] It was based on the premise that the commercial banking system and the domestic capital market were over-regulated and under-governed. This presumption was broadly correct. However, the belief that market forces would suffice to make commercial banks more profitable was unwarranted, given the significant proportion of non-performing assets in their portfolio, their inadequate equity base, and their inappropriate management structures. Similarly, the assumption that market forces would suffice to discipline the capital market was somewhat heroic in a situation

---

[14]For details, see Government of India (1991a and 1993).
[15]This proposition is discussed, in greater depth, elsewhere by the author (Nayyar 1996).

where trading malpractices abounded, disclosure rules were almost non-existent, and investor protection was slender. The process of reform dispensed with the over-regulation but the system remained under-governed because institutional and legal frameworks that would govern the market were not put in place at the same time. This mismatch was fraught with risk. And it was borne out by a series of scams which surfaced in the financial sector.[16]

The third lesson to emerge from the experience with economic reforms is that the speed and the sequence of change matter. For one, the speed of change must be calibrated, so that it can be absorbed by the economy. For another, the sequence of change must be planned with reference to an order of priorities. In both, whether speed or sequence, deregulation and openness must be compatible with the initial conditions and must be consistent with each other.

The significance of speed and sequence emerges clearly in the sphere of trade policy reform. It is often presumed that exposure to international competition will force domestic firms to become more efficient. In fact, if the speed of import liberalization is too rapid, it may enforce closures rather than create efficiency at a micro level. The conception of such reform also makes a commonplace theoretical error in the design of policies. It confuses *comparison* (of equilibrium positions) with *change* (from one equilibrium position to another). In the real world, economic policy must be concerned not only with comparison but with how to direct the process of change. Thus, even if a reduction in tariffs or other forms of protection can, in principle, lead to more cost-efficient firms, which are competitive in the world market, success at transition depends upon the speed and sequence of trade liberalization.[17]

The significance of speed and sequence emerges even more clearly from the experience with capital account liberalization. The approach was cautious. What was liberalized was specified. Everything else remained restricted or prohibited. And the sequence of change was calibrated with care.[18] The fungibility between current account transactions and capital account transactions was substantively pre-empted by two restrictions. First, dollar-denominated transactions between residents were prohibited. Second, offshore rupee transactions were prohibited. The object was to ensure that there would be no dollarization of the domestic economy and no internationalization of the

---

[16]See Bhaduri and Nayyar (1996).

[17]For a more detailed discussion of this issue, see Nayyar (1997); also see Bhaduri and Nayyar (1996).

[18]For an analysis of the Indian experience with capital account liberalization, see Rangarajan and Prasad (1999), Reddy (1999), and Nayyar (2002).

domestic currency. Capital controls with three sets of asymmetries provided checks and balances.[19] First, there was an asymmetry between capital outflows, where there were extensive controls, and capital inflows, where there was considerable liberalization. Second, there was an asymmetry between residents, who were subject to strict controls, and non-residents, for whom there was some relaxation in capital account liberalization. Third, there was an asymmetry between individuals, who were subject to prohibitive controls on transactions in the capital account, and corporates, for whom there was a significant liberalization of transactions in the capital account. The road to capital account convertibility was thus interspersed with speed-breakers. In sum, it was recognized, almost at the outset, that it would be wise to hasten slowly on capital account liberalization. In retrospect, a decade later, this lesson from the Indian experience is seen as relevant for developing countries and transitional economies.

THE LESSONS NOT LEARNT

There are three lessons that should be drawn from the experience with economic reforms, which have not yet been learnt: that a prudent macro-management of the economy is essential; that infrastructure is of critical importance; and that it is necessary to redefine the role for the State in a market economy. It is widely accepted that a prudent macro-management of the economy is both necessary and desirable. Yet, the understanding of the problem, as also the attempted solution, is limited. This is so for two reasons.

First, the almost exclusive emphasis on reducing the fiscal deficit of the central government is both inappropriate and misplaced. It is inappropriate because we should be concerned with the fiscal deficit of the central government, the state governments, and the public sector, taken together. It is misplaced because, even for the central government, the macroeconomic cause for concern lies elsewhere. The more serious problem is that the revenue deficit of the government (the excess of consumption over income supported by borrowing) has grown steadily larger.[20] It was 2.6 per cent of GDP during the second half of the 1980s, 3.1 per cent of GDP during the 1990s, and 4.2 per

---

[19]This argument is developed, at some length, in Nayyar (2002).

[20]The gross fiscal deficit measures the difference between revenue receipts plus grants and total expenditure plus net domestic lending where the latter exceeds the former. The revenue surplus or revenue deficit measures the difference between the revenue receipts (income) of the government (made up of tax revenues plus non-tax revenues) and the non-investment expenditure (consumption) of the government. The distinction between the revenue account and the capital account is most simply stated as follows: transactions which affect the income or expenditure of the central government enter into the revenue account, while transactions which affect the net wealth or debt position of the central government enter into the capital account.

cent of GDP during the first half of the 2010s.[21] Thus, the government borrowed more and more, as a percentage of GDP every year, to finance its consumption expenditure. Indeed, the proportion of total borrowing by the central government which was used to support its consumption expenditure rose from less than one-third during the second half of the 1980s, which was a period of fiscal profligacy, to more than one-half during the 1990s, which was supposedly a period of fiscal austerity, and almost three-fourths during the first half of the 2010s.[22] In an ideal world, there should be a revenue surplus large enough to finance capital expenditure on defence and on the social sectors where there are no tangible returns. This would ensure that borrowing is used only to finance investment expenditure which yields a future income flow to the exchequer. So long as the income flow is greater than the burden of servicing accumulated debt, government burden remains sustainable. The reality in India, despite fiscal adjustment, is just the opposite. The present fiscal regime which borrows to support consumption is simply not sustainable over time.

Second, it must be stressed that the size of the fiscal deficit or the amount of borrowing, are symptoms and not the disease. And there is nothing in macroeconomics which stipulates an optimum level to which the fiscal deficit must be reduced as a proportion of GDP. Indeed, it is possible that a fiscal deficit at 6 per cent of GDP is sustainable in one situation, while a fiscal deficit at 4 per cent of GDP is not sustainable in another situation. The real issue is the use to which government borrowing is put in relation to the cost of borrowing by the government. Thus, government borrowing is always sustainable if it is used to finance investment and if the rate of return on such investment is greater than the interest rate payable. However, the evidence available and simple macroeconomics suggest that fiscal adjustment in India cannot provide a sustainable solution to the fiscal crisis despite the reduction in the gross fiscal deficit of the central government as a proportion of GDP. For one, the cost of government borrowing rose significantly during the 1990s. This was so for two reasons. The government cut back sharply on its borrowing at low interest rates from the central bank. And, compared with the past, the government borrowed much larger amounts, at a significantly higher cost,

[21]For time-series data on the revenue deficit of the central government, as a percentage of GDP at market prices, see Reserve Bank of India, *Annual Report*, various issues. The averages, for the quinquenniums, as also the decade, have been calculated.

[22]The ratio of the revenue deficit to the gross fiscal deficit of the central government, as a percentage of GDP at market prices, measures the proportion of total government borrowing that was used to support its consumption expenditure. The proportions reported here are calculated, for the selected periods, from Reserve Bank of India, *Annual Reports*, various issues.

from the commercial banking system and the domestic capital market because interest rates on government securities were raised to market levels. For another, the use of government borrowing during the 1990s remained as unproductive as before. If anything, a much higher proportion of government borrowing was used to finance consumption expenditure which yields no return. At the same time, there is no evidence to suggest that there has been any increase in the productivity of public expenditure.

It needs to be said that the distinction between deficit financing of public consumption versus public investment is perhaps overdrawn. The reason is simple. The conventional accounting notion of public consumption includes expenditures on health and education which, if well executed, have a large investment component. Similarly, the conventional accounting notion of public investment includes expenditure on, say, luxury hotels, which seldom yields a rate of return sufficient to cover the cost of borrowing. Therefore, strictly speaking, deficit-financed public expenditure is justified so long as the social return from such expenditure is higher than the social cost of borrowing.

Yet, it is important to recognize the fallacies of deficit fetishism. The fetish about reducing the fiscal deficit, despite a burgeoning revenue deficit, or eliminating the monetized deficit, despite the much higher cost of borrowing, is entirely misplaced and this approach can only postpone the day of reckoning. And the fiscal situation is even less sustainable than it was earlier. Even if fiscal crises are more like treadmills than like timebombs, correction is imperative.

The second lesson which has not yet been learnt relates to the critical importance of infrastructure. It is obvious that the process of fiscal adjustment created a massive squeeze on public investment. The resource crunch was more acute for public investment in physical infrastructure. These cuts in public investment, particularly those for infrastructure, are bound to constrain the supply response of the economy in the medium-term and the long-run. The problem may be accentuated because available evidence in India suggests that public investment crowds in rather than crowds out in private investment. The government must, therefore, find the resources for stepping up public investment in physical infrastructure, especially power, transport, and communications. The withdrawal of the government from these sectors in keeping with the ideology of privatization and liberalization, is premature because sufficient private investment, whether domestic or foreign, is simply not forthcoming.

Similarly, the development of a social infrastructure which provides the poor with access to shelter, health care, clean water, or sanitation and ensures a steady increase in social consumption, is almost entirely dependent on the government. Yet, fiscal adjustment squeezed allocations for social sectors not only in the central government but also in the state governments, which were not immune from the consequences of macroeconomic reforms. Thus, as a proportion of GDP, government expenditure on social sectors for the Centre and the states, taken together, experienced a stagnation or decline during the 1990s.[23] But it is clear that in a country such as India, the social infrastructure for the majority of people would have to be financed by the government and the services rendered would have to be provided through institutions maintained by the government. Therefore, it is necessary to improve the performance of the government. But it is also necessary to ensure that it does not abdicate its responsibilities in the name of liberalization.

The third, and perhaps the most important, lesson that has not yet been learnt is about the role of the State in economic development. There is a complete swing of the pendulum in thinking. We appear to have moved from a widespread belief prevalent in the 1950s that the State could do nothing wrong to a gathering conviction, fashionable in the 1990s, that the State can do nothing right. These are, of course, caricatures of perceptions. Both market failure and government failure are facts of life. For neither markets nor governments are, or can ever be, perfect. Indeed, markets are invariably imperfect and governments are without exception fallible. The juxtaposition of government failure and market failure in an either or mode, or a judgment about which is worse, as if there is a choice to be made, is misleading because it creates a false debate. It is important to introduce correctives against both market failure and government failure. These failures are seldom absolute and a reasonable degree of correction is possible in either case. It is, of course, important to learn from mistakes but it is just as important to avoid over-correction in learning from mistakes. In India, as in Eastern Europe, perceptions have been so strongly influenced by the counterproductive role of State intervention in the past that the possibilities of a creative interaction between the State and the market are not quite recognized. Hence, there is no systematic attempt at redefining the economic role of the State in a market economy. Yet, such rethinking is essential.

The starting point for such rethinking is a simple hypothesis which rests on two basic propositions.[24] First, the State and the market are, in general,

---

[23]The implications and consequences of fiscal adjustment for government expenditure on social sectors are discussed by Guhan (1995) who considers the evidence on the central government and Prabhu (1996) who considers the evidence on the state governments.

[24]The logic of these propositions is set out in Bhaduri and Nayyar (1996) and Nayyar (1997).

complements rather than substitutes. Second, the relationship between the State and the market cannot be defined once-and-for-all in any dogmatic manner but must change over time in an adaptive manner. Indeed, these two institutions must adapt to each other, in co-operation rather than in confrontation, as circumstances change. These propositions explain the difference between success and failure in countries that are latecomers to development.

The next step is to redefine the role of the State *vis-à-vis* the market in a changed national and international context.[25] In the earlier stages of industrialization, State intervention creates the conditions for the development of industrial capitalism. It creates a physical infrastructure through government investment, which reduces the cost of inputs used by the private sector or increases the demand for goods produced by the private sector. It develops human resources through education, which raises private profitability as it lowers the private cost of training workers. It facilitates institutional change, through agrarian reforms, which increases productivity and incomes in the agricultural sector to foster industrialization through supply–demand linkages.

In the later stages of industrialization, it is not just the degree but also the nature of State intervention that must change. Such intervention may be functional, institutional, or strategic. Functional intervention by the State seeks to correct for market failures. Institutional intervention by the State seeks to govern the market, for markets are good servants but bad masters. It does so by setting the rules of the game for players in the market. In particular, it creates frameworks for regulating markets and creates institutions to monitor the functioning of markets. It is possible to cite many examples. Import liberalization needs supporting anti-dumping laws. Industrial deregulation requires corresponding anti-trust laws. Financial liberalization requires matching regulatory laws. Strategic State intervention, interlinked across activities or sectors, may seek to attain broader, long-term objectives of development. It is necessary to cite some examples. Exchange rate policy is not simply a tactical matter of getting-prices-right but may turn out to be a strategic matter if deliberately undervalued exchange rates, maintained over a period of time, provide an entry into the world market for differentiated manufactured goods. The structure of interest rates is not just about allowing market forces to determine the price of capital, but may be a strategic method of guiding the allocation of scarce investible resources. Restrictions on the use of foreign brand names is not so much an inward-looking attitude if it is

---

[25]The discussion that follows draws upon earlier work of the author. See Bhaduri and Nayyar (1996), Nayyar (1996 and 1997). See also Amsden (1989), Wade (1991), and Chang and Rowthorn (1995).

perceived as a strategic means of buying time to develop national brand names that become acceptable in world markets after a lag. In this manner, State intervention may constitute an integral part of any strategy of industrialization that endeavours to strengthen capabilities and develop institutions rather than rely on incentives or markets alone.[26] This is the most important lesson that emerges from the East Asian experience. Strategic intervention by the State, not only in the realm of industrial policy and technology policy but also in the sphere of trade policy, rather than a reliance on market forces alone, is a vital factor underlying efficiency and dynamism in industrialization and growth.[27]

Rethinking on this subject must recognize the complementarity between the State and the market. The relationship must be characterized by cooperation, not conflict. It must also evolve with time. Given that the entrepreneurial talents of the private sector and the capabilities of the State, as also the needs of economy and society, change over time, this relationship must be flexible and adaptive. The crux of the problem is to assess the costs of government failure and market failure at critical points of time, so as to minimize the cost to society. And those who never tire of emphasizing the costs of State intervention must also recognize the costs of State inaction at such critical points. In the present context, therefore, it is necessary to reformulate the questions about the economic role of the State. The real question is no longer about the size of the State (how big?) or the degree of State intervention (how much?). The question is now about the nature of State intervention (what sort?) and the quality of the performance of the State (how good?).

THE FORGOTTEN ESSENTIALS

The debate on economic reforms tends to focus on what is said or done but does not always consider what is not said or not done. In the process, some essentials are forgotten.

The restructuring of an economy over time has three dimensions: the management of demand, the management of incentives, and the development of capabilities and institutions.[28] The object of managing the demand is to influence the level and the composition of demand—hence output and employment—in the economy, mostly in the short-term. The object of designing incentives is to induce supply responses and coax productivity increases, mostly

---

[26]See Lall (1990), Stiglitz (1989), Killick (1990), and Shapiro and Taylor (1990).
[27]See Amsden (1989), Wade (1991), World Bank (1993), and Chang (1996).
[28]This hypothesis is developed in Nayyar (1996).

in the medium-term. The object of building capabilities at a micro-level and institutions at a meso-level is to create a milieu that imparts efficiency and dynamism to the growth process, mostly in the long-term.

Each of these dimensions of restructuring has a close correspondence with the respective time horizons. But it is not possible to separate demand, supply, and capabilities or institutions in this manner because there is an interdependence and an interaction which leads to spillovers. It would take too long to set up a complete matrix. Some examples would suffice. For instance, aggregate demand management in the short-term, which is part of a stabilization programme, may squeeze supply responses in the medium-term. Similarly, incentive management, say in the form of import liberalization, may impact on the level of demand in the short-term at a macro-level if it switches expenditure away from home-produced goods and may affect capabilities in the long-term if it enforces closures rather than efficiency at a micro-level. Or, State intervention meant to support the development of capabilities and institutions in the long-term, say strategic industrial policy, may affect incentive structures in the medium-term and aggregate demand in the short-term.

It would seem that economic liberalization in India, which is attempting to restructure the economy, is overwhelmingly concerned with the management of incentives and the supply side in a medium-term perspective. Some attention was paid to the management of demand in the short-term but this was limited to the quest for stabilization. There is no recognition yet that the development of capabilities and institutions has a long-term significance. This approach, evolved by the Bretton Woods institutions—which has been adopted in India and elsewhere—cannot make for success. The restructuring of incentives in isolation often has an adverse effect on demand in the short-term and capabilities in the long-term. The better alternative, which considers all three dimensions, should recognize possible contradictions so as to avoid them and should recognize potential complementarities so as to exploit them.[29]

It is clear that the debate on economic reforms does not pay sufficient attention to transition paths over time and to interactions across time horizons. But that is not all. There are four other manifestations of what is forgotten which deserve mention.

First, the debate on economic reforms does not make a clear distinction between means and ends. For example, it does not recognize that markets, as much as States, are institutions, which are means and it is development which

[29]For a detailed discussion, see Nayyar (1996).

is the end. What is more, there is a presumption that what is necessary is also sufficient. The management of incentives motivated by the objective of minimizing cost and maximizing efficiency at a micro-level, is based on a set of policies that are intended to increase competition between firms in the marketplace. Domestic competition is sought to be provided through deregulation in investment decisions, in the financial sector, and in labour markets. Foreign competition is sought to be provided through openness in trade, investment, and technology flows. It must, however, be recognized that policies may be necessary but not sufficient. For there is nothing automatic about competition. Policy regimes can allow things to happen but cannot cause things to happen. The creation of competitive markets that enforce efficiency may, in fact, require strategic intervention through industrial policy, trade policy, and financial policy just as it may need the creation of institutions.

Second, it is not quite recognized that economic growth is necessary but not sufficient to bring about a reduction in poverty. It cannot suffice to say that the outcomes of economic policies should be moderated by social policies. The dichotomy between economic and social policies is inadequate just as the dichotomy between economic and social development is inappropriate. In fact, no such distinction is made in industrialized countries. And the experience of the industrialized world suggests that there is a clear need for an integration, rather than separation, of economic and social policies. Thus, it is important to create institutional mechanisms that mediate between economic growth and social development.

Third, it is often forgotten that the well-being of humankind is the essence of development. Thus, distributional outcomes are important. So are employment and livelihoods. Structural reforms associated with economic liberalization have important implications for employment creation and income opportunities. For one, insofar as such reforms increase the average productivity of labour, through the use of capital-intensive or labour-saving technologies, or through a restructuring of firms, which increases efficiency, it reduces the contribution of any given rate of economic growth to employment growth. For another, insofar as trade liberalization enforces closures rather than efficiency at a micro-level, or switches domestic demand away from home-produced goods to foreign goods at a macro-level, it has an adverse effect on output, hence employment, which is magnified through the multiplier effect. This has important consequences in the medium-term. There is a contraction of employment in some sectors without a compensatory expansion of employment in other sectors. And, as employment elasticities of output decline, employment creation slows down. For any given level of employment, the globalization of prices without a globalization of incomes also threatens livelihoods.[30] The poor at the margin are the most vulnerable. But the non-rich are not immune. It is only natural that people see the world through the optic of their employment or livelihood. Thus, people do not judge economic liberalization in terms of what it does for economic growth or economic efficiency. The real litmus test for economic liberalization is whether or not it improves the living conditions or the daily lives of ordinary people. And, insofar as there are some winners and many losers, distributional outcomes in the sphere of economics shape electoral outcomes in the realm of politics.

Fourth, the fundamental importance of good governance is not quite recognized. Governance is largely about rules and institutions that regulate the public realm in civil society. A democratic system seeks to provide for equal participation of the rich and the poor, or of the strong and the weak, individuals as citizens in political processes. The basis for good governance, then, is a democratic political system that ensures representative and honest governments responsive to the needs of people. This involves more than simply free and fair elections. Good governance, where governments are accountable to citizens and people are centrestage in the process of development, is essential for creating capabilities, providing opportunities, and ensuring rights for the common man. Governance capabilities matter. Indeed, the quality of governance is an important determinant of success or failure with economic reforms. The most striking illustration of this proposition is provided by the wide diversity in economic performance across states in India, despite common policies, similar institutions, and the economic union. The moral of the story is not *less government* but *good governance*.

CONCLUSION

The experience of the past 25 years suggests that the strategy of economic development in India is characterized by both continuity and change. Yet, the changes in the early 1990s were systemic as compared with the earlier episodes of liberalization which were piecemeal. Indeed, the economic reforms which began life in the early 1990s constituted fundamental departures from the earlier strategy of development in India.

The conjuncture was an important underlying factor. The external debt crisis, juxtaposed with the uncertain political situation, allowed the reforms to be introduced, while the changed international context supported this

---

[30]The implications of the globalization of prices without a globalization of incomes are considered elsewhere by the author, see Nayyar (2000).

process. The oft-stated view that there was a political consensus on economic reforms, at the time, is not quite correct because such a consensus existed only among the rich, the literati, and the influential. It extended to most political leaders although not to the rank and file of most political parties. But it did not have an acceptance among ordinary people, most of whom were poor or silent and, thus, unheard. The political consensus has become broader and stronger with the passage of time. There is, of course, strong support from those who have derived benefits from the process. It is reinforced by a voice that borders on advocacy in the media. A growing enthusiasm for liberalization in consonance with the dominant ideology of our times, combined with the gathering momentum of globalization in the world outside, has also sustained the process. It is not clear, however, that economic reforms have found an acceptance among people at large. The ordinary people are silent. The poor do not have a voice. Yet, from time to time, people, who judge economic liberalization in terms of what it has done for their living conditions, question the apparent political consensus to exercise a strong influence at election time which shapes electoral outcomes.[31] It is important to remember that the people who are excluded by the economics of markets are included by the politics of democracy.[32]

It is just as important to recognize that economic reforms, which were introduced in India more than a decade ago, have been implemented and sustained. In this, India has met with more success than most developing countries and transitional economies. This success is, to a significant extent, attributable to institutional capacities and political democracy. Many institutional capacities existed at the time that the reforms were introduced. And the essential foundations were provided by the preceding four decades of economic development in India. The entrepreneurial abilities were created. A system of higher education was developed. The social institutions and the legal framework necessary for a market economy were in place. In this milieu, it was possible to create new institutional capacities with relative ease. Given the importance of initial conditions, it must be stressed that economic reforms

---

[31]It is plausible to argue, though impossible to prove, that the outcome of the mid-2004 elections in India was influenced by this factor. At the national level, the 'India Shining' campaign of the NDA government, was perhaps rejected by ordinary people who felt excluded from this world of prosperity. At the state level, in Andhra Pradesh, the incumbent government was trounced at the polls, perhaps because of the crisis in the rural hinterland of the state, even though the chief minister was much admired for economic reforms not only in India but also in the outside world.

[32]For an analysis of the interaction between the economics of markets and the politics of democracy, in independent India, see Nayyar (1998a).

in India turned out to be a success, in large part, because of the foundations laid in the preceding four decades. In this context, despite the differences, it is important to make a comparison with China, where economic reforms were introduced much earlier in 1978. Economic reforms in China, too, would not have succeeded without the preceding 30 years which laid the foundations and created the initial conditions. The politics of democracy was the other critical factor which sustained the process of economic reforms in India. There was room for dissent. And dissenting voices could be heard. Essential correctives could, therefore, be introduced through moderation and adaptation in the process of economic reforms. Most important, perhaps, political democracy provided the necessary checks and balances through a wide range of institutional mechanisms.

REFERENCES

Amsden, Alice (1989), *Asia's Next Giant: South Korea and Late Industrialization*, Oxford University Press, New York.

Amsden, A.H., J. Kochanowicz, and L. Taylor (1994), *The Market Meets Its Match: Restructuring the Economies of Eastern Europe*, Harvard University Press, Cambridge.

Bhaduri, Amit and Deepak Nayyar (1996), *The Intelligent Person's Guide to Liberalization*, Penguin Books, New Delhi.

Bhagwati, Jagdish (1993), *India in Transition*, Clarendon Press, Oxford.

Bhagwati, Jagdish and T.N. Srinivasan (1993), *Indian Economic Reforms*, Ministry of Finance, New Delhi, July.

Chang, Ha-Joon (1996), *The Political Economy of Industrial Policy*, Macmillan, London.

Chang, Ha-Joon and Robert Rowthorn (eds) (1995), *The Role of the State in Economic Change*, Clarendon Press, Oxford.

Cornia, G. Andrea, Richard Jolly, and Frances Stewart (1987), *Adjustment with a Human Face*, Clarendon Press, Oxford.

Dreze, Jean and Amartya Sen (1995), *India: Economic Development and Social Opportunity*, Oxford University Press, Oxford.

Government of India (1991a), *Statement on Industrial Policy*, Ministry of Industry, New Delhi, 24 July.

——— (1991b), *Statement on Trade Policy*, Ministry of Commerce, New Delhi, 13 August.

——— (1993), *Economic Reforms: Two Years After and the Task Ahead*, Ministry of Finance, New Delhi, June.

Guhan, S. (1995), 'Social Expenditures in the Union Budget: 1991–1996', *Economic and Political Weekly*, Vol. 30, Nos 18–19, pp.1095–101.

Jenkins, R. (1999), *Democratic Politics and Economic Reform in India*, Cambridge University Press, Cambridge.

Joshi, Vijay and I.M.D. Little (1994), *India: Macroeconomics and Political Economy*, World Bank and Oxford University Press, Washington, DC and New Delhi.

—— (1996), *India's Economic Reforms: 1991–2001*, Oxford University Press, Oxford.

Killick, Tony (1990), *A Reaction Too Far: Economic Theory and the Role of the State in Developing Countries*, Overseas Development Institute, London.

Lall, Sanjaya (1990), *Building Industrial Competitiveness in Developing Countries*, OECD Development Centre, Paris.

Lewis, John P. (1995), *India's Political Economy*, Oxford University Press, Oxford.

Nayyar, Deepak (1994), 'The Foreign Trade Sector, Planning and Industrialization in India', in T.J. Byres (ed.), *The State and Development Planning in India*, Oxford University Press, New Delhi.

—— (1996), *Economic Liberalization in India: Analytics, Experience and Lessons*, R.C. Dutt Lectures on Political Economy, Orient Longman, Calcutta.

—— (1997), 'Themes in Trade and Industrialization', in Deepak Nayyar (ed.), *Trade and Industrialization*, Oxford University Press, New Delhi.

—— (1998a), 'Economic Development and Political Democracy: Interaction of Economics and Politics in Independent India', *Economic and Political Weekly*, Vol. 33, No. 49, pp. 3121–31.

—— (1998b), 'Short-termism, Public Policies and Economic Development', *Economies et Societes*, Vol. 33, No.1, pp.107–18.

—— (2000), 'Globalization: What Does it Mean for Development?', in KS Jomo and S. Nagaraj (eds), *Globalization versus Development*, Palgrave, London.

—— (2001), 'Macroeconomic Reforms in India: Short-term Effects and Long-run Implications', in Wahiduddin Mahmud (ed.), *Adjustment and Beyond: The Reform Experience in South Asia*, Palgrave, London.

—— (2002), 'Capital Controls and the World Financial Authority: What Can We Learn from the Indian Experience?', in John Eatwell and Lance Taylor (eds), *International Capital Markets: Systems in Transition*, Oxford University Press, New York.

Ocampo, Jose Antonio (2004), 'Latin America's Growth and Equity Frustrations during Structural Reforms', *Journal of Economic Perspectives*, Vol. 18, No. 2, pp. 67–88.

Prabhu, K. Seeta (1996), 'The Impact of Structural Adjustment on Social Sector Expenditure: Evidence from Indian States', in C.H.H. Rao and H. Linneman (eds), *Economic Reforms and Poverty Alleviation in India*, Sage Publications, New Delhi.

Rangarajan, C. and A. Prasad (1999), 'Capital Account Liberalization and Controls: Lessons from the East Asian Crisis', *Money and Finance*, No. 9, pp. 13–45.

Reddy, Y. Venugopal (1999), 'Managing Capital Flows', *Reserve Bank of India Bulletin*, September, pp. 701–8.

Shapiro, Helen and Lance Taylor (1990), 'The State and Industrial Strategy', *World Development*, Vol. 18, No. 6, pp. 861–78.

Stiglitz, Joseph E. (1989), 'Economic Role of the State: Efficiency and Effectiveness', in A. Heertje (ed.), *The Economic Role of the State,* Basil Blackwell, Oxford.

Taylor, Lance (1988), *Varieties of Stabilization Experience: Towards Sensible Macroeconomics in the Third World,* Clarendon Press, Oxford.

Taylor, Lance (ed.) (1993), *The Rocky Road to Reform: Adjustment, Income Distribution and Growth in the Developing World,* The MIT Press, Cambridge.

Wade, Robert (1991), *Governing the Market,* Princeton University Press, Princeton.

Williamson, John (ed.) (1990), *Latin American Adjustment: How Much has Happened?,* Institute for International Economics, Washington, DC.

World Bank (1993), *The East Asian Miracle: Economic Growth and Policy,* World Bank, Washington, DC.

Chapter 14

ECONOMIC DEVELOPMENT
AND POLITICAL DEMOCRACY
*Interaction of Economics and Politics in Independent India**

INTRODUCTION

There is a vast literature on the theme of economic development in independent India. The literature on the subject of political democracy in India since independence is just as extensive. Both are rich in terms of range and depth. But they constitute two different worlds, divided into the disciplines of economics and political science. The intersections are few and far between. This essay makes a modest attempt to reflect on the interconnections. It situates the process of economic development in the wider context of political democracy to explore the interaction between economics and politics in India over 50 years beginning 1947. The first section sets out an analytical framework. It explains why markets and democracy provide no magic wand, to suggest that the real issue is the tension between the economics of markets and the politics of democracy. The problem, it argues, is compounded because markets exclude people, particularly the poor. The essay then divides the five decades into three phases. Any such periodization is obviously arbitrary but it serves an analytical purpose. The second section examines the first phase, 1947–66, in which the strategy of development was shaped by a political consensus and characterized by a long-term perspective. The spirit of nationalism meant that there was less need to manage conflict, but there was a conscious effort to accommodate the poor even if it was long on words and short on substance. The third section analyses the second phase, 1967–90, which witnessed a qualitative change in the interaction of economics and politics. Economic policies and economic development were strongly influenced by

*I am indebted to Amit Bhaduri, Arvind Das, Satish Jain, and Shrirang Shukla for helpful discussion on some of the ideas developed here. I would also like to thank Partha Chatterjee, Ashok Mitra, and Achin Vanaik for valuable comments on a preliminary draft. I am particularly grateful to Rajni Kothari and Arjun Sengupta for searching questions and constructive suggestions which persuaded me to think further about the subject.

the compulsions of political democracy. Those with a political voice made economic claims on the State. But the process of mediation and reconciliation had long-term economic and political consequences. The fourth section discusses the third phase, beginning 1991, characterized by an absence of consensus and a presence of short-termism, in which the economics of liberalization and the politics of empowerment seem to be moving the economy and the polity in opposite directions. The need for conflict resolution is greater than ever before. But the task has become more difficult. And, strangely enough, the effort is much less.

DEMOCRACY AND MARKETS

In this new millennium, *market economy* and *political democracy* are buzz words: not only in turbulent Eastern Europe attempting a transition to capitalism, but also across a wide spectrum of countries in the developing world from Latin America through Africa to Asia. This is partly a consequence of the collapse of planned economies and excessive or inappropriate State intervention in market economies. And it is partly attributable to a concern about authoritarian regimes, particularly in countries where there has been no improvement in living conditions of the common people, but even in countries where economic development has been impressive despite which there is no movement towards a democratic polity. Consequently, the mood of the moment is such that markets and democracy are perceived as both virtue and necessity. In this process, some countries are in search of new models of development, while others are attempting to adapt their erstwhile models of development. For the new orthodoxy believes that, insofar as democracy is about political freedom for individuals and markets are about economic freedom for individuals, the two together must serve the interests of the people. However, there is little basis for this inference either in theory or in practice.

For one, democracies function on the principle of majority rule or some variant thereof. This is clearly preferable to monarchies or oligarchies associated with the rule of an individual or of a few. But democracy can lead to the *tyranny of majorities*.[1] What is more, in countries characterized by social and economic inequalities that run deep, it is not clear how adult franchise alone can create political equality. We must not forget that universal suffrage is a twentieth century phenomenon even in Europe. Indeed, we would do well

---

[1] The principle that the will of the majority should always prevail in a democracy has been a matter of debate for a long time. John Stuart Mill, for example, argued that 'the government of the whole by a mere majority of the people', the principle of majority rule, is undemocratic. This was, then, developed into an argument for proportional representation (Mill 1859 and 1861).

to remember that it was property rights, rather than equality, which were at the foundation of liberalism. And, for a long time, it was property that endowed people with a right to vote so that access to political democracy was the privilege of a few and not the right of everyone.

For another, the proposition that markets create equal opportunities for all depends on the critical assumption that the initial distribution of property rights is equal. Thus, any defence of the market on the premise that it is good in terms of actual outcomes must rest on a defence of the initial distribution of property rights. The argument that markets protect the interests of individuals or minorities, which even democracies cannot, is limited,[2] for such individuals or minorities are not guaranteed access to the market as buyers if they have no incomes or sellers if they have nothing to sell. It is important to recognize that while democracy may be about the *tyranny of majorities,* markets are inevitably about the *tyranny of minorities.*[3]

In practice, we know that the combination of democracy and markets is neither necessary nor sufficient to bring about an improvement in the living conditions of the majority of the people in a society. Consider egalitarian development, which brings about material well-being of people together with some equality of economic opportunities. We have seen such egalitarian development in planned economies without political democracy, as in the erstwhile socialist countries of Eastern Europe, and in market economies without political democracy, as in some East Asian and South East Asian countries. In sharp contrast, markets and democracy together, where these institutions are not sufficiently developed and have not evolved over a long period of time, as in countries of Eastern Europe, have only produced chaos. The outcome is prosperity for a few and misery for the many. Clearly, there are no magic wands. Democracy and markets are both institutions. The outcome depends on how they are used.

The real issue, in my view, is somewhat different. The essence of the tension between the economics of markets and the politics of democracy must be recognized. In an economic democracy, people vote with their money in the

---

[2]The argument is that even when a minority group is treated with hostility by the majority (say a group of people with extremist political views who wish to produce a newspaper), the market system offers the minority significant protection (say buying newsprint and employing journalists). Friedman (1962) provides a historical example, when he suggests that Jewish people were able to survive the hostile environment in medieval Europe largely because they were engaged in commerce and trade. And the economic (self) interest of the population prevailed over religious discrimination.

[3]I owe this formulation to my colleague Satish Jain.

market place. But a political democracy works on the basis of one-person-one-vote. The distribution of votes, unlike the distribution of incomes or assets, is equal. One adult has one vote in politics, even though a rich man has more votes than a poor man, in terms of purchasing power, in the market. Governments are elected by the people. Even where they are not, the State needs legitimation from the people (most of whom are not rich or are poor). Markets, on the other hand, are driven by demand and not need. For this important reason, among others, successive generations of economic thinkers and social philosophers have stressed the role of the State in bringing the ideals of political democracy and economic democracy closer together. The State may or may not succeed in this task. It is clear, however, that in reconciling economic and political democracy, a sensible compromise must be reached between the economic directions which the market sets on the basis of purchasing power and the priorities which a political system sets on the basis of one-person-one-vote.[4]

This is easier said than done. Markets may, in fact, exclude a significant proportion of the people, particularly the poor, from the process of development. Joan Robinson once said: 'There is only one thing that is worse than being exploited by capitalists. And that is not being exploited by capitalists'. The same goes for participation in markets. For there is an *exclusion* in the process. Markets may exclude people as consumers or producers or both.

Markets exclude people as consumers or buyers if they do not have any incomes, or sufficient incomes, which can be translated into purchasing power. This exclusion is attributable to a lack of *entitlements*.[5] Such people are excluded from the consumption of goods and services which are sold in the market.

Markets exclude people as producers or sellers if they have neither *assets* nor *capabilities*.[6] People experience such exclusion if they do not have assets,

---

[4]For a discussion of this problem in the Indian context, see Bhaduri and Nayyar (1996). For a discussion of the complex relationship between democracy and development, with reference to theory and reality, see Bagchi (1995).

[5]This term was first used by Sen (1981) in his work on poverty and famines.

[6]In this paper, I use the word *capabilities* to characterize the mix of natural talents, skills acquired through training, learning from experience, and abilities or expertise based on education, embodied in a person, that enable him or her to use these (capabilities as a producer or a worker) for which there is not only a price but also a demand in the market. It follows that even persons with capabilities may be excluded from employment if there is no demand for their capabilities in the (labour) market. It is essential to note that the same word, *capabilities*, has been used in a very different sense by Amartya Sen, who argues that the well-being of a person depends on what the person succeeds in *doing* with the commodities (and their characteristics) at his command. For example: food can provide nutrition to a healthy person

physical or financial, which can be used (or sold) to yield an income in the form of rent, interest or profits. The prime example of this for the rural poor in the developing world is exclusion from land. Even those without assets could enter the market as producers or sellers, using their labour, if they have some capabilities. Such capabilities which are acquired through education, training, or experience are different from abilities which are endowed. But the distribution of capabilities may be just as unequal if not more so. It is these capabilities which can, in turn, yield an income in the form of wages. Hence, people without capabilities, the poor, who cannot find employment are excluded. It must be recognized that even people with capabilities may be excluded from employment if there is no demand for their capabilities in the (labour) market.

Markets exclude people both as consumers and producers or as buyers and sellers if they do not accept, or conform to, the *values* of a market system. The most obvious example of such exclusion is tribal populations or forest communities in market economies. The same can be said, perhaps, for pockets of pre-capitalist formations in what are essentially capitalist systems. Such exclusion may also take other forms. There may be people who are unable or unwilling to sell their assets: for instance, a person may be unable or unwilling to sell an ancestral house in the market. Or, there may be people who are unable or unwilling to sell their capabilities: for instance, a person may be unable or unwilling to charge fees as an astrologer or a musician because of a belief system that such talents cannot and should not be sold. In other words, people who are excluded because of their set of norms can find some kind of inclusion in the market once they accept a different set of norms. In general, the terms of such inclusion are such that it intensifies insecurity and exploitation at least for some time.

As a concept, exclusion may describe a situation or characterize a process.[7] In describing a situation, whether it refers to a point in time or to a permanent

---

but not to a person with a parasitic disease; or, a bicycle can provide transportation to an able-bodied person but not to a disabled person. Thus, for Sen (1985), *capabilities* characterize the combination of functionings a person can achieve, given his personal features (conversion of characteristics into functioning) and his command over commodities (entitlements).

[7]The term *exclusion* has become a part of the lexicon of economists recently, although it has been in the jargon of sociology and the vocabulary of politics in Europe for somewhat longer. The European Commission, for example, uses the phrase *social exclusion* to describe a situation, as also to focus on a process, which excludes individuals or groups from livelihoods and rights, thus depriving them of sources of well-being that have been assumed, if not taken for granted, in industrialized countries. The essential point is that economic stratification is

state, the concept of exclusion is much the same as the concept of poverty. The object is to identify the excluded and the poor, respectively. In characterizing a process, the concept of exclusion goes further to focus on how the operation of economic and social forces recreates or accentuates exclusion over time. This may be attributable to the logic of markets, which give to those who have and take away from those who have not, as the process of cumulative causation leads to market-driven virtuous and vicious circles. This may be the outcome of patterns of development where economic growth is uneven between regions and the distribution of its benefits is unequal between people, so that there is growing affluence for some combined with persistent poverty for many. This may be the consequence of strategies of development, as a similar economic performance in the aggregate could lead to egalitarian development in one situation, and growth which bypasses the majority of the people in another situation. It is clear that institutional arrangements which mediate between economic development on the one hand and social development on the other are critical. For these institutional mechanisms may accentuate exclusion or foster inclusion, just as they may limit the gains to an affluent minority or spread the gains to the poor majority. The initial distribution of assets and the subsequent distribution of incomes are important determinants of whether the vulnerable sections of the population are marginalized and excluded or are uplifted and included.

It is only to be expected that there is an interaction between exclusion from the market in the economic sphere and the non-economic dimensions of exclusion in the social, political, and cultural spheres. The social manifestations of exclusion can be powerful. This is best illustrated with an example where the underprivileged in society, such as the scheduled castes or the lower castes in India, are poor because they have little in the form of entitlements, assets, or capabilities. But even where they are better endowed in terms of these attributes, their exclusion from markets, particularly from the markets for land and labour in rural India, persists for social rather than economic reasons. At the same time, economic exclusion accentuates social exclusion. The marketization of economies has meant a roll-back of the State which has diluted social security provisions made available by governments, just as it has meant a weakening of the community and the extended family as institutions

---

inevitable in market economies and societies, which systematically integrate some and marginalize others to distribute the benefits of economic growth in ways which include some and exclude others. For an extensive discussion on social exclusion, ranging from conceptual issues through country studies to policy issues, see Rodgers et al. (1995).

which were safety nets provided by society. In the sphere of politics, an economic exclusion from livelihood often creates or accentuates a political exclusion from rights. Thus, for the poor in India, the right to vote may exist in principle but in practice it may be taken away by coercion or coaxed away by material incentives at the time of elections. Sometimes, the underprivileged or the poor are not allowed to vote. At other times, their votes may be cast by someone else. And, in some situations, their votes are purchased. This reality does not conform to the principle of one-person-one-vote. It also suggests that people do not vote with their money in the market place alone. Similarly, the very poor are vulnerable to exploitation and oppression because their civil rights or equality before the law exist in principle but are difficult to protect or preserve in practice. The reason is simple. They do not have the resources to claim or the power to assert their rights. Similarly, cultural exclusion such as that of immigrant groups, minority communities, or ethnic groups interacts with economic exclusion from the market. In all of this, there is an asymmetry that is worth noting. Economic exclusion exacerbates other forms of exclusion, but economic participation does not eliminate other forms of exclusion which have social, political, or cultural roots.

The preceding discussion may suggest that exclusion is bad and inclusion is good. But it is not meant to. It must be said that the nature of inclusion or exclusion matters. Inclusion is not always good. Coercive inclusion by markets, whether child labour, tribal populations, or immigrant workers can be exploitative. The employment of women as wage labour on terms inferior to those of men, or the employment of migrants from rural areas in the unorganized urban sector at wages lower than those of workers in the organized sector, provide other examples. The basic point is that inclusion which is coercive or on inferior terms is not desirable. For similar reasons, exclusion is not always bad. To those who do not accept the values of the market system, any voluntary exclusion from markets, on the part of individuals or groups, should be perfectly acceptable.

NATIONALISM AND DEVELOPMENT: 1947–66

The conception and the birth of political democracy in independent India was unique in its wider historical context. For democracy did not follow but preceded capitalist industrialization and development. What is more, democracy came to India neither as a response to an absolutist State nor as the realization of an individualist conception of society. In each of these attributes, it provided a sharp contrast with the experience elsewhere, particularly in Europe.[8] In fact, it was not even an obvious outcome of the nationalist movement. The struggle for independence was much more about autonomous space for the nation than about freedom for the individual. Indeed, the Gandhian notion of a just State was premised on the idea that the collective interest must take precedence over individual interests.[9] And the legacy of nationalism was such that the end of colonialism may have imparted a sense of pride and hope to the people, but independence meant freedom and sovereignty for the nation as a collective of people rather than for individuals who together made up the people. Yet, the Constitution adopted by independent India created a democratic republic and pledged to secure justice, liberty, equality, and fraternity for all its citizens. Universal adult franchise was provided at one stroke. The republicanism of the Western World was perhaps the role model. This was, in a sense, India invented.[10] A liberal democracy was constructed by an enlightened elite in accordance with its conception of a modern nation state. It was democracy from above provided to the people.[11] And not democracy from below claimed by the people. This is perhaps an oversimplified view. The reality was, obviously, more complex. For the nationalist movement meant a dialectical relationship between the provision from above and the claim from below. All the same, democracy in independent India was unique insofar as it introduced universal suffrage in a predominantly agrarian society with an inadequate crystallization of class forces. In this construct, the State was the essential mediator. It had to perform a critical role in reconciling the conflict between political democracy and economic democracy as also in mediating between economic development and social needs. Thus, if the logic of markets meant exclusion of a significant proportion of people, particularly the poor, it was necessary for the State to ensure inclusion of such people in the economic sphere.

In this milieu, the strategy of economic development was shaped by the colonial past and the nationalist present. For one, there was a conscious attempt to limit the degree of openness and of integration with the world economy, in pursuit of a more autonomous, if not self-reliant, development. For another, the State was assigned a strategic role in development because the market, by

[8]This argument is developed by Kaviraj (1995). See also, Bagchi (1995).

[9]Kaviraj (1995). For a perceptive analysis of the ideological forms and substance of Indian nationalism, see Chatterjee (1993).

[10]The phrase 'India Invented' is, in fact, the title of, as also an important theme in, a book by Das (1994).

[11]This view is articulated by Kaviraj (1995) as also Khilnani (1997).

itself, was not perceived as sufficient to meet the aspirations of a latecomer to industrialization. Both represented points of departure from the colonial era which was characterized by open economies and unregulated markets. But this approach also represented a consensus in thinking about the most appropriate strategy for industrialization. It was, in fact, the Development Consensus at the time.

The objectives were clear enough: to catch up with the industrialized world and to improve the living conditions of the people. So were the perceived constraints.[12] The scarcity of capital was seen as the fundamental constraint on growth but the low capacity to save limited the rate of capital accumulation, and even if savings could be raised there were structural constraints on transforming savings into investment. It was believed that the primacy of the market mechanism would lead to excess-consumption by the rich and under-investment in sectors critical for development. At the same time, it was assumed that agriculture was subject to diminishing returns whereas industrialization promised not only increasing returns but also productive employment for surplus labour from the rural sector. These perceptions shaped the contours of economic policies—the lead role of public investment, industrialization based on import substitution, the emphasis on the capital goods sector, industrial licensing to guide the allocation of investible resources in the private sector, or even the relative neglect of agriculture. And State intervention was meant to create the conditions for the development of industrial capitalism.[13] It did so. Large doses of public investment created a physical infrastructure and set up intermediate goods industries, which reduced the cost of inputs used by the private sector and increased the demand for goods produced by the private sector. Import substitution, implemented through protection, not only guaranteed existing markets for domestic capitalists but also ensured a future insofar as the excess demand attributable to import restrictions would continue to provide markets. This *modus operandi* of fostering industrialization, a State-led capitalism, was no different from State capitalism elsewhere in the world.[14]

At this juncture in independent India, industrialization was thought of as synonymous with development while it was presumed that national interest and the people's interest were the same. There was not only a consensus about the strategy of economic development that was adopted. There was also a

---

[12]For a discussion on how such structural constraints shaped the strategy of development, see Chakravarty (1987). See also, Bettelheim (1968).

[13]Nayyar (1978). See also, Gough and Sharma (1973).

[14]See Bettelheim (1968) and Kothari (1970).

political consensus on what was attempted. This was attributable in part to the legacy of nationalism which emphasized unity in diversity and in part to the nature of the Congress Party which represented a composite coalition of interests. It was not as if there was no conflict of economic interests. There was. And it was recognized. Some steps were debated but ruled out. It was decided, for example, not to expropriate foreign capitalists or local landlords. Similarly, even though economic inequalities posed a problem, a redistribution of assets was not seen as desirable because it would be detrimental to savings while a redistribution of incomes was not seen as feasible because India could only redistribute its poverty. Other steps were taken in a half-hearted manner. Land reform legislations were passed. However, these were either replete with loopholes or simply not implemented.[15] The abolition of absentee landlordism was a significant outcome.[16] But these reforms did not give land to the cultivators. Instead, they forced owners to turn into cultivators. Some steps were devised to address the exclusion of the poor and the exploited. The community development programme was introduced to create an infrastructure in rural India. A system of *panchayats* was created to facilitate institutional change at the village level. Social legislation, which introduced reservations in educational institutions and government employment for the scheduled castes and scheduled tribes, made for affirmative action.

The consensus of the time meant that there was less need for conflict resolution. Yet, there was a conscious attempt by the State to reconcile economic policies with the compulsions of the political process, to minimize the conflicts in the interaction of economics and politics. But this was possible only within limits. For the State was substantively an alliance of the industrial capitalist class, the land-owning class, and the educated elite.[17] There were, also, the people of India whose interests could not be set aside altogether, or forgotten, in a democracy. The solution was found in a politics of accomodation among the dominant economic and social classes, the rulers, on the one hand, and with the multitude of people, the ruled, on the other. The accomodation among the rulers was a complex process because there were conflicts and tensions, particularly between the rural oligarchy and the industrial bourgeoisie, which were resolved through mediation by the State in the form

[15]Frankel (1978).

[16]The origins, the nature, and the consequences of land reforms in India are discussed, at some length, by Joshi (1975).

[17]See Bardhan (1984) and Rudolph and Rudolph (1987). The complex but mutually profitable alliances of interest, combined with an interlocking system of patronage, which characterized the interaction of politics and economics in India were noted much earlier by Kothari (1970).

of mutually acceptable trade-offs in the economy or in the polity.[18] This was inevitably based on a sharing of the spoils. The accomodation of the poor, who were the ruled, however, was long on words and short on substance. The strategy of economic development was given a statist orientation, epitomized in the phrases 'commanding heights of the economy' and 'socialistic pattern of society'. The building of industrial capitalism was combined with the radical rhetoric of a political democracy as a means of reconciling economics and politics. It was no surprise, then, that the language of political discourse in this phase came to be strongly influenced by 'a virus of socialism without substance' across the ideological spectrum of political parties.[19]

All the same, it must be recognized that this strategy of development was characterized by a long-term perspective. In this phase, there was a vision, however imperfect, about the future of economy, polity, and society. In the economy, the object was to eradicate poverty of the people and put the country on the road to industrialization. In the polity, it was believed that democracy was an alternative to revolutionary class struggle in equalizing society. For political democracy would, ultimately, endow the poor with the strength to exert strong pressures on the ruling classes for moving towards economic democracy.[20] It is worth noting that this perception reversed the sequence observed elsewhere, as economic development mounted pressures on the ruling classes for moving towards political democracy. In the society, it was hoped that affirmative action would make caste wither away, secularism would dispense with religious identities, and modernization would reduce the significance of linguistic differences.

The reality, as it turned out, belied these expectations. Yet, at the beginning of this period, in the early 1950s, India was a role model. And the optimism extended beyond those who had a dream about India. For some, its mixed economy was an answer to the challenge posed by communism in China.

[18]Mitra (1977) put forward a perceptive and clear hypothesis. The exercise of political authority and State power in India represented an arrangement between the rural oligarchy on the one hand and the industrial bourgeoisie on the other. While the bourgeoisie controlled the industrial sector and dominated the working class, they also needed the rural oligarchy, which could deliver the votes from the countryside and help maintain them in power. This alliance of convenience survived on the basis of mutual trade-offs, for even though political interests often coincided, economic contradictions abounded.

[19]See Bagchi (1995, p. xxxv). Kaviraj (1995, p. 104) suggests that, at the time, political language did not provide any identification of social interests thereby 'creating a socialist night in which all parties were black'.

[20]Frankel (1978). For a discussion on politics in India during this phase, see Kothari (1970) and Morris-Jones (1971).

For others, its strategy represented a non-capitalist path to development. For yet others, who recognized the problems of industrial capitalism, India was on the road to their ideal of a social democracy and a welfare state. It is another matter that, towards the end of this period, by the mid-1960s, there was a drastic change in perceptions. India ceased to be a role model in the outside world.

DEVELOPMENT AND DEMOCRACY: 1967–90

The economic consequences and the political implications of the development process over the two decades that followed independence also surfaced at about the same time in India.

The economic reality that unfolded did not conform to the expectations and the promises. The benefits of economic growth accrued mostly to the rich, while the process of development largely bypassed the poor. Indeed, available evidence suggests that there was a sharp increase in the incidence of poverty during the 1960s as both the number of the poor and the proportion of the population below the poverty line registered a substantial rise.[21] This was in keeping with the logic of markets which excluded people without entitlements, assets, and capabilities. And, matters were brought to a head by the crisis in the economy in the mid-1960s. Successive droughts which necessitated large-scale imports of food from the United States under PL 480 created images of a 'basket-case'. The devaluation of the rupee, in June 1966, made a dent on autonomy in economic decisions as the government came under the influence of foreign donors. The industrial sector was caught in a persistent recession. Savings and investment rates dropped. Economic planning was suspended for an interregnum of three years.

The political scenario that emerged was characterized by two discernible changes. First, the ideology of nationalism had begun to wane. This was partly a consequence of the passage of time as the second generation came to the fore in the Congress Party. It was also related to the regionalization of politics that surfaced because the central leadership, after Nehru, was weaker. At the same time, politics in India witnessed the first revolts of the young, manifest in the Naxalite movement and the stirring among Dalits. Second, there was a slow but steady erosion of the political consensus. The heritage

[21]There is an extensive literature and an intensive debate on estimates of poverty in India. Much of it, however, suggests a substantial increase in the incidence of poverty during the 1960s. Nayyar, Rohini (1991), for example, estimates that, in rural India, the proportion of the population living below the poverty line (based on a norm of 2200 calories per day) increased from 34 per cent in 1960–1 to 57 per cent in 1970–1. The trend was not significantly different for urban India.

of nationalism began to fade from memories and the compulsions of political democracy came home to roost. It became clear that governments were elected by the people and the mandate to rule had to be renewed at election time. But winning elections depended on votes from the poor who constituted the vast majority of the people. The general elections of 1967 established that electoral outcomes could no longer be taken for granted and that the Congress Party could no longer assume the support of the people.[22]

The rise of the rich peasantry, sometimes described as capitalist farmers, provides a powerful illustration of the economic and political changes set in motion by the process of development.[23] Semi-feudal landowners lost their economic strength and social dominance in the countryside. This power was captured by a class of farmers who cultivated their land, reinvested their surpluses in agriculture, and engaged wage labour. It was this rich peasantry which captured the benefits of the land reform legislation, the community development programme, the *Panchayati Raj* system, and the network of cooperatives. As a new entrant, it began to place demands on the ruling political coalition. Unsatisfied by what the ruling elite was willing and able to do for it, this rich peasantry deserted the Congress Party to join or to create coalitions of opposition parties. It was this that led to the defeat of the Congress Party, in almost every North Indian state, in the general elections of 1967.

It must be said that 1967 represented a watershed in an evolving situation and a continuum of developments. In retrospect, however, it is possible to discern a qualitative change in the interaction of economics and politics in independent India which surfaced around that time. It is difficult to understand, let alone analyse, the complexities of the development process in India over the next two decades or so. For an understanding, it is perhaps necessary to distinguish between two periods in this phase: the first, from 1967 to 1980 and the second, from 1980 to 1990. Such periodization is, in a sense, arbitrary but serves an analytical purpose.

Co-option and Mediation: 1967–80

The crisis in the economy and the political setback to the Congress Party, at the very begining of the first period in this phase, led to rethinking in economics

[22]See Kaviraj (1995) and Vanaik (1990). The political consequence was a sharp erosion in the cohesion of the Congress Party as dissent and discord led to its split in 1969. It was, however, the decline of the Congress Party that explained the rise of Indira Gandhi and not the other way around (Vanaik 1990).

[23]There is a rich literature on the economic origins and the political consequences of the rise of the rich peasantry. See, for example, Mitra (1977), Brass (1980), Byres (1988), and Vanaik (1990).

and politics. There was a recognition of two realities. For one, the rich peasanty had emerged as a new force demanding its due share in benefits derived from economic policies and seeking an upward mobility in the political process. For another, the poor, who had not seen any improvement in their living conditions, did exercise their right to vote in a political democracy. The system responded in accordance with its perceptions of this reality. This response can be characterized as a politics of co-option.

In the sphere of economics, the response was two-fold. First, there was a strong, new emphasis on agriculture. The new strategy for agricultural development, which culminated in the Green Revolution, was motivated by the imperative of increasing the output of foodgrains. This quest for food security was driven, in part, by a concern that the nation could not continue its 'ship-to-mouth' existence and, in part, by a concern that if there was a shortage of food it was the poor who went without. The end shaped the means. The better endowed farmers and regions were provided extensive support to increase their marketable surplus of food. This came in a variety of forms: mostly as lower (subsidized) prices of inputs whether fertilizers, seeds, water, power, or credit, but also as higher prices of output through a system of procurement prices for producers and a manipulation of the inter-sectoral terms of trade in favour of agriculture.[24] Economic benefits of this regime of subsidies, explicit and implicit, accrued to the rich peasanty. It was not without political purpose. Second, poverty alleviation programmes began life in independent India, albeit on a modest scale. The Crash Scheme for Rural Employment, the Drought-prone Areas Programme, the Small Farmers Development Agency, and the Marginal Farmers and Agricultural Labourers Development Agency were among the first to be introduced. These were followed, some years later, by the Employment Guarantee Scheme in Maharashtra and the Food for Work Programme in other states. Most of these programmes sought to create employment for the poor while a few sought to provide them with assets for self-employment.[25] The poor were thus provided with entitlements or assets to combat their exclusion.

In the realm of politics, the response had three dimensions. First, there was a conscious effort to co-opt the rich peasantry into the ruling coalition and, wherever possible, the Congress Party. Second, the dissent and the regionalism in the Congress Party was met by a strategy of 'divide-and-rule', where one

[24]This argument is developed, at some length, by Mitra (1977), who argues that the steady increase in the relative prices of food and raw materials sold by the surplus farmers was a principal manifestation of the trade-off principle (referred to above). See also Frankel (1971).

[25]For a discussion on, and evaluation of, these poverty alleviation programmes, see Nayyar, Rohini (1991).

faction was pitted against another to be neutralized and then vanquished. Third, populist rhetoric was born in an endeavour to woo the people. The slogan of *garibi hatao*, even if it was mere words, captured the popular imagination. But the rehetoric went further to the nationalization of banks and the abolition of privy purses. It was these steps which gave Indira Gandhi, who dominated politics in this period through the democratic, populist, and authoritarian phases of her rule, a stranglehold on the political process.[26]

These responses led to some expected outcomes in the economy and some unexpected outcomes in the polity. In the economy, rapid growth in the agricultural sector ensured food security. A surge in savings and investment boosted growth. The balance of payments situation surmounted the oil shock. Industrial growth revived. In the polity, the rich peasanty returned to the fold, the Congress Party won a decisive mandate in the general elections of 1971, and Indira Gandhi consolidated her control over both the party and the government by reaching out directly to the people. As it turned out, the economic bliss and the political equilibrium did not last long. Crises in the economy led to agitations in the polity. An erosion of the political mandate strengthened the opposition both inside and outside the Congress Party. In response, Indira Gandhi sought to control and curb the political opposition, to establish herself as an undisputed leader in the mode of Caesar. The majoritarianism soon turned into an authoritarianism. But this was not consistent with the checks and balances needed in a political democracy. And, it was this, rather than an economic crisis, which led to the Emergency. However, the authoritarian regime did not last even two years.[27] Democracy reasserted itself. There were two reasons. For one, the suppression of dissent and opposition was ultimately not sustainable because political democracy was, by then, embedded in the system. For another, the mediation between the constituents of the ruling elite that sustained the coalition of class interests required an institutional mechanism which had, until then, been provided by political democracy. Thus, it needs to be said that the Janata government was the beneficiary rather than the cause of the return of democracy in India. In most respects, it was much like the Congress government before 1975. But, towards the end of its regime, the second oil shock and an inept management of the economy led to unprecedented inflation. The management of the polity was not even functional as the coalition failed to provide governance. The people were hurt by inflation and tired of squabbling among political leaders

---

[26]Kaviraj (1995). For a perceptive analysis of this phase of politics in India, see also Vanaik (1990) and Brass (1992).

[27]The factors underlying the imposition and the collapse of the Emergency are examined, among others, by Chatterjee (1997, pp. 58–66). See also, Vanaik (1990) and Kaviraj (1995).

of the Janata regime. And, in 1980, the electorate voted a largely unrepentant Indira Gandhi back to power.

Populism and Patronage: 1980–90

The next period in this phase, the 1980s, was in a sense more of the same but not quite. The compulsions of political democracy exercised an even stronger influence on economic policies and economic development. It turned out to be the age of populism in both economics and politics.

In the sphere of economics, this led to some important changes in policies. First, there was a proliferation of subsidies. Some, such as the subsidies on food, fertilizers, and exports, were explicit. These meant expenditure disbursed.[28] Others were implicit in under-priced services of public utilities such as irrigation, electricity, and road transport, or in under-priced goods produced in public sector such as steel and coal. These meant revenue foregone. There was something for everybody.[29] The rich peasantry, of course, continued to benefit from implicit and explicit subsidies. But the industrial capitalist class was not far behind. The public sector provided them with cheap inputs and carried the losses. The nationalized banks extended loans which turned into non-performing assets. And, in effect, *loan waivers* for big firms in the industrial sector quietly came into existence much before they were announced for small farmers in the agricultural sector. *Loan melas*, which began life then, were just a more explicit example of such directed lending as patronage. The government took over sick firms from the private sector which privatized the benefits and socialized the costs. Second, beyond these subsidies, there was a rapid increase in public consumption expenditure, which provided a sharp contrast with the expansion in public investment expenditure during the first phase.[30] Some of it supported an increase in social consumption and, thus, contributed to an inclusion of the poor. However, a lot of such public

[28]The explicit subsidies provided by the central government alone increased from 8.3 per cent of its total expenditure and the equivalent of 1.4 per cent of GDP in 1980–1 to 11.4 per cent of its total expenditure and the equivalent of 2.4 per cent of GDP in 1989–90 (*Economic and Functional Classification of the Central Government Budget*, annual issues). The corresponding proportions would be much larger if we could add the implicit subsidies and include the state governments.

[29]The situation in the early 1980s, which was just the beginning of this phase, is described by Bardhan (1984, p. 70) as follows: '... a patron–client regime fostered by a flabby and heterogeneous dominant coalition preoccupied in a spree of anarchical grabbing of public resources ...'.

[30]The total expenditure of the central government increased from 16 per cent of GDP in 1980–1 to 20 per cent of GDP in 1985–6 and stayed above that level through the second half of the 1980s. Much of this was attributable to the increase in consumption expenditure and transfer payments, as the share of gross capital formation in total expenditure dropped from more than 40 per cent in 1980–1 to about 33 per cent in 1989–90. See Nayyar (1996).

expenditure, particularly that on salaries of those employed in the government and in the public sector, supported increases in private consumption. All of it contributed to an increase in aggregate demand and, to the extent that supply constraints were not dominant, an increase in output. Third, there was a massive expansion in poverty alleviation programmes. The National Rural Employment Programme and the Rural Landless Employment Guarantee Programme were launched in 1980. The object was to create employment and provide incomes to the poor. These programmes were extended, modified, or renamed in subsequent years but remained the same in substance. The Integrated Rural Development Programme, on the other hand, attempted to provide assets or training to the poor as a sustainable source of income through self-employment. This was a systematic attempt at creating a safety net for the poor, who experienced exclusion, by providing them with entitlements, assets, or capabilities. It needs to be said that this effort at the inclusion of the poor was far more extensive and substantive than it had been in the 1970s. Yet, it must be recognized that economic development did not create social opportunities for people at large. There were transfer payments to sustain minimum levels of consumption. But the provision of basic education, health care, and social security was simply inadequate.[31]

In the realm of politics, there were two discernible changes. For one, electoral compulsions, which required the support of the people through their votes, unleashed a competitive politics of populism. Political parties and political leaders across-the-board sought to woo the people with sops. In this quest, no group with a political voice was left unsolicited or untouched. And there was not much difference between the Centre, where one party ruled for most of the time, and the states, where different parties ruled at different times. The number of promises made multiplied but the number of promises kept dwindled. For another, a State that was increasingly unable to mediate between conflicting interests and competing demands resorted more and more to a politics of patronage. This patronage, which came to be extended in a bewildering variety of ways, was a means of sharing the spoils among the constituents of the ruling elite.

These changes led to some visible, as also some invisible, economic and political consequences. The rate of growth of the economy during the 1980s was unprecedented. In real terms, national income increased at a rate of

---

[31]This is the theme of an excellent book by Dreze and Sen (1995). For a detailed discussion of the poverty alleviation programmes, during the 1980s, see Planning Commission (1985, pp. 49–63) and Planning Commission (1992, pp. 27–35). For an evaluation, see also, Nayyar, Rohini (1991).

more than 5 per cent per annum and per capita income increased at a rate of more than 3 per cent per annum. At the same time, there was a substantial reduction in the incidence of poverty. The proportion of the population living below the poverty line dropped from 51.3 per cent in 1977–8 to 38.9 per cent in 1987–8. And, even with the rapid growth in population, the number of the poor declined a little from 329 million in 1977–8 to 307 million in 1987–8.[32] In economics, this was attributable to rapid growth, moderate inflation, and the spread of anti-poverty programmes. In politics, this was attributable to the compulsions of democracy for, after a time, elections could no longer be won by slogans alone. But there was also the other side of the coin. The seeds of the fiscal crisis and the debt crisis were also sown during this period.[33] There were no obvious dividends in politics, except that this period represented a concerted attempt at reconciling the distribution of gains from economic growth with the context of political democracy. There was, however, a visible consequence in the political process.[34] The arena of conflict shifted from the rich versus the poor to the Centre versus the states. Dissent in democracy took the form of regional movements which turned to militancy and terrorism in Punjab, Assam, and Kashmir. There was also an invisible political consequence in the consolidation of the subaltern classes who recognized that their political identity made their right to vote that much more potent.

The Solution as a Problem

In retrospect, it is clear that in the second phase as a whole, from 1967 to 1990, conflicts of interests were that much sharper and the need for resolution that much greater. This was attributable partly to the eroding consensus and partly to the development process. It was also inevitable given the essential tension between the economics of markets and the politics of democracy. The exclusion of the poor by market had to be reconciled with the inclusion of the poor by democracy. There was, indeed, a conscious attempt by the State to reconcile the process of economic development with the compulsions of political democracy. That the mediation did not lead to a resolution is another matter.

---

[32]The evidence on the proportion and the number of the poor, cited in this paragraph, is from Planning Commission (1993).

[33]The origins of the fiscal crisis and the debt crisis are analysed elsewhere by the author (Nayyar 1996). See also, Bhaduri and Nayyar (1996).

[34]For different perspectives on political developments in India during the 1980s, see Kothari (1988), Kohli (1990), Vanaik (1990), Das (1994), Kaviraj (1995), Chatterjee (1997), and Khilnani (1997).

During the first period of this phase, from 1967 to1980, the intervention was purposive. There was an attempt to build new coalitions in terms of economic interests and sustain them through a consolidation of political power. This process was laced with a dose of electoral populism. But the economics remained within limits of prudence. The macro-management of the economy by the government was conservative. Inflation remained within limits of economic and political tolerance. The balance of payments situation was not allowed to get out of hand. It is not as if there were no hiccups. There were. But the system had the ability to cope with the shocks, whether the oil price increases in the economy or the Emergency in the polity. In other words, the economy and the polity both had a resilience.

The solutions, however, became a part of the problem. The management of the political process in this period had profound consequences with long-term implications. First, even though the government became stronger, the centralization of authority and power at the apex weakened the institutional base of the pyramid, so that the ability of the government to mediate between conflicting interests was much reduced.[35] Second, the same culture spread rapidly to institutions and structures in the political process so that there was no room for dissent or debate within political parties. In this situation, the choice was to stay but accept authority without question or to leave the mainstream and strike out on your own. Third, the politics of co-option meant inclusion for some but, at the same time, exclusion for others. This did lead to a *tyranny of majorities* which is always a possible danger in a democracy. It needs to be said that each of these changes in the political process was to have a lasting impact.

There was, also, an interaction between economics and politics which, slowly but surely, transformed the solution into a problem. It surfaced at the beginning of the first period in this phase, gathered momentum through the 1970s, and was established practice by the end of the second period in this phase. It was also to have a lasting impact, as the role of money extended beyond the economics of markets to exercise a profound influence on the politics of democracy. To begin with, votes were purchased at election time, not everywhere but in close contests or important constituencies. The practice spread. Those with money progressively acquired an advantage over those without money in the battle of the ballot. This created barriers to entry in politics, which are, by now, formidable. The process did not quite stop there. It was soon realized that, after elections, even legislators could be bought and sold. If the price was right, a legislator conveniently forgot the mandate on

[35]Kaviraj (1995) and Chatterjee (1997). See also Kohli (1990).

which he was elected and crossed over to support a programme, a party, or a government, in direct conflict with the interests of those who elected him in the first place. It did not take very long for such practices to spread from legislators to parliamentarians.

The consequences are no surprise and are observable in the reality of contemporary India. Election season is about mobilizing gigantic vote banks. This is often based on money power. There are, of course, vote banks mobilized on the basis of caste, religion, or ethnicity, but these can also be swayed in this or that direction, at critical moments, by the lure of money. Similarly, the scenario after elections, if there is no decisive mandate, is predictable as 'money-bags' descend upon state capitals, or even the national capital, to make or unmake coalition governments. It needs to be said that these attributes now almost characterize the political system in India. And, it should be clear that once profit maximization becomes an important motive for political acts or deeds, the conflict between the economics of markets and the politics of democracy is neither reconciled nor resolved. It is side-stepped or circumvented.

During the second period of this phase, from 1980 to 1990, the politics of co-option relied almost entirely on a politics of patronage. It was neither supported nor supplemented by an effective political mediation. The co-option during the first period of this phase, from 1967 to 1980, was based on an understanding, even if imperfect, of the interaction between economics and politics. It had a clear objective. The drift to an overwhelming reliance on patronage in the 1980s, however, simply represented a path of least resistance and a strategy of survival in State power. It was a means of buying time. This populist politics and cynical economics, taken together, translated into soft options, which had the most serious consequences for the economy. It was possible for the government and the country to live beyond its means, on borrowed money, for some time, but it was not possible to postpone the day of reckoning forever. The inevitable crunch did come at the end of this phase.

LIBERALIZATION AND EMPOWERMENT: BEGINNING 1991

The external debt crisis, which surfaced in early 1991, brought India close to default in meeting its international payments obligations. The balance of payments situation was almost unmanageable. The fear of an acceleration in the rate of inflation loomed large. The underlying fiscal crisis was acute. This juxtaposition was neither an accident nor a coincidence. It was a consequence of the cavalier macro-management of the economy during the 1980s. The balance of payments crisis was man-made and policy-induced. Export performance remained modest, remittances from migrants tapered off, and import substitution in the petroleum sector slowed down. The liberalization in the regime of trade policies and industrial policies created incentives for import-intensive industrialization. There was also a surge in defence imports. This was sustained by borrowing abroad which led to a continuous rise in external debt. The fiscal crisis was attributable to inadequate resource mobilization and a profligate increase in public expenditure. Direct taxes were progressively reduced while indirect taxes, which already contributed the bulk of tax revenues, could not be raised any further because such a step could be inflationary or regressive or both. At the same time, transfer payments on subsidies and government consumption expenditure proliferated, driven in part by the competitive politics of populism and in part by the cynical economics of soft options. Such a fiscal regime, which borrowed to support expenditure that did not yield any returns to the exchequer, was simply not sustainable for long.[36]

In response to the crisis situation, the government set in motion a process of macroeconomic stabilization combined with fiscal adjustment and structural reform. This strategy was nothing new. In conformity with orthodoxy of the IMF and the World Bank, it replicated broadly the response of several developing countries in Latin America and sub-Saharan Africa to the debt crisis in the 1980s. But it constituted a fundamental departure from the past in independent India.[37] First, economic growth combined with economic efficiency became the objective function. The object of bringing about a reduction in poverty and inequality was not set aside but such concerns about equity were subsumed in the pursuit of growth on the premise that it is both necessary and sufficient for an improvement in the living conditions of the people. Second, there was a conscious decision to substantively reduce the role of the State in the process of economic development and rely far more on the market. Public investment, seen as a catalyst if not a leader until then, it was argued, pre-empts scarce resources at the expense of private investment and leads to inefficient resource utilization which constitutes a drain on the exchequer. Third, the degree of openness of the economy was increased significantly and at a rapid pace. The object was not simply to enforce a cost-discipline on the supply side through international competition, but also to narrow the difference between domestic and world prices. Foreign

[36]The factors underlying the fiscal crisis and the debt crisis are analysed, at some length, in Nayyar (1996) and Bhaduri and Nayyar (1996). See also Joshi and Little (1994).

[37]Nayyar (1996). For an analysis and an evaluation of India's development experience, from the early 1950s to the late 1980s, see Byres (1994).

capital and foreign technology were assigned a lead role in the process. Every aspect of this quest for integration with the world economy provided a striking contrast with the Development Consensus that emerged soon after independence. In sum, India moved from a quest for State-led capitalism to a world of market-driven capitalism.

It is clear that economic liberalization in India began on a dramatic note with sudden and fundamental changes in the strategy of development. In the context of a democracy, it is essential to understand the political foundations of such economic change. There are two obvious questions which arise.[38] First, why did a relatively minor crisis in the economy evoke this response while decades of persistent poverty had so little impact? Second, how were such far-reaching changes introduced by what was then a minority government while predecessor governments with overwhelming majorities were unable to do so? These complex political questions seem to have a relatively simple economic answer. The change was dictated by the immediate economic compulsions of crisis management. The external debt crisis which erupted in 1991 meant that the fear of default hung as the Sword of Damocles. There was a sudden realization that governments can and do become insolvent even if countries do not go bankrupt. The problem was accentuated by a change in the international context at about the same time. The collapse of communism meant that competing ideologies gave way to a dominant ideology, while the collapse of the erstwhile USSR removed the countervailing force, an important prop for India in the past, from the international system. It is not as if there were no other underlying factors. The emerging concerns about efficiency and productivity—even if not about poverty and inequality— had led to a debate and some rethinking in India about the development strategy through the 1980s. This had permeated vaguely through the political system inasmuch as the manifesto of every political party for the 1991 elections, across the ideological spectrum, talked about the need for restructuring the economy. In sum, it was a combination of the reality in the national context and the conjuncture in the international context which provided the impetus for sudden change. But there can be no doubt that the response was driven, even dictated, by the crisis. It was not planned.

It would seem that 1991 was a watershed much more for the economy than for the polity. The economic liberalization introduced as a big bang was crisis-driven and not strategy-based. Yet, it was superimposed on a process of economic development and political democracy that had evolved in

[38]For a more detailed discussion on these questions, see Bhaduri and Nayyar (1996).

independent India over a period spanning four decades. It was, therefore, bound to influence the interaction of economics and politics.

Given the complexity of India's economic development experience, it would be idle to pretend that everything it did was right but it would be naive to suggest that everything it did was wrong. A discussion of this issue would mean too much of a digression. Suffice it to say that there were both successes and failures.[39] In a long-term perspective, the most important success was the significant step up in savings, investment, and growth, which provided a sharp contrast with the near-stagnation in the colonial era, particularly during the first half of the twentieth century. This was combined with the development of a diversified industrial sector, although the declining productivity of investment and the lack of international competitiveness emerged as problems that required a reformulation of policies and a restructuring of the economy. There was, also, a sustained expansion in the agricultural output which ensured food security, even if it did not lead to a significant reduction in absolute poverty. But there is the other side of the balance sheet. The most important failure, situated in a long-term perspective, was that this process of development did not improve the living conditions, or the quality of life, for the common people. Persistent poverty and absolute deprivation remained the reality for a large proportion of the population.[40] So much so that, after 50 years of freedom from colonial rule, India was unable to meet the basic needs of more than 300 million people who lived in poverty. And the poor do not even have enough food and clothing, let alone shelter, health care, and education. It needs to be said that, despite the significant reduction in the incidence of poverty during the 1980s, the number of the poor *circa* 1990 was larger than the total population of India at the time of independence. In retrospect, it is clear that the objectives of eradicating poverty of the people and placing the country on the path of sustained industrialization were not quite realized. Economic liberalization, however, is no panacea. It is limited in both conception and design.[41] At one level, it is concerned with the economic problems of the government such as the balance of payments situation, the rate of inflation, and the fiscal crisis. At another level, it is concerned with the efficiency of industrialization. But it is not concerned with the economic priorities of the people such as employment and poverty, agriculture and the rural sector, or physical and social infrastructure. Long-term development

[39]Nayyar (1996).

[40]For a lucid assessment and a perceptive analysis of India's failure to eliminate basic deprivation in the decades since independence, see Dreze and Sen (1995).

[41]For an articulation of this view and critical perspectives on liberalization, see Dreze and Sen (1995) and Bhaduri and Nayyar (1996).

objectives, such as education and human resource development or the acquisition of technological and managerial capabilities, are simply neglected. What is more, the reform process stresses the need to eliminate weaknesses or what went wrong but neglects the possibilities of building on strengths or what turned out right.[42] This, too, is a serious shortcoming.

The story of the evolution of political democracy in India, during this period, is as complex but somewhat more positive. The real achievement is that democracy has taken roots at the level of the people. There is a political consciousness among voters who judge political parties and their performance. It is also possible to discern an increasing, almost silent, participation in the political process, combined with an emerging mobilization on some issues. In this respect, the expectations of the founding fathers of the republic have been more than realized. For one, there is an absolute institutionalization of adult franchise which is irreversible. For another, democracy which was provided largely from above is now being claimed increasingly from below by the people. Taken together, these two attributes reflect an increasing empowerment of the people in the political process. In other respects, however, the expected did not happen. The polity did not transform society. Caste did not wither away. In fact, reservations ultimately led to a politicization of caste. Secularism did not dispense with religious identities. If anything, religion became an increasingly important factor in politics. The significance of linguistic or cultural differences did not diminish. It persisted as ethnic identities and regional movements became an important form of dissent in politics. If the main vocabulary of politics turned out to be caste and religion, or other forms of social identity, rather than class, democracy did, in a sense, bring politics to the people. The irony is that, although democracy struck roots among the people, it was not so embedded in political parties. Indeed, intra-party democracy diminished slowly but surely with the passage of time. Thus, dissent did not lead to debates or factions within parties. It led to splinters. In this world, politics in political parties became more and more personalized so that ideology was less and less a point of reference. The economic liberalization which was introduced in 1991 and gathered momentum thereafter, was simply not related to the institutional framework of political democracy. It was, therefore, neither shaped by political processes nor rooted in social formations, which could have provided constituencies in polity and society.

It is always difficult to analyse the present without the benefit of distance in time. It is, however, plausible to suggest that the 1990s witnessed an accentuation of conflict both in economic interests and in political interests.

---

[42]For further discussion, see Nayyar (1996).

The former is implicit while the latter is explicit. This is bound to make the interaction of economics and politics even more complex.

The retreat of the State, which is almost a corollary of economic liberalization, hurts the poor in a material sense. And India is no different. The soft options in fiscal adjustment lead to cuts in public expenditure in social sectors, as the resources allocated for poverty alleviation, health care, education, and welfare programmes decrease, or do not increase as much as they should, in real terms, so that there is a squeeze on social consumption. Cuts in subsidies are often at the expense of the poor. So are many of the increases in user charges for public utilities. The story does not end there as the State withdraws from investment in infrastructure. It is the poor who go without. But that is not all. Markets and globalization have a logic of their own, which leads to inclusion for some and exclusion for others or affluence for some and poverty for others. There are some winners. There are many losers. It is perhaps necessary to identify, in broad categories, the winners and the losers. If we think of people, asset-owners, profit-earners, rentiers, the educated, the mobile, and those with professional, managerial, or technical skills are the winners, whereas asset-less, wage-earners, debtors, the uneducated, the immobile, and the semi-skilled or the unskilled are the losers. Globalization has introduced a new dimension to the exclusion of people from consumption possibilities. Exclusion is no longer simply about the inability to satisfy the most basic human needs in terms of food, clothing, and shelter for large numbers of people. It is much more complicated. For the consumption patterns and the lifestyles of the rich associated with globalization have powerful demonstration effects. People everywhere, even the poor and the excluded, are exposed to these consumption possibility frontiers because the electronic media has spread the consumerist message far and wide. This creates expectations and aspirations. But the simple fact of life is that those who do not have incomes cannot buy goods and services in the market. Thus, when the paradise of consumerism is unrealizable or unattainable, which is the case for the common people, it only creates frustration or alienation.

This process is juxtaposed with a politics of segmentation arising out of conflicts in the political process. For one, religion has become a major factor in political mobilization, reflected primarily in the rise of the Bharatiya Janata Party. For another, caste identities are now crucial in political parties and the electoral process, reflected not only in Dalit mobilization by the Bahujan Samaj Party but also in the co-option of backward castes into most political parties sometimes referred to as the 'Mandalization' of politics. At the same time, the decline of national political parties is leading to a regionalization of politics, reflected in the fact that regional parties now rule a large proportion of the states in India. This politics of segmentation means that there is no dominant political party and no stable coalition. The reality is constantly shifting coalitions or unstable governments. Yet, there is a functional stability in political democracy because each of these segments has a stake in the system and aspires to a share in State power. It is not about empowerment alone. There are the material spoils of office, with or without corruption.

These tensions are compounded by conflicts between the sphere of economics and the realm of politics. People who are excluded by the economics of markets are included by the politics of democracy. Hence, inclusion and exclusion are asymmetrical in politics and economics. The distribution of capabilities is also uneven in the economic and political spheres. The rich dominate the economy now more than earlier, but the poor have a strong voice in the polity now more than earlier. And there is a mismatch.

It is, then, plausible to suggest that this latest phase in independent India is characterized by an intensification of conflict in the economy, in the polity, and in the interaction between economy and polity. There can be little doubt that the need for conflict resolution is much greater than ever before. But the task has become more difficult. And the effort is much less.

It is more difficult to mediate in the conflicts between economic development and political democracy for two reasons. First, there is no consensus. In the sphere of economics, the old consensus has broken down while a new consensus has not emerged. The oft-stated view that there is a political consensus on economic reforms in India is not quite correct because such a consensus exists only among the rich, the literati, and the influential. It extends to most political leaders, whose discourse on the economy has come to be strongly influenced by a 'virus of liberalization without understanding' although not to the rank and file of most political parties. But it does not have an acceptance at the level of the people, most of whom are poor or silent and thus unheard. In the realm of politics, too, the old consensus has turned into a new dissensus, as divisive issues such as caste, religion, language, and regionalism have multiplied. Second, a short-termism has replaced the long-term perspective of yesteryears. In the sphere of economics, the preoccupation with stabilization in the short-term and adjustment or reform in the medium-term, which is natural for the IMF and the World Bank respectively, leads to confusion between tactics and strategies or means and ends in the minds of governments. In the realm of politics, where governments are no longer sure about their tenure, a visible myopia has crept in. In this milieu, political parties and political leaders can think only about the next month or the next year or, at most, the next election. The next quinquennium or the next decade are simply irrelevant. Such short-termism leads to a neglect of long-term development objectives. There are two reasons for this. First, such objectives cannot be defined in terms of performance criteria in the sphere of economics laid down by the multilateral financial institutions. Second, such objectives do not bring tangible gains in the realm of politics which can be exploited by governments within one term as they seek to renew their mandate in the next election. This short-termism may also lead to 'hysteresis'—the effects of short-term policies or actions which persist over time to influence outcomes in the long-term—in both the economy and the polity.[43] The past influences the present, just as the present shapes the future, if economic policies or political actions have consequences which are irreversible after a time lag.

The effort to mediate in conflicts between economic development and political democracy is also much less. Curiously enough, the willingness and the ability of the State to mediate is not quite there. Its willingness to mediate is dampened by the use of money power to influence or to use the State apparatus for particular purposes. In most democracies, governments can be sectarian in their actions as they seek to protect or promote the interests of classes, or groups, whom they represent. The apparatus of governments is often used deliberately to promote the interests of the ruling elite. This does not surprise anyone. In India, however, the governmental system is increasingly being used to further, sometimes crudely and openly, the interests of powerful individuals through corruption and nepotism. In this milieu, people with money lobby hard and exercise influence in pursuit of their interests.[44] But people without

[43]The experience in independent India, beginning *circa* 1970, provides some powerful illustrations of such 'hysteresis' effects. In the polity, the centralization of authority and power at the apex, which began with Indira Gandhi in the early 1970s, weakened the institutional base of the pyramid, so that the ability of the State to mediate between conflicting interests was much reduced. We live with its consequences even now. In the economy, the populism of the 1980s translated into soft options where the solutions conceived for the short-run turned into problems in the longer-run. The fiscal cirsis and the debt crisis, which surfaced in early 1991, were the consequences. Similarly, it is possible that the economic liberalization of the 1990s, in particular the trade liberalization and the financial liberalization, may have an adverse effect on the performance of the economy in the long-term through 'hysteresis'. This argument about the long-term consequences of short-termism, in the context of public policies and economic development, is developed at some length in Nayyar (1998).

[44]In extreme situations, the State may be used almost as private property. There is some cumulative causation here. Politics is about the seizure of power. And, power is a source of gathering income and accumulating wealth which, in turn, facilitates the capture of political power. In this milieu, the political freedom provided by democracy is curbed by the uneven spread of money power, just as the economic freedom provided by the market is vitiated by the unequal distribution of income and wealth.

money do not have the voice or the resources to support their cause. Thus, the desire of the State to mediate surfaces only in election season. Its ability to mediate is constrained by the spread of markets and the march of globalization. This process is not only eroding the autonomy of the nation state in the international context, but is also creating a situation where the political process is losing control over the economy in the national context. The credibility of the State as an institution has eroded and the government, it appears, is abdicating its role in reconciling economic and political democracy.

In sum, the economics of liberalization and the politics of empowerment represent an unstable, if not volatile, mix. It would seem that these forces are moving the economy and the polity, for the first time in independent India, in opposite directions, without any concerted attempt at a reconciliation or a mediation. This is fraught with risk.

REFERENCES

Bagchi, Amiya K. (ed.) (1995), 'Introduction: Democracy and Development: Heritage, Aspirations and Reality', *Democracy and Development*, Macmillan, London.

Bardhan, Pranab (1984), *The Political Economy of Development in India*, Basil Blackwell, Oxford.

Bettelheim, Charles (1968), *India Independent*, Monthly Review Press, New York.

Bhaduri, Amit and Deepak Nayyar (1996), *The Intelligent Person's Guide to Liberalization*, Penguin Books, New Delhi.

Brass, Paul R. (1980), 'The Politicisation of the Peasantry in a North Indian State', *Journal of Peasant Studies*, Vol. 7, No. 4, pp. 395–426 and Vol. 8, No. 1, pp. 3–36.

_____ (1992), *The Politics of India since Independence*, Cambridge University Press, Cambridge.

Byres, Terence J. (1988), 'Charan Singh: 1902–1987: An Assessment', *Journal of Peasant Studies*, Vol. 15, No. 2, pp. 139–89.

_____ (ed.) (1994), *The State and Development Planning in India*, Oxford University Press, New Delhi.

Chakravarty, Sukhamoy (1987), *Development Planning: The Indian Experience*, Clarendon Press, Oxford.

Chatterjee, Partha (1993), *The Nation and its Fragments: Colonial and Post-colonial Histories*, Princeton University Press, Princeton.

_____ (1997), *A Possible India: Essays in Political Criticism*, Oxford University Press, New Delhi.

Das, Arvind N. (1994), *India Invented: A Nation in the Making*, Manohar, New Delhi.

Dreze, Jean and Amartya Sen (1995), *India: Economic Development and Social Opportunity*, Oxford University Press, New Delhi.

Frankel, Francine R. (1971), *India's Green Revolution: Economic Gains and Political Costs*, Princeton University Press, Princeton.

_____ (1978), *India's Political Economy: 1947–1977: The Gradual Revolution*, Princeton University Press, Princeton.

Friedman, Milton (1962), *Capitalism and Freedom*, University of Chicago Press, Chicago.

Gough, K. and H. Sharma (eds) (1973), *Imperialism and Revolution in South Asia*, Monthly Review Press, New York.

Joshi, P.C. (1975), *Land Reforms in India*, Allied Publishers, Bombay.

Joshi, Vijay and Ian Little (1994), *India: Macroeconomics and Political Economy: 1964–1991*, Oxford University Press, New Delhi.

Kaviraj, Sudipto (1995), 'Democracy and Development in India', in A.K. Bagchi (ed.), *Democracy and Development*, Macmillan, London.

Khilnani, Sunil (1997), *The Idea of India*, Hamish Hamilton, London.

Kohli, Atul (1990), *Democracy and Discontent: India's Growing Crisis of Governability*, Cambridge University Press, Cambridge.

Kothari, Rajni (1970), *Politics in India*, Little, Brown, Boston.

_____ (1988), *State Against Democracy*, Ajanta Books, New Delhi.

Mill, John Stuart (1859) *On Liberty* and (1861) *Considerations on Representative Government*, with an introduction by R.D. McCallum, Oxford University Press, Oxford, 1946.

Mitra, Ashok (1977), *Terms of Trade and Class Relations*, Frank Cass, London.

Morris-Jones, W.H. (1971), *The Government and Politics of India*, Hutchinson, London.

Nayyar, Deepak (1978), 'Industrial Development in India: Some Reflections on Growth and Stagnation', *Economic and Political Weekly*, Vol. 13, Nos 31–3, pp. 1265–78.

_____ (1996), *Economic Liberalization in India: Analytics, Experience and Lessons*, R.C. Dutt Lectures on Political Economy, Orient Longman, Calcutta.

_____ (1998), 'Short-termism, Public Policies and Economic Development', *Economies et Societies*, Vol. 32, No. 1, pp. 107–18.

Nayyar, Rohini (1991), *Rural Poverty in India: An Analysis of Inter-State Differences*, Oxford University Press, New Delhi.

Planning Commission (1985), *Seventh Five Year Plan*, Volume II, Government of India, New Delhi.

_____ (1992), *Eighth Five Year Plan*, Volume II, Government of India, New Delhi.

_____ (1993), *Report of the Expert Group on Estimation of Proportion and Number of Poor*, Government of India, New Delhi.

Rodgers, G., C. Gore, and J.B. Figueiredo (eds) (1995), *Social Exclusion: Rhetoric, Reality, Responses*, International Labour Organization, Geneva.

Rudolph, L.I. and S.H. Rudolph (1987), *In Pursuit of Lakshmi: The Political Economy of the Indian State*, University of Chicago Press, Chicago.

Sen, Amartya (1981), *Poverty and Famines: An Essay on Entitlement and Deprivation*, Clarendon Press, Oxford.

_____ (1985), *Commodities and Capabilities*, North-Holland, Amsterdam.

Vanaik, Achin (1990), *The Painful Transition: Bourgeois Democracy in India*, Verso, London.

Chapter 15

INDIA'S UNFINISHED JOURNEY
*Transforming Growth into Development**

T his essay is about independent India's unfinished journey in development. The destination, not yet reached, is the well-being of its people. The object is to assess the performance of the economy, since independence, situated in the wider context of polity and society. In doing so, the essay evaluates the past and contemplates the future to analyse the implications for economic development and social progress in India. The structure of the discussion is as follows. The first section outlines the dramatic changes in perceptions about the story of economic development in India, in retrospect and prospect, to set the stage before the play begins. The second section examines the turning points in India's economic performance during the twentieth century by situating it in historical perspective to provide a comparison with the colonial era. The third section provides an assessment of economic growth in India since independence, with reference to the past and compared with the performance of other countries, to suggest that it was respectable to begin with and impressive thereafter. The fourth section shows that India did not succeed in transforming this growth into development, for there was almost no improvement in the living conditions of a large number of people and a significant proportion of the population. The fifth section explores the opportunities and the challenges of bringing about this transformation in the future. The sixth section discusses some essentials that have been forgotten. The seventh section draws together some conclusions.

THE CONTEXT: RETROSPECT AND PROSPECT

The second half of the twentieth century witnessed remarkable swings of the pendulum in perceptions about economic development in independent India.

*This paper is based on the text of the author's Kingsley Martin Lecture at the University of Cambridge on 7 November 2005. I would like to thank Amit Bhaduri and Romila Thapar for helpful suggestions.

In the early 1950s, India was a path-setter, if not a role model. And the optimism extended beyond those who had a dream about India.[1] For some, its mixed economy was an answer to the challenge posed by communism in China. For others, its strategy represented a non-capitalist path to development. For yet others, who recognized the problems of industrial capitalism, India was on the road to their ideal of a social democracy and a welfare state. Just 25 years later, in the mid-1970s, perceptions were almost the polar opposite. India became an exemplar of everything gone wrong.[2] For some, the slow growth and the persistent poverty in the economy represented failure. For others, the inefficient industrialization was a disaster. For yet others, the political democracy was unaffordable if not unviable. Another 25 years later, in the early 2000s, there was a dramatic change in perceptions once again. The same India came to be seen as a star performer, if not a role model.[3] For some, rapid economic growth turned the lumbering elephant into a running tiger. For others, the impressive economic performance combined with strong institutions which have matured over time in a political democracy mean that India may be the next Asian giant competing with, if not displacing, China.[4] For yet others, India's economy is the latest poster child to demonstrate the virtues of markets and openness.

These are, of course, caricatures of perceptions. Even so, these do reflect the popular mood at each of the junctures in time. It would be natural to ask: what has changed? In part, the process of development has changed realities in India over five decades. But, in part, changes in thinking about development have shaped perceptions over time. And it needs to be said that perceptions have changed more than realities.

The present juncture, strongly influenced by the dominant ideology of our times, has not only shaped thinking about the future but has also reshaped thinking about the past. In caricature form, the orthodox story about the economy of independent India, half a century later, runs as follows. The era of planned development, which began life in 1950, was characterized by misguided, possibly counterproductive, economic policies. The strategy of industrialization, which protected domestic industries from foreign competition

---

[1]For a discussion on perceptions about India in the early 1950s, see Nayyar (1998).

[2]This strongly critical view of India is articulated by Lal (1998).

[3]Such optimism about India is more characteristic of international business and captured attention in the media following the study on BRICs by Goldman Sachs (Wilson and Purushothaman 2003). But it is beginning to find mention in the academic literature on the subject.

[4]See, for example, Khanna and Huang (2003).

and led to excessive State intervention, in the market, was responsible for high costs and low growth in the economy. The prime culprits were inward-looking policies, particularly in the sphere of trade, which stifled competition, and extraordinarily cumbersome licensing with controls on domestic economic activity that suffocated entrepreneurship and initiative in the private sector.[5] Some blame the first prime minister, Jawaharlal Nehru, who was strongly influenced by the colonial past and the socialist present, in this error of judgment. Others lay the blame at the door of post-colonial elites who were followers of Fabian socialists in Britain. And a few blame the political process in which mobilizing the poor through rhetoric was seen as more important than resolving their problems through growth.[6] In this world view, which almost ignores the significant achievements of that era, more than four decades were simply wasted. For them, the economic liberalization in the early 1990s, which reduced the role of the State to rely more on the market, dismantled controls to rely more on prices, cut back on the public sector to rely more on the private sector, and increased the degree of openness of the economy at a rapid pace, represented a new dawn. It is almost as if the economy began life in 1991. And the ideologues are convinced that the economic reforms of the early 1990s unleashed economic growth and led to the superb economic performance that is now much admired.[7]

This world view is also beginning to shape thinking about the future. It has led to many aspirations for India 2025. The incorrigible optimists hope for a developed India that has caught up with industrial societies. Political leaders aspire for recognition as a nuclear power in the P-5 club, membership of the Security Council in the United Nations, and a seat at the dinner table with the G-8. Their ultimate aspiration is India as a superpower in the world. The corporate elite hope for dynamic entrepreneurship, technological capabilities, and wealth creation. Their ultimate aspiration is India as a lead player in the global market with its own transnational firms. The pink pages of our newspapers and the electronic media have similar, even if somewhat more nuanced, hopes for India two decades hence. Such beliefs about India in the world stem primarily from aspirations about the economy in 2025: that it would become the third largest economy in the world in terms of

[5]Bhagwati and Desai (1970) developed this view in their elaborate critique of the industrialization experience in India.

[6]These perceptions, which border on rhetoric, are summed up nicely by De Long (2003).

[7]India's impressive economic performance is attributed to the economic reforms of the early 1990s by several economists. See, in particular, Ahluwalia (2002), Srinivasan and Tendulkar (2003), and Panagariya (2004).

national income at PPP; that it would become a middle-income country in terms of per capita income; and that poverty would be banished from the republic. And if China is the world's factory, India would be the world's office.

In my view, this belief system about the story of economic development in independent India is open to serious question for two reasons. First, it represents a misreading, if not a misinterpretation of the past. Second, it rests on oversimplified thinking about the future.

THE LONG TWENTIETH CENTURY

In seeking to establish turning points in the performance of the economy, or structural breaks in the pace of economic growth, most studies focus on the period since 1950. This is not quite appropriate. Indeed, any meaningful assessment of economic performance in independent India must situate it in a long-term historical perspective to provide at least some comparison with the colonial era. Therefore, it would be logical to consider the performance of the economy before and after independence during the twentieth century.

In this historical perspective, available evidence shows that the turning point came in the early 1950s. The trends in national income and per capita income, at constant prices, during the period from 1900–1 to 1946–7 are outlined in Figure 15.1. It reveals that during the first half of the twentieth century, there was a near-stagnation in per capita income while the growth in national income was minimal. The trends in GDP and GDP per capita, at constant prices, during the period 1950–1 to 2004–5 are outlined in Figure 15.2. The contrast is clear. There was a steady growth in both GDP and GDP per capita during the second half of the twentieth century. This is confirmed by Table 15.1 which sets out average annual rates of growth in national income and per capita income during each of the two periods. There are two sets of growth rates for the period 1900–1 to 1946–7 based on two different estimates of national income. The Sivasubramonian estimates suggest that, in real terms, the growth in national income was 1 per cent per annum whereas the growth in per capita income was 0.2 per cent per annum. The Maddison estimates suggest that the growth in national income was 0.8 per cent per annum whereas the growth in per capita income was almost negligible at 0.04 per cent per annum. The growth rates for the period from 1950–1 to 2004–5 provide a sharp contrast. In real terms, the growth in GDP was 4.2 per cent per annum while the growth in per capita income was 2.1 per cent per annum. The step-up in sectoral growth rates was just as substantial. The magnitude of the increase over the entire period is also revealing. Between

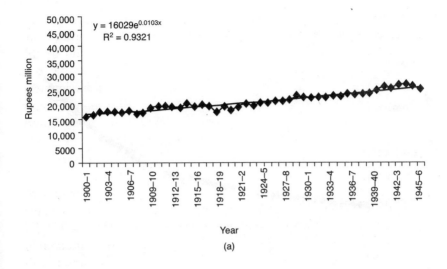

$y = 16029e^{0.0103x}$
$R^2 = 0.9321$

Year

(a)

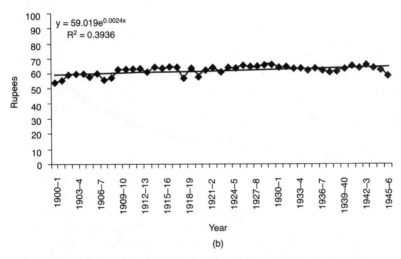

$y = 59.019e^{0.0024x}$
$R^2 = 0.3936$

Year

(b)

Figure 15.1(a): Trends in National Income, India, 1900–1 to 1946–7 (in rupees million at 1938–9 prices); (b): Trends in Per Capita Income, India, 1900–1 to 1946–7 (in rupees at 1938–9 prices)

Source: Sivasubramonian (2000).

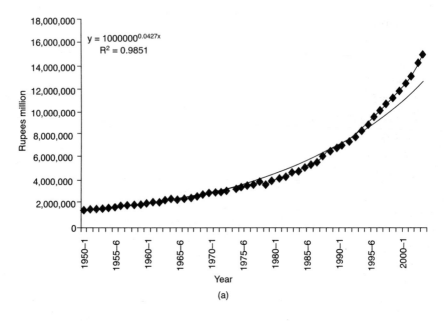

(a)

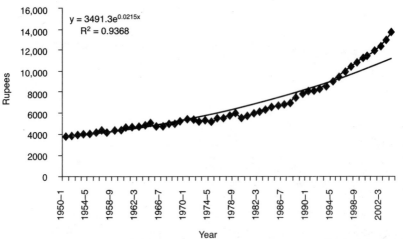

Figure 15.2(a): Trends in GDP, India, 1950–1 to 2004–5 (at factor cost in rupees million at 1993–4 prices); (b): Trends in GDP Per Capita, India, 1950–1 to 2004–5 (at factor cost in rupees at 1993–4 prices)

Source: CSO and EPW Research Foundation, *National Accounts Statistics of India*.

Table 15.1a: Rates of Economic Growth in India, 1900–1 to 1946–7

(per cent per annum)

| Sector | Estimates | |
	Sivasubramonian	Maddison
Primary Sector	0.4	0.8
Secondary Sector	1.7	1.1
Tertiary Sector	1.7	0.8
National Income	1.0	0.8
Per Capita Income	0.2	0.04

Table 15.1b: Rates of Economic Growth
in India, 1950–1 to 2004–5

(per cent per annum)

Sector	Rate of Growth
Primary Sector	2.5
Secondary Sector	5.3
Tertiary Sector	5.4
GDP Total	4.2
GDP per capita	2.1

Note: The average annual rates of growth, sectoral and aggregate, for the period 1950–1 to 2004–5, have been calculated by fitting a semi-log linear regression equation Ln Y = a + bt and estimating the values of b.
Sources: For 1900–1 to 1946–7, Sivasubramonian (2000) and Maddison (1985). For 1950–1 to 2004–5, CSO and EPW Research Foundation, *National Accounts Statistics of India*.

1900–1 and 1946–7, at constant 1938–9 prices, national income for undivided India increased from Rs 15.4 billion to Rs 24.9 billion by 60 per cent, whereas per capita income increased from Rs 54 to Rs 60 by a mere 11 per cent.[8] Between 1950–1 and 2004–5, at constant 1993–4 prices, GDP increased by 1000 per cent, while GDP per capita increased by 250 per cent.[9] For those who are not persuaded by the trends in graphs, the step-up in growth

[8]Sivasubramonian (2000, pp. 369–71).
[9]Between 1950–1 and 2004–5, GDP at factor cost in 1993–4 prices increased from Rs 1405 billion to Rs 15,294 billion while GDP per capita increased from Rs 3913 to Rs 14,018.

rates, or the proportionate increases in income, there is conclusive evidence provide by statistical analysis. There is a complete time series for national income aggregates, GDP at constant 1948–9 prices, for the entire period 1900–1 to 1999–2000. Econometric analysis based on this data set shows that the most important structural break, which is statistically the most significant, for the growth rate in national income is 1951–2.[10]

Interestingly enough, even if we focus on the performance of the economy in India since independence, it is clear that the turning point in economic growth is *circa* 1980, more than a decade before economic liberalization began in 1991.

Figure 15.3 outlines the trends in GDP and GDP per capita, at constant prices, in India during the period from 1950–1 to 2004–5. In doing so, it makes a distinction between two sub-periods 1950–1 to 1979–80 and 1980–1 to 2004–5. The break in the trend is clearly discernible in 1980–1 with a marked acceleration in economic growth thereafter. This is also borne out by Figure 15.4, which outlines trends in GDP and GDP per capita, at constant prices, during the period from 1980–1 to 2004–5. In doing so, it makes a distinction between two sub-periods: 1980–1 to 1990–1 and 1991–2 to 2004–5. The picture that emerges is clear enough. Almost the same trend continues, without any break, throughout the period. The evidence presented in Table 15.2, on average annual rates of growth in GDP and GDP per capita, for each of these sub-periods, provides further confirmation. During the period from 1950–1 to 1979–80, growth in GDP was 3.5 per cent per annum while growth in GDP per capita was 1.4 per cent per annum. During the period from 1980–1 to 2004–5, growth in GDP was 5.6 per cent per annum while growth in GDP per capita was 3.6 per cent per annum. The sharp step-up in growth rates, not only aggregate but also sectoral, suggests that 1980–1 was the turning point. This conclusion is reinforced by a comparison of growth rates, aggregate and sectoral, during the sub-periods 1980–1 to 1990–1 and

---

[10]See Hatekar and Dongre (2005). The authors situate the debate on structural breaks in India's economic growth in a longer-term perspective by considering the period from 1900–1 to 1999–2000. This exercise is based on the Sivasubramonian estimates of national income at 1948–9 prices. It needs to be said that the time-series before 1947, which relates to undivided India, is not strictly comparable with that after 1947, which relates to partitioned India. In addition, there are also some definitional differences in national income accounts for India before and after independence. Even so, the statistical analysis carried out by Hatekar and Dongre is based on plausible assumptions which minimize the problems of comparability and provide the basis for robust conclusions.

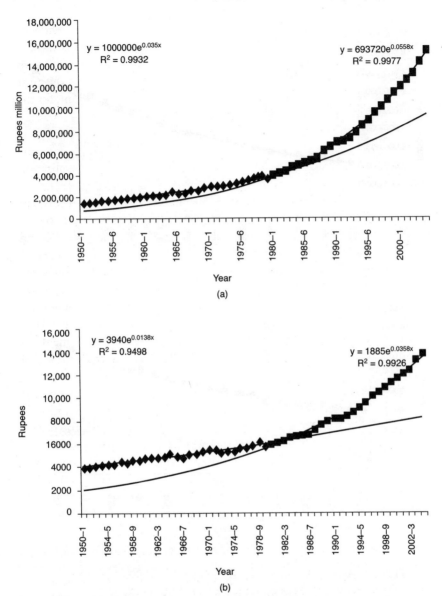

Figure 15.3: Two Phases of Economic Growth in India, 1950–1 to 1979–80 and 1980–1 to 2004–5 . (a): GDP (at factor cost in rupees million at 1993–4 prices); (b): GDP Per Capita (at factor cost in rupees at 1993–4 prices)

Source: CSO and EPW Research Foundation, *National Accounts Statistics of India*.

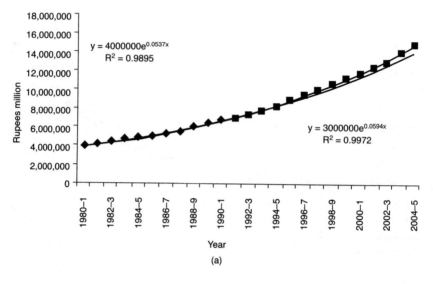

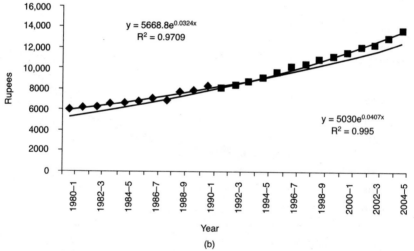

Figure 15.4(a): Trends in India's GDP, 1980–1 to 1990–1 and 1991–2 to 2004–5 (at factor cost in rupees million at 1993–4 prices); (b): Trends in India's GDP Per Capita, 1980–1 to 1990–1 and 1991–2 to 2004–5 (at factor cost in rupees at 1993–4 prices)

Notes: GDP at factor cost in rupees million at 1993–4 prices; GDP per capita at factor cost in rupees at 1993–4 prices.
Source: CSO, *National Accounts Statistics of India*.

Table 15.2: Sectoral and Aggregate Economic Growth
in India since Independence

(per cent per annum)

Sector/Period	1950–1 to 1979–80	1980–1 to 2004–5	1980–1 to 1990–1	1991–2 to 2004–5
Primary Sector	2.2	2.9	3.1	2.5
Secondary Sector	5.3	6.1	6.7	6.0
Tertiary Sector	4.5	7.1	6.6	7.8
GDP Total	3.5	5.6	5.4	5.9
GDP per capita	1.4	3.6	3.2	4.1

Notes: (a) This table is based on data for GDP at factor cost and at 1993–4 prices.
(b) The primary sector includes agriculture, forestry, and fishing. The secondary sector includes mining and quarrying, manufacturing, electricity, gas and water, and construction. The tertiary sector includes trade, hotels and restaurants, transport, storage and communication, financing, insurance, real estate, and business services, and community, social, and personal services.
(c) The average annual rates of growth, sectoral and aggregate, for each of the selected periods, have been calculated by fitting a semi-log linear regression equation $LnY = a + bt$ and estimating the values of b.
Source: CSO and EPW Research Foundation, National Accounts Statistics of India.

1991–2 to 2004–5. The growth rates were almost the same. In fact, during the period from 1991–2 to 2004–5, growth in the primary sector and the secondary sector was somewhat slower while growth in the tertiary sector was somewhat faster in comparison with the period from 1980–1 to 1990–1. Growth in GDP was 5.9 per cent per annum as compared with 5.4 per cent per annum, while growth in GDP per capita was 4.1 per cent per annum as compared with 3.2 per cent per annum. There was some acceleration in the rate of growth of GDP per capita which was largely attributable to the slow-down in population growth. For those not persuaded by trends in graphs or comparison of growth rates, statistical analysis should be conclusive. And there is now some literature on this subject.[11] Econometric analysis of time series data on GDP and GDP per capita for the period from the early 1950s to the early 2000s establishes that the structural break in economic

[11]Indeed, there are several papers that seek to establish structural breaks in economic growth in India since independence: De Long (2003), Wallack (2003), Rodrik and Subramanian (2004), Sinha and Tejani (2004), and Virmani (2004).

growth since independence, which is statistically the most significant, occurs around 1980.[12]

There are two conclusions that emerge from the available evidence and the preceding discussion. First, if we consider the twentieth century in its entirety, the turning point in economic performance, or the structural break in economic growth, is 1951–2. Second, if we consider India since independence, during the second half of the twentieth century, the turning point in economic performance, or structural break in economic growth, is 1980–1. In either case, 1991–2 is not a turning point. Therefore, it is simply not possible to attribute India's growth performance to economic liberalization even on a *post hoc ergo propter hoc* basis. It is also clear that the turning point in the early 1950s was much more significant than the structural break during the early 1980s. This proposition is validated by econometric analysis.[13] It is also worth noting that the proportionate change in growth rates, both aggregate and sectoral, was much larger *circa* 1950 than it was *circa* 1980.

It needs to be stressed that this turning point in the early 1950s was not just statistical, nor was it simply about growth rates. It was far more significant for the polity and economy of independent India in a substantive sense.

The conception and the birth of political democracy in independent India was unique in its wider historical context.[14] For democracy did not follow but preceded capitalist industrialization and development. What is more, democracy came to India neither as a response to an absolutist State nor as the realization of an individualist conception of society. In each of these attributes, it provided a sharp contrast with the experience elsewhere, particularly Europe. In fact, it was not even an obvious outcome of the nationalist movement. The struggle for independence was much more about autonomous space for the nation than about freedom for the individual. Indeed, the Gandhian notion of a just State was premised on the idea that the collective interest must take precedence over individual interests. Yet, the Constitution adopted by independent India created a democratic republic and pledged to secure justice, liberty, equality, and fraternity for all its citizens. Universal adult franchise was provided at one stroke. The republicanism of the Western world was perhaps the role model. This was, in a sense, India invented. A liberal democracy was constructed by an enlightened elite in accordance with its conception of a modern nation state. It was democracy from above provided

[12]See Wallack (2003) and Rodrik and Subramanian (2004). See also De Long (2003) and Sinha and Tejani (2004).

[13]Hatekar and Dongre (2005).

[14]For a more detailed discussion, see Nayyar (1998).

to the people. And not democracy from below claimed by the people. This is perhaps an oversimplified view. The reality was obviously more complex. For the nationalist movement meant a dialectical relationship between the provision from above and the claim from below. In this construct, the State was the essential mediator. It had to perform a critical role in reconciling the conflict between market economy and political economy as also mediating between economic development and social needs.

In this milieu, the strategy of economic development was shaped by the colonial past and the nationalist present. For one, there was a conscious attempt to limit the degree of openness and of integration with the world economy, in pursuit of a more autonomous path to development. For another, the State was assigned a strategic role in development because the market, by itself, was not perceived as sufficient to meet the aspirations of a latecomer to industrialization. Both represented points of departure from the colonial era which was characterized by open economies and unregulated markets. But this approach also represented a consensus in thinking about the most appropriate strategy for industrialization. It was, in fact, the Development Consensus of the times. The objectives were clear enough: to catch up with the industrialized world and to improve the living conditions of the people.

It should be obvious that the economic liberalization which began in the early 1990s did not match the significance of the changes in the realm of politics and the sphere of economics in the early 1950s. In fact, the changes that were introduced in the early 1990s were concerned with economic policies and did not even touch upon the political domain. In the wider context of the economy, the changes were significant.[15] And it is worth highlighting three dimensions of the changes. First, economic growth combined with economic efficiency became the explicit objective. The earlier concern about preventing a concentration of economic power or attempting a redistribution of wealth, never more than rhetoric, was explicitly abandoned. The objective of bringing about a reduction in poverty and inequality was not set aside but such concerns about equity were subsumed in the pursuit of growth on the premise that it is both necessary and sufficient for an improvement in the living conditions of people. Second, there was a conscious decision to substantively reduce the role of the State in the process of economic development and rely far more on the market. The government no longer sought to guide the allocation of scarce investible resources, whether directly through industrial licensing or indirectly through intervention in the financial sector, and left this role to

[15]This issue is discussed, at some length, in Nayyar (1996). See also Bhaduri and Nayyar (1996).

the market. Third, the degree of openness of the economy was increased significantly and at a rapid pace. The object was not simply to enforce a cost-discipline on the supply side through international competition, but also to narrow the difference between domestic and world prices. Foreign capital and foreign technology were expected to perform a strategic role in the process of integration with the world economy. These changes in policies did represent a radical departure from the past. But these were changes in economic policies. In contrast, the regime change during the early 1950s was wide-ranging and far-reaching. It was in part about policies but only in part. It was about establishing institutions, not only economic but also social and political. It was about creating the initial conditions for development in a country that was a latecomer to industrialization. It was about the pursuit of national development objectives in a long-term perspective.

PHASES OF GROWTH: AN ASSESSMENT

Growth matters because it is cumulative. If GDP growth, in real terms, is 3.5 per cent per annum income doubles over 20 years, if it is 5 per cent per annum income doubles over 14 years, if it is 7 per cent per annum income doubles over 10 years, and if it is 10 per cent per annum income doubles over seven years. Of course, the complexity of economic growth cannot be reduced to a simple arithmetic of compound growth rates, for there is nothing automatic about growth. In retrospect, however, the cumulative impact of growth on output is a fact.

There are two discernible phases of economic growth in India since independence: 1950 to 1980 and 1980 to 2005. It is worth providing an assessment of economic performance during these periods. An assessment of performance, in terms of economic growth, should address two questions. First, how does this performance compare with performance in the past? Second, how does this performance compare with the performance of other countries?

It is clear that the pace of economic growth during the period from 1950 to 1980 constituted a radical departure from the colonial past. For the period 1900 to 1947, there are two sets of growth rates based on alternative estimates of national income. If the economy had continued to grow at the rate based on the Sivasubramonian estimates, national income would have doubled in 70 years whereas per capita income would have doubled in 350 years. If the economy had continued to grow at the lower rate, based on the Maddison estimates, national income would have doubled in 87.5 years whereas per capita income would have doubled in 1750 years. The reality in independent India turned out to be different. The growth rates achieved during the period from 1950 to 1980 meant that GDP doubled in 20 years while GDP per capita would have doubled in 50 years. In fact, between 1950 and 1980, GDP multiplied by 2.86 while GDP per capita multiplied by 1.5.[16] The latter was not as modest as it seems because, during this phase, the rate of population growth was more than 2 per cent per annum.

Obviously, this growth was impressive with reference to the near-stagnation during the colonial era. It was also much better than the performance of the now industrialized countries at comparable stages of their development.[17] However, this growth was not enough to meet the needs of a country where the initial level of income was so low. For this reason, perhaps, it was described as the *Hindu rate of growth* by Raj Krishna. This phrase, which became larger than life with the passage of time, meant different things to different people. For some, it meant a performance that was disappointing but not bad. For others, it meant an acceptance of the performance in a spirit of contentment without an effort to change. Interestingly enough, the phrase which was used to describe a reality was used by a few to deride the same reality. But this was not warranted.

It has been shown that, during this period, India's performance in terms of economic growth was about the same as in most countries in the world.[18] It was certainly not as good as in East Asia. But it was definitely not as bad as that in Africa. It was average. In fact, the actual rate of growth of output per worker in India was very close to the average across the world. What is more, the rate of growth predicted for India, based on its initial output per worker, its share of investment in GDP, and its population growth rate, was also very close to the world's average.[19] Is it possible to reconcile this conclusion with the view that India did badly in this era? There are two possible explanations: either that inefficiencies of the regime in India were paralleled by similar shortcomings in most countries of the world, or that without its misguided policies India would have experienced a miracle in growth.[20] Neither of these explanations is plausible. It would seem that the story that depicts an

[16]Between 1950–1 and 1980–1, GDP at factor cost in 1993–4 prices increased from Rs 1405 billion to Rs 4011 billion while GDP per capita increased from Rs 3913 to Rs 5908.

[17]See Bairoch (1993) and Maddison (1995). See also Chang (2002).

[18]For a lucid analysis of, with evidence on, this proposition, see De Long (2003).

[19]This is established by De Long (2003).

[20]These two possible explanations are suggested by De Long (2003), who also puts forward a third explanation which is somewhat more plausible. It suggests that if there was a failure of economic policies it was in large part offset by the success at mobilizing resources which raised levels of saving and investment in the economy. In other words, even if resource-allocation or resource-utilization constrained growth, resource-mobilization fostered growth. This macroeconomic perspective, somewhat different from the orthodox view, is developed elsewhere by the author (Nayyar 1994 and 1997).

average India is much more plausible than the caricature which portrays a failed India.

It is clear that there was a sharp acceleration in the rate of growth *circa* 1980. It went almost unnoticed but for a few of us. And India grew almost by stealth. It came into the limelight in the early 2000s. Some analysts, as also many casual observers, attributed this performance to economic liberalization which began in the early 1990s.[21] However, discerning scholars recognized the reality that the structural break, which was a second turning point in the economic performance of independent India, occurred around 1980.[22]

In comparison with the preceding 30 years, there was a distinct step-up in rates of growth for GDP and GDP per capita. The growth rates achieved on an average, during the period from 1980 to 2005, meant that GDP doubled in 12.5 years where GDP per capita doubled in 20 years. In fact, between 1980–1 and 2004–5, GDP multiplied by 3.81 while GDP per capita multiplied by 2.37.[23] This growth was impressive, not only in comparison with the past in India but also in comparison with the performance of most countries in the world. Indeed, in terms of growth, India performed much better than the industrialized countries which experienced a slowdown in growth, the transition economies which did badly, and much of the developing world. And it was only East Asia, particularly China, which performed better.

There is an emerging literature on the subject which seeks to analyse this rapid economic growth in India that has been sustained for 25 years. Interestingly enough, the search for explanations is competitive. And some hypotheses are driven by an ideological world view. It would be impossible to provide an exhaustive analysis. It would also mean too much of a digression. Nevertheless, some explanations deserve mention.

The earliest explanation suggested that the expansion of aggregate demand, mostly through a rapid increase in public expenditure on investment and consumption, was the major factor underlying rapid economic growth during the 1980s.[24] This is widely accepted. Even so, orthodoxy argues that this growth supported by the expansionary macroeconomic policies was not sustainable and culminated in the crisis of 1991.[25] But this view is not quite correct. Insofar

[21]See, for example, Ahluwalia (2002) and Srinivasan and Tendulkar (2003).

[22]See, in particular, De Long (2003) and Rodrik and Subramanian (2004), who highlighted the fact that the structural break in economic growth in India since independence occurred around 1980 and not in 1991.

[23]Between 1980–1 and 2004–5, GDP at factor cost in 1993–4 prices increased from Rs 4011 billion to Rs 15,294 billion while GDP per capita increased from Rs 5908 to Rs 14,018.

[24]See Nayyar (1994) and Joshi and Little (1994).

[25]Ahluwalia (2002), Srinivasan and Tendulkar (2003), and Panagariya (2004).

as the increase in fiscal deficits did not translate into a corresponding increase in current account deficits, the increase in aggregate demand would, in the presence of excess capacity and unemployment, have led to an increase in output. Such an increase in capacity utilization would have also raised the productivity of investment which is reflected in significant productivity growth during the 1980s.[26] And even if the macroeconomic crisis of 1991 was induced in large part by the fiscal imbalances, the expansion in aggregate demand does provide a plausible expansion for the rapid growth during the 1980s.

The most fashionable explanation, advocated by orthodoxy, is that the rapid economic growth in India is largely attributable to economic reforms. There is, however, a fly in the ointment. The turning point in growth was 1980, whereas economic liberalization began in 1991. Confronted with this reality, orthodoxy relies on two explanations. First, it argues that the economic growth of the 1980s was not sustainable.[27] But there was growth. Second, it argues that the growth could have been unleashed by the mild doses of industrial deregulation and trade liberalization.[28] But this process started only in the mid-1980s. Therefore, such hypotheses which seek to explain the step-up in economic growth entirely in terms of economic reforms are simply not plausible.

There is yet another explanation.[29] It argues that there was an attitudinal change on the part of government in the early 1980s, which signalled a shift in favour of the private sector although this was not quite reflected in actual policy changes. The limited policy changes that were introduced were pro-business rather than pro-competition or pro-market so that the benefit accrued to existing players rather than to new entrants. Even these small changes elicited a large productivity response because India was far away from its production possibility frontier. And existing manufacturing capacities established earlier performed a critical role in shaping responses. This explanation is both interesting and perceptive, although it is somewhat far-fetched. And there are some obvious questions that arise. Why did the change in attitudes alone spur growth starting 1980 even though the mild policy changes were introduced

[26]Rodrik and Subramanian (2004) develop this argument to question the orthodox view, but conclude that the increase in capacity utilization was not enough to explain the actual productivity increase in the period since 1980.

[27]See Ahluwalia (2002) and Srinivasan and Tendulkar (2003).

[28]See Panagariya (2004). Joshi and Little (1994), on the other hand, believe that these changes were more than trivial but were piecemeal and limited. Hence they do not attribute rapid growth to this mild dose of reforms. It is also worth noting that Rodrik and Subramanian (2004) do not accept this as a possible explanation for the step-up in growth during the 1980s.

[29]This is the main hypothesis put forward by Rodrik and Subramanian (2004), who argue that none of the other explanations are plausible or convincing.

in the mid-1980s? Why did the economic liberalization of the early 1990s not produce a similar response in terms of productivity increase and output growth because, even in 1991, India was somewhere inside its production possibility frontier?

In my judgment, the search for a single explanation which seeks to exclude, or to deny, competing explanations is futile. There is, perhaps, a bit of truth in every nook. Hence, a convincing explanation must recognize that the acceleration in economic growth, *circa* 1980, was attributable to several factors. First, expansionary macroeconomic policies which led to an increase in aggregate demand did stimulate an increase in the rate of growth of output.[30] Second, beginning in the late 1970s, there was a significant increase in the investment–GDP ratio which was sustained through the 1980s.[31] Unless there was a decline in the productivity of investment, which was not the case, this would also have contributed to the step-up in economic growth during the 1980s. Third, starting in the late 1970s, there was also a significant increase in public investment which was sustained through the 1980s.[32] Obviously, this contributed to the increase in aggregate demand. However, insofar as such public investment created new infrastructure or improved existing infrastructure, it could have stimulated growth in output by alleviating supply constraints. Fourth, trade liberalization beginning in the late 1970s, combined with some deregulation in industrial policies introduced in the early 1980s, also probably contributed to productivity increase and economic growth.[33] In particular, liberalization

[30]In fact, this proposition is accepted by Ahluwalia (2002, p. 67), as also Srinivasan and Tendulkar (2003, p. 9), even if they argue that the growth was not sustainable.

[31]Gross capital formation as a proportion of GDP at current prices rose from 18.7 per cent in 1980–1 to 24.1 per cent in 1990–1. Adjusted for errors and omissions, this proportion rose from 20.3 per cent in 1980–1 to 26.3 per cent in 1990–1. See *National Accounts Statistics of India 1950–51 to 2002–03*, EPW Research Foundation, Mumbai, 2004.

[32]Gross capital formation in the public sector as a proportion of GDP at current prices rose from an average level of 7.7 per cent during the period 1971–2 to 1975–6, to 9.1 per cent during 1976–7 to 1980–1 and 10.3 per cent during 1981–2 to 1985–6. This average level was 9.8 per cent during the period 1986–7 to 1990–1. See *National Accounts Statistics of India, 1950–51 to 2002–03*, EPW Research Foundation, Mumbai, 2004. If the effects of public investment, particularly in infrastructure, are lagged, by say five years, the surge in public investment does provide an important part of the explanation for economic growth in India during the 1980s. Statistical analysis by Rodrik and Subramanian (2004) confirms this proposition, who argue that the contribution of public investment to economic growth would have been small if there were no time lags in its effects.

[33]The Rodrik and Subramanian (2004) hypothesis, which is an interesting variation around this theme, could, perhaps, constitute a part of the explanation. The problem is their claim that it is the only possible explanation. Similarly, the Panagariya (2004) conclusion

of the regime for the import of capital goods and broad-banding which reduced industrial licensing, could have played a contributory role.

It is also misleading, perhaps, to search for explanations which focus on observed changes *circa* 1980 that might explain the turning point in economic growth. Insofar as outcomes are shaped by initial conditions, the cumulative impact of economic policies or public actions over the preceding 30 years possibly played an important role in the turnaround.[34] Institutional capacities were created. The social institutions and the legal framework for a market economy were put in place. A system of higher education was developed. Entrepreneurial talents and managerial capabilities were fostered. Science and technology was accorded a priority. The capital goods sector was established. Much of this did not exist in colonial India. But it was in place by 1980 and probably provided the essential foundations. In other words, the second turning point in the economic performance of independent India may not have been possible starting from scratch.

This wonderful story about economic growth in India is not quite a fairy tale. And everybody does not live happily hereafter. Both phases of economic growth had something in common. It is essential to recognize that economic growth in independent India, respectable in the first phase and impressive in the second phase, was not transformed into development.

THE FAILURE IN THE PAST

There is a vast literature on economic development which is rich in terms of range and depth. Yet, there is not enough clarity about the meaning of development. There are many different views. And perceptions have changed over time. In the early 1950s, conventional thinking identified development with growth in national income or income per capita. The earlier literature emphasized economic growth and capital accumulation at a macro level. The contemporary literature emphasizes economic efficiency and productivity increases at a micro level. Industrialization has always been seen as an essential

---

could provide a part of the explanation but his claim in terms of cause and effect is exaggerated. The difficulty is that the step-up in economic growth occurred about five years before the much cited economic reforms of the mid-1980s. But there were some earlier piecemeal changes in trade policies and industrial policies, such as the liberalization in the regime for the import of capital goods, which could also have contributed to growth, in conjunction with the other factors outlined in this paragraph. In fact, Sinha and Tejani (2004) suggest that imported capital goods probably contributed to increases in the productivity of labour, hence economic growth, during the 1980s.

[34]For a discussion, see Nayyar (2004).

attribute of development. The emphasis has simply shifted from the pace of industrialization to the efficiency of industrialization. From time to time, dissenting voices questioned conventional wisdom to suggest other indicators of development, but these were largely ignored by mainstream economics. And, even 50 years later, economic growth, or increases in per capita income remain the most important measure of development.

The early 1970s witnessed the emergence of a literature that suggested other indicators of development such as a reduction in poverty, inequality, and unemployment, which would capture changes in the quality of life.[35] This thinking moved further. Development, it was argued, must bring about an improvement in the living conditions of people. It should, therefore, ensure the provision of basic human needs for all: not just food and clothing but also shelter, health care, and education.[36] This simple but powerful proposition is often forgotten in the conventional concerns of economics. Such thinking culminated in writings on, and an index of, human development.[37]

In the late 1990s, Amartya Sen provided the broadest conception of development as freedom: a process of expanding real freedoms that people enjoy for their economic well-being, social opportunities, and political rights.[38] Freedoms, then, are not just the primary ends of development (constitutive), they are also among its principal means (instrumental). And there are strong interactions that link different freedoms with one another. Political freedoms help promote economic security. Social opportunities facilitate economic participation. And so on.

It is essential, then, to make a distinction between means and ends. Economic growth and economic efficiency, or for that matter industrialization, are means. It is development which is an end. The purpose of development, after all, is to create a milieu that enables people, ordinary people, to lead a good life. Development must, therefore, provide all men and women the rights, the opportunities and the capabilities they need to exercise their own choice for a decent life.

In conventional terms, India made enormous economic progress during the second half of the twentieth century. Over the period 1950–2005, GDP has multiplied by 10.9 while per capita income has multiplied by 3.6. India's growth performance was respectable in the period 1950–80 and impressive in the period 1980–2005. Of course, in both phases, it could have been better.

[35]See, for example, Baster (1972) and Seers (1972).
[36]Streeten (1981).
[37]See Anand and Sen (1994). See also, UNDP, *Human Development Report*, various issues.
[38]Sen (1999).

Table 15.3: Selected Indicators
of Social Development in India

	1951	1981	2001
Life Expectancy (at birth in years)			
Male	32	54	64
Female	32	55	67
Infant mortality Rate (per 1000 births)	146	110	66
Literacy Rate (percentage of population)	18	44	65
Adult Literacy (percentage of population in the age group 15 years and above)	28	41	61

Source: Census of India 1951, 1981, and 2001.

But counterfactuals serve little purpose even in academic debate. Nevertheless, it is clear that this growth was not enough in relation to India's needs. What is more, it did not quite match the performance of the stunning success stories in East Asia, particularly China. The real failure, however, was that India was unable to transform its growth into development.

Selected indicators of social development, set out in Table 15.3, suggest that India has made significant progress in the five decades from 1951 to 2001. Life expectancy at birth has more than doubled from 32 years to 65 years. Infant mortality rates have dropped by more than half from 146 to 66 per thousand births. The literacy rate has more than trebled from 18 per cent to 65 per cent of the population. The adult literacy rate has more than doubled from 28 per cent to 61 per cent. There is also evidence of significant progress in health care, housing, and education. The proportion of the population that has access to electricity, drinking water, and sanitation facilities is notably higher. This progress has been steady, even if slow, in both phases, 1951–81 and 1981–2001. Yet, much remains to be done and, in terms of social development, India has miles to go.

It is important to ask: what was the impact of economic growth and social progress, during the second half of the twentieth century, on the poor? The level of per capita income is only an arithmetic mean. Social indicators are also statistical averages. And neither captures the well-being of the poor.

In this context, it is worth considering the available evidence on absolute poverty in India. It suggests that there was no change for the better during the first two decades from the early 1950s to the early 1970s. In fact, the proportion of the population living below the poverty line remained high. It was 45.3 per cent in 1951–2, 47.4 per cent in 1955–6, 45.3 per cent in 1960–1, 56.8 per cent in 1965–6, and 52.9 per cent in 1970–1.[39] Indeed, in some years, during the late 1950s and the late 1960s, the incidence of poverty was even higher when poor monsoons depressed agricultural output and incomes.

This was a failure which had economic and political consequences.[40] In the sphere of economics, the response was two-fold. First, there was a strong, new emphasis on agriculture. The new strategy for agricultural development, which culminated in the Green Revolution, was motivated by the imperative of increasing the output of foodgrains. This quest for food security was driven, in part, by a concern that the nation could not continue its ship-to-mouth existence and, in part, by a concern that if there was a shortage of food it was the poor who went without. Second, poverty alleviation programmes began life, albeit on a modest scale. Most of these programmes sought to create employment for the poor, while some sought to provide them with assets for self-employment. In the realm of politics, it was recognized that the poor who had not seen any improvement in their living conditions, did exercise their right to vote in a political democracy. And populist rhetoric was born in an endeavour to woo the people. The slogan *Garibi Hatao*, even if it was mere words, captured the popular imagination. Rapid growth in the agricultural sector, combined with the spread of anti-poverty programmes, did make a dent on the problem.

The database for poverty estimates is provided by National Sample Survey tables on consumer expenditure, which are now compiled only on a quinquennial basis. Estimates of the proportion of the population and the number of people living below the poverty line, during the period 1973–4 to 1999–2000, are presented in Table 15.4. It shows that the incidence of absolute poverty in both rural and urban India registered a steady and continuous decline from the early 1970s to the late 1990s. The proportion of the population living below the poverty line dropped from 54.9 per cent in 1973–4 to 51.3 per cent in 1977–8, 44.5 per cent in 1983, 38.9 per cent in 1987–8, 36 per cent in 1993–4, and 26.1 per cent in 1999–2000. The estimates for 1999–2000 are a point of contention. And it has been convincingly argued that the incidence of poverty in 1999–2000 was

[39]See Dev (1997).
[40]For a more detailed discussion, see Nayyar (1998).

Table 15.4: Incidence of Poverty in India, 1973–4 to 1999–2000

Year	1973–4	1977–8	1983	1987–8	1993–4	1999–2000
Proportion below the poverty line (in percentage)						
Rural	56.4	53.1	45.7	39.1	37.3	27.1
Urban	49.0	45.2	40.8	38.2	32.4	23.6
Total	54.9	51.3	44.5	38.9	36.0	26.1
Number below the poverty line (in million)						
Rural	261.3	264.2	252.0	231.9	244.0	193.2
Urban	60.0	64.6	70.9	75.1	76.3	67.0
Total	321.3	329.0	323.0	307.0	320.4	260.2

Note: Estimates based on quinquennial rounds.
Source: National Sample Survey and Planning Commision.

significantly higher than the 26.1 per cent of the population suggested by official estimates.[41] If that is correct, the pace of reduction in poverty may have slowed down during the late 1990s. Even so, there can be no doubt that the last quarter of the twentieth century witnessed a significant reduction in the incidence of poverty in India. This reduction in poverty, to begin with, during the 1970s, was attributable to the spread of the Green Revolution and increased public expenditure on infrastructure as also social sectors, which created employment opportunities for the poor. The decline in poverty continued, at a faster pace through the 1980s and the 1990s. This was attributable, in part, to rapid economic growth and, in part, to the spread and the reach of anti-poverty programmes. Yet, this was not enough, with at least one-fourth, and possibly one-third, of India's one billion people still living in absolute poverty. What is more, sustainable livelihoods for the poor remain a distant dream.

Even after six decades of independence from colonial rule, India is unable to meet the basic needs of hundreds of millions of citizens. It is estimated that at least 260 million people, possibly 330 million people, live in absolute poverty. The poor do not even have enough food, let alone clothing, shelter, health care, and education. In fact, there are more poor people in India now than the total population at the time of independence. It is worth citing some evidence, *circa* 2001, which is also the latest available, on social indicators of development.[42] More than one-third of our population is still illiterate.

[41]Sen and Himanshu (2004). See also, Deaton and Kozel (2005) in which there are several essays, with different views, on trends in poverty in India during the 1990s.
[42]The evidence on social indicators, cited in this paragraph, is from the *Census of India, 2001*.

This proportion is significantly higher in rural India at 40 per cent and much higher for women at 45 per cent. The infant mortality rate at 66 per 1000 is among the highest in the world. The maternal mortality rate at 407 per 100,000 live births is far higher than that in most developing countries. 22 per cent of the population does not have access to drinking water while 64 per cent of the population does not have access to sanitation facilities; these aggregate figures conceal the reality that the problem is far more acute in rural India even if the situation is somewhat better in urban India. Although enrolment rates in primary school are more than 95 per cent, drop-out rates are as high as 40 per cent. Enrolment rates in secondary school are 33 per cent, but drop-out rates are 66 per cent. Thus, more than 65 million children who should be in school are not; of these, 55 million are in rural India and 10 million are in urban India. Only 6 per cent of the population enters into the world of higher education. And 39 per cent of the adult population, as many as 225 million people, remain illiterate.

In my view, the most important failure during the past 25 years was that the rapid economic growth did not create sufficient employment opportunities. In this context, it is important to recognize that the growth of the labour force in India has always been higher than the growth in employment, so that the backlog of unemployment has grown steadily over time. What is more, employment growth has not kept pace with output growth. The available evidence on employment elasticities of output is presented in Table 15.5. It shows that the already low employment elasticities registered a significant decline between the early 1970s and the late 1980s, for the economy as a whole as also for the agricultural sector and the industrial sector. It appears that this trend continued during the period from the late 1980s to the late 1990s. The employment elasticities of output for the economy as a whole declined from 0.61 during the period 1972–3 to 1977–8 to 0.30 during the period 1983 to 1987–8 and 0.16 during the period 1993–4 to 1999–2000. In agriculture, the employment elasticities dropped to near zero. Jobless growth is a caricature description but it does capture the unfolding reality in India. It is, perhaps, the reason why equivalent rates of growth during the 1990s did not translate into equivalent poverty reduction during the 1990s as compared with 1980s.

Ironically enough, this asymmetry between output growth and employment growth was reflected in an impressive growth in output per worker, which registered an increase at the rate of 3.6 per cent per annum during 1980–99 as compared with 1.28 per cent per annum during the period 1960–80. It is worth noting that 57 per cent of the growth in output per worker

Table 15.5: Employment Elasticities of Output in India

Period	Agriculture	Manufacturing	Total (for all sectors)
1972–3 to 1977–8	0.64	0.55	0.61
1977–8 to 1983	0.49	0.68	0.54
1983 to 1987–8	0.36	0.26	0.30
1987–8 to 1993–4	0.43	0.29	0.39
1993–4 to 1999–2000	0.01	0.33	0.16

Source: Planning Commission, Government of India.

during the period 1980–99 was attributable to growth in total factor productivity, while 33 per cent was attributable to capital accumulation, and just 10 per cent was attributable to education. In the light of this evidence, labour productivity growth is seen as the principal factor underlying the rapid economic growth since 1980.[43] The sharp slowdown in employment growth during the same period is a corollary.[44] The irony of this paradoxical situation is striking.

Such an outcome is not inevitable. The simplest analytical construct derived from Solow suggests that there are three proximate determinants of economic growth: the investment–GDP ratio, the population growth rate, and the initial level of output per worker. The determinants of growth, of course, are manifold and complex. However, theoretical analysis suggests that economic growth depends on the share of investment in GDP and the productivity of investment. Orthodoxy believes that the productivity of investment is determined by the state of technology. There is a serious lacuna in this thinking. If excess capacity and unemployment exist, an increase in investment which creates a larger domestic market can increase capacity utilization and, therefore, raise the productivity of investment. Orthodox thinking misses this obvious point because it assumes that there is always enough demand to ensure full employment of all resources of the economy. This assumption is not quite tenable in the Indian context. There is, perhaps, a more useful way of thinking about GDP growth directly in terms of employment growth. The level of employment and the growth in labour productivity,

[43]This hypothesis, based on empirical evidence, is developed by Rodrik and Subramanian (2004).

[44]For a complete picture and a detailed discussion of the employment situation in India, during this period, see Vaidyanathan (2001).

measured as output per worker, together add up to the growth in GDP. If the employment growth rate is increased by 1 per cent, the GDP growth rate would also increase, provided labour productivity does not fall by 1 per cent or more. In other words, if it is possible to raise the employment growth rate, without inducing a drastic reduction in labour productivity growth, the growth rate of the economy can only be higher.[45]

THE CHALLENGE FOR THE FUTURE

In the first decade of the twenty-first century, there is a striking optimism about the emerging India. The country which only had a past is beginning to be seen as a country with a future. The land of scarcities is being thought of as a land of opportunities. The land of snake charmers is now considered a land of fashion designers. The land of traditional crafts is increasingly perceived as a land of information technology. The land of bullock-carts, or steam trains, is beginning to be seen as a land of automobiles, or jet planes. This dramatic change of mood is particularly discernible among the rich and the literati in India. There is a similar change in thinking about India in the outside world, mostly among interested individuals or concerned institutions. The mood is contagious, and the images are larger than life, because those who articulate such views have both voice and influence.

It would seem that perceptions about India are changing rapidly. The realities are also changing, but much more slowly. And there is a mismatch. The perceptions, as also the realities, depend on who you are, what you do, and where you live. Captains of industry, editors of newspapers, or ministers of governments see one India. So does the software engineer in Bangalore, the stockbroker in Mumbai, the lobbyist in Delhi, or the entrepreneur in provincial India. The picture is similar, even if shallower, for the investment banker in London, the mutual fund manager in New York, or the chief executive in the board room in Tokyo. These images shape thinking about India 2025 in the world. But there are also contrasting images of India, which constitute an altogether different world. Poor tribals in Orissa or Madhya Pradesh, landless labourers in Bihar, Dalits in Uttar Pradesh, peasants in villages everywhere, migrant construction workers in Delhi, slum children in Mumbai, pavement dwellers in Kolkata, or street vendors in Chennai, see quite another India. Their daily lives are such a struggle that they simply cannot think about, or imagine, a different India in 2025.

It is not just that there are two sharply contrasting views of India in the world. There are two different, almost dichotomized worlds in India. There

[45]For a detailed discussion on this issue, see Bhaduri (2005).

is an India that is global and there is a *Bharat* that is local. What is more, there is a virtual disconnect between these two worlds. Of course, India is a society in which different cultures (traditional and modern), different divides (caste, class, and religion), or even different centuries (nineteenth and twenty-first), co-exist. There is no clash between modernity and tradition. At the same time, the diversity and the pluralism are necessary as also desirable. But the dichotomy between India and Bharat is not.

This is not the India I want. What is more, thinking ahead to 2025, such an India is neither ethically acceptable nor politically sustainable. Therefore, my vision of India 2025 is somewhat different. Its focus is on people, rather than on the nation. I want a society in which India and Bharat become one: connected and integrated. The India of my dreams, then, is one that provides capabilities, opportunities, and rights to people, ordinary people, so that they can exercise their choices for a decent life. In the pursuit of this objective, it is essential that we provide not only food and clothing but also shelter, health care, and education, for all, to create a world without poverty, deprivation, and exclusion. This will need employment creation and sustainable livelihoods. But development must also enhance the well-being of people in terms of expanding freedoms. This must extend beyond freedom from hunger, disease, and illiteracy, so that development creates economic opportunities, promotes social inclusion, and ensures political liberties for people.

There could be a temptation, on the part of some, to dismiss this as the thinking of an incurable romantic or a committed ideologue. But I am neither. And it needs to be said that this is the dream of a concerned citizen. It is no less plausible than other visions of India 2025. Indeed, this is a realizable vision. It is possible to overcome hunger, disease, and illiteracy, just as it is possible to eradicate poverty, deprivation, and exclusion, during the first quarter of the twenty-first century. So many countries in Asia have done so in shorter spans of time. The resources exist. Mahatma Gandhi put it very simply: 'There is enough in the world for everybody's need, but there cannot be enough in the world for everybody's greed'. And I am convinced that a better world is possible. But, by themselves, growth and markets cannot deliver such a world. It needs far more. Above all, it needs good governance in economy, polity, and society, which we had *circa* 1950, where governments are accountable to people and people are centre stage in the process of development. This may be different from, but is not inconsistent with, other, grander yet narrower, visions of India. I believe that we cannot imagine India as a superpower in politics, which some do, or as a powerhouse in economics, which others do, unless it is built on the strong foundations of our most abundant resource and most valuable asset: people.

Economic growth is clearly necessary but not sufficient to bring about a reduction in poverty. This may be attributable to the logic of markets which give to those who have and take away from those who have not, as the process of cumulative causation leads to market driven virtuous circles and vicious circles. This may be the outcome of patterns of development where economic growth is uneven between regions and the distribution of its benefits is unequal among people, so that there is a growing affluence for some and persistent poverty for many. This may be the consequence of initial conditions and institutional frameworks, as similar economic performances in the aggregate could lead to egalitarian economic development in one situation and growth which bypasses the majority of people in another situation.

It cannot suffice to say that outcomes of economic policies should be moderated by social policies, in the form of safety nets. The dichotomy between economic and social policies is inadequate, just as the dichotomy between economic and social development is inappropriate. In fact, no such distinction is ever made in industrial societies. And the experience of the industrialized world suggests that there is a clear need for integration, rather than a separation, of economic and social policies. Thus, I believe, it is important to create institutional mechanisms that mediate between economic and social development.

There are two essential correctives: foster inclusion where markets exist, and create markets where they do not exist.[46] The inclusion of poor people, where markets exist, requires a spread of education and an increase in social consumption. To foster inclusion, we need to develop the capabilities of people, particularly through education, just as we need to develop a social infrastructure which provides the poor with access to shelter, health care, clean water, sanitation, and ensures a steady increase in social consumption that depends almost entirely on the government in a country such as India. The creation of markets, where they are missing, requires a substantial investment in physical infrastructure, particularly in rural areas and backward regions.

In this era of markets and globalization, surprisingly enough, the role of the State is more critical than ever before. This role extends beyond regulating domestic markets or correcting for market failures. It is about creating the initial conditions to capture the benefits from globalization, about managing the process of integration into the world economy in terms of pace and sequence, about providing social protection and safeguarding the vulnerable in the process of change, and about ensuring that economic growth also creates employment and livelihoods for the well-being of people. It is also about acting as a guardian

---

[46]These correctives are discussed, at some length, in Nayyar (2003).

of civil society. In sum, governments need to regulate and complement markets so as to make them people-friendly. The reason is simple. Governments are accountable to people, whereas markets are not.

The object of any sensible strategy of development in a world of globalization, over the next 25 years, should be to create economic space for the pursuit of national interests and development objectives. In pursuit of this goal, it is necessary to think big and to think long. Such thinking must extend across several spheres: first, the creation of a world class infrastructure, to remove supply constraints and support social consumption, where any premature withdrawal of the State is a recipe for disaster; second, the development of human resources, through education, both as a means and as an end, because investing in human beings is important at every stage of development; and, third, the fostering of managerial capabilities in individuals and technological capabilities in firms at a micro level, which are the essential foundations on which international competitiveness is built and without which no latecomer to industrialization has ever succeeded.

It follows that the role of the State in the process of development will continue to be important for sometime to come, even as the scope of the market increases through liberalization in the wider context of globalization.[47] Most would find this argument persuasive. Yet, many would doubt whether such a role is feasible in terms of politics. And the mood of the moment is not receptive to such ideas anywhere, for there is disillusionment with the economic role of the State. It is essential to recognize that there are some things that markets can and should do. Even so, there are other things that governments can and must do. If governments do those things badly, it does not mean that we can dispense with governments. We have to ensure that governments perform better.

The real issue is not about more or less government. It is about the quality of government performance. And the importance of good governance cannot be stressed enough. Governance is largely about rules and institutions that regulate the public realm in civil society. A democratic system seeks to provide for equal participation of the rich and the poor, or the strong and the weak, individuals as citizens in political processes. And good governance is a process characterized by communication and consultation, through which disputes are resolved, consensus is built, and performance is reviewed on a continuous basis. The basis for good governance is a democratic political system that ensures representative and honest governments responsive to the needs of people. This

[47]Nayyar (1997). See also Bhaduri and Nayyar (1996).

involves more than simply free and fair elections. It implies a respect for economic, social, and political rights of citizens. The rule of law is a foundation. An equitable legal framework, applied consistently to everyone, defends people from the abuse of power by State and non-State actors. It empowers people to assert their rights. The need for good governance extends to economic, social, and political institutions. A vibrant civil society is just as important for good governance insofar as it provides checks and balances when governments do not act as they should. In this context, it is essential to stress the importance of values. In effect, values provide the foundations of ethical principles and social norms which, in turn, ensure the effectiveness of institutions and the accountability of actors. Much of this exists in principle. In practice, however, good governance is not possible without transparency and accountability in the political system.

SOME FORGOTTEN ESSENTIALS

The debate in India tends to focus on what is said or done, but does not always consider what is not said or not done. In the process some essentials are forgotten.[48]

First, it is essential to remember that the well-being of humankind is the essence of development. Therefore, development must bring about an improvement in the living conditions of people, ordinary people. It should ensure the provision of basic human needs for all, not just food and clothing but also shelter, health care, and education. This simple but powerful proposition is often forgotten in the pursuit of material wealth and the conventional concerns of economics. Yet, people view the world through the optic of their living conditions and daily lives. The litmus test for the performance of an economy, hence government, is neither economic growth, nor economic efficiency, indeed not even equity in an abstract sense, but whether or not it meets the basic needs and the growing aspirations of people. Austerity now for prosperity later is neither credible nor acceptable. The essence of the tension between the economics of markets that works on the principle of one-rupee-one-vote, and the politics of democracy that works on the principle of one-person-one-vote, must be recognized. For those excluded by the economics of markets are included by the politics of democracy.

The second essential we have almost forgotten is that there is a rural hinterland. Indeed, India lives in its villages. Yet, the discourse proceeds as if the rural sector does not exist, or if it exists it does not matter. This is incredible

[48]The discussion in this section draws upon some earlier work of the author (Nayyar 2004).

in an economy where two-thirds of the workforce is employed in agriculture and where three-fourths of the population lives in the rural sector. The rural–urban divide is wider than ever before. And farmers' suicides, or starvation deaths, are symptoms of an acute problem. Indeed, there is a quiet crisis in agriculture that runs deep. Even if the share of rural India in national income is less than its share in the population, its share of votes is directly proportional. And rural India decides for the republic at election time. The electoral, if not political, compulsions of a democracy cannot be set aside for long.

Third, it is not recognized that distributional outcomes are important. So are employment and livelihoods. Structural reforms associated with economic liberalization have important implications for employment creation and income opportunities. For example, insofar as such reform increases the average productivity of labour, through the use of capital-intensive or labour-saving technologies, or through a restructuring of firms which increases efficiency, it reduces the contribution of any given rate of economic growth to employment growth. There is a contraction of employment in some sectors without a compensatory expansion of employment in other sectors. As employment elasticities of output decline, employment creation slows down. For any given level of employment, a globalization of prices without a globalization of incomes also threatens livelihoods. The poor at the margin are most vulnerable, but the non-rich are not immune. And, insofar as there are some winners and many losers, distributional outcomes in the sphere of economics shape electoral outcomes in the realm of politics.

Fourth, the debate on economic reforms does not make a clear distinction between means and ends. For example, it does not recognize that markets, as much as States, are institutions evolved by humankind, that are means and it is development that is the end. What is more, there is a presumption that what is necessary is also sufficient. The management of incentives, motivated by the objective of minimizing costs and maximizing efficiency, or even unleashing creativity and innovation at a micro level, is based on a set of policies that are intended to increase competition in the market place. Competition is obviously desirable, but there is nothing automatic about competition. Policy regimes can allow things to happen, but cannot cause things to happen. The creation of competitive markets that enforce efficiency may, in fact, require strategic intervention on the part of the government. The essential missing link is that this debate does not consider transition paths. It confuses *comparison* of one equilibrium position with another, with *change* from one equilibrium position to another. But it does not tell us anything about how we move from one position to the other.

Fifth, the fundamental importance of good governance is not quite recognized. Good governance, where governments are accountable to citizens and people are centre stage in development, is essential for creating capabilities, providing opportunities, and ensuring rights for people. Governance capabilities matter in a much more concrete sense, whereas the role of the State is somewhat more abstract. Indeed, the quality of governance is an important determinant of success or failure at development. The most striking illustration of this proposition is provided by the wide diversity in economic performance across states in India despite common policies, similar institutions, and an economic union.

CONCLUSION

The story of economic development in independent India is often distorted by beliefs in fashion or caricatures of perceptions which shape conventional wisdom. I have argued that this is misleading, not only in analysing the past but also in contemplating the future. If we consider India during the twentieth century as a whole, the turning point in economic growth was *circa* 1951. If we consider India since independence, the turning point in economic growth was *circa* 1980. And it is clear that the turning point in the early 1950s was much more significant than the structural break in the early 1980s. In any case, 1991 was not a watershed. Thus, it is not possible to attribute the turnaround in India's growth performance to economic liberalization. Economic growth in India was respectable during the period 1950–80. It was a radical departure from the colonial past. And it was no worse than the growth performance of most countries during that period. But it was simply not enough in relation to India's needs. Economic growth in India was impressive during the period 1980–2005. Indeed, it was much better than that in most countries. But even this was not enough. The real failure, throughout the second half of the twentieth century, was that India failed to transform its growth into development, which would have brought about an improvement in the living conditions of people, ordinary people.

India's unfinished journey in development would not be complete so long as poverty, deprivation, and exclusion persist. The destination, then, is clear. It must be said that such an India which provides capabilities, opportunities, and rights to people, ordinary people, can also deliver power and prosperity for the nation so cherished by some. In this endeavour, economic growth is essential. But it cannot be sufficient. What is more, it is neither feasible nor desirable to separate economic growth from distributional outcomes because they are inextricably linked with each other. This link is provided by employment creation. Jobless growth is not sustainable either in economics or in politics. If we create employment, it would only reinforce economic growth through a virtuous circle of cumulative causation. There is a critical role for the State in the process. This role cannot be more of the same. It must be redefined to recognize the complementarities between the State and the market. The moral of my story in our quest for development is not less government but good governance. Indeed, without good governance, this dream about India simply cannot become a reality. Even if it is an imperative, however, there is no magic wand that can deliver good governance. In the realization of this objective, political democracy, which provides not only checks and balances but also early-warnings and alarm-bells, is our real asset. What it needs is transparency and accountability. Despite its flaws, the deeply embedded political democracy is the basis of my optimism about the future of India.

REFERENCES

Ahluwalia, Montek S. (2002), 'Economic Reforms in India since 1991: Has Gradualism Worked?', *Journal of Economic Perspectives*, Vol. 16, No. 7, pp. 67–88.

Anand, Sudhir and Amartya Sen (1994), 'Human Development Index: Methodology and Measurement', HDRO Occasional Paper 12, UNDP, New York.

Bairoch, Paul (1993), *Economics and World History: Myths and Paradoxes*, University of Chicago Press, Chicago.

Baster, Nancy (1972), 'Development Indicators', *Journal of Development Studies*, Vol. 8, No. 3, pp. 1–20.

Bhaduri, Amit (2005), *Development with Dignity: A Case for Full Employment*, National Book Trust, New Delhi.

Bhaduri, Amit and Deepak Nayyar (1996), *The Intelligent Person's Guide to Liberalization*, Penguin Books, New Delhi.

Bhagwati, Jagdish and Padma Desai (1970), *India: Planning for Industrialization*, Oxford University Press, London.

Chang, Ha-Joon (2002), *Kicking Away the Ladder: Development Strategy in Historical Perspective*, Anthem Press, London.

Deaton, Angus and Valerie Kozel (eds) (2005), *The Great Indian Poverty Debate*, Macmillan India, New Delhi.

De Long, J. Bradford (2003), 'India since Independence: An Analytic Growth Narrative', in Dani Rodrik (ed.), *In Search of Prosperity: Analytic Narratives on Economic Growth*, Princeton University Press, New Jersey.

Dev, S. Mahendra (1997), 'Growth, Employment, Poverty and Human Development: An Evaluation of Change in India since Independence', *Review of Development and Change*, Vol. 2, No. 2, pp. 209–50.

EPW Research Foundation (2004), *National Accounts Statistics of India, 1950–51 to 2002–03, Linked Series with 1993–94 as the Base Year*, Economic and Political Weekly Research Foundation, Mumbai.

Hatekar, Neeraj and Amrish Dongre (2005), 'Structural Breaks in India's Growth', *Economic and Political Weekly*, Vol. 40, No.14, pp.1432–5.

Joshi, Vijay and I.M.D. Little (1994), *India: Macroeconomics and Political Economy, 1964–1991*, World Bank and Oxford University Press, Washington, DC and New Delhi.

Khanna, Tarun and Yasheng Huang (2003), 'Can India Overtake China?', *Foreign Policy*, July–August, Issue 137, pp. 74–81.

Lal, Deepak (1998), *Unfinished Business: India in the World Economy*, Oxford University Press, New York.

Maddison, Angus (1995), *Monitoring the World Economy: 1820–1992*, OECD Development Centre, Paris.

Nayyar, Deepak (ed.) (1994), *Industrial Growth and Stagnation: The Debate in India*, Oxford University Press, Bombay.

——— (1996), *Economic Liberalization in India: Analytics, Experience and Lessons*, R.C. Dutt Lectures on Political Economy, Orient Longman, Calcutta.

——— (1997), 'Themes in Trade and Industrialization', in Deepak Nayyar (ed.), *Trade and Industrialization*, Oxford University Press, New Delhi.

——— (1998), 'Economic Development and Political Democracy: Interaction of Economics and Politics in Independent India', *Economic and Political Weekly*, Vol. 33, No. 49, pp. 3121–31.

——— (2003), 'Globalization and Development Strategies' in John Toye (ed.), *Trade and Development*, Edward Elgar, Cheltenham.

——— (2004), 'Economic Reforms in India: Understanding the Process and Learning from Experience', *International Journal of Development Issues*, Vol. 3, No. 2, pp. 31–55.

Panagariya, Arvind (2004), 'Growth and Reforms during 1980s and 1990s', *Economic and Political Weekly*, Vol. 39, No. 25, pp. 2581–94.

Rodrik, Dani and Arvind Subramanian (2004), 'From Hindu Growth to Productivity Surge: The Mystery of the Indian Growth Transition', IMF Working Paper WP/04/77, International Monetary Fund, Washington, DC.

Seers, Dudley (1972), 'What are We Trying to Measure?', *Journal of Development Studies*, Vol. 8, No. 3, pp. 21–36.

Sen, Amartya (1999), *Development as Freedom*, Oxford University Press, Oxford.

Sen, Abhijit and Himanshu (2004). 'Poverty and Inequality in India', *Economic and Political Weekly*, Vol. 39, Nos 38–39, pp. 4247–63 and pp. 4361–75.

Sinha, Ajit and Shirin Tejani (2004), 'Trend Breaks in India's GDP Growth Rate', *Economic and Political Weekly*, Vol. 39, No. 52, pp. 5634–9.

Sivasubramonian, S. (2000), *The National Income of India during the Twentieth Century*, Oxford University Press, New Delhi.

Srinivasan, T.N. and Suresh Tendulkar (2003), *Reintegrating India with the World Economy*, Institute for International Economics, Washington, DC.

Streeten, Paul (1981), *First Things First: Meeting Basic Human Needs in Developing Countries*, Oxford University Press, Oxford.

Vaidyanathan, A. (2001), 'Employment in India, 1977/1978 to 1999/2000: Characteristics and Trends', *Journal of the Indian School of Political Economy*, Vol. 13, No. 2, pp. 217–54.

Virmani, Arvind (2004), 'India's Economic Growth: From Socialist Rate of Growth to Bharatiya Rate of Growth', ICRIER Working Paper No. 122, Indian Council for Research on International Economic Relations, New Delhi.

Wallack, Jessica S. (2003), 'Structural Breaks in Indian Macroeconomic Data', *Economic and Political Weekly*, Vol. 38, No. 41, pp. 4312–15.

Wilson, D. and R. Purushothaman (2003), 'Dreaming with BRICs: The Path to 2050', Global Economics Paper No. 99, Goldman Sachs, London.

ACKNOWLEDGEMENTS

The author would like to acknowledge the following academic journals and books where these essays were first published.

1. 'Macroeconomics in Developing Countries', *Banca Nazionale del Lavoro Quarterly Review*, September 2007, Vol. LIX, No. 242, pp. 249–69.
2. 'Macroeconomics of Structural Adjustment and Public Finances in Developing Countries', *International Journal of Development Issues*, June 2008, Vol. 7, No. 1, pp. 4–28.
3. 'On Exclusion and Inclusion: Democracy, Markets and People', in Amitava Krishna Dutt and Jamie Ros (eds), *Development Economics and Structuralist Macroeconomics*, Edward Elgar, Cheltenham, 2003, pp. 94–106.
4. 'Development through Globalization?', in George Mavrotas and Anthony Shorrocks (eds), *Advancing Development: Core Themes in Global Economics*, Palgrave, London, 2007, pp. 593–613.
5. 'Learning to Unlearn from Development', *Oxford Development Studies*, September 2008, Vol. 36, No. 3, pp. 259–80.
6. 'Short-Termism, Public Policies and Economic Development', *Economies et Societies*, 1998, Vol. 32, No. 1, pp. 107–18.
7. 'Work, Livelihoods and Rights', *Indian Journal of Labour Economics*, January 2003, Vol. 46, No. 1, pp. 3–13.
8. 'International Relocation of Production and Industrialization in LDCs', Review of Political Economy, *Economic and Political Weekly*, July 1983, Vol. XVIII, No. 31, pp. 13–26
9. 'Themes in Trade and Industrialization', in Deepak Nayyar (ed.), *Trade and Industrialization*, Oxford University Press, Delhi, 1997, pp. 1–42.
10. 'Industrial Development in India: Growth or Stagnation?', *Economic and Political Weekly*, Special Number, August 1978, Vol. XIII,

Nos 31–3, pp. 1265–78. Reprinted in A.K. Bagchi and N. Banerji (eds), *Change and Choice in Indian Industry, Calcutta,* 1980, pp. 91–117.

11. 'The Foreign Trade Sector, Planning and Industrialization in India', in T.J. Byres (ed.), *The State and Development Planning in India,* Oxford University Press, Delhi, 1994, pp. 433–61.

12. 'Macroeconomic Reforms in India: Short-term Effects and Long-run Implications', in W. Mahmud (ed.), *Adjustment and Beyond: The Reform Experience in South Asia,* Palgrave, London 2001, pp. 20–46.

13. 'Economic Reforms in India: Understanding the Process and Learning from Experience', *International Journal of Development Issues,* December 2004, Vol. 3, No. 2, pp. 31–55.

14. 'Economic Development and Political Democracy: The Interaction of Economics and Politics in Independent India', *Economic and Political Weekly,* December 1998, Vol. XXXIII, No. 49, pp. 3121–31. Reprinted in N.G. Jayal (ed.), *Democracy in India,* Oxford University Press, Delhi 2001, pp. 361–96, and Rakesh Mohan (ed.), *Facets of the Indian Economy,* Oxford University Press, Delhi, pp. 136–65.

15. 'India's Unfinished Journey: Transforming Growth into Development', *Modern Asian Studies,* July 2006, Vol. 40, No. 3, pp. 797–832.

INDEX